**Varieties of
American English**

Varieties of
American English

Essays by Raven I. McDavid, Jr.

**Selected and Introduced
by Anwar S. Dil**

Stanford University Press, Stanford, California   1980

Language Science and National Development

A Series Sponsored by the
Linguistic Research Group of Pakistan

General Editor: Anwar S. Dil

Stanford University Press
Stanford, California
© 1980 by Raven I. McDavid, Jr.
Printed in the United States of America
ISBN 0-8047-0982-3
LC 78-59374

Contents

Acknowledgments

The Linguistic Research Group of Pakistan and the General Editor of the Language Science and National Development Series are deeply grateful to Professor Raven I. McDavid, Jr. for giving us the privilege of presenting his selected writings as the thirteenth volume in our series established in 1970 to commemorate the International Education Year.

We are indebted to the editors and publishers of the following publications. The ready permission on the part of the holders of the copyrights, acknowledged in each case, is a proof of the existing international cooperation and goodwill that gives hope for better collaboration among scholars of all nations for international exchange of knowledge.

Postvocalic /-r/ in South Carolina: A Social Analysis. American Speech 23. 194-203 (1948), with permission of the publisher. © 1948 Columbia University Press.

The Relationship of the Speech of American Negroes to the Speech of Whites; with Virginia G. McDavid. American Speech 26. 3-17 (1951), with permission of the publisher. © 1951 Columbia University Press.

Dialect Differences and Social Differences in an Urban Society. Sociolinguistics, ed. by William Bright (The Hague: Mouton Publishers, 1966), pp. 72-83, with permission of the publisher. © 1966 Mouton Publishers, The Hague.

Changing Patterns of Southern Dialects. Essays in Honor of Claude M. Wise, ed. by Arthur J. Bronstein, et al. (Hannibal,

Missouri: Standard Printing [sponsored by the Speech Association of America]), pp. 206-228, with permission of the Editor. © 1970 Speech Communication Association, Washington, D.C.

The Dialects of Negro Americans; with Lawrence M. Davis. Studies in Linguistics in Honor of George L. Trager, ed. by M. Estellie Smith (The Hague: Mouton Publishers, 1972), pp. 303-312, with permission of the publisher. © 1972 Mouton Publishers, The Hague.

The Folk Vocabulary of Eastern Kentucky; with Virginia G. McDavid. Zeitschrift für Dialektologie und Linguistik, Beihefte, NF 9 [Lexicography and Dialectology: Festgabe for Hans Kurath, ed. by Harald Scholler and John Reidy] (Wiesbaden, West Germany: Franz Steiner Verlag GmbH, 1973), pp. 147-164, with permission of the publisher. © 1973 Franz Steiner Verlag GmbH, Wiesbaden, West Germany.

The Urbanization of American English. Philologica Pragensia, Volume 18, No. 4, pp. 228-238 (1975), published by ACADEMIA, Publishing House of the Czechoslovakia Academy of Sciences, Prague, Czechoslovakia. © 1975 Czechoslovak Academy of Sciences.

Prejudice and Pride: Linguistic Acceptability in South Carolina; with Raymond K. O'Cain. Acceptability in Language, ed. by Sidney Greenbaum (The Hague: Mouton Publishers, 1977), pp. 103-132, with permission of the publisher. © 1977 Mouton Publishers, The Hague.

Social Differences in White Speech. Language and Society, ed. by William McCormack and Stephen A. Wurm (The Hague: Mouton Publishers, 1979), pp. 249-261, with permission of the publisher. © 1979 Mouton Publishers, The Hague.

The Sociology of Language. Linguistics in School Programs, National Society for the Study of Education Yearbook 69.2, ed. by Albert H. Marckwardt (Chicago, Illinois: The National Society for the Study of Education, 1970), pp. 85-108, with permission of the publisher. © 1970 The National Society for the Study of Education.

Two Studies of Dialects of English. Studies in Honor of Harold Orton, Leeds Studies in English NS 2, ed. by Stanley Ellis (Leeds, England: Leeds Studies in English, University of Leeds, 1968), pp. 23-45, with permission of the Editor. © 1968 University of Leeds.

Planning the Grid. American Speech 46. 9-26 (1971), with permission of the publisher. © 1971 Columbia University Press.

New Directions in American Dialectology. English Studies Today 5. 53-85 (1973), with permission of the President of the International Association of University Professors of English. © 1973 International Association of University Professors of English. Revised, enlarged, and updated by the author for this volume.

The Social Role of the Dictionary appears for the first time in this volume.

False Scents and Cold Trails: The Pre-Publication Criticism of the Merriam Third. Journal of English Linguistics 5. 101-121 (1971), with permission of the publisher. © 1971 Journal of English Linguistics.

Poor Whites and Rustics; with Sarah Ann Witham. Names 22. 93-103 (1974), with permission of the publisher. © 1974 The American Name Society.

Dr. Afia Dil, Lecturer in Linguistics, United States International University, San Diego, must be thanked for help in many ways. Kamran Dil of Mt. Carmel High School, San Diego, assisted the Editor in library research and several matters of detail. Typing of the camera-ready manuscript has been done by Dr. Jacquelyn Rose Bailey of the United States International University and she certainly deserves a word of appreciation.

Among those who helped the author in completing work on this volume, special gratitude is due to William A. Kretzschmar, Jr., Sara Sanders, Michael Witkoski, and Raymond O'Cain. The author is also grateful to the Newberry Library of Chicago, the Joseph Regenstein Library of the University of Chicago, and the English Department and Library of Louisiana State University for assistance in all stages of the preparation of this work and of the articles from which it is derived.

This volume is affectionately dedicated to

DR. VIRGINIA G. McDAVID

who has been the major influence on the

author's career as a scholar

EDITOR'S NOTE

These essays have been reprinted from the originals with only minor changes made in the interest of uniformity of style and appearance. In cases where substantive revisions have been made proper notation has been added. Misprints and mistakes appearing in the originals have been corrected in consultation with the author. In come cases references, notes and bibliographical entries have been updated. Footnotes marked by asterisks have been added by the Editor.

Introduction

Raven Ioor McDavid, Jr. was born in Greenville, South Carolina, on October 16, 1911. He received his bachelor's degree from Furman University in 1931. For his graduate studies he went to Duke University, where he received his Master's degree in 1933 and his Ph. D. degree in 1935 with a dissertation on Milton as a political thinker. After three years as an instructor at The Citadel, a year at Michigan State, and two years at Southwestern Louisiana, he became involved in the Intensive Language Program for the Armed Services from 1942 to 1945. For the next five years he did fieldwork for various linguistic atlases, with incidental teaching at Illinois, Colorado, Cornell, Montana State, and Michigan. In 1957, after five years at Western Reserve University, he joined the faculty of the University of Chicago, where he was Professor of English and Linguistics till his retirement in 1978.

McDavid has been active in the Modern Language Association, the American Dialect Society, the American Name Society, the Linguistic Society of America, and the International Association of University Professors of English. He was president of the American Dialect Society in 1967-68. He has served as a linguist for the U.S. Board on Geographical Names, and as a consultant to the U.S. Office of Education. He is a Fellow of the American Anthropological Association and the American Association for the Advancement of Science. He has been awarded honorary degrees of Litt. D. by Furman University (1966) and Duke University (1972), and membership in Phi Beta Kappa (Duke, 1975). In 1969 he was the recipient of the David Russell Award of the National Council of Teachers of English.

H. L. Mencken's book <u>The American Language</u> was instrumental in changing McDavid's interest from literature to language. First published in 1919, the book was largely responsible for what McDavid describes as "a realization among professional scholars that American English demanded serious and systematic investigation by the best minds, and that the fruits of this investigation might not only be interesting in themselves but have beneficent effects upon American letters and the American educational system." In the 1940's McDavid received Mencken's personal encouragement in studying the relationships between linguistic patterns and sociocultural forces in American society; and in 1963, with assistance from David W. Maurer, he published a one-volume abridged edition of Mencken's fourth edition of 1936 and the two supplements of 1945 and 1948, with annotations and modifications to reflect developments after 1948. McDavid has also made a number of contributions to Mencken studies, notably a 1966 paper on Mencken's impact on American linguistics and a 1967 essay on Mencken's onomastics.

Another important event in McDavid's career was his participation as a demonstration informant in Bernard Bloch's course on dialect field methods at the 1937 Linguistic Institute at the University of Michigan, which catalyzed an interest in language variety developed in childhood and intensified by his teaching in Charleston and in Louisiana. In 1941, encouraged by Bernard Bloch and by Hans Kurath, director of the Linguistic Atlas project, he began the linguistic fieldwork investigations that led to his life work in linguistic geography. The first major outcome of his collaboration with Kurath was <u>The Pronunciation of English in the Atlantic States</u> (1961), to which McDavid contributed an important chapter entitled "Regional and Social Differences in the Incidence of Vowels and Consonants." At present, he is editor-in-chief of the <u>Linguistic Atlas of the Middle and South Atlantic States,</u> on which he has been working since Kurath's retirement in 1964; of the <u>Linguistic Atlas of the North-Central States,</u> on which he began work in 1948, becoming chief editor after Albert Marckwardt's death in 1975; and, since the death in 1977 of William R. Van Riper, with whom he had long collaborated, of the <u>Linguistic Atlas of Oklahoma.</u>

McDavid believes strongly that full and accurate collecting and recording of variations in language usage are essential to theoretical and interpretative linguistic studies. As he remarks, theories and interpretations come and go but data on how people in real-life situations speak their language remain forever useful. Although his outspoken stand in this regard has provoked criticism from some quarters, none of his critics can match the breadth and depth of his contribution to the data bank of American English speech patterns.

Yet another area that has occupied McDavid's scholarly attention is lexicography. Since his work on Charles Hockett's Dictionary of Spoken Chinese, published by the U.S. War Department in 1945, he has been deeply interested in dictionaries and dictionary making. His best-known work in this field is his investigation of the history and structure of the Merriam establishment, represented in this volume by his paper "False Scents and Cold Trails" (1971). Lexicography in English (1973), which he edited in collaboration with Audrey R. Duckert, is recognized as a standard text on the subject.

Areal and social variations in language are studied today with growing interest, not only in the context of American English, but also, and for more urgent reasons, in many other languages and nation-states. From his 1940 paper "Low-Back Vowels in the South Carolina Piedmont," through the two classic papers that open this volume, right up to his recent paper "New Directions in American Dialectology," Raven McDavid has brought to this important study his own unique combination of Mencken's energetic enthusiasm and Kurath's impeccable scholarship. The study of language variation is an endless delight for McDavid, and his exemplary work on American English makes it a delight for us all.

Anwar S. Dil

United States International University
San Diego, California
April 17, 1979

**Varieties of
American English**

Part I. American English: Social and Regional Varieties

1 | Postvocalic / -r / in South Carolina: A Social Analysis

The relationship between speech forms and the cultural con-
figurations and prestige values within a civilization has been indicated
by linguistic scientists, but so far most of the study of that relationship has been directed toward languages outside the Indo-European
family.[1] It is, however, just as proper to utilize the data of linguistics, as derived from a study of dialects of our own language, in analyzing some of the problems within our own culture.[2]

As an example of a situation in which linguistic data and
other cultural data must be correlated, one may examine the distribution in South Carolina and the adjacent parts of Georgia of postvocalic /-r/ as constriction in such words as thirty, Thursday,
worm, barn, beard, father.[3] (In popular terminology, speakers
lacking constriction in words of these types are said not to pronounce
their /-r/.) A social analysis proved necessary for this particular
linguistic feature, because the data proved too complicated to be explained by merely a geographical statement or a statement of settlement history. In this particular problem, moreover, the social
analysis seems more significant than it might seem in others, because the presence of absence of postvocalic /-r/ as constriction
becomes an overt prestige symbol only on a very high level of sophis-
tication. With little experience a speaker learns that the folk forms
[ˈlaɪtəd], lightwood, and [ˈfaɚˌboəd], fireboard, do not have the
prestige of the corresponding standard forms kindling and mantelpiece[4] — that the folk forms are generally recognized as 'countrified'
or 'common.' Folk verb forms, like I seen what he done when he run
into your car, are under a strong social taboo, and as a rule may be
used by highly cultured speakers only for deliberate, humorous effects.

MAP I
REGIONS
OF
SOUTH CAROLINA

Even some pronunciations, such as [ˈaɪðə(r], [ˈnaɪðə(r], instead
of [ˈiːðə(r], [ˈniːðə(r), either, neither, or the so-called 'broad
a' pronunciation [ˈhaf ͵ past] instead of the more common [ˈhæf ͵ pæst],
half past, are fairly generally known as symbols of real or fancied
elegance. But there is little or no direct concern with a person's
postvocalic /-r/ except as part of the occupational training for such
highly sophisticated crafts as elocution, pedagogy, concert singing,
acting, radio announcing, and some branches of the ministry. Since
the traditions of these professions generally require that their prac-
titioners tinker with their speech in other ways, persons deliberately
concerned about the presence or absence of constriction in their postvocalic /-r/ would not be used as representatives of natural local
usage on any cultural level. In short, constriction — or lack of it —
in the speech of Atlas informants may be considered due to the normal
operation of social forces and not to any conscious notions of elegance.

The first of the accompanying maps shows the geographical details essential to an understanding of the distribution of postvocalic /-r/ in South Carolina. The tidewater area, extending inland about thirty miles through a network of islands and peninsulas and tidal creeks, except along the beach front of Horry County, was the area in which the first cultural centers were planted: Georgetown, Charleston, Beaufort, and Savannah. About thirty miles inland is a belt of pine barrens, which have never been suitable for large-scale plantation agriculture, and where small-scale farming is the prevailing pattern.[5] Above the pine barrens the rich coastal plain spreads inland for about seventy miles, to the infertile sand hills along and just below the fall line. Above the fall line — the old head of navigation on the rivers, and the shore line in an earlier geological period — the rolling Piedmont begins, gradually becoming more broken until in the northwestern corner of the state it merges into a fringe of the Blue Ridge Mountains. From the coast to the fall line is generally known as the Low Country; above the fall line, as the Up Country.

The conventional statement about the Southern postvocalic /-r/ is that it does not occur as constriction in words of the type here under examination. The fact that in every Southern state one may find locally rooted native speakers with constriction in at least some of these words has been either overlooked or deliberately ignored.[6] The usual statement is still that Southern and New England speech differs from so-called 'general American' in that the two former types do not have constriction of postvocalic /-r/.[7]

However, records made for the Linguistic Atlas of the South Atlantic States showed very early that postvocalic /-r/ does occur with constriction in many Southern communities, including several of those first investigated in South Carolina for the Atlas by Guy S. Lowman. These data led Professor Hans Kurath, director of the Atlas, to set off tentatively two areas in South Carolina within which constriction occurred: the middle and upper Piedmont, and the area north of the Santee River.[8] A simple explanation of the evidence seemed possible at that time: The area north of the Santee was settled predominantly by Scotch-Irish planted from the coast, was adjacent to the Highlander settlements in the Cape Fear Valley of North Carolina, and could be looked upon generally as a cultural continuation

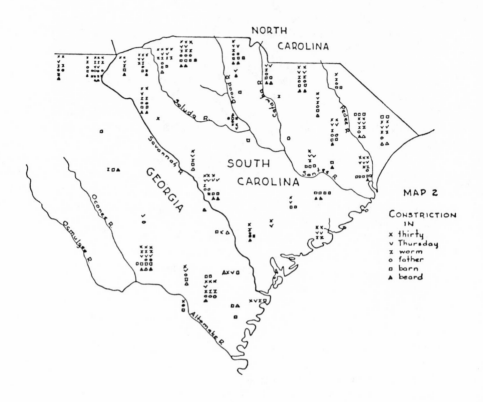

MAP 2

CONSTRICTION
IN
x thirty
v Thursday
z worm
o father
□ barn
▲ beard

of the Cape Fear settlements. The northwestern corner of the state
was settled originally by the main Scotch-Irish migration southward
from Pennsylvania, and would naturally represent a southward prong
of the extensive 'Midland' area that Kurath has set up as stemming
from the Pennsylvania settlements.[9] The explanation was still on the
basis of geography and the area of original settlement.

But if a geographical interpretation of the postvocalic /-r/
was the proper one, it might have been expected that further field
work would substantiate and simplify the picture. Instead, with

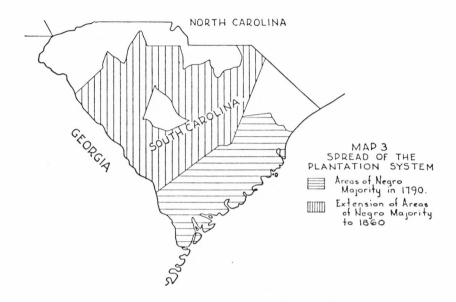

MAP 3
SPREAD OF THE
PLANTATION SYSTEM

▤ Areas of Negro
   Majority in 1790.

▥ Extension of Areas
   of Negro Majority
   to 1860

further research the picture has become more complicated, as the second map indicates. Many speakers — even whole communities — are found with constriction of postvocalic /-r/ in the area where the 1941 evidence did not indicate constriction to exist, and many speakers lack constriction in areas where constriction seemed indicated as normal. A purely geographical interpretation of the distribution is likely to be meaningless: it is difficult to see how, in a geographical sense, Barnwell and Orangeburg counties can be less 'Midland' than Hampton and Berkeley, where constriction occurs. It is therefore necessary to make a statement of other social phenomena in order to explain the distribution of postvocalic /-r/ in South Carolina.

In the communities where postvocalic /-r/ occurs with constriction, it has been noticed that three variables operate toward

decreasing the amount: normally, the more education an informant
has, the less constriction; and within the same cultural level, younger informants generally have less constriction than older ones, and
urban informants less than rural.

Moreover, the communities in which constriction occurs
have in common a proportionately large white population — generally
a majority, even in 1860, when the proportion of Negroes in South
Carolina was largest. [10] These communities are counties or parts
of counties where farming, often scratch-farming, was the rule, and
where the cultural orientation was toward the county seat and the local religious congregation. They comprise the pine barrens, the
hinterland of the Horry beach, the sand hills, and the mountain mar-
gin — lands where the plantation system could not be even temporarily profitable — and the Dutch Fork between the Saluda and Broad
rivers, where a cohesive, religious-centered Lutheran community
with a tradition of self-sufficient farming was able to resist the lure
of alleged money crops. Constriction in the speech of textile workers
in Piedmont metropolitan centers is only superficially an exception to
the observation that constriction is a mark of cultural isolation: the
textile workers were originally recruited from the culturally peripheral areas, and the paternalistic company village that characterizes
the Southern textile industry has created a pattern of cultural segregation as real and almost as strong as that setting off whites from
Negroes. [11]

When one studies both the early settlement history and the
current distribution of speech forms other than the postvocalic /-r/ ,
it is apparent that the original area without constriction was only a
small part of the state. [12] The area settled by southern British
speakers hardly reached above tidewater; further inland, whether
the settlers came in the great migration from Pennsylvania or first
landed at Charleston or other ports, the early population was made
up almost entirely of Scotch-Irish and Germans, who might be expected to retain their postvocalic constriction of /-r/ , just as they have
retained much of their characteristic vocabulary. [13] Only in Beaufort, Charleston, and Georgetown districts — and only in the tidewater riceland sections of those districts — were the southern
British settlers, in whose dialect constriction would have first been

lost, the dominant group in 1790; and in those same sections plantation agriculture and large slave majorities prevailed.[14] Clearly, the
spread of the loss of constriction accompanied the spread of the plantation system, both representing the imposition on the majority of the
patterns, if not the will, of a minority.

The spread inland of the minority speech pattern, so far as
constriction is concerned, naturally involved several types of social
readjustment. The following social forces are known to have operated; given the established prestige of the original group that lacked
constriction, the tidewater plantation caste,[15] each of these forces
would have tended to reinforce the prestige of the constrictionless
type of speech as a model:

1. Following the establishment of American independence,
the reopening of the slave trade,[16] and the invention of the cotton gin,
plantation agriculture spread inland from the coast, displacing many
of the small farmers, who in their turn moved west into the frontier
communities.[17]

2. Some successful Up Country farmers became planters,
and intermarried with the older plantation caste.[18]

3. As inland towns arose, they tended to become cultural
outposts of Charleston. The original fall line trading posts — Augus-
ta, Columbia, Camden, and Cheraw — were financed by Charleston
capital for the Indian trade.[19] As the trading posts grew into towns,
the local business and financial leaders had an increasing number of
contacts with the group in Charleston that has always controlled the
financial life of the state. Sometimes, Charlestonians even migrated
to the Up Country to establish offshoots of their family banks or business houses. The cotton of the Up Country was marketed through
Charleston factors until well into the twentieth century.[20]

Not only financial ties attached the Up Country townspeople
to Charleston. Both health and fashion contrived to make the Low
Country planters migrate inland during the malaria season to such
health resorts as Aiken, Pendleton, Greenville, and Spartanburg.[21]
Some of the Low Country visitors settled permanently, to become the
local elite. Even the Civil War did not disturb this trend; in fact, the

siege of Charleston caused many Charlestonians to become refugees
in the Up Country, and some did not return with the cessation of hos-
tilities. For the Charlestonian not completely above the salt in his
home town, the Up Country provided a greater sense of social prestige than he could have known between the Ashley and the Cooper.
Even Irish Catholics transplanted to the Up Country, though remaining exotic in the Protestant environment, found that a Charleston
origin and a trace of Charleston accent helped them to become accepted as part of the socially preferred group.[22]

Charleston long continued to dominate the cultural and professional life of South Carolina. The state medical college is still
located in Charleston, and apprenticeship in the office of a Charleston
lawyer has long been considered the best type of legal training.[23]
The moving of the state capital to Columbia, and the setting up of the
state university there, did not change the picture materially; from
the beginning, the dominant group in Columbia society was the plantation caste, the rulers of South Carolina.

The many Protestant colleges in the Up Country did little to
counteract the trend — partly because after 1830 (and almost all the
Up Country colleges were established after that date) there was but
one approved social system and no room for competitors; partly because a rising educational institution tended to conform by way of
showing its cultural legitimacy; partly because many of the founders
and early faculty members of these inland institutions were themselves from tidewater areas, or at least educated in institutions
located in these areas.[24]

None of these influences operated alone; they make up a complex, rooted in the desire of every ambitious South Carolinian to be
accepted by, and, if possible, taken into, the ruling caste. Politically, this same desire was manifested in the ardor with which many
Up Country leaders adopted and championed the cause of Charleston
and the interests of the large slaveholders.[25] In any event, the prestige of the old plantation caste has meant the spread inland of many
of their speechways, including the lack of constriction of postvocalic
/-r/, and the trend toward the loss of constriction continues. It
even serves to reinforce Southern xenophobia, for among the phoneti-
cally sophisticated the lack of constriction has become a point of
caste and local pride.[26]

It is true, of course, that prestige values can change. It should not be surprising, therefore, that indications already exist that constriction of postvocalic /-r/ may some day become respectable in South Carolina. The presence in local military posts of many Northern and Western servicemen, with strong constriction of their /-r/, as well as with a different and more sophisticated line of conversation, has led many Southern girls to the conclusion that a person with constriction can be acceptable as a date for the daughter of generations of plantation owners, or even possibly as a husband. Even in the heart of the Low Country, a number of girls in their late teens or early twenties are still speaking with a newly acquired constriction of postvocalic /-r/, long after the training camps have closed.[27] Perhaps the trend is about to be reversed.

In the meantime, since practical applications of scientific information are always sought, there are some ways in which this analysis of the social distribution of postvocalic /-r/ in South Carolina might be put to use by other social scientists. Just as in South Carolina, so probably in most of the other states of the Deep South, constriction is a linguistically peripheral feature found in culturally peripheral communities, generally on poor land among people who were driven onto the land — or, as with the textile workers, into their occupation — by the pressure of competition from the plantation system and Negro labor. It is among those people, whose cultural situation was originally brought about by Negro competition, that the fear of continuing Negro competition is keenest, and is most easily exploited by demagogues. It is from those people that the Ku Klux Klan, the Bleases and Talmadges and Bilbos, and the lynching mobs have tended to draw their strength.[28] Consequently, a Southern official whose job dealt with interracial problems might screen with a little extra care those native applicants for, say, police jobs whose speech showed strong constriction. And those interested in changing the racial attitudes of the whites might well concentrate their efforts on those areas where constriction has survived in greatest strength. Perhaps this suggestion is extreme, but it shows the possibilities.[29] For language is primarily a vehicle of social intercommunication, and linguistic phenomena must always be examined for their correlation with other cultural phenomena — as for the correlation between the spread of the unconstricted postvocalic /-r/ in South Carolina and the rise of the plantation system.

NOTES

This paper was presented at the symposium on linguistics and culture sponsored by Section H (Anthropology) of the AAAS at Chicago, Dec. 27, 1947.

[1]See, for example, the work of the late Benjamin L. Whorf, particularly 'The Relation of Habitual Thought and Behavior to Language,' in Language, Culture and Personality, Sapir memorial volume (Menasha, Wis., 1941), pp. 75-93.

[2]Raven I. McDavid, Jr., 'Dialect Geography and Social Science Problems,' Social Forces, XXV (1946), 168-72.

The data for this study have been derived from the field records collected for the Linguistic Atlas of the South Atlantic States prior to 1941 by Lowman, chief field worker, and since then by McDavid. The latter's field work was made possible first by a fellowship in 1941 from the Julius Rosenwald Fund and later by an honorary fellowship from Duke University and grants from the American Council of Learned Societies.

[3]The term 'constriction' includes turning up of the tongue tip (retroflexion, perhaps the rarest type of constriction in English), retraction of the tongue, spreading of the tongue, and other tongue movements providing friction during the articulation of a vowel. Traditionally, 'retroflexion' has been used where this paper uses 'constriction.'

[4]These transcriptions are for the type of dialect in which these lexical items generally occur.

[5]The difference between a farm and a plantation is not merely one of size, but rather of the attitude of the owner toward participation in the work of farming. Even on the largest farms, in the Up Country and north of the Santee, the farmer and his family normally did a great deal of the manual labor; on the plantations, the work of the planters was almost exclusively managerial.

[6]It is a tradition among some schools of scientific investigation not to insist on facts and examples, and to ignore them when they conflict with previously formulated theories.

[7]See, for example, George Philip Krapp, The English Language in America (New York, 1925), I, 38; Albert C. Baugh, History of the English Language (New York, 1935), pp. 444-449; Eilert Ekwall, British and American Pronunciation, the American Institute

in the University of Upsala, 'Essays and Studies on American Language and Literature' (Upsala, 1946), II, 13.

[8]Chart accompanying talk before the annual meeting of the Linguistic Society of America, New York, 1944.

[9]The concept of the Midland group of dialects, spreading westward and southward from the Philadelphia area, is perhaps the most fruitful contribution Kurath has made to the study of American dialects. The division into Northern, Midland, and Southern types is generally a better explanation of the historical facts and the present distribution of vocabulary items than the older grouping of Eastern, Southern, and 'General American,' and is at least as good a framework for an analysis on the basis of phonetic types.

[10]See Map 3. Since the available statistics are for counties, the large slaveholdings on the Sea Islands and the river ricelands obscure the presence of the many small farmers in the pinelands of Beaufort and Charleston districts.

[11]The mill villages, regardless of size — some are over ten thousand in population — are usually unincorporated, with all municipal functions handled by the mill management. The company store, with bills deducted from millworkers' wages, has existed on a scale unparalleled in any other industry, except possibly coal mining. Separate schools are provided for mill children — at Greenville, even a separate high school — and each mill village has its separate Protestant churches. See Liston Pope, Millhands and Preachers; a Study of Gastonia (New Haven, 1941).

In South Carolina, the paternalistic textile village dates from the founding of the Graniteville mill, in Aiken County, by William Gregg, in 1845. Gregg is also traditionally responsible for the pattern of employing only white labor in production operations in Southern textile mills. He advocated the building up of a textile industry as a philanthropic enterprise which would provide the poor whites with a means of livelihood secure from Negro (slave) competition.

[12]The loss of initial /h-/ in wheelbarrow, whetstone, whip — a feature of southern British 'received' pronunciation today — hardly occurs outside the immediate vicinity of the coastal centers, and is by no means universal even there. Such Midland vocabulary items as a little piece ('a short distance'), jacket ('vest'), coal oil or lamp oil ('kerosene'), and quarter till (the hour) may still be found in many Low Country communities.

Original settlement from southern Britain does not necessarily imply a tendency toward loss of constriction. Field records
made in England by Dr. Lowman show constriction in many southern
British folk dialects today. It does not, of course, weaken the argument for the influence of prestige factors to assert that the loss of constriction occurred principally in American communities which maintained close cultural contacts with the city of London; in fact, this
assertion only reemphasizes that influence.

[13]Expansion inland from the coast in the eighteenth century
was not the work of groups within the older communities as it was in
New England. Instead, frontier townships were laid out, and groups
of immigrants settled directly upon them. As a rule, the townships
north of the Santee were settled originally by Scotch-Irish, those
south of the Santee by Germans and German-Swiss. See Robert Lee
Meriwether, The Expansion of South Carolina 1729-1765 (Kingsport,
Tenn., 1940).

[14]See Map 3.

[15]Although by the time of the American Revolution the bulk of
the white population of South Carolina was to be found in the frontier
townships and in the new settlements made by the immigrants from
Pennsylvania, political power was held by the plantation group around
Charleston. All the delegates to the Continental Congress and to the
Constitutional Convention came from this group.

The tidewater planters and merchants kept up their ties with
England after the American Revolution, and a fair number of their
sons were educated in England. Even today the socially elite in
Charleston and Savannah tend toward uncritical admiration of things
English, at least of the practices of the English upper classes.

[16]Under the royal government several efforts were made to
restrict the importation of slaves, generally by imposing high import
duties, but profits from rice and indigo plantations kept these efforts
from being very effective. See Julian J. Petty, The Growth and Distribution of Population in South Carolina, Bulletin No. 11, State Planning Board (Columbia, S.C., 1943), pp. 50-57.

[17]Ibid., pp. 70-81.

[18]A case history is cited by Wilbur Joseph Cash, The Mind of
the South (New York, 1941), pp. 14-17.

[19]See, for example, Meriwether, op. cit., pp. 69-71.

[20]Interest rates were usually very high. For Up Country resentment toward Charleston, especially toward the symbols of

Charleston influence, the merchant and the banker, see Ben
Robertson, Red Hills and Cotton (New York, 1942), pp. 81-84, 91-
107.

To my paternal grandfather, an Up Country farmer, Charleston was a symbol of sharp business practices, if not of outright dishonesty.

[21]See Lawrence Fay Brewster, Summer Migrations and Resorts of South Carolina Low Country Planters, Historical Papers of the Trinity College Historical Society (Durham, N.C., 1942).

[22]Refugees from Charleston contributed particularly to the growth of Greenville. The Roman Catholic group in Greenville dates from the Civil War. Paradoxically, although the Roman Catholic Church has repeatedly served as a whipping boy for Up Country Ku Klux Klan organizers, demagogues, and Protestant ministers, Roman Catholics as individuals have achieved far more complete cultural integration in Greenville than in the outwardly more tolerant culture of Charleston.

Even today, Charlestonians not fully accepted in their native city have found their origin a password to social acceptance in the up-country. Typical of the colonial attitude of the older families in up-country towns is their reverence for the exclusive balls given by the St. Cecilia Society of Charleston. In Greenville, for instance, there is much more talk of the possibilities of being invited than one would hear in Charleston from people of the same social standing.

[23]As for example, the apprenticeship served by the Hon. James F. Byrnes, in the firm of Mordecai and Gaston.

[24]This was true even among the Baptists, the most loosely organized of the major Protestant sects. See William Joseph McGlothlin, Baptist Beginnings in Education: a History of Furman University (Nashville [1926]).

[25]John C. Calhoun, the most eloquent orator for slavery and nullification and Southern separatism, was born on the South Carolina frontier, and in the early stages of his political career was a spokesman for the frontier philosophy represented nationally by Andrew Jackson. After marrying into a Charleston family, he became the spokesman for the plantation interests. Robertson, op. cit., pp. 101-2.

[26]A former student of mine, the son of a Darlington County informant, explained, 'The reason we Southerners resent the way the Yankees roll their /-r/ is that it reminds us of the way the crackers

talk.' In South Carolina the term crackers is used (though less than
formerly) by the townspeople, the plantation caste, and plantation-
reared Negroes as a derogatory designation for the poor whites —
nonslaveholders, or descendants of nonslaveholders — in areas where
large slaveholdings once prevailed.

[27]This phenomenon has been observed particularly in such
constrictionless Low Country towns as Walterboro and Sumter. The
radio and the movies will probably reinforce this new trend. Similar
effects may be expected from the recent and continuing migrations of
Negroes northward and of Up Country whites to coastal towns.

An apparent tendency to replace the Low Country ingliding
diphthongs in date, boat [de·ət,|bo·ət] with the Up Country upgliding
type [de·ɪt, bo·ut] also suggests a reversal of the trend in prestige
values. One must remember, however, that in linguistic geography
each phonological or lexical item must be judged on its own merits,
and nothing could be more dangerous than to predict the fate of the
postvocalic /-r/ in South Carolina from the fate of the Low Country
diphthongs in date and boat.

[28]South Carolina political observers have noticed that Horry
County, the northeasternmost coastal county, has generally voted
the same way as the upper Piedmont in state elections, and always
gave a heavy Blease majority. Linguistic evidence — not only the
preservation of constriction, but of many lexical items as well —
indicates the cultural tie between the two sections.

[29]It is not necessarily true, of course, that only those persons
in the Deep South lacking postvocalic constriction of /-r/ would be
likely not to mistreat Negroes. Many of the plantation caste would
resent the notion of equality, much as they would resist anti-Negro
mob violence by poor whites. But since the revision of racial attitudes is largely a matter of education, it can hardly be without significance that in South Carolina the postvocalic /-r/ loses constriction among the group with the greater amount of education. It is also
worthy of note that almost every lynching in South Carolina in the last
twenty-five years occurred in counties where the field work for the
South Atlantic Atlas has disclosed strong constriction of postvocalic
/-r/.

[The prediction that postvocalic /-r/ might be rehabilitated
in South Carolina has been borne out by recent studies, notably R. K.
O'Cain, A Social Dialect Study of Charleston, South Carolina, Dissertation, University of Chicago, 1972.]

2 | The Relationship of the Speech of American Negroes to the Speech of Whites

In Collaboration with Virginia Glenn McDavid

Almost without exception, any scholar studying American Negro speech, whether as an end in itself or as part of a larger project, must dispose of two widely held superstitions: (1) he must indicate that there is no speech form identifiable as of Negro origin solely on the basis of Negro physical characteristics; (2) he must show that it is probable that some speech forms of Negroes—and even of some whites — may be derived from an African cultural background by the normal processes of cultural transmission. Such a necessity of refuting folk beliefs seldom arises when one is studying the English of other American minority groups. For these, it is generally assumed, though not necessarily in the terms anthropologists would use, that all linguistic patterns are culturally transmitted, that where a group with a foreign-language background — such as the Pennsylvania Germans — has been speaking a divergent variety of English for several generations in an overwhelmingly English-speaking area, there is nothing in their speech that cannot be explained on the basis of the culture contacts between the speakers of two languages. We are generous in recognizing Scandinavian linguistic survivals in Minnesota and the Dakotas, German in Wisconsin and Pennsylvania, and Dutch in the Hudson Valley. We do not explain this influence on the basis of Scandinavian hair color, German skull configuration, or Dutch mouth shape, but on the grounds that two languages were spoken side by side, so that bilingualism developed in the community. [1]

In forming judgments on the speech of the American Negro, however, the process has been reversed: the cultural transmission of speech forms of African origin has been traditionally denied, and the explanation of Negro dialects given in terms of a 'simple, child-like mind, [2] or of physical inability to pronounce the sounds of socially approved English. So widely spread is this superstition that Gunnar

Myrdal felt obliged to explain that Negro speech, like all other speech, is culturally transmitted;[3] as late as 1949 the author of a widely syndicated 'popular science' newspaper quiz explained that the Negro cannot pronounce a post vocalic / -r/ in such words as car, beard, or bird because his lips are too thick.[4]

There are reasons for this popular misinterpretation. One of the most obvious is that the Negro, unlike the other groups of foreign-language origin, is readily identifiable by skin pigmentation. Whatever differences the naïve observer notices between his speech and that of the average Negro he encounters, he interprets as a function of the identifiable physical difference. The fact that the contacts between whites and educated Negroes are limited, the normal contact between the two races being in terms of the situation of white master and Negro servant, means that Negro speech is generally judged on the basis of nonstandard speakers, or at best on the basis of speakers from a different dialect area.[5]

Other reasons for such misconceptions can be seen in the history of Negro-white relationships. Most obvious is the historical fact that the Negroes constituted the only large group of the American population that came here against their will, and with their cultural heritage overtly overridden in the effort to fit them into the new pattern of the basic unskilled labor for the plantation system.[6] Rationalizing the institution of chattel slavery as a benefit to the Negroes required that the whites deny any consequential African cultural heritage. Then when slavery was abolished as an institution but replaced—both in the South and elsewhere—by a racially determined caste system, supported by discriminatory legislation or extralegal covenants, the need for rationalization continued.[7]

It is therefore difficult for the white scholar to approach dispassionately the problem of African survivals in American Negro culture in general and speech in particular. The scholar who accepts the theory of Negro inferiority tends to explain any apparent differences between Negro and white speech on the basis of the Negro's childlike mind or imperfectly developed speech organs. Or if he tries to be fair, he will probably deny that there are any essential differences. This was the position of the late George Philip Krapp:

... The Negro speaks English of the same kind and, class for class, of the same degree, as the English of the most authentic descendants of the first settlers at Jamestown and Plymouth.

The Negroes, indeed, in acquiring English have done their work so thoroughly that they have retained not a trace of any native African speech. Neither have they transferred anything of importance from their native tongues to the general language. A few words, such as <u>voodoo</u>, <u>hoodoo</u>, and <u>buckra</u>, may have come into English from some original African dialect, but most of the words commonly supposed to be of Negro origin, e.g. <u>tote</u>, <u>jazz</u>, and <u>mosey</u>, are really derived from ancient English or other European sources. The native African dialects have been completely lost. [8]

But neither has the Negro scholar found the task an easy one. For a considerable period, he was as reluctant as the white scholar to admit a consequential African cultural heritage, reckoning Africa 'a badge of shame ... the reminder of a savage past not sufficiently remote, as is that of the European savagery, to have become hallowed.'[9] The inevitable overemphasis of possible African survivals, which one sometimes discovers in the works of recent Negro scholars, is perhaps no nearer an objective presentation than the old attitude, but ultimately should be as salutary a corrective of perspective as it is inevitable.

At the beginning of the century, the opinions held concerning the relationships between Negro and white speech may be summed up in two ethnocentric statements, both frequently heard today:

1. The regionally ethnocentric statement by Northerners that the 'quaintness' and 'primitiveness' of what they considered Southern speech[10] was due to the influence of the Negro.

2. The racially ethnocentric statement that the Negro contributed nothing of himself from his African heritage except a few exotic words, but that the essential characteristics of Negro speech— even of Gullah[11]—were to be derived from British provincial speech or from lapses into quasi baby talk by a simple people physically and intellectually incapable of mastering the sounds and structure of English.

Both of these statements, we will find, contained elements of truth. But neither was the whole truth. The first statement has had comparatively little currency and done little damage.[12] But the second has been institutionalized as part of what Herskovits calls 'the Myth of the Negro past.'[13]

To cite a multiplicity of examples of these attitudes would add little to the argument. But from two examples one may see the myth in action.

In his single essay at linguistic analysis,[14] Cleanth Brooks sought in Wright's English Dialect Grammar and Dictionary for the origins of what he called the 'Alabama-Georgia dialect,' recorded by his definition in Leonidas W. Payne's 'A World-List from East Alabama'[15] and the Uncle Remus stories of Joel Chandler Harris. As a basic premise, Brooks assumes that no Africanisms have survived,[16] and that the speech of Negroes and whites may therefore be considered as the same.[17]

The first study of Gullah was that made by John Bennett.[18] His general conclusions were that Gullah was essentially derived from seventeenth-century British folk speech, as adopted or misinterpreted by a culturally inferior group physically incapable of making English speech-sounds:

> To express other than the simplest ideas, plain actualities, is, however, difficult ...[19]
> Intellectual indolence, or laziness, mental and physical, which shows itself in the shortening of words, the elision of syllables, and modification of every difficult enunciation...[20]
> It is the indolence, mental and physical, of the Gullah dialect that is its most characteristic feature ...[21]

Until the studies of Lorenzo Turner, students of Gullah—or those referring to Gullah speech in the course of other work—largely took over Bennett's conclusions and words, with some slight rephrasing.[22] It would seem that the linguistic investigator had often formed his conclusions before he began his field work.

Even where the investigator is seriously interested in gathering new evidence for reinterpreting the old, he is likely to run into

difficulties in the field. A Negro community that has been too often
pointed out as a Negro community, and exploited as such by political
and propaganda groups, is reluctant to accept the outside investigator,
no matter how well intentioned.[23] If the speech of the Negro group
has a situational dialect variety employed to conceal information or
attitudes from the white man, there is reluctance to give away the in-
group secret to the investigator.[24] Where the Negro is accustomed to
telling the white man what he thinks the white man wants to be told—
where, in fact, his survival often depends on his skill in guessing
that—the investigator may find informants too cooperative, too ready
to offer evidence supporting a stereotype.[25] And in communities
where the caste lines are most sharply drawn, even an experienced
field worker may inadvertently lose rapport with his Negro informants
by transgressing taboos of speech or manner.[26]

    In spite of these difficulties, the last half century has seen
much information gathered about both white and Negro speech, and
the cultures in which they are used, so that we are now able to speak
more intelligently, if somewhat more tentatively, than before. Perhaps the most important force in the revision of older attitudes has
been the development of the culture concept by anthropologists,[27] with
the realization that long-established ways of saying and doing things
or thinking about them can persist in the face of almost inconceivable
disadvantages, simply because they are what people are used to. More
particularly, there has been a great deal of serious study of Negro
communities in Africa and various parts of the New World, and a
large-scale study of the American Negro under the direction of the
Swedish sociologist Gunnar Myrdal and the auspices of the Carnegie
Corporation.[28] There have been scientific studies, both descriptive
and comparative, of African languages[29] and of pidgin and creolized
languages, especially the studies of Melanesian pidgin, Chinese pidgin,
Taki-Taki, and Haitian Creole by Hall,[30] of Haitian Creole by Sylvain-
Comhaire,[31] of Louisiana Negro-French by Lane,[32] and of Papiamento
(the creolized Negro-Dutch-Spanish of Curaçao) by Frederick Agard
and C. Cleland Harris.[33] The South Atlantic records for the Linguistic Atlas of the United States and Canada provide material for comparing white and Negro speech in the same communities, and Turner has
made a significant contribution by his seventeen years of research in
Gullah.

    The study of African languages has served two purposes, in
addition to the obvious one of indicating actual or potential etyma for

vocabulary items in American Negro speech. By providing a record
of the structural features of African languages—phonemics, morphology, and syntax—it has enabled us to see that some features of
American Negro speech may not be baby talk of the misinterpretations of ignorant savages, but rather the persistence of something
from African speech. Moreover, the comparative work in African
languages has revealed a high degree of structural similarity between
the languages of the area from which most of the slaves were taken,
so as to make for common trends in the speech of American Negroes,
regardless of the mutual unintelligibility of their original languages. [34]

The study of pidgins and creolized languages has likewise
facilitated the intelligent study of the relationship between white and
Negro speech. It has been repeatedly shown that these languages are
not linguistic freaks, with quaint and curious ways of saying things,
but that each of them has its own definite structure, and that they are
as worthy of serious study as the better-known languages of Western
Europe. Consequently, the investigator of Negro speech in this country has precedent for making a scientific description, as one should
make of any dialect. More immediately pertinent, the research into
Taki-Taki, Brazilian Negro Portuguese, and Haitian Creole enables
the student of American Negro speech to assay whether a particular
structural feature is of African origin or not. If a certain feature of
Gullah syntax, say, is also found in Brazilian Negro Portuguese, in
Haitian Creole, and in Papiamento, and resembles a structural feature
of several West African languages, it is likely that it is not taken from
British peasant speech. [35]

The Linguistic Atlas project provides a tremendous mass of
data for evaluating dialect-relationships within English-speaking North
America; and thanks to the cooperation promised by British scholars,
it may soon enable us to state the interrelationships of all forms of
present-day English. In their present state, the records for the
Atlantic seaboard area of original settlement, in which Hans Kurath—
the director of the project—is particularly interested, show the comparable results of 1,500 interviews in over 700 communities from
southern New Brunswick to the Altamaha Valley and northeastern
Florida. The regional surveys—under Albert Marckwardt in the North
Central states, under Harold Allen in the upper Midwest, under Henry
Alexander in the Maritime Provinces, and those recently begun elsewhere include some 2400 more interviews of actual usage by living
informants native to the communities investigated. These records

include 40 Negro informants in the South Atlantic states, a few in
New England and New Brunswick, and a large number in the Gulf
States. These studies have attempted to obtain data from Negro and
white informants of the same economic and educational level in the
same community; in such a way one can avoid the comparison so
properly resented by Negro leaders and by serious scholars of all
races, of juxtaposing the most cultured white and the least sophisticated Negro.[36] And with such data available, one finds—as anthropologists have predicted—that vocabulary and phonology are not matters
of skin pigmentation but of the social contacts and economic opportunities of the informant.

Perhaps the greatest single contribution to an intelligent
reappraisal of the relationships between white and Negro speech has
been the investigation of the speech of the Gullah Negroes by Lorenzo
D. Turner. Though embodying only part of his findings, his 1949
book, Africanisms in the Gullah Dialect, dispels effectively the notion
that the American Negro lost all his language and his culture under
the impact of chattel slavery and the plantation system. Turner's
overt statement is impressive enough: that an investigation of Gullah
speech discloses several thousand items presumably derived from the
languages of the parts of Africa from which the slaves were taken.
But the implicit conclusions are yet more impressive: that many
structural features of Gullah are also to be found in creolized languages
of South America and the Caribbean, in the pidgin-like trade English
of West Africa, and in many African languages—this preservation of
fundamental structural traits is a more cogent argument for the importance of the African element in the Gullah dialect (and, by inference, in the totality of Gullah culture) than any number of details of
vocabulary.[37] Perhaps most significant of all, though hardly hinted
at by Turner, is the evidence from phonological structure: like the
languages of West Africa described by Westermann and Ward, Gullah
has a far less complex system of vowel phonemes than any known
variety of English; furthermore, Gullah has a remarkable uniformity,
not only in phonemic structure but in the phonetic shape of vowel
allophones, along a stretch of nearly four hundred miles of the South
Atlantic coast, in the very region where there is a greater variety
among the dialects of white speech than one can find elsewhere in
English-speaking North America—a uniformity difficult to explain
by chance, or by any of the older explanations of Negro speech.[38]
Turner's work has already made scholars aware of the importance

of the African background in American Negro speech; though his
descriptive grammar of Gullah was never completed, one can make a
tolerable grammatical sketch from the texts in the Africanisms.

As by-products of the field work for the Linguistic Atlas and
other dialect studies, several bits of evidence have been found that
suggest how a comparative study of Negro and white speech may be
useful in indicating areas of actual or potential interracial tension.
It is not without significance that Chicago-born Negro students at the
University of Illinois have preserved many characteristic Southern
words that are unknown to white students of the same age and city,
or that Michigan-born Negroes in the age group between twenty and
thirty have the South Midland diphthongs in dance and law, although the
dialect of older-generation Michigan-born Negroes is indistinguishable
from that of their white contemporaries. Nor can one overlook the
fact that educated Negroes in such Southern communities as Greenville
and Atlanta tend to avoid the forms having prestige in local white
speech in favor of their conception of New England speech. Even though
this evidence is spotty and unsystematized, it already indicates that
future community social analyses should include a study of dialect
differences within the community—and especially if the community
contains a large Negro group. [39]

In summary, we must evaluate the relationships between
Negro and white speech in the same scientific spirit as any anthropologist studies acculturation. We must lay aside ethnocentric prejudices
of all kinds—no less the traditional Southern assumption of Negro
inferiority than the equally glib statement of career Negroes (perhaps
oftener in Africa than in the United States) that no study of Negro culture by whites can be valid because 'the white man doesn't understand
the black man's mind.' We must remember that conclusions are valid
only in so far as they are based on valid data, and that the discovery
of new data may call for new conclusions—though we can hardly expect
so drastic a modification of attitudes as that made possible in the last
generation by the use of evidence from African languages and from
creolized Negro speech elsewhere in the New World. What new conclusions we reach will probably come by revision of details within the
following framework.

First, the overwhelming bulk of the material of American
Negro speech—in vocabulary as well as in grammar and phonology—

is, as one would expect, borrowed from the speech of the white groups
with which Negroes come in contact. Sometimes these contacts have
been such that Negroes simply speak the local variety of standard
English.[40] It is also likely that many relic forms from English dialects are better preserved in the speech of some American Negro
groups than in American white speech—not merely items of vocabulary
but also items of grammar and even of pronunciation, so far as the
occurrence of a given phoneme in a given group of words is concerned.
After all, the preservation of relic forms is made possible by geographical or cultural isolation. If Africanisms survive, say, in Gullah
because of the long inaccessibility of the Gullah-speaking communities
and because of the Southern caste system which limited contacts between white and Negro speakers, so can relic forms from seventeenth-century English.

Nevertheless, the borrowing has not been all in one direction.
The Linguistic Atlas indicates that many words noted by Turner as of
African origin have been taken over by Southern whites and spread far
beyond the areas in which the plantation system flourished.[41] The
foci from which these words have apparently spread had large Negro
populations early in their history.[42] Pinto, 'coffin,' has been recorded
sporadically from the PeeDee River to Savannah—chiefly from Negroes,
but sometimes offered by white informants as a characteristic 'Negro
word.'[43] Buckra, 'white man,' has spread into the South Carolina
Piedmont, especially in the contemptuous designation of poor whites
as poor buckra. Joggling board (cf. Gullah [ʄɔgɔl-bod, ʄɔglʊ-bod]),
less often applied to a seesaw than to a long limber plank anchored
at both ends and used, as a swing might be used, by nurses dandling
infants, by children at play, and by courting couples, is known throughout the plantation country from Georgetown to the Altamaha River, and
in inland communities frequented by plantation families in the malaria
season. Jinky board, janky board (cf. Gullah ['cika-bod]) is a name
for the seesaw in Berkeley County, S. C. Pinder 'peanut' has been
recorded in all parts of South Carolina; goober, 'peanut,' is found
from Chesapeake Bay and the Potomac River southwest through the
Piedmont of South Carolina and Georgia, and along the coastal plain
from Georgetown south. Cooter, 'turtle,' is found throughout the
coastal plain and the lower piedmont from the Cape Fear River to
Florida. Cush, 'a kind of mush,' is frequently recorded in the coastal
plain.[44] Of words not recorded in the Atlas, hoodoo (noun and verb)

has spread far beyond the South; okra is a staple Southern vegetable;
gumbo, 'a thick soup with an okra base' (cf. Gullah [ˈgʌmbo] 'okra')
is nationally known; benne, 'sesame,' is a common ingredient of
cookies and candy in the Charleston and Savannah areas; da is the
usual Charleston name for a child's Negro nurse; Geechee is commonly used, with mildly insulting connotations, by Up Country South
Carolinians as a nickname for any Low Countryman, especially one
from the Charleston area; jigger (or chigger) is the common Southern
name for a minute insect with a proclivity for burrowing in human
flesh; war mouth, also known as more-mouth (cf. Gullah [ˈwɔmɛut],
Mende [wɔ]'large'), is a common coastal plain name for a kind of
catfish; pojo, 'heron,' is widely known in the Charleston area; tabby,
'a type of structural material made of cement and oyster shells, often
with pieces of brick intermixed,' is frequently used for foundations or
house walls in South Carolinian and Georgia coastal communities;
shout, 'religious dance,' is a typical practice of the less formally
organized Protestant groups in the South, white as well as Negro.[45]

So far as Gullah word formation is concerned, dialect geography supports Turner's suggestion that many Gullah compounds and
onomatopoetic expressions may reflect African practice: yard ax,
'poorly trained irregular preacher,' and its synonym table tapper have
been recorded chiefly in the Georgetown and Charleston areas and in
the Santee Valley; huhu owl, 'hoot owl, large owl,' is found occasionally in the South Carolina coastal plain; bloody-noun, 'large bullfrog' (cf. Gullah [ˈblʌdiˌnɔn]) has been recorded in the Santee and
Savannah valleys, and along the coast from Georgetown to the Florida
line.[46] Not recorded in the Atlas but commonly considered to be of
Negro origin are such metaphors as sweet-mouth, 'to flatter,' and
bad-mouth, 'to curse.'[47]

From Negroes—whether the form is in origin an Africanism
or a relic of early English usage—many white folk speakers along the
South Carolina coast have taken for as the particle with the infinitive
of purpose, as he come for tell you rather than the standard to or the
widespread folk form for to. It may possibly be that the Negro playmates of well-to-do white children (especially boys) and the Negro
servants to whom they have been accustomed are at least partially
responsible for the more frequent occurrence and the higher degree
of cultural tolerance for nonstandard forms in cultured speech in the

South than elsewhere.[48] In phonology, many white folk informants in
and near the Gullah country use the bilabial /f,v/ [Φ,β] or replace
both /v,w/ by one bilabial voiced spirant [β], as Turner indicates
happens in Gullah.[49] Perhaps the greater tendency in Southern speech
to simplify final consonant clusters is encouraged by the fact that
Gullah and African languages have relatively less complex final clusters than English dialects in other parts of the United States. Furthermore, the striking intonation patterns noticed in such communities as
Charleston and Georgetown suggest the possibility that Negro influence
in this feature might well be investigated.

With so much apparent, the next step is to plan future work.
Herskovits has already made suggestions as to places to be investigated and types of linguistic investigation to be conducted.[50] To these
one might make a few additions. Americo-Liberian English certainly
should be studied, to see both the extent of reacculturation to Africa
and the survivals of traits of Southern American English.[51] One
should investigate such old Negro communities outside the South as
the Dowagiac-Cassopolis area in Michigan or Dresden in Ontario
(both settled by refugee slaves brought out of the South along the Under-
ground Railroad) or the relics of the New Brunswick settlements by
the slaves of New York Loyalists and the Nova Scotia settlements by
Jamaica Negroes.[52] For controls—communities where relic forms
might be expected to occur, but where Negro influence is improbable—
we should have an early survey of Newfoundland, and intensive study
of selected communities in the Maritime Provices and of the Banks
Islands on the North Carolina coast between Manteo and Wilmington.
Furthermore, in community studies where Negroes are interviewed,
the field worker should not only interview representatives of several
age groups and educational groups, but should also make a selection
in terms of the number of generations the families of informants have
been resident in the community.

In this way it should be possible to establish a procedure for
determining whether a form found among Negroes in the South is likely
to be African or folk English in origin. The investigator should check
its occurrence in Newfoundland, the Banks Islands, New Hampshire
and Maine, Cape Ann, Cape Cod and the offshore islands—all known
to be relic areas without probable Negro influence. If the form is
found in the latter communities, whether or not it is found in the

British Isles, it is reasonable to suspect that its etymon is not African,
though one may concede a reinforcement by African influence.[53] Conversely, forms not found in such communities but found, say, in Gullah
and Papiamento probably have African origins.

As with many other aspects of dialect investigation, the half
century of investigations of Negro speech and its affiliations with white
speech has left many questions unanswered. But it has provided a
framework within which these questions can be both asked and answered
more intelligently than heretofore.[54] The linguistic scientist has
learned not to look down upon other forms of speech that happen to
differ from his own; he can hope that the public will cease to look down
upon the speech of those whose skin pigmentation or hair form may be
different, or to fancy any necessary correlation between the pigmentation of a speaker's skin and the phonemic system of his dialect.

NOTES

[1] Einar Haugen, 'The Analysis of Linguistic Borrowing,'
Language, XXVI (1950), 210-31.
      [2] The most widely publicized arguments for the allegedly
childlike mentality of the Negro and of his general inferiority are
Jerome Dowd, The Negro in American Life (New York, 1926), and
J. A. Tillinghast, The Negro in Africa and America (New York,
1902). Even so sympathetic a student of the Negro as Howard Odum
accepted the stereotype of Negro inferiority in his early work, Social
and Mental Traits of the Negro (New York, 1910).
      [3] An American Dilemma (New York, 1944), as on p. 965:
'There is absolutely no biological basis for it [Negro dialect]; Negroes
are as capable of pronouncing English words perfectly as whites
are ...'
      [4] Albert E. Wiggam, 'Let's Explore Your Mind,' as in the
Cleveland Plain Dealer, July 3, 1949.
      [5] Myrdal, op. cit., p. 965.
      [6] Allen Walker Read in his study, 'The Speech of Negroes in
Colonial America,' Journal of Negro History, XXIV (1939), 247-58,
drawing his material from the advertisements for runaway slaves,
throws a clear light on the process of the Negroes' learning of English.
He concludes, p. 258: 'The present study shows that during colonial

times there were Negroes in all stages of proficiency in their knowledge
of English: a constant stratum of recently arrived ones without any
English, those who were learning English during their first years in
the new country, and a group who had learned successfully. The
Negroes born in this country invariably used, according to these
records, good English. The colored race were faced, against their
will, with a huge problem in adopting a new language in a strange
country, and their success, in the light of their opportunities, was
equal to that of any other immigrant body. '

[7]The generation after the Civil War also witnessed the
last period of European colonial expansion at the expense of the non-
white races, the period in which the Nordic myth was so widely publicized by Gobineau, Chamberlain, Madison Grant in his The Passing
of the Great Race (New York, 1918), and Homer Lea in his The Day
of the Saxon (New York, 1912), and in which European imperialism
was rationalized by Kipling and others as a benign paternalism—'the
white man's burden. '

[8]'The English of the Negro, ' American Mercury, II (1924),
190-95, at p. 190. See also Krapp, The English Language in America
(New York, 1925), I, 161-63; II, 226.

[9]Melville J. Herskovits, The Myth of the Negro Past (New
York, 1941), p. 32.

[10]Much of what has been popularly labeled as 'Southern
speech, ' such as the dialects of the southern Appalachians, is properly not Southern at all, but South Midland, derivative from Pennsylvania. 'The common notion of a linguistic Mason and Dixon's Line
separating "Northern" from "Southern" speech is simply due to an
erroneous inference from an oversimplified version of the political
history of the nineteenth century ... ' Hans Kurath, A Word Geography
of the Eastern United States (Ann Arbor, 1949), p. vi. See also R.
McDavid's review of Kurath, New York History, XXXI (1950), 442-44.

[11]'Gullah' is the creolized variety of English spoken by the
descendants of Negro slaves in the area of rice, indigo, and Sea Island
cotton plantations along the South Carolina and Georgia coasts. The
term Geechee is sometimes used, either as a synonym for Gullah or
as a designation for the Gullah spoken in Georgia.

[12]To some extent it has been used by elocutionists and their
satellites to shame cultured Southerners—or those who would like
outsiders to consider them as cultured Southerners—into giving up
their own dialectal patterns in favor of southern British, eastern New

England, or whatever dialect the elocutionist speaks or sets up as a
model of elegance. For the same motive—a desire to depart from the
regional patterns of the other race—plus the identification of eastern
New England with abolitionism and other efforts to break the caste
system in the South, educated Southern Negroes sometimes model their
own speech on that of eastern New England. Likewise, some Negro
school systems are inclined to favor such New England speech characteristics as the [aɪð̆ə, naɪð̆ə] forms of either, neither, and the so-
called 'broad a' [a,ɑ] forms of half past, dance, grass, etc.

[13] Herskovits, op. cit., pp. 1-2.

[14] The Relation of the Alabama-Georgia Dialect to the Provincial Dialects of Great Britain (Baton Rouge, 1935).

[15] 'A Word-List from East Alabama,' Dialect Notes, III (1908-
9), 279-328, 343-91.

[16] Brooks, op. cit., p. 64.

[17] One must always use Wright with caution, since a large
part of the evidence on which both the Grammar and the Dictionary are based was collected by amateurs with uneven training and
without any systematic procedure. The unevenness of the results can
readily be perceived if one attempts to chart for the British Isles the
vocabulary variants which Kurath's Word Geography of the Eastern
United States indicates as significant for the Atlantic seaboard. For
instance, of the variety of terms for the earthworm which Kurath has
found representative of major or minor American dialect areas—and
of which most must have been found in the British Isles—only angledog
and eaceworm are recorded in Wright.

In selecting his American sources Brooks likewise shows a
lack of discrimination. The part of Georgia in which Harris grew up
was not near the Alabama line but in the eastern part of the state.
Both Alabama and inland Georgia were areas of tertiary—or at best
secondary—settlement, whose settlers came from areas where dialect mixture already had occurred. Finally, the informant whose
speech is represented in Harris's stories may not have been representative of any variety of Georgia speech since Uncle Remus speaks of
himself as having been raised in Virginia, or 'Ferginny' as he would
say it.

[18] 'Gullah: a Negro Patois,' South Atlantic Quarterly, VII
(1908), 332-47; VIII (1909), 39-52.

[19] Ibid., VII, 338.

[20] Ibid., VIII, 40.

[21]Ibid., p. 49.

[22]'Slovenly and careless of speech, these Gullahs seized upon the peasant English used by some of the early settlers and by the white servants of the wealthier colonists, wrapped their clumsy tongues about it as well as they could, and, enriched with certain expressive African words, it issued through their flat noses and thick lips as so workable a form of speech that it was gradually adopted by the other slaves ...' Ambrose E. Gonzales, The Black Border: Gullah Stories of the Carolina Coast (Columbia, S.C., 1922), p. 10. 'Simple language concepts of the unseasoned slaves ... with their simple dialects ...' Mason Crum, Gullah: Negro Life in the Carolina Sea Islands (Durham, N.C., 1940), p. 113.

[23]We encountered this reaction in Dresden, Ontario, in the summer of 1950. In the spring of 1949 there had been local controversy over discrimination against Negroes in restaurants and barber shops, a situation which was widely publicized by the Canadian press and utilized by Communist front organizations for their own ends. Although some of the younger leaders of the Negro community were sympathetic to the purposes of the Atlas, efforts to interview older Negroes were unsuccessful, because the community was sensitive about the type of publicity it had already received.

[24]Lorenzo D. Turner reports that his earlier Gullah records contained far fewer Africanisms—especially the African-derived personal names—than his later ones. See his Africanisms in the Gullah Dialect (Chicago, 1949), p. 12.

[25]I found among Negro informants a somewhat greater willing-ness than among whites to accept as authentic the responses suggested by the field worker, no matter how deliberately far-fetched some of these suggestions might be. On the other hand, I found at least one Negro informant who conformed to the traditional stereotype of Negro speech during the part of the interview conducted in the presence of his white patron, but who abandoned that role when we were alone. (R.I.M.)

[26]Turner, op. cit., pp. 11-12.

[27]A. L. Kroeber, 'Anthropology,' Scientific American, CLXXXIII, No. 3 (1950), 87-94.

[28]Myrdal was chosen as director of the project because Sweden is a nation without colonies, and therefore without institu-tionalized attitudes toward the nonwhite races. The Negro problem is summarized in An American Dilemma; no person unfamiliar with

this book can claim to 'know the Negro.' Herskovits's The Myth of the
Negro Past is one of the special studies prepared for the project.

[29] Joseph H. Greenberg, 'Some Problems in Hausa Phonology,'
Language, XVII (1941), 316–23; 'Studies in African Linguistic Classification,' Southwestern Journal of Anthropology, V (1949), 79–100,
190–98, 309–17; VI (1950), 47–63, 143–60. C. T. Hodge and E. E.
Hause, 'Hausa Tone,' Journal of the American Oriental Society, LXIV
(1944), 51–52. C. T. Hodge, 'An Outline of Hausa Grammar' (Language Dissertation No. 41), Language, Vol. XXIII, No. 4, Suppl.
(1947). W. E. Welmers, 'A Descriptive Grammar of Fanti' (Language
Dissertation No. 39), Language, Vol. XXII, No. 3, Suppl. (1946).
'New Light on Consonant Change in Kpella,' Zeitschrift für Phonetik
und Allgemeine Wissenschaft, IV (1950), 105–17. 'Notes on Two
Languages of the Senufo Group, I. Senadi; II. Sup'ide,' Language,
XXVI (1950), 126–46, 494–531. 'Secret Medicines, Magic, and Rites
of the Kpella Tribe of Liberia,' Southwestern Journal of Anthropology,
V (1949), 208–43. 'Tones and Tone Writing in Menika,' Studies in
Linguistics, VII (1949), 1–17. W. E. Welmers and Z. S. Harris,
'The Phonemes of Fanti,' Journal of the American Oriental Society,
LXII (1942), 318–33. [Since 1951 such studies have multiplied.]

[30] Robert A. Hall, Jr., 'Chinese Pidgin English Grammar
and Texts,' Journal of the American Oriental Society, LXIV (1944),
95–113. 'The Linguistic Structure of Taki-Taki,' Language, XXIV
(1948), 100–101, 109. Melanesian Pidgin English: Grammar, Texts,
Vocabulary (Baltimore, 1943).

[31] Suzanne Sylvain-Comhaire, Le Créole haïtien: morphologie
et syntaxe (Wetteren and Port-au-Prince, 1936).

[32] George S. Lane, 'Notes on Louisiana French,' Language,
X (1934), 323–33; XI (1935), 5–16.

[33] The research in Papiamento is now in progress at Cornell
University.

[34] Herskovits, op. cit., pp. 79–81.

[35] Robert A. Hall, Jr., 'The African Substratum in Negro
English' (review of Africanisms in the Gullah Dialect), American
Speech, XXV (1950), 51–54.

[36] The availability of accurate data on the actual speech of
the Atlantic seaboard has enabled scholars to make intelligent approaches to the problems of 'literary dialect'—to interpreting the devices
through which poets and novelists attempt to represent regional or

local speech by respellings in the conventional alphabet. At least four recent doctoral dissertations treat this problem, making use of Atlas data to discover the kind of dialect the writer was trying to represent: by James N. Tidwell (Ohio State), on literary representations of Southern speech; by Sumner Ives (Texas), on the dialect of the Uncle Remus stories; by James W. Downer (Michigan), on the dialect of the Biglow Papers; and by Charles William Foster on the stories of Charles W. Chesnutt.

[37] Evidence that the American Negro stems from an advanced cultural background in Africa and has managed to preserve significant traits from that background does not help the case of those who attempt to rationalize discriminatory practices as justified by Negro cultural and psychological inferiority.

[38] This uniformity is attested both in Turner's own field records and in corroborative recordings made for Kurath by Guy S. Lowman, Jr., principal field investigator for the Linguistic Atlas. [For a more recent appraisal, see Kurath, Studies in Area Linguistics (Bloomington, Indiana, 1972), pp. 118-121.]

[39] Comparative studies of Negro and white usage, as recorded in Atlas field records, have been made by Solveig Greibesland (University of Chicago, 1970), for three Potomac Valley Communities, and by George Dorrill (University of South Carolina, 1975), for two communities in central South Carolina.

[40] William Gilmore Simms, whose representations of dialect are rather accurate, regularly indicates quasi-Gullah characteristics of the speech of Negro huntsmen, stable-boys, and field hands. But in Katherine Walton, where most of the action takes place in Charleston, he properly indicates no 'dialect' forms in the speech of a Negro butler and major-domo, who would normally speak the standard English of Charleston.

[41] The sentences here following are closely paraphrased or quoted from the review of Turner's book by Raven I. McDavid, Jr., in Language, XXVI (1950), 328-30.

[42] See Julian J. Petty, The Growth and Distribution of Population in South Carolina, State Planning Board, Bulletin 11 (Columbia, S.C., 1943).

[43] Pinto is used chiefly for the old-fashioned hexagonal coffin (occasionally pentagonal, with the omission of the footboard); informants often explain the name by commenting that the narrowness of the

coffin pins the corpse's toes together—a spurious etymology which was seldom questioned prior to Turner's investigations.

[44] Turner does not list tacky, 'horse,' generally recorded along the South Carolina coast in the form marsh tacky, and often supposed to be of African origin. Presumably the proposed African etyma are dubious.

[45] It would have been very useful if Turner had indicated the geographical distribution within the Gullah country of each lexical item, including personal names. In an earlier report, he suggested that groups of words and names traceable to particular African languages were found clustered in particular Gullah communities, and that this geographical distribution can be correlated with the pattern of slave settlement. See 'Linguistic Research and African Survivals,' American Council of Learned Societies Bulletin, XXXII (1941), 73.

[46] An onomatopoetic variant /búdidəŋk, bə́-, -dʊŋk/ seems to be confined to the Georgetown area.

[47] Such phrases as put the mouth on, 'hex,' are also frequently heard, and are considered to be of Negro origin.

[48] Nearly every cultured informant interviewed in South Carolina and Georgia used ain't at some time during the interview. In fact, one of the touchstones often used by Southerners to distinguish the genuine cultured speaker from the pretenders is that the latter are too socially insecure to know the proper occasions for using ain't, the double negative, and other such folk forms, and hence avoid them altogether.

[49] Turner, op. cit., pp. 241-42.

[50] Herskovits, op. cit., pp. 327-337.

[51] Welmers reports many speech forms in Americo-Liberian that have been recorded for the Linguistic Atlas in the South Atlantic states.

[52] Herskovits, op. cit., p. 94.

[53] In Some Sources of Southernisms (University, Alabama, 1948), M. M. Mathews attempts to derive the folk term doney 'sweetheart' through a Gullah personal name from the latter's suggested African etymon, Bambara [doni] 'a burden.' However, the Linguistic Atlas records doney most frequently in areas where there is least reason to suspect Negro influence: the Shenandoah Valley and central and western North Carolina. Similarly, despite the absence of an attested Middle English etymon, it seems improbable that tote 'carry,' is exclusively of African origin, since tote, 'haul,' is well attested in

areas of New England and the inland North outside the area of probable
Negro influence, along with such compounds as tote-road, tote-sled,
tote-wagon, and tote-team.

      [54]H. L. Mencken, in The American Language (4th ed.; New
York, 1936), pp. 112-13, accepted the earlier theory of the paucity
of African survivals in American Negro speech. However, in his
Supplement I (New York, 1945), pp. 198-99, Turner's work had
enabled him to revise his judgment.

3 | Dialect Differences and Social Differences in an Urban Society

When kings have become philosophers and philosophers have become kings, when the average American citizen becomes less intensely competitive with his neighbors and more willing to give each one a chance to do to his fullest capacity the work for which he has the greatest aptitude and interest, then — as class markers lose significance — it will hardly be necessary to talk about social dialects. But until that time, while a person's social standing will be assessed in terms of the way in which his use of English measures up to what the dominant culture consider the marks of educated speech, it will be important to understand the linguistic indicators of social difference in any given community. Everyone knows from his own experience that such indicators exist, though he may misjudge the actual significance of a particular item. As an example of the kind of mistake one can make, until I was nearly thirty I could not imagine that a truly educated and cultivated person would fail to distinguish between such pairs as horse and hoarse or dew and do, or such triads as merry, marry and Mary. [1]

But in compensation for such limits, I learned intuitively that in my native community (Greenville, South Carolina) one's vowels were clear markers of one's social standing. This experience prepared me for what I encountered in teaching in a wide spectrum of other communities — Charleston, South Carolina; Lafayette, Louisiana; Cleveland and Chicago — where complex social dialect situations could be readily observed. [2]

The intuitive and informal observations in these situations have been reinforced by some three thousand hours of field interviewing for the Linguistic Atlas project, and by the more intensive studies that younger investigators have undertaken — some of them,

I am proud to state, students of mine. This paper presents a syn-
thesis of some of the evidence gathered in these investigations; if any
specific remark impinges on a sensitive corn, say that of a metropolitan school superintendent, the cornbearer should not blame the evidence but the society in which the evidence was gathered.

A dialect, in the sense in which American scholars use it,
is simply an habitual variety of a language, set off from other such
varieties by a complex of features of pronunciation (/drin/ vs.
/dren/ "drain"), grammar (I dove vs. I dived) or vocabulary (doughnut vs. fried cake). Dialects arise through regional or social barriers in the communications system: the stronger the barrier, the
sharper the dialect differences. Most often we think of a dialect as
the way some stranger talks; we generally assume that we speak
"normal English" — or French or Russian or Burmese or Ojibwa, as
the case may be.

The most obvious dialects, to most of us, are the regional
varieties — the Eastern New England type, of the late President
Kennedy; the Southwestern variety, of President Johnson; or the
Charleston variety, which everyone in the Up Country of South Carolina used to mock in something like the following:

[wi·l hav ə leˑ·ᵊt deˑ·ᵊt ət eˑ·ᵊt and goˑ·ᵊ aut tənəit ɔn ðə boˑ·ᵊt
ənd rɔid bɔi ðə batrɪ ənd θroˑ·ᵊ brɪkbats ət ðə batlʃɪps]

"We'll have a late date at eight and go out tonight on the boat, and
ride by the Battery and throw brickbats at the battleships."

Other regional varieties may be less conspicuous than these, but we
generally do fairly well in sorting out the stranger from the person
who grew up in our home town.

In addition to regional dialects, however, we have social
dialects. A social dialect, as I define it, is an habitual sub-variety
of the speech of a given community, restricted by the operation of
social forces to representatives of a particular ethnic, religious,
economic or educational group. By and large, the more that any
one sub-variety is esteemed above all others in a given community,
the sharper will be the distinction between it and its less-favored

competitors. No community is without social dialects; but in general, the fewer the locally sanctioned class barriers, the more difficult to find the true class markers, in speech as in anything else. Since it is impossible to give in detail all kinds of social dialect situations, my discussion here is confined to two examples — Greenville and Chicago. Both illustrate the traditional pattern of urban growth from in-migration, though the scales and the details are different. For Greenville I draw on years of intuitive observations as a child and adolescent (observations the more likely to be objective since as a child I felt no identity with any local class or clique or cult), followed by field investigations for the Atlas. For Chicago I rely on conscious observations, especially on the dissertation of Lee Pederson.[3]

Greenville: A Microcosm

Greenville, like most of the Upland South, was originally settled by Ulster Scots and Pennsylvania Germans, who came southward along the Shenandoah Valley and the eastern slopes of the Blue Ridge. A few of the most adventurous drifted northwest with Daniel Boone and his associates, to colonize the Ohio Valley; another group, fiercely individualistic, infiltrated the Appalachians, where they made some of the best whiskey in the world (illegal, of course) until the industrialization of moonshining during the unlamented Noble Experiment. Most, however, settled down to family farming in the Piedmont. The town of Greenville, in the geographical center of the county, developed out of a village that grew up around a grist mill established by a local trader during the American Revolution. Here the county seat was located, with the establishment of counties in the 1790's; and a small professional élite, partly from the cultural focus of Charleston, partly from the other focus of Eastern Virginia, founded law firms, banks and other businesses. Early in the Nineteenth Century the village became a summer resort for rice planters and their families during the malaria season (roughly May 1-November 1); a few of these summer people became permanent residents and members of the local élite. Others from the Charleston area, including representatives of humbler families, refugeed in Greenville during the Civil War. From the house servants of these Charleston-oriented families are descended many of the present-day leaders in the local Negro community.

With the spread of cotton culture following Eli Whitney's invention of the gin, the plantation system — and its concomitant,

Negro slavery — spread to the southern half of the county, and the
Negro population increased by 1860 to about 1/3 of the total. But the
plantation interests never dominated the county. In particular, the
mountainous northern half was unsuited to plantation agriculture, and
the mountaineers were particularly resentful of Negro slave competition. The county was a stronghold of Unionist sympathy before and
during and after the Civil War; contrary to the official myth, the percentage of desertions from the Confederate Army was high, and there
were many echoes of the popular designation of the Lost Cause as "a
rich man's war and a poor man's fight". A Greenvillian, Benjamin
Perry, was governor of South Carolina during the short-lived period
of reconciliation before Congress established the Reconstruction government. With emancipation, most of the plantation slaves became
tenant farmers, and many Negroes continue in that status today, despite the drift from farm to city and thence to the North.

During the period of industrialization that set in toward the
end of the Nineteenth Century, the county in general and the city of
Greenville in particular became one of the centers of the Southern textile industry. The mills maintained the traditional segregated employment patterns of Southern industry established by William Gregg, at
Graniteville, S.C., in the 1830's. Gregg had looked to the textile industry as the salvation of the poor white farmers crowded off the land
by the spread of the plantation system, and as a refuge where they
would be protected against the unfair competition of slave labor. The
continuing pattern has been for new mills to be staffed by displaced or
unsuccessful farmers from the mountains and other unproductive
areas, though by now textile employment has become a hereditary way
of life for the fourth generation, who may move from mill to mill
over a hundred-mile span, but who remain tied to the industry, basically one for low-skilled and low-paid labor, susceptible to long periods of depression and unemployment and bitter competition from the
newer mills in the Deep South. Except for menial tasks, Southern
cotton mills hire few or no Negroes, and the traditional threat of
Negro employment is cannily exploited by mill management whenever
the unions launch organizing drives.[4] As a result, the cotton mills
around Greenville, as elsewhere in the South, remain essentially un-
unionized. Until recently, most mill operatives have lived in company
villages with company stores furnishing long-term credit on terms
sometimes little short of peonage. These villages, like the mills,

were set up outside the city limits to avoid city taxes. However,
since World War II the company villages have begun to disappear, as
the mills have sold off the mill-village houses to operatives and others.

The mill schools were rather poor at first, thanks to a district school system that till the 1920's received little help from the
state.[5] About 1920, when the population of the mill belt had reached
some twenty thousand, little less than that of the city proper, the
management of the various mills joined to support a united and segregated school district, largely restricted to the children of mill operatives. This school system was independent of that of the city proper,
which at that time provided a competent traditional education for local
whites and a separate and inferior one for Negroes. So strong were
the economic and social barriers setting off the mill district from
the town that it used to be said, not altogether in jest, that Greenville
was a community of three races — whites, Negroes and cotton-mill
workers. The mill hands and the city people were as mutually dis-
trustful as either group of whites and the Negroes — and the former
distrust was repeatedly exploited by low-grade demagogues. Within
the Negro community, of course, there were also competing groups;
but of those the local whites were largely ignorant.

Negro speech, like educated white speech of the town, generally had loss of constriction of postvocalic /-r/; rural white, cotton mill and mountain speech generally retained constriction. Educated speech had [raɨt] but [ra·d]; uneducated speech normally had
[ra·t]. Thus nice white rice became a social shibboleth; for Negro,
cotton mill, mountain and rural uneducated white speech most commonly had [na·s hwa·t ra·s], while a few speakers with Charleston
or eastern Virginia connections (or pretensions) had [nəis hwəit rəis].
A very few Charleston- and Virginia-oriented speakers (mostly women) affected the so-called "broad a" in such words as half past and
dance. This pronunciation had no prestige; in fact, it was often an
excuse for ribald humor. The Charleston intonation and vowel qualities would be tolerated in elderly distinguished citizens, but cruelly
ridiculed in the young. Folk verb forms were common on all levels
of speech in all styles, except in the most formal situations for the
most cultivated. An educated speaker who would not use ain't in familiar conversation with his social equals was looked on with suspicion, as if attempting to cover up an unsavory past. Local and regional lexical items were used in everyday speech as a matter of

course; a child might read about the chipmunk Nurse Jane in the
Uncle Wiggly stories without identifying it with the ground squirrel
in the city park.

Chicago: The Macrocosm

From this microcosm it seems a far cry to the macrocosm
that is Chicago. Yet here too we may trace the chain of influence
from the historical background to the sources of local speech patterns
and the relationships of those speech patterns to the social order.

Northern Illinois — like northern Indiana, southern Michigan
and southeastern Wisconsin — was first settled from the Inland Northern dialect region: western New England, by way of Upstate New
York. In many of the small towns in Chicago's exurbia, the older
families still show distinctly New England speech-traits, such as the
centralized diphthongs [əu] and [əɨ] in down and ride, or /u/ in spoon
and soon. But the city of Chicago developed a more polyglot tradition
from the beginning. The city was established at the time when the
Erie Canal made it easy for the economic and political refugees from
Western Europe to reach the American heartland. The Irish brought
reliable labor for the new railroads and a continuing tradition of lively
politics; the Germans contributed their interest in beer, education,
art, music and finance. Almost immediately Chicago also became a
magnet for the younger sons of the agricultural settlements in southern Illinois and southern Indiana — Midlanders, whose speech patterns
derived from western Pennsylvania. Scandinavians followed Germans
and Irish; toward the end of the Nineteenth Century the population of
the metropolitan area was swelled by mass peasant immigration from
Southern and Eastern Europe — the strong backs and putatively weak
brains on which Chicago's mighty steel industry was built. When this
immigration tailed off during World War I, a new supply of basic labor was sought in the Southern Negro. Negro immigration has increased until Chicago is possibly the largest Negro city in the world.
More recently the Negroes have been joined by Latin Americans (Mex-
icans, Cubans, Puerto Ricans), and last by rural whites from the
Southern Appalachians. In response partly to the pressure of the increasing non-white population, partly to easy credit and slick promotion, Chicago whites like those in other cities have spread into the

suburbs, many of which are at least informally restricted to a single
economic and social (sometimes even an ethnic or religious) group. [6]

    In Chicago as in most large cities, the development of social
dialects has been a by-product of what might be called differential acculturation: differences in the facility and speed with which representatives of various social groups develop the ability to live alongside
each other as individuals, without stereotyped group identification. In
favor of the trend is the traditional American principle of individual
dignity, and the belief that each man should be allowed to improve his
lot as far as his ability and his luck permit. Against it is the tendency of people to flock together according to their nature and common
ties — whether Filipinos, Orthodox Jews, Irishmen, hipsters or college professors — a tendency abetted by those with a stake in keeping
the flock from scattering and by the tendency of each group to reject
the conspicuous outsider. In the early Nineteenth Century, the Penn-
sylvanians and downstaters, with a few generations of Americanizing
under their belts, soon mingled freely with all but the wealthiest and
most genealogically conscious Northerners. Acculturation was more
difficult for the "clannish" Irish, Germans and Scandinavians. [7] The
Irish were usually Roman Catholics; the Scandinavians spoke a foreign language; many Germans suffered from both handicaps, and all
three groups had broken with the native cultures only recently and
maintained many of their native customs. Nevertheless, all three of
these groups had enough in common with the "Older American Stock"
— all coming from northwestern Europe — to make some sort of sym-
biotic assimilation easy, though all of these older immigrant groups
were to suffer during the xenophobic hysteria of 1917-19 and after. [8]
In general they managed to participate freely in the community, while
retaining their cultural societies, newspapers and even foreign-
language schools.

    The later immigrants from Southern and Eastern Europe suf-
fered, in general, from the twin disabilities of foreign language and
Roman Catholicism. Moreover, they were largely peasants and illiterate, without the strong sense of their cultural tradition that the
Germans and Scandinavians had brought. [9] All these groups found
themselves at the focus of a complicated polyhedron of forces. In an
effort to help their acclimatization — and no doubt to avoid the erosion
of traditional ecclesiastical allegiance — the Roman hierarchy fostered

the "ethnic parish", designed specifically for a single nationality or
linguistic group. Whether or not this institution served its immediate
purpose, it had the side effects of further identifying foreignness and
Roman Catholicism, of separating the new groups from the American
Protestants, from the "native Catholics" (chiefly of Irish and German
descent), and from each other, and of fostering ethnic blocs in local
politics. [10] The blocs persist; but the common tendency of Chicagoans
(as of Clevelanders) of Southern and Eastern European descent is to
abandon their ancestral languages and turn their backs on their ancestral cultures, even in the first American-born generation. The
notable exceptions are the Jews, with the attachment to the synagogue,
to the synagogue-centered subculture, and to the family as a religious
and culturally focused institution. But it is possible for an individual
from any of these new immigrant groups to give up as much of his
ethnic identity as he may wish, and to mingle relatively unnoticed in
apartment building or housing development alongside members of
the earlier established groups.

In contrast to both of these groups of European immigrants,
the American Negro in Chicago is a native speaker of American
English, normally of at least five generations of residence in North
America (cf. McDavid, 1951); little survives of his ancestral African
culture, though undoubtedly more than American Caucasoids are
generally willing to admit. Early Negro settlers in Chicago were
able to settle as individuals — whether freemen or manumitted or
fugitive before the Civil War, or emancipated migrants afterward;
furthermore, a large number of the earliest Negro immigrants were
skilled craftsmen, who might expect to find a place in an expanding
economy, and with some education to smooth off the rough corners
of their dialects. However, even as an individual settler the Negro
was more easily identified than any of the whites who had preceded
him; and many Negroes exhibited traumata from slavery and mass
discrimination. With the mass migrations of Negroes, other forces
began to operate: the arrivals from 1915 on were largely a black
peasantry, somewhat exposed to urban or small-town life but almost
never actively participating in the dominant culture. Their own American cultural traditions — gastronomic, ecclesiastical and everything
between — often diverged sharply from those of middle-class Chicago.
Their speech, though American English, was likewise sharply different from that of their new neighbors. Even an educated Missis-
sippian has a system of vowels strikingly different from the Chicago

pattern. An uneducated Mississippi Negro would have had his poor
sample of learning in the least favored part of the Southern tradition
of separate and unequal schools; his grammar would differ more
sharply from the grammar of educated speech in his region far more
than would the grammar of any Northern nonstandard dialect differ
from the local white standard. Furthermore, the easy identification
of the Negro immigrant would provoke open or tacit pressure to
reinforce the tendency of living with one's kind — a situation which,
for the Chicago Negro, is likely to strengthen the linguistic and cultural features alien to the dominant local dialect pattern. Finally,
the displacement of unskilled labor by automation has injured the Negroes — less educated and less skilled, on the whole — more than it
has other groups. The specter of a permanently unemployable Negro
proletariat has begun to haunt political leaders in Chicago as in other
Northern cities, with inferior educational achievement and inferior
employment opportunities reinforcing each other, and in the process
strengthening the linguistic differences between whites and Negroes.

Of the Latin American, it can be said that he adds a language barrier to the problem of physical identification which he often
shares with the Negro. Of the displaced Southern mountaineer, it
has often been observed that he is even less acculturated to urban
living than the Negro or the Latin; however, his physical traits will
make it easy for his children to blend into the urban landscape, if
they can only survive.

What then are the effects of this linguistic melting pot on
the speech of metropolitan Chicago? And — since I wear the hat of
English teacher as well as that of social dialectologist — what are
the implications for the schools?

First, the speech of the city proper has apparently become
differentiated from that of the surrounding area, as the result of four
generations of mingling of Inland Northern, Midland, and Irish, and
the gradual assimilation of the descendants of continental European
immigrants. The outer suburbs call the city /ʃɪkágo/, butcher
/hagz/, and suffer from spring /fag/; to most of its inhabitants the
city is /ʃɪkɔ́go/, quondam /hɔg/ butcher to the world, beset by
Sandburg's cat-footed /fɔg/. To the city-bred, prairie and gangway
and clout have connotations quite different from those they bear in the

hinterlands.[11] Little if anything survives in the city of such Inland
Northern speech forms as [əi] and [əu] in <u>high</u> and <u>how</u>, [ʊ] in <u>soon</u>
and <u>spoon</u>, or /éjə/ as an oral gesture of assent. Even the second
generation of Irish, lace-curtained or otherwise, have largely lost
their brogue; such pronunciations as /ohɛrə/ for <u>O'Hare</u> Field seem
to be socially rather than ethnically identifiable.[12]

Among the older generation with foreign-language backgrounds, one finds sporadic traces of old-country tongues, such as
lack of certain consonant distinctions (e.g., /t/ and /θ/, /d/ and
/ð/) that are regular in standard English. Among the younger generation of educated speakers some of the Jewish informants stand out,
not only for the traditional American Jewish vocabulary, from <u>bar</u>
<u>mitzvah</u> and <u>blintz</u> to <u>tsorris</u> and <u>yentz</u>, but for the dentalization or
affrication of / t, d, n, s, z, r, l/. The former features have spread
to other local groups, but the latter has not. The so-called Scandinavian intonation of English is rarely encountered, even among informants of Scandinavian descent; it has not been picked up by other
groups as it has in Minneapolis.

Negroes born in Chicago before 1900 vary less from their
Caucasoid contemporaries than the latter do among themselves, attesting to something like genuinely integrated residential patterns in
the past. However, Chicago-born Negroes under 50 show many features of Southern and South Midland pronunciation, notably in the consistent use of /ʃɪkágo/ in outland fashion, in often having /griz/ and
/grizi/ as verb and adjective,[13] in the frequent loss of postvocalic
/r/ in <u>barn</u>, <u>beard</u> and the like, in contrasts between <u>horse</u> and
hoarse, and in relatively greater length of stressed vowels. These
Negroes also show distinctive extralinguistic speech traits: a quaver
of ingratiation when speaking to someone presumed to be in authority
— a feature not shared by whites — and the general Southern wide
spread between strongest and weakest stress, between highest and
lowest pitch, a spread far greater than what is found in Inland
Northern speech. In grammar, the Chicago-born Negro who grows
up in an environment of poverty and limited cultural opportunities —
as most Chicago Negroes grow up — has a tendency to use forms that
identify him easily and to his disadvantage, in writing as well as in
speech. Most of these are forms of common verbs — absence of the
third-singular present marker, as in <u>he do</u>, <u>it make</u>; old-fashioned

preterites and participles, as <u>holp</u> "helped"; or the appearance of an
-<u>s</u> marker in unexpected places as <u>we says</u>, <u>they does</u> — or in plurals
of nouns, like <u>two postes</u> /-əz/.   Many of these features of pronunciation and grammar, especially the lengthened stressed vowels, are
also found among the recent immigrants from Appalachia, who have
their own paralinguistic phenomena, such as strong nasalization, and
a few grammatical peculiarities like the sentence-opening <u>used to</u>:
"Used to, everybody in these-here hills made they own liquor." But
because the recently arrived Appalachian whites are relatively few
in number, because their residential patterns are not so rigorously
segregated as those of the Negroes, and because they are not so
readily identified as to physical type, their linguistic features do not
seem to be perpetuated into the younger generation, and probably will
never be.

Implications for Language Engineering

As far as the teaching of English is concerned, the overt commitment of American education — whether or not it is always recognized, let alone successfully practiced — is that each student should
acquire a command of standard English, the English of educated people, sufficient to enable him to achieve the social and economic position
to which his ambition and intelligence and ability entitle him. This does
not mean that everyone should talk like the works of Henry James or
Walter Pater; it does mean that everyone should be aware that certain words or grammatical forms or pronunciations will tag them,
justly or not, as unfit. We also have an American tradition — again,
one not always honored — of respect for the dignity of the individual
and the integrity of the family, no matter how deviant their behavior
by the standards of Madison Avenue or <u>Better Homes and Gardens</u>.
No educational program should aim at forcibly alienating the individual from his cultural background; if he must make a break, he must
make it with understanding of all the forces involved.

It would therefore seem in order for a language program to
start from an examination of the data, probably of a much more massive collection of data than we have access to as yet. In fact, the
gathering of data should be recognized as a continuing responsibility,
for the culture and the language — and the values of cultural and linguistic traits — will continue to change.

With the data collected, it should be possible to determine which words or grammatical features or pronunciations are typical of the various social groups in the community. Once this objective social identification of speech forms is established, it should be possible to compare such forms with the common subjective reactions in the community, both as to the accuracy of the subjective identifications and as to the pleasantness or unpleasantness of associations. [14]

Forms, words, pronunciations which are obviously characteristic of a disadvantaged minority and which produce unfavorable reactions in members of the dominant culture should be the systematic target of the early programs in the schools. The emphasis should not be negative, on error-chasing exercises, but positive, on habit-producing drill.

Where the home language is something other than English, or is a variety of English sharply removed from the local standard, it would probably be desirable to teach standard English as a whole, as a foreign idiom, to be used in certain situations where the culture demands it. We would thus produce many bilinguals and bidialectals, capable of communicating with ease in two or more different cultural worlds. We have ample precedent: Eugene Talmadge, of McRae Georgia, was the son of a plantation owner and won a Phi Beta Kappa key at the state university, but knowing that plantation owners and Phi Betes have little voting power in Georgia statewide elections, he perfected his command of rural Georgia folk speech to induce the "wool hats" to support him as their spokesman. Huey Long, on the contrary, was a "red neck" (poor white) from northern Louisiana, who had educated himself to a command of standard English (when he chose to use it) comparable to that of the Lodges and Saltonstalls. And those of us who have grown up in the South can cite many examples of Negro house-servants who — operating intuitively according to the classical tradition of decorum — could speak the folk dialect to the yard man and cultivated English to the quality without making a lapse in either mode. It should be possible through education to give a larger number the advantages that a few have acquired through intelligence or luck or both.

Where traces of a foreign language pronunciation exist in a student's English, these should also be approached systematically by teachers who know the structure of the English pronunciation system, and if possible the system of the home language as well.[15] To linguists and other cultural anthropologists it is superfluous to remark that the problem is cultural, not physiological. Yet too often in the schools it is not recognized that the child whose parental language lacks the phonemic contrasts between /s/ and /z/ constitutes a different kind of problem from one with a cleft palate.

English classes for speakers of other languages should be organized under professionally competent direction, with knowledge of what has been done recently to improve techniques and materials.[16] If there are many children from homes where a language other than English is spoken, special programs in English must be provided from the beginning of the child's school experience. Instruction toward reading English might be deferred until speaking and auditory comprehension are developed; instruction in reading the home language might be given instead. Conceivably, the Latin-American child could, by the fourth grade, be reading in Spanish two years ahead of what his Anglo competitors are doing in English and then could be more rapidly phased into reading English than if he had had reading thrust upon him before he had any competence in speaking or comprehension. Here, however, the design of programs is complicated, and the need for cross-disciplinary cooperation is particularly great.

An obvious difficulty in setting up special reading programs in the home language — perhaps in the long run more important than the lack of trained teachers or imaginative administrators — is the shibboleth of "segregation." But it is an established policy for the schools to provide special programs for children suffering from physical handicaps: the blind, the deaf, the lame. It would be equally humane to provide special programs for children suffering from cultural handicaps — a foreign language or a sharply divergent variety of English — which have some chance of being eliminated by intelligent diagnosis and purposeful instruction; no amount of taking thought can restore sight to the blind. Furthermore, there is a great difference between genuine integration and mere physical juxtaposition; the earlier in the school career a positive language program is adopted, the sooner students will be able to perform as equals, regardless of race or ethnic background — the only situation in which true integration can be said to have been achieved.

Once the schools become aware of the need for specific programs to cope with the problems of social dialects, two by-products for the school curriculum could develop naturally. First, the most obviously "culturally deprived" are those whose parents and grandparents, in the heat of the melting pot and the passions of war, were alienated from their native cultures and led to think of everything foreign as inferior. Depending on the size of the school system, there should be room in elementary programs for a broad spectrum of foreign languages, not merely those with the snob appeal of French, German, Italian, Spanish and now Russian, but little-discussed tongues like Croatian, Hungarian, Lithuanian and Ukrainian. To develop such a program would require cultural sensitivity and some intricate arrangements for shared time, but the cost would be relatively low and the potential gain in self-respect would be high.

The second by-product, even more easily achieved, and I like to think even more significant, is a deeper understanding of the meaning of dialect differences. Too many students, too many parents, too many teachers, shy away from alien varieties of English as from the plague; they feel that any variety different from their own is ipso facto inferior. In Detroit, even superior students have undergone the brainwashing of courses in "corrective speech" if their native pronunciation has been that of Oklahoma. But once the problem of social dialects is honestly faced, it should be possible to explain that differences arise not from mental or moral inferiority but from differences in cultural experience, and that the most divergent dialect, however ill suited for educated middle-class conversation, has a dignity and beauty of its own. Faced in this way, the social dialects of a metropolitan area become not a liability but an asset, a positive contribution to educating our students in understanding the variety of experience that enriches a democratic society.

NOTES

[1]Such distinctions are characteristic of the Southern and South Midland dialect areas of the Atlantic Seaboard (Kurath and McDavid, 1961). A summary of features of some of the principal areas of the Atlantic Seaboard was prepared by the late E. Bagby Atwood, from materials in the Atlas archives; it has been freely adapted as a general reference, as in Chapter 9 of Francis, 1958.

[2] Phonetic summaries of cultivated Charleston and Greenville speech appear in Kurath and McDavid, 1961. Lafayette, as a bilingual community (English-Acadian French) has been studied by Wallace A. Lambert, of the psychology department of McGill University; Chicago has been studied by Pederson, 1965, and Cleveland by Drake, 1961. A study of the effects of urbanization on the speech of Akron, Ohio, by Gerald Udell, was completed in 1966.

[3] In addition to his dissertation, Pederson has been actively involved in the Chicago social dialects project, 1963-5, and has collected a massive quantity of lexical evidence from the metropolitan area.

[4] This was particularly evident during the fiasco "Operation Dixie", a widely publicized but poorly planned drive of the Textile Workers Union, CIO, following World War II. For evidence I am indebted to Earl Taylor, then of the Greenville TWU office.

[5] In this connection it must be recalled that there was no constitutional commitment to public education in South Carolina before the Reconstruction Constitution of 1868. With public education a much more recent commitment than, say, in the old Northwest Territory, it is not surprising that some spokesmen for the alleged "Southern Way of Life" have talked casually about abandoning the public school system, as an alternative to desegregation.

[6] For the socio-economic ranking of Chicago suburbs, see Pederson, 1965.

[7] It is obvious that only outsiders are clannish; in-groups are merely closely knit.

[8] Since the Germans were the largest functioning foreign-language group, and since their position in the cultural life of the community was so high, it is almost impossible to calculate to what extent the teaching of languages and literature, and the position of the scholar, suffered as a result of these witch-hunts. The abolition of Germanic studies at the University of Texas, as a gesture of patriotism, was only one of many such acts.

[9] Paradoxically, one of the most successful adaptations of native cultural traditions to the opportunities of the American setting — that of the South Italians of Chicago to the public demands during Prohibition — tended to stigmatize the whole group, whether or not they actively participated in the Syndicate's version of venture capitalism.

[10]In his Language Loyalty in the United States, Joshua Fishman repeatedly attacks the heavily Irish American hierarchy of the Roman church for discouraging the ethnic parish in the past generation. In contrast, the late Msgr. Joseph L. O'Brien, director of parochial education in the Charleston diocese, was outspoken in his belief (based on his home community in Pennsylvania) that the ethnic parish tended to prevent the development of a truly Catholic church in the United States. The Irish, after all, had found their ethnicity one of their greatest obstacles to full participation in American society.

[11]Evidence on these features is basically that of Pederson's dissertation and his lexical research.

[12]The pronunciation /ohɛrə/, definitely substandard in Chicago, was however the normal one for Mayor Richard J. Daley, probably the most powerful municipal politician in the United States. To urban Chicagoans a prairie is a vacant lot; a gangway is a passage between two apartment buildings; clout is political influence.

[13]Grease and greasy have been studied by Atwood, 1950 and previously by Hempl, 1896.

[14]An instrument to evaluate such reactions has been prepared by Vernon S. and Carolyn H. Larsen, as a part of "Communication Barriers to the Culturally Deprived," Contract No. 2107, Cooperative Research Branch, U.S. Office of Education. A preliminary run showed that where the pronunciations of single words were concerned, Middle Westerners of the middle class could not distinguish between Negro and Southern white speech. Apparently the stereotype is to equate anything "Southern" with "rural" and "uneducated," for the Southern white whose voice was included in the instrument was the most highly educated and had lived only in urban areas.

[15]A series of contrastive studies, for English and specific other languages, has been published by the University of Chicago Press.

[16]The problem of preparing materials for special groups demands continuous experimentation and interdisciplinary cooperation. The needs of elementary school children in urban areas are least satisfactorily met so far, but any special group needs attention to the peculiarities of its learning situation.

REFERENCES

Atwood, E. Bagby, "Grease and greasy — a study of geographical
    variation", University of Texas Studies in English, 29 (1950),
    249-60.
Drake, James A., "The effect of urbanization on regional vocabu-
    lary", American Speech, 36 (1961), 17-33.
Fishman, Joshua A., Language Loyalty in the United States. The
    Hague, Mouton, 1966.
Francis, W. Nelson, The Structure of American English. New York,
    Ronald Press, 1958,
Hempl, George, "Grease and greasy", Dialect Notes, 1 (1896),
    438-44.
Kurath, Hans, and Raven I. McDavid, Jr., The Pronunciation of
    English in the Atlantic States. Ann Arbor, University of
    Michigan Press, 1961.
McDavid, Raven I., Jr., and Virginia, "The relationship of the
    speech of American Negroes to the speech of Whites",
    American Speech 26 (1951), 3-17.
Pederson, Lee, The Pronunciation of English in Chicago: Conso-
    nants and Vowels. PADS 44, 1965.
Udell, Gerald, The speech of Akron, Ohio. Dissertation, Univer-
    sity of Chicago, 1966.

4 | Changing Patterns of Southern Dialects

In Honor of Claude M. Wise

I

The times have never been more favorable for analyzing the patterns of Southern speech. First, we now have massive quantities of data, which we never had before; some of it is already accessible to scholars, whatever their residence, and there will be more to come as the <u>Linguistic Atlas of the Middle and South Atlantic States</u> finds its way into print. Second, there is nationwide concern with some of the varieties of Southern speech; as the less-educated Southerners flock to Northern and Eastern cities in search of new opportunities, their pronunciation seems out of place in their new habitat, and their grammar stands in the way of their getting as far in school or in business as their abilities would normally justify. Finally, many of the most important national concerns have been expressed in Southern accents. Despite the bitterness of professional Bostonians, no president has worked harder than Lyndon Johnson for the general welfare, and his efforts have been eloquently supported by those of Martin Luther King and Ralph Abernathy. Nor does the change in administration greatly alter the realities of the situation. Given all his faults, Richard Nixon at least abandoned the bloody shirt as the Republican emblem and decided to accept Southerners as members of the human race and citizens deserving the respect customarily extended to those from other regions. The election of Jimmy Carter further served to bring the South back into the nation.

II

So now, in looking at the speech of the South against the background of other varieties of English — United States, Canadian,

British and Commonwealth — we may begin by deflating a few old
myths, some related particularly to Southern speech, but most of
them with far wider inplications.

The uniformity of Southern speech is grossly exaggerated.
Many of our friends from further North speak of "the Southern accent" as if it were something monolithic. Actually, within the territory where Southern traditions are important, there is evidence of
at least three major speech types: (1) Southern proper, the speech
of the old plantation country; (2) South Midland, the speech of the
Southern uplands, ultimately affiliated with that of Western Pennsylvania; and (3) North Midland, the speech of Pennsylvania and its immediate dependencies. Within these regional patterns one finds at
least nine clearly marked areas of consequence in the pre-Revolutionary South alone and a number of minor areas; [1] even a preliminary examination shows more than half a dozen areas in Louisiana
and Texas; when the returns are in we can expect to find at least
thirty important sub-varieties of Southern speech, to say nothing of
reflexes of foreign language settlements of European origin and the
semi-creolized dialect of the Gullah Negroes. Truly, as Hans
Kurath has repeatedly remarked, the South has the greatest diversity
of speech forms to be found in English-speaking North America, with
the possible exception of Newfoundland.

The origins of Southern dialects are also generally misunderstood. Many casual observers assert that the warm climate is
responsible for a languid drawl. But even if a drawl were a general
characteristic of Southern speech — as it is not — those who believe
in the effects of hot climate would be confounded by the rapid-fire
dialogue of the Bengali in eastern India. Similarly, the nasality of
Southern upland speech cannot be explained by either excessive rain-
fall or excessive dryness — and both explanations have been offered.
More prosaic causes — social forces — are responsible.

Nor are there physiological reasons. Though many laymen
will assert that there are racial differences in speech, independent
of region or education, the solid evidence is all on the other side. In
controlled tests, Chicago middle-class whites have consistently identified as the voice of a rural uneducated Negro that of an urban educated Southern-born white — and Southerners are no more accurate. [2]

Educated Negroes in Charleston sound much more like the Pinckneys and Rutledges than either group sounds like the uneducated of either race. Concededly, centuries of separate and unequal opportunities have left the average Southern Negro with a larger residue of folk pronunciations and non-standard grammatical forms; but where investigators have interviewed Negroes and whites in the same community, with equivalent education and income, there is no consistent difference. In a few situations the values are even reversed: before 1954, West Virginia State College had an elite Negro student body — for the most part the children of highly skilled craftsmen and high-level service employees — and a distinguished faculty with degrees from such universities as Northwestern and Chicago. With desegregation, the school began to attract the disadvantaged from the mountains and has had a constant struggle to maintain standards in the face of increasing white enrollment.

It is thus no wonder that popular accounts of the features of Southern dialect should often be wide of the mark. What is referred to as "the Southern drawl" is probably not a feature of language per se; it is rather something else — a relatively greater length of strong-stressed syllables in comparison with weak-stressed ones. For example, in the American Middle West, the first syllable of highness will be perhaps twice as long as the last; in much of the South it will be three or four times as long. But even in the South drawl is not universal. It does not appear in Charleston speech, nor in Gullah — and even where it occurs, the tempo may be far from languid; the effect of drawl may be created by lengthening the strong-stressed syllables and shortening the weak-stressed ones, while the overall tempo remains rapid. The loss of post-vocalic /-r/ in barn, beard and the like — traditionally associated with "Southern speech" — is also far from universal in the South; its distribution is complex, part regional and part social. And the so-called "broad a" [ɑ] in half, past, dance and tomatoes is normal for only a small number of Southerners, even among the oldest and best families.

III

We are thus driven away from our folk beliefs toward the same forces that have created dialect differences elsewhere and at other times.

The most important cause is the pattern of settlement.

Immigrants to a new area bring their speech with them.
Students of German dialects still take as their starting point the settlements of Germanic tribes in the Fifth and Sixth Centuries and
label certain features of present-day German as Franconian or Ale-
mannic in origin. In the same way it is often possible to identify an
American dialect feature with early settlements, say, from East
Anglia or Northern Ireland. Since the impact of languages other
than English is greatest in the areas where those languages were
spoken, one can expect a high incidence of Spanish loans in West
Texas, of French loans in Southern Louisiana, of German loans in
the Shenandoah Valley and on the Yadkin, and of Africanisms in the
Sea Islands.

Similarly, speech forms are normally transmitted along
major routes of migration and communication. Features of Parisian
speech have followed the Rhone to the Mediterranean; features of
Pittsburgh speech have moved down the Ohio into the Mississippi
Valley. Conversely, a barrier to migration may become a dialect
boundary: the Blue Ridge prevented expansion of the Virginia Piedmont in the Eighteenth Century, and today there is no sharper dialect
boundary in the English-speaking world. Not only linguistic traits
but other cultural ones are affected by such boundaries. Notice that
the Virginia Piedmont prevailingly has the small Southern haystack
built around a center pole; the Shenandoah generally has the long
Pennsylvania rick or the square stack without a center pole. In vocabulary, in pronunciation, in haystack shapes, in folk songs, in all
aspects of traditional life the influence of the old geographic barrier
is still felt.

Ancient political boundaries sometimes become dialect
boundaries. In the Rhineland, as Leonard Bloomfield has pointed
out, linguistic differences often follow the boundaries of medieval
German principalities that were liquidated by Napoleon. In the
United States, where political boundaries have rarely constituted a
barrier to the movements of people or goods, state lines are much
less important; nonetheless, county site is common in Georgia as a
synonym for county seat, but unknown in South Carolina. And if two
adjacent states differ in the quality of their educational systems, the

political boundary may mark the limits of linguistic features; time
and again, Pennsylvania will lack old-fashioned pronunciations or
grammatical features that are very common in Maryland and the
states further south. The schoolmasters of Pennsylvania simply did
a more thorough job.

Where a city or a cluster of cities becomes an important cultural focus, its speech forms will spread into the surrounding area
and even beyond. The fall line cities of the Virginia Piedmont —
Fredericksburg-Falmouth, Richmond and Petersburg — have dominated Virginia speech; and the pronunciations of their first families
have been emulated in Winchester, in Roanoke, and even in Charleston, West Virginia. In South Carolina, Charleston has played a role
similar to that of Richmond and its sister cities in Virginia. In the
Gulf States and Mississippi Valley the plantation pronunciation of [ɜɪ]
in bird and the like (a pronunciation strongly resembling what was
once common in Metropolitan New York, but lacking the stigma of the
latter) is found in southeastern Alabama and the Tennessee Valley
(but not around Birmingham), in New Orleans and in Vicksburg — to
cite a few instances. Has this radiated from Montgomery or from
New Orleans or both ?

Finally, the social structure of an area will determine where
the sharpest social distinctions in language happen to lie. In the Old
South there was a sharp difference between the "old families" and the
rest of the population; in Virginia, when the original surveys for the
Atlas were conducted, only in this group did one find the "broad a"
in dance or the /æ/ vowel of patch in catch, instead of the more common /ɛ/ of fetch. In inland communities the class markers in language were most likely to be those associated with education, notably
the consistent use of the standard preterites and participles of irregular verbs: I saw, did, ran and the like.

IV

If we take the Southern evidence from the first stage of the
Linguistic Atlas project, and extrapolate for areas yet uninvestigated,
we find a few clear patterns. For our practical purposes we will consider the territorial South as consisting of the fifteen slave states of

1860, plus Oklahoma.[3] Our conclusions are surest for the area from
the Mason-Dixon line to the Ocmulgee and northeastern Florida, and
almost as sure for Kentucky.

Along the northern boundary we find considerable influence
of the North Midland region — the area settled by the westward expansion of Pennsylvania. West Virginia north of the Kanawha watershed is North Midland, though without a focus to balance against the
influence of the Pittsburgh area; its most characteristic feature to
outlanders is the intrusive /r/ in wash, push, bushel, judge, mush.
Further east, the Pennsylvania German area and the Delaware Valley with the cultural focus at Philadelphia have long influenced parts
of Maryland and Virginia. There are offshoots of the Pennsylvania
settlements in both central Maryland and the Shenandoah Valley. In
Delaware there is a major speech boundary between Wilmington and
the more rural southern part of the state; the strength of this boundary suggests that Wilmington has been a cultural satellite of Philadelphia since before the Revolution. Baltimore, a latecomer as Atlantic Seaboard communities go, had a well defined core of old Southern families, but soon came under the influence of Philadelphia. Today, with industrialization, its ties to the North Midland are growing
stronger, those to the South growing weaker. This tendency was evident even as early as the 1930's, when for practical purposes the
regional boundary ran through the city, but younger and better educated speakers favored North Midland forms. Postvocalic /-r/ was
pronounced; horse and hoarse were homonyms; whip and the like began with /w-/, not with /hw-/.

The South Midland region also derives from Pennsylvania,
but less directly. In the middle of the Eighteenth Century, when the
Ulster Scots in Pennsylvania reached the Alleghenies and found further progress westward blocked by the French and their Indian allies,
they turned southwest into the Shenandoah. Some of them recrossed
the Blue Ridge and followed the eastern slopes into the Piedmont of
the Carolinas and Georgia; others descended the Clinch and Holston
to the neighborhood of Knoxville and beyond; still others followed the
Kanawha into the Ohio Valley. In the beginning, these Ulstermen
were strongly opposed to the institutions and mores of the Plantation
South; they were independent subsistence farmers, with little use for
money crops or chattel slavery; their traditions are reflected by the

migration of the Lincolns into the free land north of the Ohio, by the fission of West Virginia from the parent state and by the continuing political cleavage between planter and mountaineer in nearly every part of the South. The picture is obscured, however, by other facts of cultural and political history: in all of the South, as cotton became profitable and the decay of chattel slavery was arrested, money crop agriculture spread into the upper Piedmont and the rich bottom lands of the inland rivers; local government fell into the hands of those who accommodated themselves to the interests of the plantation economy; local autonomy was suppressed behind a facade of "states rights" and "the Solid South." Despite the extent of the South Midland settlements — from Harper's Ferry to San Antonio — it was not until after the Confederate War that the region developed cultural foci comparable to Philadelphia and Pittsburgh in the North Midland. Louisville, Lexington, Nashville, Memphis were outposts of the cultural values enunciated in Richmond, Charleston, Savannah, Montgomery and New Orleans. Linguistically, the South Midland has been passive until recent years, receptive to speech forms from outside foci — occasionally the North Midland but more generally the planting and mercantile coastal South. The prevalent loss of postvocalic /-r/ in the uplands among younger and more sophisticated speakers — as in park your car — is a case in point: in my boyhood in Greenville, S. C., this loss was characteristic of young people of better families in the city; outside the city, the small farmers, mountaineers and textile workers retained the /-r/ essentially unimpaired. The receptivity of the South Midland to plantation speech-forms has led to debate among scholars as to whether it belongs dialectally with the Midland or the South.[4] In either event, its transitional quality is undeniable.

Passive though the South Midland is in comparison with the South, it has its own subdivisions. At least three of these have been identified along the Atlantic Seaboard: (1) The Shenandoah Valley, (2) Southern West Virginia, with Southwestern Virginia and Eastern Kentucky, (3) the Carolina and Georgia mountains. Each has a few characteristic features, though — as with the South Midland in general — features not shared with other areas are fewer than one might expect.

The Shenandoah Valley was historically a route of diffusion of Midland settlers from Pennsylvania into the Southern uplands.

Few words mark this route: flannel cake 'pancake,' focusing in
Philadelphia and extending to the head of the Valley; family pie 'cob-
bler,' beginning in the Shenandoah and spreading into the Carolina
Piedmont.

West Virginia from the Kanawha south, along with southwestern Virginia and the easternmost counties of Kentucky, has a few
peculiar words of its own. Perhaps the most characteristic is hobby or hobby bread, to designate a small handshaped loaf of cornbread,
smaller than the traditional pone, and generally baked three to an
oven or skillet. Less widespread in West Virginia, but extending
through the Carolina mountains, is redworm, a regional term for
earthworm. A few mountain terms extend toward the seacoast, along
the valleys of the Yadkin-Pee Dee and the Cape Fear, with the speech
of mountain Ulstermen and Cape Fear Highlanders for once reinforcing
each other. Among these words are big house for the living room and
fireboard for the mantelpiece. Yet none of these South Midland areas
is well defined; all are under pressure from both the older plantation
centers and the newer cities.

The areas of the South proper have been much more distinctive than those of the South Midland, because (as noted) every focal
community lay in the plantation area; plantation families that prospered with the plantations set the prestige patterns.

Throughout the South there are a few words of general currency. One of the most typical — if somewhat less frequently heard
today, in a generation of technological change — is lightwood
/laitəd/ (homonymous with the plantation pronunciation of lightered)
for fatty pine kindling. But even within the South there a few well-
defined belts. Along the coast below the Fall Line, the dragon fly is
mosquito hawk, a clingstone peach is a press peach, and budget,
bulge, bulk have the vowel of cut; above the Fall Line, we find, respectively, snake doctor, plum peach and the vowel of put.

The two strongest focal areas in the Old South, the Virginia
Piedmont and the Charleston area, have several things in common.
In pronunciation, the two areas share with Canadian speech striking
alternations of the diphthongs /ai/ and /au/ according to the phonetic
environment, with a strongly centralized variety occurring before

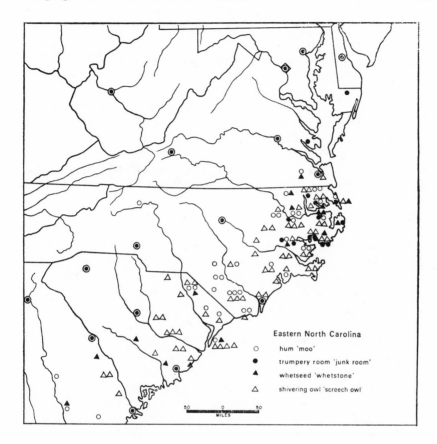

Eastern North Carolina
- ○   hum 'moo'
- ●   trumpery room 'junk room'
- ▲   whetseed 'whetstone'
- △   shivering owl 'screech owl'

voiceless consonants, as in <u>ice</u> and <u>house</u>. A few vocabulary items are also shared, such as <u>corn house</u> for corncrib and <u>croker sack</u> for burlap bag. In other respects, however, the two areas are sharply different: Virginia has the Africanism <u>goober</u> for peanut; South Carolina has <u>pinder</u>: Virginians call spoonbread <u>batterbread</u> — a term unknown in South Carolina; conversely <u>mutton corn</u> for the more common <u>roasting ears</u> is a South Carolina term unfamiliar to Virginians.

Such traditional Virginia pronunciations as /ə'frɛd/ for <u>afraid</u> and
/hʌm/ for <u>home</u> are not found in Charleston, whose peculiar ingliding /e/ and /o/, as in <u>date</u> and <u>boat</u>, sound as exotic in Richmond as in Dubuque.

In contrast to focal areas like the Virginia Piedmont and the
South Carolina Low-Country, the Old South has its relic areas, lacking influential centers to make their words and pronunciations fashionable; as a result their characteristic speech forms are chiefly retained by the older and less sophisticated, with others taking on the
usage of the Virginia Piedmont, the South in general, or the nation
as a whole.

One of the most striking relic areas has been Chesapeake
Bay, heavily indented with bays and tidal rivers that have inhibited
communication until the last two decades. Here we find <u>cow pound</u>
for the more common <u>cow lot</u>, <u>caps</u> for <u>corn shucks</u>, <u>cornstack</u> for
<u>corn crib</u>, <u>baseborn (child)</u> for <u>bastard</u>, <u>mongst-ye</u> instead of <u>you-
all</u> as the polite plural, and the archaic <u>housen</u> for <u>houses</u>. Eastern
North Carolina, caught between the two adjacent mountains of con-
ceit, tenuously preserves <u>shivering owl</u> for <u>screech owl</u> and <u>hum</u> as a
synonym for <u>moo</u>; <u>trumpery room</u> (instead of the Virginia <u>lumber
room</u> or the more common <u>junk room</u>) and <u>whetseed</u> for <u>whetstone</u>,
are practically confined to the shores of Albemarle Sound. Further
south, there are relics of German settlement around Salisbury, North
Carolina, and Newberry, South Carolina — with survivals of <u>rain-
worm</u> for <u>earthworm</u> and <u>smearcase</u> for <u>cottage cheese</u>. The Ulster
Scots settlement around Kingstree, South Carolina, has kept the
Northern Irish <u>chay</u>! as a call to cows. The descendants of the Salz-
burgers in the Savannah Valley still use <u>cripple</u> to designate the deli-
cacy known in Philadelphia as <u>scrapple</u> — the term apparently coming
from a South German word meaning drippings. The Savannah Valley
also uses <u>stoop</u> for <u>porch</u>, especially an unroofed one; since <u>stoop</u> is
traditionally derived from Dutch and associated with the Hudson Val-
ley, its occurrence along the Savannah — where there was no Holland
Dutch settlement — so far is inexplicable. Perhaps the term was
brought South by the architects who designed the mansions of the Savannah well-to-do — houses with more than a casual resemblance to
the brownstones of New York City. Further south, with their territory undefined, we encounter <u>gopher</u> designating a kind of burrowing

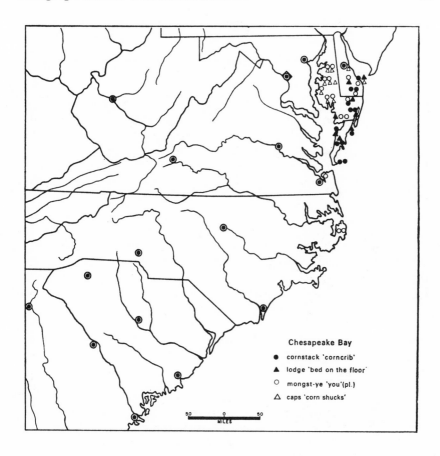

Chesapeake Bay

● cornstack 'corncrib'
▲ lodge 'bed on the floor'
○ mongst-ye 'you'(pl.)
△ caps 'corn shucks'

turtle and <u>prairie</u> designating a damp meadowland — their oldest meanings in North American English, if somewhat overshadowed by what they refer to in the Upper Mississippi Valley.

Although there is little evidence to distinguish the speech of Southern Negroes from that of Southern Whites with comparable social advantages, there is one striking exception: the Gullah country of the South Carolina-Georgia coast. In this area, large numbers of slaves were imported in a relatively short time to work such money

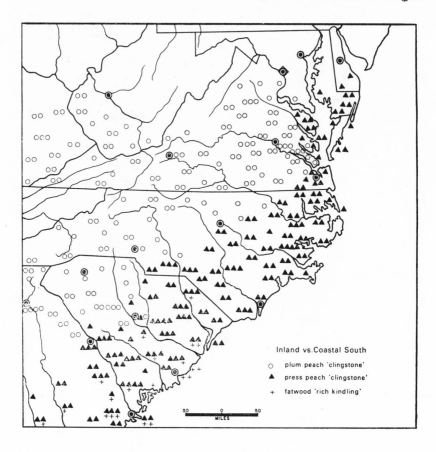

Inland vs.Coastal South

○   plum peach 'clingstone'

▲   press peach 'clingstone'

+   fatwood 'rich kindling'

crops as indigo, rice and Sea Island cotton; endemic malaria discouraged white settlers, and encouraged long summer absences on the
part of the few who lived there. Slavery, peonage, swamps and tidal
rivers discouraged movement. For these reasons many speech forms
of probably African origin are still established in these communities,
though hardly known inland; in the same area, the forces of geographical and cultural isolation also preserved old and humble speech
forms that the slaves acquired from the whites among whom they
worked.[5]

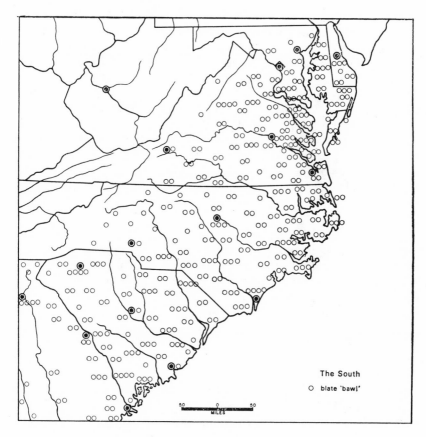

The South

O blate 'bawl'

V

To this point we speak on the basis of systematic evidence elicited in personal interviews by trained investigators. Once we cross the Appalachians, however, we are without this kind of evidence so far, save for Kentucky and Oklahoma and a few local studies. Nevertheless, the evidence we have is sufficient for an observer to make certain general observations on the patterns of Southern dialects before the age of mass-production industry and the subsequent age of automation.

In the New South, as in the old, social differences in language were more sharply marked than in the regions to the North. Status was determined by family background, education and wealth,

with family at least ostensibly the most important — since the older
families dominated the economy and had most of the opportunities for
education and other indices of cultural prestige. Many schools designed for the less affluent soon became oriented to the dominant system of values; typical was Sweet Briar, originally founded to educate
Virginia mountain girls, but by the 1920's popularly regarded as an
advanced finishing school. The outsiders who built up new fortunes
by skill or luck or a convenient lack of scruples adjusted so skillfully
to the prevailing patterns of prestige that the community often forgot
their humble beginnings — even in the first generation of promi-
nence. [6] And the common economic ruin following the Confederate
War only emphasized the inalienable advantages of family and culture,
as contrasted with the ephemeral status of wealth.

As the South expanded westward, Southern society continued
to be dominated by the planters and merchants. When cotton culture
expanded in the early Nineteenth Century, the plantation system —
and with it, a relatively large slave population — spread into rich upland areas. Some of the original South Midland small farmers rose
into the planter class; others were pushed into the unproductive hills
and pine barrens, crossed the Ohio into territory where slavery was
forbidden (the Lincolns are the most notable representatives), or
pushed further west. The social distinction between the planter and
the redneck was fundamental in Southern society; the planters, a
small minority, manipulated the political attitudes of the region
for at least a generation after Reconstruction, and by such political
contrivances as the creation of new counties with disproportionate
representation kept at least a veto on significant legislative change
until the recent decisions of the Federal courts.

But the planter group of the inland South was far more diverse than its coastal counterpart. A few of the older families, like
the Hamptons and Hugers, either added new plantations in the Mississippi Valley to their older holdings along the coast or transferred the
bulk of their operations from exhausted soil to new. They found,
however, a local planter group — mostly French — already established and were soon augmented by the successful entrepreneurs who
had made wealth on the frontier — as gory and violent as any of the
later manifestations of the American tradition of the Wild West. As
a consequence of this mobility, many features originally associated

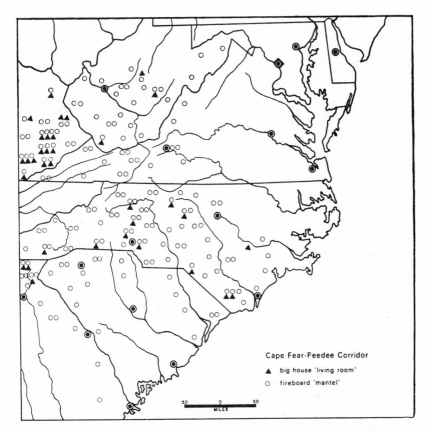

Cape Fear-Peedee Corridor

▲ big house 'living room'

○ fireboard 'mantel'

with the South Midland found their way into plantation speech, even
in those areas most heavily settled from the plantation belt of the
Old South.

The westward dialectal expansion of the Old South is a crazy
quilt if compared to the orderly and well marked belts of coastal
plain, Piedmont and mountains that we find along the Atlantic. Even
in eastern Georgia the pattern begins to be confused, with the plantation areas expanding inland largely between the Savannah and the
Ogeechee, and then sweeping west across the Piedmont; however,
barely thirty miles west of Brunswick and St. Marys we encounter
swamps, wiregrass and piney woods, settled by marginal farmers.
Cherokees and Creeks long blocked expansion into the lower valleys

of the Chattahoochee and Flint, which were first settled by land-hun-
gry uplanders rather than by the westward extension of plantation
holdings. The fertile bottomlands of the Mississippi and its tribu-
taries produced an intricate interlacing of plantation and small farming areas, with the respective domination by Southern and South Midland features. To take one characteristic example, the Black Belt of
Alabama, the lower Mississippi Valley, and the Tennessee Valley
towns as far upriver as Athens and Decatur show the loss of /r/
coloring in <u>barn</u>, <u>beard</u> and <u>bird</u> — and often in the last the diphthong
associated with older New York City speech; but the hill country
around Birmingham and the pinelands of eastern Mississippi exhibit
an /r/ as strong as anything to be found in the Middle West. A similar crazy-quilt pattern would not be unlikely in Arkansas and Missouri.

   The territorial expansion of the South, of course, was not
conducted solely by Southerners and South Midlanders. Pennsylvan-
ians, Yankees and York Staters pushed into Missouri; in combination
with the German exiles and the mountaineers who had always opposed
slavery, they were able to keep the Show Me State in the Union —
though at the price of local feuds that started Jesse James on his
short career as an outlaw and on his longer one as the first juvenile
delinquent to become a folk hero. And though the American Indians
— except in Oklahoma — were largely brushed aside, two other
groups maintained their identity, and indeed modified the invading
Anglo-American culture: the Spanish-Americans of Texas and the
French of Louisiana. Loans from these two groups, in fact, mark
respectively the two principal focal areas of the Gulf States: the ha-
cienda country of the Southwest and the plantation area of Southern
Louisiana, with its metropolitan focus at New Orleans. Since these
patterns persist in the vocabulary despite the cultural changes of the
last fifty years, it is likely that they will also be found in pronunciation and even in grammar. Other probable focal areas in the New
South — though the extent of their influence has not yet been determined — are the Kentucky Bluegrass, Metropolitan St. Louis, Memphis, the Nashville Basin and the Montgomery-Mobile axis in Southern Alabama.

VI

Since dialect patterns are rarely static, particularly in
times when the population is rapidly growing, we should have expected this outline of Southern dialect patterns to have been modified
over the past generation by the simple passage of time. But modification has been accelerated by a number of fundamental economic
and social changes whose impact is likely to be even greater in the
future.

The three principal forces operating in American society to
create a different dialect situation from that to be found in Europe
have been industrialization, urbanization, and general education.
For a long time these forces were less active in the South than in
other regions. In comparison with the other parts of the United
States, the Southern regions have been the most predominantly agricultural (with a large proportion of small, marginal farms), the
most predominantly rural, the least literate and sophisticated. Although in all of these respects the South as a whole is still behind the
rest of the nation, the discrepancy is far less than it used to be. In
industry and education the best Southern achievements rank with the
best achievements in other regions, though they are much less
numerous.

Industrialization began in the 1830's, when such leaders as
William Gregg developed cotton mills to provide employment for
poor whites crowded off the land by the competition of slave labor
and the low fertility of subsistence farms; to Gregg is due the un-
happy tradition of Southern textiles as the most segregated and least
unionized American industry. But it was not till after Reconstruction
that the era of textile expansion began. Throughout the Piedmont of
the South Atlantic States, almost every county seat and many smaller
places became ringed with cotton mills, whose operatives — in company villages, with company stores, company schools and company
churches — became a de facto third race in the pattern of segregation. Drawn from the pine barrens, the sandhills, the mountains
and other areas of marginal farming, the textile workers swelled the
population of urban areas; though their speech had little prestige,
they altered the structure of urban society in such a way that through

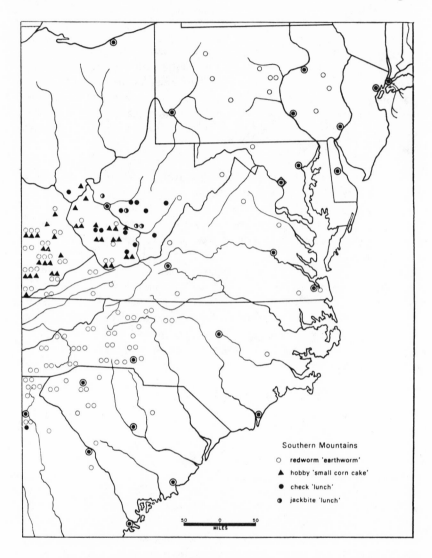

Southern Mountains

○   redworm 'earthworm'
▲   hobby 'small corn cake'
●   check 'lunch'
◑   jackbite 'lunch'

the educational opportunities of their children and grandchildren they
would inevitably affect the patterns of local cultivated speech.

Though textiles was the first industry to become established in the South, it was not alone. Tobacco manufacturing and coal
mining soon followed — both, like textiles, employing relatively

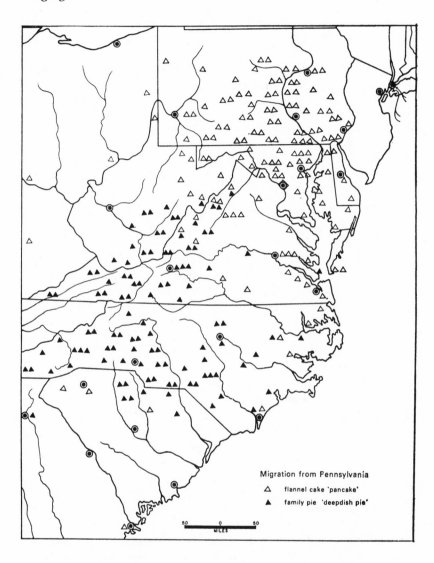

Migration from Pennsylvania

△   flannel cake 'pancake'

▲   family pie 'deepdish pie'

low-skilled labor at the outset and suffering disproportionately from
economic cycles. But more sophisticated industries ultimately developed — steel, paper, shipbuilding, aircraft manufacturing among
them. Especially on the Gulf coast, large fields of oil and gas
brought rapid industrialization, centering first on refining and then on

petrochemicals. And the tendency of giant corporations to decentralize only hastened the industrialization of the South.

Industrialization requires the easy movement of raw materials to the factory and of finished products to the consumer. The in-
dustrializing South eagerly improved its means of transportation —
railroads, roads, waterways. Moreover, since the distribution of
industrial products is most efficiently handled through larger centers, industrialization inevitably led to the growth of cities. The urbanization of the South was also furthered by the general mechanization of agriculture and by the specific decline in cotton growing and
the rise of timber cropping and cattle-raising, which required fewer
hands and sent large numbers to the towns. The stores and services
— from groceries to gin-mills — that sprang up to supply the mill
workers and handle industrial products absorbed much of the labor
surplus; some of the new arrivals quickly moved into the growing
middle class, which was also swelled by newcomers from other regions. The expansion of Southern cities has been uneven; but this
has been true in other regions as well. Some, despite their size,
have remained little more than overgrown mill villages; some —
like the Texas metropolises — have ostentatiously displayed great
wealth and a reactionary social philosophy; a few, notably Atlanta,
have walked open-eyed into the Twentieth Century and developed a
character of their own. But throughout the South the typical cultural
leader everywhere is now not the planter but the urban businessman,
often not a Southerner except by adoption.

For the industrialization and urbanization of the South could
not have been accomplished on Southern resources alone. With plentiful natural resources and a large labor supply, the region had a
shortage of capital and of management talent. Although a few giant
corporations were developed by Southern capital and leadership to
the point where they could compete successfully on the national scene,
most Southern industries soon passed into the control of Eastern
capital; the vast majority of Southern factories are now owned by
national corporations, and managed by representatives from the central organization.

This side of the change in Southern population is often overlooked. Everyone knows that hundreds of thousands of Southern

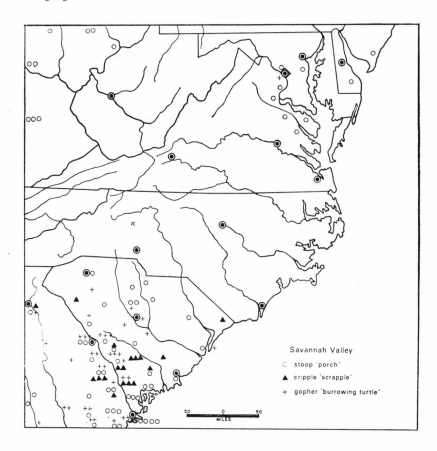

Savannah Valley

○ stoop 'porch'

▲ cripple 'scrapple'

+ gopher 'burrowing turtle'

Negroes have moved North — so that there are now more Negroes in
the Chicago metropolitan area than in all of South Carolina.   In
Cleveland, Detroit, Philadelphia, New York, Negroes from the South
and their children are a large part of the population; in such cities
they are also one of the major economic problems since the demand
for unskilled labor is declining and many of them lack the training
for the new clerical and technical jobs that automation is creating.
We are all aware that many poor whites have also gone North — to
the assembly lines of Detroit, the rubber shops of Akron and the air-

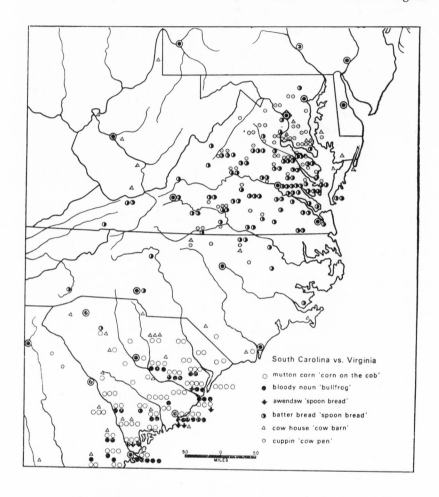

South Carolina vs. Virginia

○ mutton corn 'corn on the cob'

● bloody noun 'bullfrog'

✦ awendaw 'spoon bread'

◐ batter bread 'spoon bread'

△ cow house 'cow barn'

○ cuppin 'cow pen'

plane factories of Dayton — and have created their share of social problems. We are also aware that within the South there has been a flow of both races from the country to the city — to Louisville and Little Rock, to Memphis and Birmingham and Atlanta. If we think of Northern migration southward, we are likely to think of the resort

traffic and retirement colonies that have made the southern half of
Florida an exclave of the Middle Atlantic States and the Middle West.
We forget the more diffuse — and for that reason, probably the more
influential — migration of plant superintendents, bank cashiers,
store managers, industrial chemists, tool and die makers, and now
of college professors, as the needs of the South outran local supplies
and new opportunities made positions competitive with those available
in other regions.[7]

This has been most noticeable as the quality of Southern education has improved. Not unfittingly, some of the first steps were
taken by the Reconstruction governments; the constitution of 1868
was the first one that committed South Carolina to general education.
The ensuing century has seen the South, by and large, contributing
to education a much larger proportion of its wealth than other regions
— though the discrepancy in resources to tax meant that expenditures
per pupil in Mississippi were nowhere near what they have been in
Ohio or California. Progress has not been easy, as nostalgia, funda-
mentalism and petty politics have often hamstrung the best designed
programs. But no one can deny that the general quality of Southern
education has improved, at all levels. If the Johns Hopkins, the first
real graduate university in the United States, failed to keep its preeminence (and in any event it is situated in a city whose Southern affiliations are rather weak), Duke is now unquestionably in the first
rank today, and from Charlottesville to Austin, from Miami to Louisville, the better institutions have as high standards and as cosmopolitan an atmosphere as anyone could desire. As with industrialization and urbanization, education has advanced unevenly in the South,
as indeed in other regions. But this development, too, will have a
profound effect on Southern speechways.

The combined force of these developments promises to affect Southern speech in several ways.

First of all, the balance of population and wealth has shifted
irreversibly from the plantation. The textile and tobacco centers of
the Piedmont — increasingly diversified — centers of heavy industry like Birmingham, petrochemical foci like Baton Rouge, and the
variegated industrial complexes like Atlanta and Louisville and

Houston have reduced many of the old Southern towns to backwaters, surviving on the custom of Florida-bound tourists. Where seaports flourish — as Norfolk and Savannah and New Orleans — it is because they have exploited their geographical advantages to facilitate industrialization.

With industrialization and urbanization, wealth can be expected to replace family as a force for social prestige; since most of the new managerial class — whether Southerners or not — come from outside the plantation area, the influence of plantation speech will be diluted. Industrialization and urbanization will accelerate the disappearance of the more local terms in the vocabulary, especially those associated with the mule-powered farm. Not all the readers of this article can tell a froe from a hamestring, and I suspect all are less likely to make curds at home than to buy cottage cheese at the supermarket.

As higher education becomes more general, a smaller proportion of those attending college will be the children and grandchildren of college graduates. In this way the influence of the old elite will be further attenuated, and the characteristics of educated Southern speech will become somewhat different. Since the majority of the white population of the South is found in areas where the South Midland influence is strong, the enlargement of the ranks of the educated is bound to increase the importance of the South Midland component of Southern speech, at the expense of coastal Southern. Education will also tend to eliminate such folk grammatical forms as div or seed, and such pronunciations as /dif/ for deaf or /waundid/ for wounded. It is probable, given the prevailing attitude in American schools, that many Southerners will adopt the fashion of full rather than reduced vowels in final syllables, so that Tuesday and borrow will come to have final /-e/ and /-o/ respectively. And even educated Charlestonians may come to avoid ain't in polite conversation with their equals.

Some of this change is already under way. As early as 1946 I noticed that upland vowels were common among native Savannians; in 1949, I found that Knoxvillians were losing the distinction between horse and hoarse, between merry and marry and Mary. Seven years ago, I discovered that the younger speakers in the Kanawha Valley

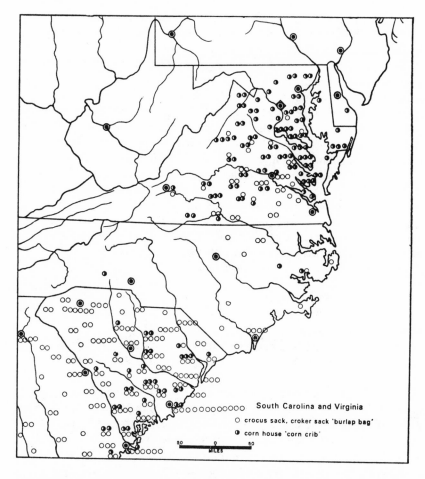

South Carolina and Virginia

○ crocus sack, croker sack 'burlap bag'

◑ corn house 'corn crib'

were pronouncing <u>tube</u> and <u>due</u> and <u>new</u> as /tub/, /du/ and /nu/ in
the fashion of northern West Virginia. In 1965, in a sample of recordings from high school students in Charleston I found little of the
traditional pronunciation of <u>date</u> and <u>boat</u>; and the daughter of a
couple from Gloucester County, but grown up in Arlington, spoke to
me without a trace of the Piedmont <u>out</u> and <u>night</u>. But even within the
South there are a few well-defined belts. Along the coast below the
Fall Line, the dragon fly is a <u>mosquito hawk</u>, a clingstone peach is a
<u>press peach</u>, and <u>budget</u>, <u>bulge</u>, <u>bulk</u> have the vowel of <u>cut</u>; above the
Fall Line, we find, respectively, <u>snake doctor</u>, <u>plum peach</u>, and the
vowel of <u>put</u>.

Let us not be nostalgic, however; change in language is inevitable — and always moved by social forces. Besides, the South is still so linguistically diverse that many of our local speech forms will survive in spite of outside pressures. And our traditions of speech are so powerful that some distinctive Southern varieties of speech are likely to endure for the foreseeable future. This, in fact, may be a source of strength toward solving our educational problems; unlike Chicago or Detroit, where uneducated arrivals from the South — of whatever race — are sharply set off from the natives by both grammar and pronunciation, each Southern community finds its basic pronunciation patterns shared by all races and social classes, and the grammatical problems the same where educational and cultural backgrounds are similar. We do not need separate programs for separate groups — only one program intelligently designed and effectively taught. Our knowledge of Southern dialects may help Southern communities to show how the rest of the nation can solve the language problems of the classroom.[8]

NOTES

A version of this paper was presented at the Institute for Southern Culture, Longwood College, Farmville, Virginia, April 1966.

[1]See particularly Hans Kurath, A Word Geography of the Eastern U.S., Ann Arbor, University of Michigan Press, 1949. For a summary of scholarship see "Dialects," Chapter 7, Section 4, of H. L. Mencken, The American Language, one-volume abridged edition, edited by Raven I. McDavid, Jr., with the assistance of David W. Maurer, New York, Alfred A. Knopf, Inc., 1963.

[2]These findings will be found in Communication Barriers for the Culturally Deprived, a cooperative research project of the University of Chicago and the Illinois Institute of Technology, H.E.W. Project CR-2107.

[3]Most of the field work in the pre-Revolutionary South, as far west as the Ocmulgee in Georgia, was done in the two periods 1933-9 and 1945-8; that in Kentucky, mostly 1952-5; in Oklahoma 1958-62. Louisiana has been investigated, less professionally, by the students of C. M. Wise, mostly 1933-48. Texas vocabulary was fairly well investigated by the students of E. Bagby Atwood; its pro-

nunciation less systematically, though there have been several first-rate studies. Field work in Missouri began in 1966. Elsewhere, we have largely vocabulary evidence collected by correspondence, but very reliable so far as it goes, thanks to the high standards of the investigator, Gordon Wood of Southern Illinois University.

[4]On the basis of vocabulary, Kurath (Word Geography) considered it a part of the Midland, conceded that pronunciation features might group it with the South. In discussing the affiliations of Texas dialects, E. Bagby Atwood grouped Southern Coastal and South Midland together as General Southern; see The Regional Vocabulary of Texas, Austin, The University of Texas Press, 1962.

[5]See Lorenzo D. Turner, Africanisms in The Gullah Dialect, Chicago, The University of Chicago Press, 1949. Analogous phenomena in Louisiana Negro-French have been discussed by many observers, notably Raleigh Morgan.

[6]A not atypical example is given in W. J. Cash, The Mind of the South, New York, Alfred A. Knopf, Inc., 1940.

[7]The development of Washington has been atypical, reflecting two disparate trends. Originally it was a small Southern town, and the lower echelons of government service held a disproportionate number of Southerners. Beginning with the 1930's, however, the expansion of government activities has drawn into the metropolitan area large numbers of Middle Westerners and Easterners to fill professional, technical, administrative and policy-making positions; in the same period, the extension of equal opportunities to Negroes and the desegregation of the public schools have attracted many Negroes from the South. As middle class whites — especially families with children — have fled to the suburbs, a peculiar situation has developed. In the suburbs the speech patterns are mixed, but with something other than the local Southern cultivated standard beginning to predominate; in the city proper, Negroes constitute about 55% of the population, over 90% of the school enrollment, and the cultivated speech of local middle class Negroes (itself strongly akin to local cultivated white speech) has been largely swamped by the new immigrants. [These figures have changed in the last decade.]

[8]As of 1978, it is generally conceded that the desegregation of public schools has been more successful in the South than in other regions.

5 | The Dialects of Negro Americans

In Collaboration with Lawrence M. Davis
In Honor of George L. Trager

The tangled story of racial relationships in the United States is illustrated no more poignantly than in the various and often sharply disparate interpretations of the origins of the forms of English spoken by Negro Americans. Much of the discussion, inevitably, is concerned less with the facts of the situation than with the egos of the discussants; indeed, one may say that there has often been an excess of rhetoric over evidence. To take the extremes, one group would hold that there is nothing African in these dialects beyond a few vocabulary loans; another, that the basic structure of these dialects is so different from that of English — or at least the English with which this group is familiar — that it is safest to posit a different grammatical system which rests on a creole substratum.

Yet, as different as these points of view are, it is refreshing to realize that we are long past the kind of naive judgment which led to the following description of the origin of Gullah, and other Negro dialects as well:

Slovenly and careless of speech, these Gullahs seized upon the peasant English used by some of the early settlers and by the white servants of the wealthier colonists, wrapped their clumsy tongues about it as well as they could, and, enriched with certain expressive African words, it issued through their flat noses and thick lips as so workable a form of speech that it was gradually adopted by the other slaves and became in time the accepted Negro speech of the lower districts of South Carolina and Georgia (Gonzales 1922: 10, quoted in Turner 1949: 6). [1]

Whatever their position today, students agree that the characteristics of Negro speech, like that of any other form of language, are culturally determined and culturally transmitted and that differences between the speech of Negroes and that of whites simply reflect the differences in experiences.

So long as the Negro population of the United States was primarily rural and Southern, and so long as American scholars remained in ignorance both of African languages and of the various contact languages which have arisen in China, the South Pacific, and the Mediterranean, observers could be pardoned almost any amount of amateurish speculation. After all, whatever problems of communication these dialectal differences posed were primarily Southern problems; and however interesting the search for origins might be, it had little practical interest for the prestigious universities.

But our age is a different one. The languages of Africa, like other aspects of African cultures, are of serious concern to the makers of American policy, and almost every reputable consortium of universities has a program in African studies. The majority of Negro Americans are no longer Southern and rural, but Northern and urban; indeed, a larger proportion of Negroes than of whites are city dwellers. Negroes have come into the industrial labor market following the Irishman, the German, the Italian, and the Slav; but unlike their forerunners who could count on manual labor to raise the status of their families, the Negro finds an upgrading of job skills and an emphasis on technical training which leaves his employment marginal and precarious. Even political 'reform' has worked to the disadvantage of the urban Negro— and indeed of all others newly arrived in urban environments — as the prompt concern of the patronage system has given way to the glacial operations of a paper-clogged bureaucracy. As Mayor Richard Hatcher of Gary (Indiana) remarked, the Negroes are the first urban ethnic minority who have had to make their way against the civil service system.

As Negroes establish large urban colonies, their speech confronts Northern urban teachers with a range of phonological and grammatical structures that the teacher-training program had not prepared them to meet. And the new militancy of rising expectations, following the recent civil rights legislation and court decisions, has

led to feelings of group identity and pride in all forms of social experience, including language, so that the patronizing depreciation of
non-standard forms of speech — something from which all American
children have suffered — is deservedly rejected.

For the linguist concerned with the varieties of American
English and with the relationship of language behavior to other forms
of cultural behavior, the situation poses two questions. First, to
what extent is it justifiable to speak of 'Negro speech' as distinct
from white? Second — regardless of the answer to the first — what
are the origins of the various dialects spoken by Negro Americans?

There are, to be sure, certain psychological realities:

1. It is not only normal but desirable that every group
should have pride in its way of speaking, whether this is in origin a
national language like Norwegian, a cultural language like Yiddish,
a national dialect like Australian, a regional dialect like that of
eastern Virginia, or a social dialect like the lower-class speech of
the New York East Side. One's habitual way of speaking is among
his most intimate possessions; and, whatever other varieties of
speech he may find it necessary to learn for other purposes, he must
respect what he brings with him.

2. It is recognized that, especially in the urban scene,
young Negroes have developed their own in-group vocabulary, just as
all conscious sub-cultural groups (whether narcotics addicts or Chicago critics) are wont to do.

3. In Northern urban areas the divergence of the speech of
Negroes — especially those least educated — from local patterns of
pronunciation and grammar is so striking that one must recognize
the existence of de facto Negro dialects, however such dialects may
have originated. [2]

These concessions, however, do not really answer the questions. To answer them, one must have several kinds of evidence,
in massive quantities: (1) detailed structural descriptions of a number of dialects; (2) historical evidence from all kinds of sources —
for the passage of time may have eradicated some of the crucial

dialects — of the speech of Negroes and whites in various situations; (3) data from Negroes and whites, of comparable educational and economic and social status, in a variety of communities, rural and urban, Northern and Southern, United States and Canadian and West Indian — the data must reflect various kinds of situations and degrees of formality; (4) demographic evidence on population origins and history in different kinds of communities, with particular attention to possible changes in economic and social structure; (5) detailed evidence on the various linguistic sources which may have contributed to the present-day dialects of Negro Americans, and of whites as well.

It is manifest that we are a long way from being able to reach definitive judgements in these areas. We can assume that for at least a generation or so we will need to search for more information in all of these fields, and we should urge scholars to continue to push ahead in their respective fields with all the professional tools at their disposal.

On the other hand, if we compare our knowledge with what was available a generation ago, we can see that we are at least able to ask more perceptive questions. We have a great deal of evidence on dialect patterns in much of the United States and a good section of Canada, even though much of it is still only in files, awaiting editing and publication. And we are beginning to have serious studies of Negro speech in a variety of situations, which may throw some light on the ways in which present-day dialects have arisen.

Of these, perhaps the most important has been the study of Gullah by Lorenzo Turner. His Africanisms in the Gullah Dialect (Turner 1949) offers striking evidence of the persistence of features of vocabulary, pronunciation, and grammar in a section of South Carolina and Georgia where slaves were imported in large numbers to work the rice plantations, and where, until very recently, geographical and cultural isolation kept contact with the dominant culture at a minimum. The studies of Jamaican English (Cassidy 1961, Cassidy and LePage 1967, Bailey 1966) provide us with serious studies of the structure and development of English in a former plantation island of the West Indies where Negroes are overwhelmingly predominant in number. And, beginning with the wartime investigations of

Melanesian Pidgin by Robert Hall (Hall 1943, 1970), we have had
recognition that contact languages, wherever spoken, are worthy of
serious investigation as linguistic systems.

This new knowledge has caused a serious reappraisal in the
comparison of Negro and white speech. Although only a generation
ago it was common, even among observers trained in the social
sciences, to dismiss the dialects of Negroes as combinations of archaisms and mispronunciations, only the most ignorant would make
such a statement today. Indeed, the pendulum has swung so far that
some scholars (Bailey 1965, Stewart 1967, Dillard 1967) have argued that Negro speech, as they define it, is only superficially related to the varieties of American English spoken by whites. They
postulate a different "deep structure", deriving from an African-
based pidgin through a process of creolization.[3] They cite such features as the omission of the copula before participles, adjectives and
nouns, the alternation of zero copula, as she busy, and be as a finite
verb, as she be(s) busy, reflecting, they say, an aspectual difference
between momentaneous and habitual behavior, and the leveling of the
person-number forms of the present indicative. It is recognized
that such forms are more common in the speech of Negroes than in
that of whites, and probably more common still in the South at the
same economic and educational level.

Yet again there are counter-arguments. Gullah is not typical of Negro speech; some of its most characteristic features are
not shared by the dialects of inland Negroes, even in South Carolina
and Georgia. For example, it is frequently noted that urban Negroes
in the North substitute /t d/ for /θ ð/ in initial position, but substitute /f v/ for these sounds elsewhere; but Gullah, according to
Lorenzo Turner and others, substitutes /t d/ in all positions, and
almost never /f/ or /v/. It is also true that Jamaica is not the
United States, since the United States lacked both the Jamaican in-
sularity and the overwhelming numbers of Negro speakers.

To assert the continuity of Negro pidgin is not to prove it,
and, except for Gullah, there is little enough direct evidence for its
past existence. These problems are also related to the fact that
there was a diversity of Negro-white relationships, even under slavery. The average slave-owning was ten, in most instances about the

size of the extended family of the slaveowners. Furthermore, for
many of the putative Africanisms noted by the creolists, it is also
possible to find documented sources in white speech, in American
communities where Negro influence is extremely unlikely (McDavid
1967).[4] And the notion of deep structure itself is so tenuous that it
is currently rejected by many of the transformational group who pro-
pounded it only a few years ago (McCawley 1967).[5]

It is also worth noting here that the discovery of some African influence in Negro dialects certainly is no proof for two "deep
structures", Negro and white. What is likely, in fact, is that further research will show a great deal of African influence in all dialects in the South. We all know that the major dialect areas of the
United States reflect to a great extent the settlement history of this
country, but no one would suggest that, for example, the Midland dialects have a different deep structure from that of the dialects of New
England.

What is needed, instead of amateurish speculation, is a
close examination of the evidence. At least for the moment, the largest-scale collections are those of the Linguistic Atlas project, with
Atlantic Seaboard records from New Brunswick to northeastern Florida, inland from the southern boundary of Kentucky to the Canadian
border, westward through Nebraska and the Dakotas, Oklahoma,
Colorado, Nevada, and California. Since there are comparable Negro and white informants in nearly forty communities, one of the
first steps would be a detailed comparison of their records; a large-
scale comparison is still to be undertaken. In the meantime, the
most conclusive statement is that of Atwood 1953 that there is no
feature of the verb system widely disseminated among Negroes that
does not occur as well in the speech of whites. A preliminary step
toward the necessary kind of comparison has been undertaken in two
M. A. theses (Greibesland 1970, Dorrill 1975) comparing the phonological and grammatical evidence in three pairs of records from the
lower Potomac Valley and two pairs from central South Carolina.

One should not, however, consider the Atlas evidence as
settling the matter once and for all. First of all, the Linguistic Atlas project is preponderantly concerned with white speech; even in

the Old South there were interviews with Negro informants in only
about a fifth of the communities selected. There are valid reasons
for this decision — notably the notorious lack of funds for field work,
and the lack of Negro scholars who were interested in field work.
Still, one would like to see more data, even though there is no reason to distrust the reliability of that which we have.

Furthermore, the methods of the Linguistic Atlas exclude
certain kinds of evidence that are of concern to those who desire to
make cross-racial comparisons. Like its predecessors in France
and Italy, the Atlas has concentrated on short-answer questions, of
vocabulary, pronunciation, and morphology; syntactic items are few,
because it is difficult to frame questions that would give an unequivocal response. And, in the absence of mechanical aids, it was
hard for even the best investigator in the 1930's to record extended
phrases from free conversation. The same observation might be
made about the suprasegmentals — pitch, stress, transitions, and
terminals (Trager and Smith 1951), and about the complex of non-
linguistic modulations of speech that are called paralanguage (Austin
1965).

To correct these gaps in our data, a number of scholars
have undertaken studies of Negro speech, especially of adolescents
in northern metropolitan areas. These are the studies which attempt
to dramatize the differences between Negro and white speech, so far
as the syntax of the copula is concerned (Dillard 1967, Stewart 1967).
Where there is a body of data presented, as with Loman 1967, it is
possible for readers to determine for themselves what happens in
contexts. Such studies provide a valuable corrective to whatever erroneous perspectives may be derived from earlier studies.

Yet the new studies themselves are likely to encourage their
own kinds of erroneous perspectives. As stimulating as the evidence
from Negro adolescents is, the fact is that it is not evidence matched
by comparable data from whites of equivalent age, economic and social status, and at least analogous regional backgrounds. Admittedly, this is not always easy to achieve, since, in some cities, such
as Washington, D.C., there is no appreciable lower-class white
population; in other cities, such as Chicago, the local lower-class
whites come from a different background than the lower-class

Negroes; in both Chicago and Akron (Udell 1966), the recently im-
migrated southern poor whites have identified incompletely with that
group, and thus are often difficult to identify. And the recent, justifiable awakening of conscience that pays particular attention to Negroes has inevitably meant that more money has been available for
the study of the speech of Negroes than for the speech of poor
whites. Nevertheless, from the viewpoint of the scientist, it is unfortunate that conclusions are based on a lack of comparable evidence,
so that the basic distinctiveness, so-called, of lower-class Negro
speech is extrapolated from a comparison of lower-class Negro and
middle-class white usage of different regional origins (Wolfram 1969).
And, finally, there is the added danger, already noted, of using facts
out of context.

Two other observations might be made here also. However
interesting may be the grammar of urban Negro children, one may
wonder whether this is a matter of race or simply of age grading. Do
white children of comparable social background or otherwise go
through the same stages in language acquisition (Labov 1965, 1966) ?
If so, the persistence of certain language traits in Negro speech may
simply reflect an arresting of the process due to a narrower range of
opportunities to interact with the dominant culture. Moreover, the
range of styles, even among the most highly educated, is not the
same in all regions, and what is popularly identified as Negro speech
may simply reflect in greater or less degree the tradition of southern
informal discourse. Even such a forbidden four-letter word as ain't
is very common in conversation among educated Southerners
(Atwood 1953; V. McDavid 1956; Mencken 1963).

Actually, there is a good deal of popular evidence in support
of this skepticism. It was amusing to Southerners to notice in the
1968 campaign conversation, and even in the formal speeches, of the
segregationist George Wallace repeated instances of such speech
forms as uninflected plurals, the uninflected third singular, and the
omission of the copula (Frady 1968). Such features have been repeatedly observed in the speech of highly educated Southerners from
areas where Negro influence is unlikely.

What it all amounts to, then, is that as of the moment we do
not have the full descriptions we would like to have of any dialect of

American English, let alone the paired descriptions of comparable economic and social groups within the same regional and local setting. Until we have these — and for several situations — we cannot assume that the differences between Negro speech and white are other than of a statistical order (McDavid 1967, Shuy 1967, Davis 1970). A provocative beginning has been made in a dissertation (O'Cain 1972) based on interviews with one hundred Charlestonians (S. C.) of both races and sexes drawn from the full range of the complicated local socio-economic system. Many more such investigations are needed.

If we must proceed with caution in asserting an essential structural difference between Negro and white speech at the present time, we must proceed even more cautiously in postulating the sources of the dialects spoken by Negroes.[6] For Gullah alone it has been shown (Lorenzo Turner 1949) that there are complicated origins — an imperfectly documented English background, French, Arabic, and several West African languages. We need detailed descriptive grammars of at least a half dozen African languages, such as Mende, Yoruba, Ewe, Ibo, and Kikongo, as well as the common trade languages of the region. Since Arabic was the tongue of slave traders as well as Moslem missionaries, it must be considered, and in terms of the varieties of spoken Arabic that would have been known in West Africa in the seventeenth and eighteenth centuries. Among Romance languages, one should know at least French, Spanish, and Portuguese, and not in their present-day forms but probably in terms of several dialects as they were spoken two centuries ago. Similarly, one should be alert to the influence of contact varieties of European languages, including Sabir, possibly the original lingua franca of the Mediterranean (Whinnom 1956, quoted in Thompson 1961).

One would need a great deal more knowledge of British dialects than anyone has at present (Orton 1962 has at least as many limitations as the American atlases), and a good deal more information on their previous status. Dialects of Irish English, essentially unsurveyed as yet, must also be considered; not only were Irish immigrants heavily represented in the overseer class in plantation territory, but the use of be in Irish English to denote habitual behavior has been repeatedly recognized (Joyce 1910; Henry 1958).[7] And one should have a sound knowledge of Early Modern English in its

varieties and complexities, since verb phrases of the type <u>he might</u>
<u>coulda done been gone</u>, eschewed by schoolma'ams but still heard in
the speech of some southerners, are not New World innovations, but,
rather, four centuries old in English (Visser 1946). In short, any
substantive statements about the origins of the dialects of Negro
Americans will require investigations in breadth and depth far beyond what we now have, and still might not get beyond a Scots ver-
dict of 'not proven'.

This does not mean that the claims of creolization can be,
or indeed should be, casually dismissed. [8] As Ian Catford has observed orally, when English is adopted by speakers of other languages, it undergoes pretty much the same mutations in a wide variety of communities, regardless of the structure of the host language. The varieties of English found among the Acadians of southern Louisiana, whose ancestral language was French, show many
striking similarities to the English of southern Negroes, whether at
home or transplanted (McDavid 1967). Whether some of these features of Southern American English — shared by Negroes and whites
— are at least partly due to the establishment of English, several
centuries past, among speakers of various Celtic dialects is only an
additional complication. Certainly the concentration, in restricted
urban environments, of speakers of non-standard dialects of Southern American English, whatever the ultimate origin of those dialects,
is likely to provide an opportunity for what one may call 'neo-creolization', with the emergence, out of diversity, of relatively uniform
non-standard dialects. And, as we said at the beginning, if a group
feels that its speech constitutes a distinctive variety, it does — at
least for the members of that group. For the objective linguist, the
dialects of the Ukraine are simply varieties of Russian, about as
different from the speech of Moscow and Leningrad as is the English
of Atlanta or New Orleans from that of Chicago or Boston. But the
psychological needs of the Ukrainian nationalists exiled in the United
States are such that it is important for them to assert the identity of
the Ukrainian language.

Clearly, the structural identity of the English of Negro
Americans is a complicated problem. With all due respect for the
aspirations of a neglected minority, and with the recognition of the

need for more intelligent approaches to the problems of non-standard
dialects in the classroom (a need faced by Americans of all races),
the serious scholar must eschew facile conclusions and insist on the
steady gathering and careful evaluation of data. Laborious it is, but
of such labor is science made.

NOTES

[1] For a more detailed account of this mythology, see
McDavid and McDavid 1951.

[2] Shuy 1967 sampled opinions of native Detroiters who were
asked to identify the race of a speaker after listening to an approximately thirty-second sample of his speech. The Detroiters were correct about eighty percent of the time, but, it should be noted, there
was no southern white speech sampled.

[3] Bailey 1965:172 writes, "I would like to suggest that the
Southern Negro 'dialect' differs from other Southern speech because
its deep structure is different, having its origins as it undoubtedly
does in some Proto-Creole grammatical structure."

[4] As in Carbonear, Newfoundland (Paddock 1967).

[5] For a further critique of the creole substratum theory,
see L. M. Davis 1969.

[6] James Sledd informally pointed out many of these complications during a conference at Tuskeegee Institute in October, 1968.

[7] One cannot rule out Irish influence on Jamaican English.
The island became an English colony under the Protectorate, and
Cromwell sent over many Irish who were unenthusiastic about his
regime.

[8] Scholars are not agreed on the nature of creolization. To
some, it must involve non-European dialects; to others, it may include the mixture of diverse dialects which has characterized every
transplanted European language. J. W. Turner 1966 characterizes
Australian English as a "creolized bush pidgin."

REFERENCES

Atwood, E. Bagby
    1953   A Survey of Verb Forms in the Eastern United States (Ann
            Arbor, The University of Michigan Press).

Austin, William M.
1965   "Some Social Aspects of Paralanguage", Canadian Journal
        of Linguistics 11:31-39.
Bailey, Beryl L.
1965   "Toward a New Perspective in Negro English Dialectology",
        American Speech 40:171-177.
1966   Jamaican Creole Syntax: A Transformational Approach
        (Cambridge, Cambridge University Press).
Cassidy, F. G.
1961   Jamaica Talk (New York, St. Martin's Press).
Cassidy, F. G., and R. B. Le Page
1967   Dictionary of Jamaican English (Cambridge, Cambridge
        University Press).
Davis, Lawrence M.
1969   "Dialect Research: Mythology and Reality", Orbis 18:332-
        339.
1970   "Social Dialectology in America: A Critical Survey", Jour-
        nal of English Linguistics 4:46-56.
Dillard, J. L.
1967   "Negro Children's Dialect in the Inner City", Florida FL
        Reporter 5:3:1-4.
Frady, Marshal
1968   Wallace (New York, New American Library).
Gonzales, Ambrose E.
1922   The Black Border (Columbia, S.C., The State Co.).
Greibesland, Solveig
1970   "Black and White Folk Speech in the Potomac Valley", un-
        published M.A. Thesis (University of Chicago).
Hall, Robert A., Jr.
1943   Melanesian Pidgin English: Grammar, Texts, and Vocabu-
        lary (Baltimore, Linguistic Society of America).
1968   "Creole Linguistics", Current Trends in Linguistics: IV:
        Ibero-American and Caribbean Linguistics, Thomas Sebeok,
        ed. (The Hague, Mouton), pp. 361-371.
Henry, P. L.
1958   "A Linguistic Survey of Ireland: Preliminary Report".
        Lochlann: A Review of Celtic Studies 1:49-208.
Joyce, P. W.
1910   English as We Speak It in Ireland, 2nd ed. (Dublin, Long-
        mans).

Krapp, George Phillip
   1925   The English Language in America, 2 vols. (New York, The
          Century Co.).
Labov, William
   1965   "Stages in the Acquisition of Standard English", Social Dia-
          lects and Language Learning, A. L. Davis, ed. (Blooming-
          ton, Ind., National Council of Teachers of English).
   1966   The Social Stratification of English in New York City (Wash-
          ington, D.C., Center for Applied Linguistics).
Loman, Bengt, ed.
   1967   Conversations in a Negro American Dialect (Washington,
          D.C., Center for Applied Linguistics).
McCawley, James
   1967   "The Respective Downfalls of Deep Structure and Autono-
          mous Syntax", unpublished paper delivered at the Annual
          Meeting of the Linguistic Society of America.
McDavid, Raven I., Jr.
   1967   "Historical, Regional, and Social Variation", Journal of
          English Linguistics 1:24-40.
McDavid, Raven I., Jr., and Virginia G. McDavid
   1951   "The Relationship of the Speech of American Negroes to the
          Speech of Whites", American Speech 26:3-17.
McDavid, Virginia G.
   1956   "A Survey of Verb Forms in the North-Central States and
          the Upper Midwest", Ph.D. thesis (University of Minnesota).
Mencken, H. L.
   1963   The American Language, ed. R. I. McDavid, Jr. (New
          York, Knopf).
Orton, Harold
   1962-71 Survey of English Dialects (Leeds, E. J. Arnold and Sons).
O'Cain, Raymond K.
   1972   "A Sociolinguistic Study of Charleston Speech", unpublished
          Ph.D. thesis (University of Chicago).
Paddock, Harold
   1967   "The Speech of Carbonear, Newfoundland", M.A. thesis
          (Memorial University of Newfoundland).
Shuy, Roger
   1967   Detroit Dialect Study (Washington, D.C., U.S. Office of
          Education).

Shuy, Roger, Walter A. Wolfram, and William K. Riley
    1968   Field Techniques in an Urban Language Study (Washington,
            D. C. , Center for Applied Linguistics).
Stewart, William A.
    1967   "Sociolinguistic Factors in the History of American Negro
            Dialects", Florida FL Reporter 5:2:1-4.
Thompson, R. W.
    1961   "Creole Dialects of Old World and New", Creole Language
            Studies 2:107-113.
Trager, George L. , and Henry Lee Smith, Jr.
    1951   An Outline of English Structure (= Studies in Linguistics,
            Occasional Papers No. 3 [Reprinted by the American Coun-
            cil of Learned Societies, 1956]).
Turner, J. W.
    1966   The English Language in Australia and New Zealand (London,
            Longmans).
Turner, Lorenzo
    1949   Africanisms in the Gullah Dialect (Chicago, The University
            of Chicago Press).
Udell, Gerald
    1966   "The speech of Akron, Ohio", unpublished Ph. D. disserta-
            tion (University of Chicago).
Visser, F. T.
    1946   A Syntax of the English Language of St. Thomas More (Lou-
            vain, Librairie Universitaire).
Whinnom, Keith
    1956   Spanish Contact Vernaculars in the Philippine Islands (Hong
            Kong, London, and New York).
Wolfram, Walter A.
    1969   A Sociolinguistic Description of Detroit Negro Speech (Wash-
            ington, D. C. , Center for Applied Linguistics).

6 | The Folk Vocabulary of Eastern Kentucky

In Collaboration with Virginia Glenn McDavid
In Honor of Hans Kurath

Hans Kurath's interest in the speech of Kentucky antedates by several years his involvement in the Linguistic Atlas of the United States and Canada. As he has often told his students, with the enthusiasm that has marked all of his professional career, Kentucky was the area of his first field investigations, and indeed of the first attempt by any scholar to ascertain the variety of educated American speech in a region where the mythical General American was once thought to prevail: [1]

"Bill[2] and I spent the summer of '25 or '26 on a camping trip in his Model T Ford. We pitched our tent in some spot not too far from a farmhouse, sometimes after asking for permission, but usually not — hoping that we would have a visitor before dark, as we usually did. We always unfolded our cots and invited anybody who dropped in to have a seat. After a chat I might ask the fellow to read the little story I had doctored up. It was the famous story of the Rat that I took from Henry Sweet's phonetic reader,[3] that Ayres used for his series of phonograph records,[4] has been cussed by various fellows, and is now being recorded by Cassidy.[5]

The reason I took this story was that it had many of the kinds of test words in it that I needed for my purpose. Needless to say, I stuck in some others that might turn up phonological differences. Of course, I was primarily interested in the speech of the better educated who could read my story with some speed. My job was to jot down the vowels in three or four words per line — right below the typed words.[6] Observations on other features were jotted down after the visitor left.

Why did I go into the field ? Simply because I could find
no reliable information on regional differences in cultivated
speech that I needed for the phonological volume of G. O.
Curme's Grammar of the English Language that he had invited me to do.

I reported on my observations to English 13 of the MLA
in '26 [the report, as indicated in the proceedings of the
meeting, was particularly concerned with the need to modify
the International Phonetic Alphabet to take care of the phenomena of American English] — and that's what got me into
the Atlas business. [English 13 was already concerned with
the need for making a systematic survey of differences in
American English.]

Bill was a joy to travel with. He had quite a sense of
humor and had no end of funny stories to tell our visitors.
And of course, many of them responded in kind. Anyway,
we never had any trouble about getting them to talk.

We started from Evanston, where I was teaching at the
time and Bill was a graduate student, and made for the triangle between the Mississippi and the Illinois, where I first
heard a sort of Southern Mountain speech.[7] From there we
cut across southern Illinois and crossed the Ohio at Evans-
ville. The area around Mammoth Cave was fascinating: no
real roads but, as a native put it, 'just a way to go.' Our
shovel and chain came in handy several times. In one spot
somewhere between Lincoln's birthplace and Danville a farmer maintained a slough in the road for making a little money
by pulling cars through with his team of oxen. We were one
of his customers. We spent some time in Danville, where
an old friend of mine [Fritz Mezger] (who wound up as the
German department's head at Bryn Mawr, first as an associate of Prokosch) was teaching [at Centre College, better
renowned at the time for its recent football teams]. This
was my headquarters for the Blue Grass area. Then we
made for the Cumberland Gap. One evening we pitched our
tent in the woods near the road. Out came a man, step by
step, totin' a gun on his shoulder. I walked towards him
just as leisurely and said: 'D'ye mind if we stay here over-
night ?' After due inspection and deliberation he said: 'T's
awright. I was jis goin' to see who it was. '

> We spent some time in the Smokies and then drove north
> in the Valley of Virginia and back to Illinois through Pennsyl-
> vania. I learned a lot in those eight weeks, and not only
> about phonology".[8]

For this reason no paper could be more appropriate in a volume
honoring Kurath than one which presents a part of the evidence on
the speech of eastern Kentucky, as reflected in the field records
for the Linguistic Atlas of the North-Central States.[9]

The popular impression of the speech of eastern Kentucky
(and indeed of the entire Southern Appalachian area), as derived from
earlier and less rigorous studies,[10] is that it is saturated with relic
forms which have been lost in almost all other dialects of English,
both British and American. Even when the romantic illusions of 'purest Anglo-Saxon' or 'pure Elizabethan English' are properly discounted, two conclusions are inevitably drawn: (1) that the speech of
eastern Kentucky (and that of other Southern mountain areas, Appalachian or Ozark) is much more archaic than that of the surrounding
lowlands; (2) that it is highly uniform.

Without disparaging the valuable contributions these early
studies have made, notably those by Gordon Wilson of Bowling Green
State College — after all, there is no substitute for either careful observation or intimate knowledge of the community whose speech is
being recorded — it is only fair to point out that they were conducted
without the benefit of a frame of reference within which the data might
be interpreted. Now that such a frame of reference is available, in
the field records from eastern Kentucky for the Linguistic Atlas of
the North-Central States, we may reappraise the speech forms characteristic of eastern Kentucky in terms of the larger speech community of American English.[11] This reappraisal, of course, does not answer all questions past or present; but it may indicate what future
questions should be asked.

The method by which the evidence is obtained for the American regional atlases has been repeatedly described during the past
two decades and a half.[12] It is a method of selective sampling, devised by Jules Gilliéron for the Atlas linguistique de la France (Paris,
1902-1910), refined by Karl Jaberg and Jakob Jud for the Sprach-und-

Sachatlas Italiens und der Südschweiz (Zofingen, 1928-1940), and adapted by Kurath to American conditions:

1. Various population origins, with dialect mixture and foreign-language settlements almost from the beginning.

2. An English-speaking settlement in which the peasant types were hardly represented at all.

3. Traditions of geographic and social mobility.

4. Attrition of the extremes of folk speech through industrialization, urbanization and mass education.

The evidence is collected by trained fieldworkers, using a questionnaire of selected items of everyday experience, designed to sample vocabulary, grammar and pronunciation. The fieldworkers go into selected communities in the areas under investigation, interview selected informants native to the particular community (and representing specified age, ethnic and educational groups within the community) in a conversational situation, and record the responses in a minute phonetic notation. [13] Since this method elicits comparable data from all informants, it is possible to chart and tabulate the regional and social distribution of particular features.

Kentucky was the last state to be investigated for the Linguistic Atlas of the North-Central States. Field work in the eastern part of the state was begun in 1952 and completed in 1957. This study concentrates on an area east of a southward prolongation of the Ohio-Indiana line. Communities investigated are of three types.

(1)   Bluegrass: the focal community of Lexington, plus four peripheral communities: Harrodsburg, Owenton, Maysville, Owingsville.

(2)   A transitional belt of foothill or Knobs communities: Somerset, Irvine, Booneville, Frenchburg, Grayson.

(3)   Mountain communities: Williamsburg, Middlesboro, Hazard, Hyden, Harlan, Whitesburg, Paintsville.

Some of these communities, of course, might be reclassified on
later detailed examination.

The informants interviewed ranged in age from 23 to 104. In
every community there is a representative of old-fashioned speech;
in nearly every community, one of the middle group, generally middle-aged (45 to 65) with about a high-school education. In three communities — Lexington, Maysville and Middlesboro — there are cultured informants, college educated and representing the best cultural traditions.

Besides these communities, several from adjacent states
have been included -- seven from Ohio, seven from West Virginia,
four from southwestern Virginia — so that we may determine whether
speech-forms characteristic of eastern Kentucky are shared by
neighboring states. Of particular concern is the role of the Ohio Valley, as a dialect boundary or as a channel of linguistic dissemination.

In appraising the speech of eastern Kentucky, as with any
other region, the scholar must recognize such background influences
as terrain, communications, economic interests, settlement history
and traditional cultural affiliations.

The terrain is everywhere rolling — gentle in the Bluegrass,
increasingly rugged through the Knobs and mountains. Historically
the primary transportation systems — still important — were the
rivers: (1) the Big Sandy, Licking and Kentucky, which flow northwestward into the Ohio; (2) the Cumberland, which — though rising
like the others in southeastern Kentucky — flows southwestward
through the Nashville Basin and then northwestward to join the Ohio
near its junction with the Mississippi, thus providing the only early
communication between eastern Kentucky and the states further south.
Through railroads are few; the Chesapeake and Ohio is the only east-
west line, and that in the northern part of the area; the Southern and
the Louisville and Nashville, the major north-south lines, run through
the Bluegrass, at the extreme west; an alternate though tortuous
north-south route at the extreme east of Kentucky is provided by a
branch line of the Chesapeake and Ohio from Ashland to Elkhorn City,
where it connects with the Carolina, Clichfield, and Ohio, a subsidiary of the Louisville and Nashville, the main line of the Norfolk and

Western, from Cincinnati to Roanoke, Virginia, skirts eastern Kentucky to the north and east. Many branch lines exist, principally to tap the eastern Kentucky coalfields. The highway system was established later than in most states, owing to adverse terrain, lack of funds and restrictive condemnation laws which made it difficult to acquire land for road improvements. At the time the field work was done (in the early stages of the Interstate system), the quality of roads varied greatly from county to county (and there are 120 counties in Kentucky). In some of the mountain areas only the principal routes are traversable in wet weather; many of the secondary roads are locally and literally branch roads, following stream beds that are occasionally improved by rough grading. On such routes the low-slung cosmetic automobiles of the 1950's and 1960's are useless, with jeeps and pickup trucks furnishing the only dependable motorized competition to the still reliable mule.

The people of eastern Kentucky earn their livelihood in various ways. Agriculture is still the most important source of income. In the Bluegrass there are large commercial plantations, many of them recently taken over by Northern capitalists and converted to country estates and horse-breeding farms; in the Knobs and mountains, farms are smaller and farming is more often at a subsistence level. Tobacco is everywhere the chief money crop. There are various small industries tributary to agriculture, including distilling — legal in the Bluegrass, illicit elsewhere.[14] Industrial employment until recently was furnished principally by coal mining and its dependent industries, which have declined even more in Kentucky than in West Virginia. Petroleum extraction has become important in recent years, especially in the valley of the Big Sandy. Manufacturing is still relatively unimportant. Along the main highways the tourist trade has become lucrative since World War II;[15] paradoxically, however, it is comparatively undeveloped where the scenery is most spectacular — thanks to the real dangers from the roads and the imaginary dangers from the local population.

Though its settlement came nearly two generations later than that of Georgia, the youngest colony on the Atlantic seaboard, eastern Kentucky was the first territory west of the Appalachians to be settled by English-speaking people. Settlers came into the area from three directions: (1) down the Ohio from the Pittsburgh area; (2) across the Big Sandy from West Virginia (then still a part of Virginia);

(3) most important, through the Cumberland Gap and other mountain passes from southwest Virginia and western North Carolina. In terms of the dialect classification established for the Atlantic seaboard by Kurath's Word Geography and related works, almost all the early settlers of eastern Kentucky represented the Midland region, deriving their speech from Pennsylvania. [16] This Pennsylvania influence is of two kinds: (1) direct, 'North Midland,' from the Pittsburgh area and northern West Virginia; (2) indirect, 'South Midland,' by way of the Shenandoah Valley, southwestern Virginia, southern West Virginia and the Carolina mountains. There was essentially no Northern settlement — from New England and its western dependencies — and almost none from the plantation South, at least in the beginning.

Culturally, however, all of Kentucky has been under Southern dominance. The plantation system was established in the Bluegrass, according to the model of eastern Virginia, but it was not powerful enough to induce secession during the Confederate War, [17] though Kentuckians served in the Confederate Army as well as in the Union. Nevertheless, even in the mountains — long a stronghold of free labor, Unionist sentiment, and staunch Republicanism — there is a tendency for the 'old families' to identify with the 'Old South', and for politicians to prosper by appealing to 'Southern traditions,' real or imaginary. [18] The Negro population has never been high; and today one encounters few Negroes outside the Bluegrass, and those few in urban areas. There has been little non-English-speaking immigration in recent years, and that usually in specialized trades; the comparative few of these groups have been almost completely assimilated.

With a high birthrate and rather limited local opportunities, it is not surprising that there is heavy migration from eastern Kentucky to such urban industrial centers further north as Chicago, Cincinnati, Cleveland, Dayton and Detroit. [19] Like the rest of the United States, eastern Kentucky has participated in the recent accelerated trends of industrialization, urbanization and mass education. Nevertheless, since all three of these forces began to work fairly late in eastern Kentucky, and have there progressed more slowly than in other parts of the nation (the low tax base — as everywhere south of the Ohio River — has been a serious handicap in the development of schools), their effects have been less noticeable than, say, in the Western Reserve of Ohio or in Upstate New York.

In view of the settlement history of eastern Kentucky, we may assume — and are not disappointed in our assumptions — that certain groups of words will be found throughout the area.

I. Words occurring throughout the Midland:

armload, load (of wood)
blinds "roller shades"
buck (sheep) "ram" (also Northern)
coal oil "kerosene"
fishworm "earthworm"
to hull beans
a little piece "short distance"
quarter till (the hour) except in central Bluegrass[20]
side meat "salt pork"
skillet "frying pan"[21]
snake feeder "dragon fly" except in central Bluegrass[22]
sook! call to cows
wait on "wait for"
want off "want to get off"
worm fence "zigzag rail fence" less common in mountains
you-uns "you" (pl.) recessive

II. Words characteristic of the Midland and South:

bottoms, bottom land "low land along stream"
bucket (of metal)
Christmas gift! "Merry Christmas"
comfort "heavy tied quilt"
corn pone "cornbread in large cakes"
dog irons, fire dogs "andirons"
fishing worm "earthworm"
granny, granny woman "midwife"
ground squirrel "chipmunk"
polecat "skunk"
pully bone, pull bone "wishbone"
right (smart) moderate intensifier

roasting ears "tender young corn"
saw! call to cows at milking time
singletree, swingletree "whippletree"
slop "liquid garbage fed to hogs or chickens"

III. Words characteristic of the South and South Midland:

ash cakes "corn bread baked in the ashes"
batter cakes "pancakes"
belly-buster "coasting face downward"[23]
branch "small stream"
breakfast bacon "packaged sliced bacon"
clabber "thickened sour milk"
clabber cheese "cottage cheese" (recessive)
corn shucks "corn husks"
hay shock "haycock"
middlings, middling meat "salt pork"
pallet "bed made up on the floor"
turn of corn "load taken to mill at one time"
whet rock "whetstone"

Some words characteristic of the South Midland are found throughout
the area, such as corn dodger "small corn cake," skim of ice "first
thin layer of ice" and sugar orchard "maple grove." Others are restricted to the mountains, such as

fireboard "mantelpiece"
jacket "vest"
mantelboard "mantelpiece"
milk gap "cowpen in pasture"
plum across "all the way across"
ridy horse "seesaw"

Of West Midland terms, one finds everywhere green-beans "string
beans," sugar grove "maple grove" and sugar tree "sugar maple."
Poke "small sack, usually of paper" is found everywhere except in
the Bluegrass.

In contrast with these generally distributed words, others
occur in only limited areas of eastern Kentucky. These show characteristic, indeed predictable, patterns of distribution.

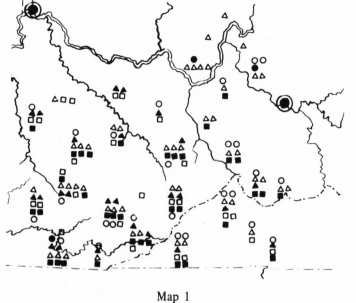

Map 1
South Midland

o <u>fireboard</u> "mantel"   △ <u>milk gap</u> "cow pen"   ▢ <u>plum across</u>
● <u>mantelboard</u> "mantel"   ▲ <u>jacket</u> "vest"   ▪ <u>ridy horse</u> "seesaw"

     Of words associated with the North and North Midland, <u>hay
cock</u> is widely scattered, as is <u>whinny</u> "noise made by a horse at
feeding time," which may be influenced by the Thoroughbred tradition
of the Bluegrass. Others, such as <u>grist of corn</u>, "load taken to mill
at one time," <u>boughten</u> "not home made" and <u>sawbuck</u> "X-shaped
frame for sawing firewood," are more sporadically distributed. The
North Midland <u>run</u> "small stream" is practically confined to the Ohio
Valley, as is the pronunciation of <u>creek</u> /krɪk/, riming with <u>lick</u>.
<u>Belling</u> "noisy celebration after a wedding," is found only in the north-
eastern corner. Of western Pennsylvania words, <u>baby buggy</u> "baby
carriage" is everywhere; but <u>hay doodle</u> "hay cock" and <u>gunny sack</u>
"burlap bag" are essentially restricted to the Ohio Valley and <u>lamp
oil</u> "kerosene" is found in only two communities in the eastern wedge.

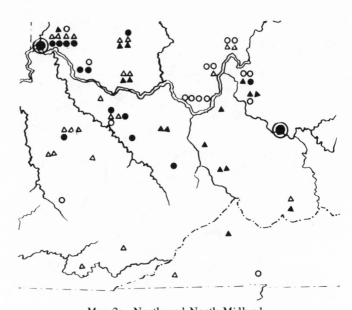

Map 2: North and North Midland

o grist of corn "load"   • sawbuck   ▵ run "small stream"   ▲ belling "shivaree"

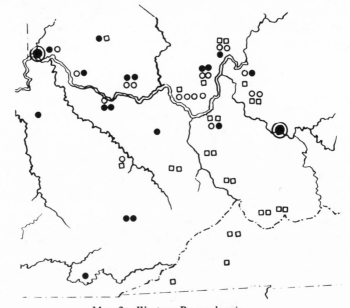

Map 3: Western Pennsylvania

o hay doodle "haycock"   • gunny sack   ▢ lamp oil "kerosene"

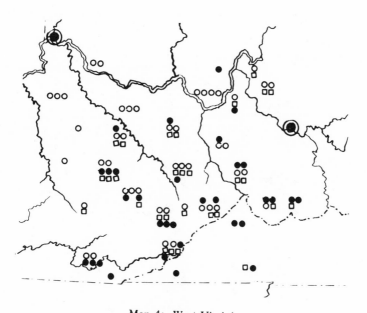

Map 4: West Virginia

O <u>coffee sack</u> "burlap bag"   □ <u>fork</u> "small stream"   ● <u>hobbies</u> "corn dodgers"

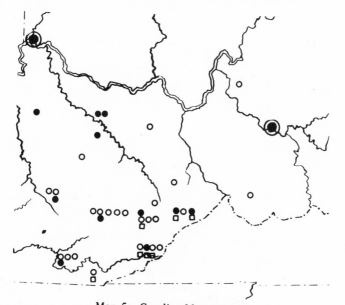

Map 5: Carolina Mountains I

O <u>big house</u> "living room"   ● <u>big room</u> "living room"   □ <u>galloping fence</u>

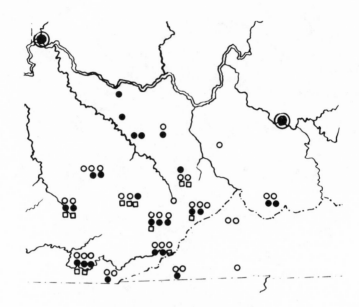

Map 6: Carolina Mountains II

○ <u>redworm</u> "earthworm" ● <u>open stone peach</u> "freestone" □ <u>hickory</u> "ox whip"

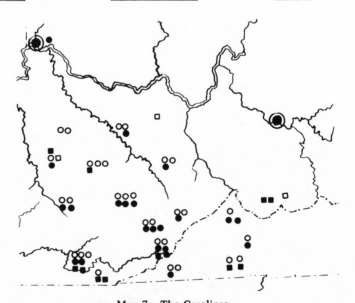

Map 7: The Carolinas

○ <u>laid out</u> "played truant" ● <u>johnnycake</u> "corn griddle cake" ◻ <u>go on!</u> "get up!"
■ <u>tow sack</u> "burlap bag"

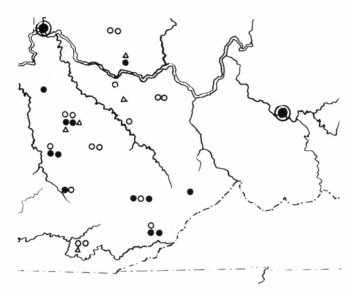

Map 8: Southern I

O <u>tote</u> "carry"   ● <u>low</u> "moo"   △ <u>carry you home</u> "convey or escort"

Words characteristic of the Southern mountains do not extend to the Bluegrass. The few characteristic West Virginia words
— <u>fork</u> "small stream, " <u>hobbies</u> "small corn cakes, " and <u>coffee sack</u>
"burlap bag" — occur throughout the foothills and mountains. Words
characteristic of the Carolina mountains are usually restricted to
southeastern Kentucky, but there are many of them, such as

> <u>big house</u>, <u>big room</u> "living room"
> <u>galloping fence</u> "rail fence laid as successive tripods"
> <u>hickory</u> "ox goad"
> <u>open stone peach</u> "freestone"
> <u>redworm</u> "earthworm"
> <u>rick</u> "haycock"

With these may be grouped such more widely distributed Carolina
words as <u>laid out</u> "played truant, " <u>tow sack</u> "burlap bag" and <u>woods
colt</u> "bastard. " Such other Carolina terms as <u>go on!</u> "get up!" and
<u>johnnycake</u> "large griddle cake of corn meal" are somewhat less com-
mon. All Carolina words seem to share a common basic pattern of
distribution, with the axis along Daniel Boone's Wilderness Road.

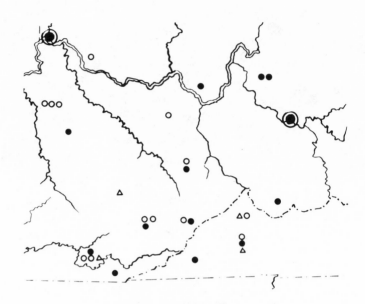

Map 9: Southern II

O clean across   ● come up!"get up!"   △ hasslet"liver and lights"

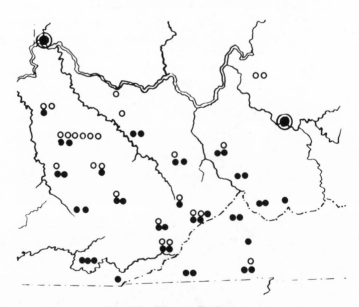

Map 10: Virginia Piedmont

O snake doctor"dragon fly"   ● plum(stone) peach "clingstone"

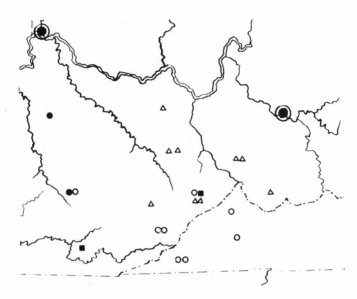

Map 11: Southern Coast

○ (sea)grass sack "burlap bag"   ● groundworm "earthworm"
△ baseborn (child) "bastard"   ■ hum "moo"

Words characteristic of the old plantation South, or parts of
it, are rare, except salat "cooked greens," which is found everywhere. Most Southern words are found, if at all, in the Bluegrass,
less commonly in the southeast. Typical of this distribution are the
Southern low "moo", goobers "peanuts" and carry you home "escort."
More widespread but nowhere dominant are clean across and come
up! "get up!" Hasslet "edible entrails of a hog" is found only in the
southeast. On the other hand, the Virginia Piedmont nicker "whinny",
plum(stone) peach "clingstone", scrich owl "screech owl" and snake
doctor "dragon fly" are found throughout eastern Kentucky and in
most of central and southern Ohio. Conversely the Virginia breakfast
meat "sliced bacon," corn house "corn crib" and cow house "cow
barn" are rare in Kentucky.

Besides the Virginia Piedmont, the Southern coast is also
represented in the vocabulary of eastern Kentucky. From Chesapeake Bay we have (sea) grass sack "burlap bag," ground worm
"earthworm," baseborn (child) "bastard," and the blend whicker

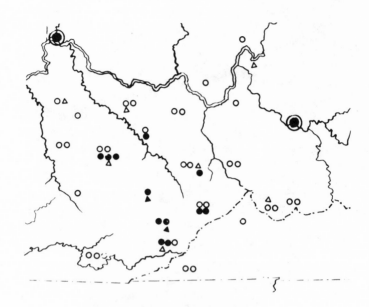

Map 12: Local Words

○ (wood) rack "sawbuck"   ● brought on "not made at home"

△ lick "small stream"   ▲ Swede fence

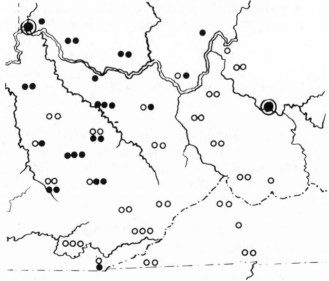

Map 13: "Maple Grove"

○ sugar grove South Midland   ● sugar camp Ohio Valley

"whinny." And from the Carolina coast is derived <u>hum</u> "moo." None of these is very common.

An apparent anomaly is the Northern <u>darning needle</u> "dragon fly," which not only has a lone occurrence in Booneville, but five instances in southern West Virginia, four in the valley of the Big Sandy. It is possible that these may derive from the New England colony at Marietta, Ohio; on the other hand, <u>darning needle</u> has also been recorded in rural communities in Northern Georgia, where there is no reason to suspect New England influence. [25]

There are also indigenous words in eastern Kentucky, or at least words of wider distribution than one finds for them along the Atlantic Seaboard. Everywhere one finds the French-derived Mississippi Valley term <u>shivaree,</u> to designate a noisy celebration after a wedding. <u>Wood rack</u>, <u>saw rack</u> "sawbuck", though found in southeastern Ohio, is far more common in Kentucky. <u>Lick</u> "small stream" is apparently a Middle Western feature. Characteristic of the Nashville Basin is the use of <u>wardrobe</u> to designate a built-in closet. And apparently restricted to eastern Kentucky are <u>branch road</u> "unimproved road in a stream bed," <u>brought on</u> "not made at home," and <u>used to</u> as a sentence-initial adverb, as in "<u>used to</u>, everybody around here baked their own bread." Whether <u>Swede fence</u> "galloping fence" belongs in this group can be determined only when all of Cassidy's evidence is in. [26]

Even from this summary of the vocabulary evidence, one should no longer assume that eastern Kentucky is a relic area, least of all an undifferentiated one. Rather, the evidence supports the inference from the historical record that it is an interesting and complicated transition area, as one should expect of the area through which most of the lower Ohio Valley was settled. This is the same picture that emerges from previous examinations of the grammatical evidence and from the preliminary examination of the phonology. From the point of view of the linguistic geographer, few areas are more deserving of intensive investigation, not only for the survival of relics but for further evidence of the mixing of speechways as Americans moved west.

NOTES

[1]Personal communication, January 15, 1970. A preliminary version of this paper was given at the Kentucky Foreign Language Conference, April 1957. For assembling the evidence we are
indebted to Lawrence M. Davis of the Illinois Institute of Technology
and Raymond K. O'Cain of the University of South Carolina.

[2]William Kurath, Hans Kurath's younger brother (1900-
1949). A student under Leonard Bloomfield at the University of Chicago and an extraordinarily successful teacher, he was dismissed
from the University after he ran afoul of the doctrinaire humanistic
technology of the Hutchins Aristotelians — a fate parallel, in a way,
to that of Bloomfield, whom Hutchins made no effort to keep. William
Kurath later became chairman of the German Department at the University of Arizona; at the time of his death he was engaged in the
study of Papago and other American Indian languages of the Southwest.

[3]"Once there was a young rat who couldn't make up his
mind. . . Thus the shirker got his due. "

[4]A series of phonograph records using this text was prepared by the late Harry Morgan Ayres in the 1930's, drawing many
subjects from the cosmopolitan student body of the Columbia summer
school. First issued by Victor and later by Linguaphone, the series
has been allowed to go out of press.

[5]For the Dictionary of American Regional English. It is also
being used for Recordings of Standard English, a project directed by
Alva L. Davis, of the Illinois Institute of Technology.

[6]This technique was also used by John S. Kenyon and Thomas
A. Knott, in gathering material for their Pronouncing Dictionary of
American English (Springfield, Mass., 1944).

[7]Actually, as often happens, the speech of the area has
proved to be more complicated than Kurath's impressions indicated.
Field work for the Linguistic Atlas of the North-Central States has
shown a number of Northern (i.e., New England derived) linguistic
forms in Calhoun County, as the apex of the triangle, including the
/-s-/ pronunciation in greasy and the verb phrase hadn't ought.

[8]Kurath and his associates, most notably Bernard Bloch,
have always emphasized the fact that language is a social instrument,
and have continually reminded field workers that an interview is a
delicate interpersonal relationship. The most successful field workers are those that are most often accepted by their informants as new
neighbors and friends of the family.

[9] The first field records from eastern Kentucky were made by K. K. Boggs in the early 1930's. They were used, chiefly for vocabulary evidence, in the preliminary editing of the proposed Linguistic Atlas of the South Atlantic States. Later the entire state was investigated for A. H. Marckwardt's Linguistic Atlas of the North-Central States, funds being provided by Western Reserve University, Ohio State University, the University of Michigan, the University of Kentucky, and Indiana University. As the principal field investigator, I extend my appreciation to these institutions for making the field work possible, as well as to the American Council of Learned Societies, which has sponsored the Linguistic Atlas project from its inception. I am also deeply grateful to Professors Kurath and Marckwardt, first for involving me in the field work and later for putting the collections at my disposal, as associate editor for the North-Central States (1954), editor-in-chief 1975; editor-in-chief for the Middle and South Atlantic States 1964.

We have confined this paper to eastern Kentucky for several reasons: (1) the original report of 1957 was restricted to that area: (2) the field records from the central part of the state were of uneven quality: (3) comparison of the Kentucky evidence with that obtained in Ohio by A. L. Davis and Guy S. Lowman, Jr., and in southwestern Virginia and southern West Virginia by Lowman is relatively easy since the three of us had similar training, similar practices in the field, and similar habits of transcribing (RIM).

[10] Such an assumption was at the basis of Joseph S. Hall's The Phonetics of Great Smoky Mountain Speech (American Speech, Reprints and Monographs 4, New York, King's Crown Press, 1942). See the review in Language 19 (1943).

[11] Such a frame of reference has been supplied in three summary volumes for the Atlantic Seaboard: Kurath, A Word Geography of the Eastern United States (Ann Arbor, 1949); E. Bagby Atwood, A Survey of Verb Forms in the Eastern United States (Ann Arbor, 1953); Kurath and McDavid, The Pronunciation of English in the Atlantic States (Ann Arbor, 1961). For the North-Central States there is an excellent broad-gauge survey by Marckwardt, "Principal and Subsidiary Dialect Areas in the North-Central States," Publication of the American Dialect Society 27.3-15 (1957). Somewhat more specialized but comparable to Atwood's study is Virginia McDavid, Verb Forms in the North-Central States and Upper Midwest, diss. U. of Minnesota, 1956.

The validity of recent sociolinguistic studies may be fairly judged by the extent to which they make use of the framework which the regional surveys provide.

[12] For example, in ch. 9 of W. N. Francis, The Structure of American English, New York, 1958.

[13] The introduction of high-fidelity lightweight recording equipment has not made the field worker obsolete. It can provide a permanent record for checking the field worker's transcriptions, and it can pick up unguarded remarks from free conversation better than the best field worker is able to do. But the field worker must still conduct the interview and elicit responses. Where he shirks this responsibility and assumes that the recorder will shorten the time of an interview, the results can be almost disastrous. See "Tape Recordings in Linguistic Geography: a Cautionary Note," Journal of the Canadian Linguistic Association 3.3-9 (1956/57).

[14] In the 1950's, of 120 counties in Kentucky, more than a hundred were officially dry, even to prohibiting the sale of beer.

[15] As a result of the expanding tourist industry, when a new highway bypassed his restaurant in Corbin and led him to sell his friends chicken at a roadside stand, Col. Harlan Sanders has become a millionaire and a national figure on television.

[16] In her M. A. thesis, using checklists distributed by mail (U. of Kentucky, 1955) Mrs. Christine Duncan Forrester concluded that the regional vocabulary of Kentucky was basically Midland.

[17] See, for example, John Fox, Jr., The Little Shepherd of Kingdom Come.

[18] Even serious students of language may let their family identification override scholarly caution. For instance, without any real examination of the data, Charles-James M. Bailey casually asserts a simple North-South division and ignores the massive Pennsylvania influence on Kentucky speech. See "Dialectal Differences in the Syllabication of Non-Nasal Consonants," General Linguistics 8.79-91 (1968). A more cautious statement is that of the late E. Bagby Atwood, in The Regional Vocabulary of Texas (Austin, 1962), which includes South Midland and coastal Southern under the classification of "General Southern," while recognizing that South Midland shares many traits with the North Midland of Pennsylvania. If a peace-loving structuralist may employ one of the counterwords of the Transformational Establishment, it is counter-intuitive (to one familiar with the generations of conflict between Up Country yeomen and Low Country planter) to assert the mystique of a common Southern dialect.

[19]The extent of this northward migration is difficult to estimate since Appalachian whites are less visible than other in-
migrants, and more reluctant to demand public assistance. Many of
them, indeed, retain their subsistence farms and their voting rights
"back home"; it was a favorite canard among Kentucky Democrats in
the election of 1954 that Eisenhower had brought some of the boys
back home from Korea, but a lot more back home from Detroit (when
the recession hit the automobile plants). For the situation in one
city, see the introductory chapter of Gerald Udell, The Speech of
Akron, Ohio, diss. University of Chicago, 1966.

[20]Quarter till has been shown by Kurath to be absent, essentially, from the plantation South. Possibly its absence in the Bluegrass may be considered due to "Southern" influence.

[21]Since it has become a commercial term, skillet now has
national currency.

[22]The Virginia Piedmont and upland Southern snake doctor
also occurs throughout the region; both terms occur side by side in
Pennsylvania. Perhaps here, too, "Southern" influence operated.

[23]As in most of the South, where coasting is rare at best,
belly-buster also designates a dive in which one hits the water flat.

[24]Since the development of stringless varieties, both the Midland green-beans and the Southern snap beans have been adopted as
general commercial terms, since they have more favorable connotations than string beans.

[25]Furthermore, mosquito hawk, a term associated with the
South Atlantic tidewater south of Chesapeake Bay, has been found in
Upstate New York and in Northern Michigan. The complicated patterns of distribution of the names for the dragon fly point to dialect
mixture in the earliest settlements; unfortunately, no systematic
study of the British Isles has published the evidence on this term.

[26]Recent field records from Georgia show the same usage,
though it is not nearly so common as in eastern Kentucky. On further
investigation it may turn out to be a feature of Southern Mountain
speech.

7 | The Urbanization of American English

There are some striking differences in the cultural conditions of Europe and America from which urbanization of rural areas has proceeded. One of the first differences one notices, on coming from America to Europe, is in the position of the village, which is a social institution utterly different from what Americans have experienced. Americans may have read about European village life in their smattering of medieval history; they may even have lamented its passing, as portrayed in Oliver Goldsmith's poem. But they have not experienced it, and have difficulty in comprehending it.

The difference is clear on approaching Prague in a plane flying over Bohemia's woods and fields. Except where the forests are thick, one can see — in every direction — nodes of settlement only a few kilometers apart, and very rarely an individual farmstead in between. For many of these villages there has been continuous settlement beyond the records of history; for others the community dates from the collapse of Rome or the rise of feudalism; each has had its own traditions and its own way of speech. Excepting the consequences of wars, few have passed out of existence, though their fortunes may have varied. From the air one can see the way in which villages have expanded — reaching out along the roadways until the fringes met and two or more coalesced into a town and ultimately a city. (Such is perhaps the fact behind the legends of the rise of Rome — the gradual merging of Latin, Sabine and Etruscan villages at the fords of the Tiber, into a city that ultimately became the dominant power in the Mediterranean.) But whatever its fate, the European village has been and still is a viable organic entity; even if under changing economic systems it becomes based on collective work, the change is probably much less than Americans suspect, for village life has

always depended on a cooperative tradition, a tradition of a balance
of shared rights and responsibilities.

In contrast with the organic tradition of the European village, the village has had a precarious place in English-speaking
America. (Things appear to be somewhat different in French Canada and in Mexico, but those nations are outside the scope of this
paper.) The village has not grown from local roots; rather, it has
been imposed on a locality by decision-makers from outside. Even
when a village — or "township", as it is sometimes called — sought
to emulate the European pattern, as in parts of New England or in
some of the transplanted New England settlements in Upstate New
York and the Middle West, it rarely emulated the European model by
being a place where people lived, who made their livelihood by cul-
tivating the surrounding farmland. Rather, it was set up as a minia-
ture city — with banks and shops and ambitions to become something
different and bigger; some developed and others faded. Sometimes
— as in the rush to exploit the mineral resources in the West —
communities of several thousand sprang into existence without any
agricultural base, or indeed without even the remote possibility of
developing such a base; when the mines gave out, these towns de-
cayed as fast as they arose, leaving the wreckage as ghost towns,
some of them rehabilitated in recent years as tourist attractions.
Even the villages in the New England tradition have become something else, often fashionable bedroom suburbs for executives of industries in nearby cities, and a few of them — like Hudson, Ohio,
with the new assembly plant for Chrysler — have found themselves
suddenly industrialized, to the distress of those who had sought a
refuge from urban dirt and noise.

The village in America, in fact, not only has rarely been organic, a part of the natural environment, but in most of the United
States the term implies a little more of the feudal relationship than
is consonant with the tradition of local democracy that one finds so
praiseworthy in the New England town meeting. This is particularly
true of the industrial village, as represented by the cotton mill or the
coal mine. The more I think of the analogy — especially as manifest
in the Southern cotton mills which had grown up around my home
town — the apter I feel it is. There was one difference: the feudal
villages often grew up around the landlord's villa — usually

transformed into a sort of castle for protection; while the mill village was laid out and built by the mill owners — who often lived somewhere else — simultaneous with the construction of the mill. But the
village homes were owned by the mill, and tenants were on suffer-
ance; the village stores were on mill property, and extended credit
to mill workers against their wages; schools and churches were supported by the mills, and if the mill owners did not actually hire the
teachers and preachers, yet their tenure was known to be at the
pleasure of management. Finally, though the mill workers could
vote in county and state elections — and their votes were eagerly
sought — they had no say in local government. The mill village was
usually outside the jurisdiction of the city, and was not incorporated,
so that all local affairs — even for a place of thirty-five thousand
population, like Kannapolis, North Carolina, the fief of Cannon
Mills — were handled by the company or by officials it appointed.

There was, indeed, little essential difference between man-
agement-worker relationships in the industrial village and those on
the agricultural plantation — whether the plantation under slavery
with black labor, or that under sharecropping with both races —
except that the plantation system was probably less impersonal and
more considerate of the individual.

In short, the term village in the United States is not one to
conjure up nostalgic reveries. Only in a few places with special
character — like Chapel Hill, North Carolina, the seat of the state
university — is the title assumed with pride. In America the village
is in constant tension between the forces of urbanization and those
fostering individual landholding, and rarely is strong enough to survive.

This difference in the population history is also reflected in
the linguistic situation. In Europe, the local dialects were those of
the villages. Everywhere, until the Renaissance, there was a clear
difference between these varieties of the vernacular, and the culture-
bearing language, which was Latin. Nationality in Europe gradually
arose around a city or a region of political or cultural preëminence,
and the variety of the language used by the wealthy and better-born
in this city or region gradually became acknowledged as the standard.
The process was sometimes very clear, as in England and France,

where the prestige of London and Paris was not questioned after the
Thirteenth Century. Sometimes it was complicated, as in Italy —
where Tuscan-Roman was generally recognized as the model six centuries before political unification — or in Germany, where the usage
of the Saxon chancellery became a satisfactory compromise in spite
of political fragmentation. But although there has been competition
from local varieties for particular purposes, in every Europen nation the standard language has been recognized as having a particular
form (in Norway there are two such forms with official status).

     In the New World the process of development was greatly
foreshortened. A number of kinds of speech were transferred simultaneously to various communities. Social differences — though undoubtedly greater than the legends of frontier democracy would allow
— were far less than in the Old World; furthermore, there has always been an opportunity to improve one's economic condition, so
that the social patterns are constantly changing. From the first,
each colony developed its own character and its own elite, and these
gave rise to local prestigious forms of the language; and at no time
since has the force of nationalism been able to overcome local pride
in traditional ways of speech; in fact, with the extension of English
across the continent, a host of new varieties of educated English has
come into existence. In other words, it is very difficult to determine
just what "standard" American English is. Spelling is essentially uniform; the syntax of the formal written variety shows little fluctuation
from one region to another. But in speech there are considerable
differences in educated usage as one looks at the practices of various
communities. And what is more, the characteristics of educated
American English in a given community are not necessarily today
what they were a generation ago.

     Yet there are certain forces that have operated on American
English from the beginning — and that are still operating — to reduce regional distinctions, at least in comparison with the distinctions that one still finds in Europe.

     1. The process of dialect selection and dialect mixture.
The American colonies had almost no representatives of the English
upper classes and very few of the English peasantry, groups that
were either so successful or so deeply rooted in the communities

that they felt no desire to move. The immigration was made up
largely of townsmen, even if they had been in town only long enough
to get in trouble with the law or to be shanghaied aboard ship (one
might aptly call the original United States a nation of misfits). If
some parts of Britain — notably East Anglia, the Home Counties,
the Southwest and Ulster — contributed larger numbers to the colonial population than others did, there was dialect mixture in all the
colonies, and the resultant patterns differed greatly among themselves, with only one constant: the differences among regions and
among social classes were far less than they had been in Britain.
Furthermore, the process of mixture has been repeated with each
subsequent migration, from the Mississippi Valley to the Pacific
Coast, with a progressive blunting of differences.

2. In almost every community, from the very beginning,
there has also been an admixture of speakers of other languages. In
few communities — notably eastern Pennsylvania — were they proportionately numerous enough to impose major changes on the regional form of English, but in many places they have left their traces.
The clearest effects have been on the vocabulary — the French
shivaree, the Dutch pot cheese, the German smearcase, the African
goober — but there have been occasional syntactic loans, such as got
awake in the German-speaking areas, and even occasional phonological effects. The southward bulge of /-s-/ in greasy, in eastern Pennsylvania, is probably due to the fact that in the German of that region
there is no phonemic contrast between voiced and voiceless spirants.

3. American society has always been characterized by mobility, both geographic and social. Leaving out of account summer
schools and temporary jobs, I have lived for periods of a year or
more in seven different states, and cast a ballot in six. Or looking
back, we discover that Daniel Boone, born in Pennsylvania, went by
way of Virginia and North Carolina to open up Kentucky to settlement
and spend his old age in Missouri. Sam Houston, a native Virginian,
launched his political career in Tennessee, spent some years in retirement among the western Indianas, and went on to found the Republic of Texas. Over 180 years about the same proportion of Americans have changed their state of residence between censuses. Or, for
social mobility, we can note that among the last eleven presidents
only three — Taft and the two Roosevelts — were from families with

long-time inherited wealth. The rest were the descendants of marginal storekeepers, sharecroppers, day laborers, railroaders, small
farmers and preachers.

4. Industrialization. This force has sought to rationalize
labor by substituting skill for brawn. The tradition goes back to the
more efficient curved ax-handle (it must be remembered that the Pil-
grim Fathers were townsmen, not farmers, and hence less bound by
traditional rural ways), through Eli Whitney's invention of interchangeable parts and Henry Ford's assembly line, down to the auto-
matic factory and the computerized blast furnace. This force has not
only introduced new words but replaced folk terms with commercial
ones.

5. Urbanization. Even by 1700 it was clear that the colonies had a new pattern of living. Instead of the society of villages,
with urban clusterings, there was a string of cities in the wilderness,
generally seaports which mediated directly between the mother country and the frontier. And in the process the dialectal extremes suffered further abrasion.

6. A commitment to general education. Described by
C. P. Snow, at the 1961 meeting of the National Council of Teachers
of English, as the earliest in the field of a generous distribution of
education, this commitment manifests itself in different ways, and
in different intensities, in various communities, but in some degree
it has been apparent ever since the Puritans sought in education a
guide to faith and conscience. Most of the early schools were privately supported, but Jefferson advocated a system of free and rigorously selective schooling for everyone, to the extent that one's
ambition and aptitude indicated. The Northwest Ordinance of 1785
was the first act in the Western World to support public education
on a large scale; if other regions were slow to follow, the model
was there, and by 1870 there was a constitutional commitment in
every state.

Nor was public support of higher education far behind. Although the oldest and most prestigious American institutions —
Harvard, Yale, Princeton, Columbia — were privately sponsored,
they were soon followed by state universities in the South, and with

the settlement of the Middle West, and the Morrill Land Grant Act of 1852, the great public universities came into being, with curricula designed to reach all kinds of students. Today, more than forty per cent of all Americans between eighteen and twenty-two are attending some sort of institution of higher education. If the results fall somewhat short of what Jefferson had hoped, the fault is not in the ideal but in the execution — in the sometimes unreasonable expectations of the young, and in the unwillingness of the old to insist on disciplined academic performance in return for their generosity.

The effect on the language from this educational commitment has been felt on various levels. On the most elementary level, it has helped to stigmatize non-standard grammatical forms and the more extreme local pronunciations. A deeper effect, however, is the social consequence: education has furthered social mobility, the mixing of dialects (regional and social) and the introduction into the already complex "standard" of forms from the speech of the newly risen. Furthermore, education accelerates other social changes. By improving farming practices, it forces the less efficient out of business and sends them to the city to enlarge the urban labor supply. And for farm and factory alike, as hand labor becomes scarce or expensive, technology — a byproduct of education — induces additional mechanization and further social change.

7. Frequency of contacts. Finally, transportation and communication have made it easier for Americans — on every level — to come in contact with their compatriots from other regions. As a modest example, I have taught or appeared at public meetings in thirty-eight states. Whatever the merits of the selective service system, it at least brings about intimate intercommunication, in situations where effective intercommunication is necessary for survival, among Americans of various origins. The mass media, too, have probably had some influence, in that they expose all kinds of Americans to the same kinds of fare; but since it is impossible to talk back to the loudspeaker or tube, the influence on one's active speech practices is problematical — as witnessed by the fact that non-standard speech forms are the most persistent among the groups of children who watch television the most.

Here we have listed the centripetal forces, those that are working toward a greater degree of uniformity in American speech practices. But there are also centrifugal forces, in the direction of greater or new diversity, even as the process of urbanization continues, and as the federal government assumes the new responsibility for equalizing educational opportunities among all citizens, in all parts of the nation.

The first of these centrifugal forces is a new ethnic consciousness on the part of some of our cultural minorities. They are insisting on the right to speak their own language, not only at home but on all occasions.

Now this, in one sense, is neither unfamiliar nor undesirable. In fact, a little of it in the past — and a fair amount of sensitivity to its implications — might have saved us from some of our present woes. We have had linguistic minorities from colonial times; three of the original colonies — New York, New Jersey and Delaware (the latter two probably including a little of what became the grant of Charles II to William Penn) — were originally settled by Holland Dutch, Swedes and Finns, only to be absorbed into the English domains in the New World. Quebec on the north was a French settlement, and has long been a source of immigrants, especially into New England; the territorial expansion of the United States brought under its flag French-speaking settlements in Louisiana and the Mississippi Valley, Spanish-speaking ones in Texas, New Mexico, California and Puerto Rico, and a polyglot culture in Hawaii. Even before the American Revolution, German-speaking settlements dotted the Atlantic Seaboard from New Hampshire to Georgia, and the numbers of Americans of German origin have been enlarged by almost continuous migration. The alumni of the unsuccessful European revolutions of 1830 and 1848 — along with many of their Hungarian and Slavic compatriots — not only established further rural colonies but helped civilize the expanding American cities, with banks, breweries, art museums and symphony orchestras. Later, Scandinavians developed the farmlands of the Upper Midwest, while Slavs and Hungarians and Italians provided the manpower for urban heavy industry and the era of mass production. All of these groups had their own ethnic communities, urban or rural, in which their home language was spoken. (For instance, my mother-in-law, a native of rural Wisconsin, spoke only Austrian German until she went to school.)

Yet it is not from these groups with their European cultural
traditions that the new ethnic consciousness springs; but from the
militant Negroes and Latin-Americans, the latest wave in the immigration to urban areas. To some of these groups, especially blacks,
all white Americans of foreign extraction — German, Slavic, Italian,
Jewish — and sometimes native whites as well, are lumped together
derisively as <u>hunkies</u> (or in a vogue pronunciation of Southern origin,
<u>honkies</u>). For most of these colonial and earlier immigrant groups
speaking languages other than English (as the research of Prague linguists testifies — and it is the greater reproach to American scholarship that we should have waited so late, and depended on our overseas
colleagues to do our work), the linguistic communities have disinte-
grated and the languages themselves are disappearing.

For the most part this change has been accomplished without external pressure. The only exception was the silly season of
World War I, when German-Americans (and other groups to less degree) were subjected to the one documentable instance of cultural
genocide, to use a currently fashionable term. In that time of super-
patriotic hysteria, all things German were proscribed, and all non-
Romance languages were lumped with German as objects of suspicion,
with even German measles being rechristened as <u>liberty measles</u>.

Far more influential was the tradition of the "melting pot",
at its height between 1885 and 1914. Yet, however it may have been
perverted in practice, the metaphor suggested not the deracination
of the immigrant but the possibility that each ethnic group might make
its own contribution to the richness and strength of the nation. In any
event the chief forces behind the disappearance of the immigrant languages seem to have been the desire of the immigrants themselves to
adapt to American ways, and the expanding economic opportunities
which broke up the old ethnic neighborhoods. In Chicago, historians
have noted, these neighborhoods served less as permanent homes
than as way stations for the fortunate, as they moved out among a
more diverse population. In the process, the second and third generation rarely retained the ancestral language. (In my five years at
Western Reserve University in Cleveland, although three-fifths of
my students — judging by their names — were of recent immigrant
stock, fewer than a dozen, at the most liberal estimate, had the
slightest knowledge of the language of their grandparents.)

But the physical types of the central European immigrants were within a range more or less similar to that of the older American stock. What has set off the Negro from other ethnic groups has been his physical visibility; and if this were not enough, the heritage of slavery, segregation and discrimination has given the Negro an imperfect participation in the dominant culture and an imperfect command of the tools by which achievement in the dominant culture is gained, including that of language. Now, with the greatly enlarged economic and educational opportunities that a number of forces have made available, many Negroes are insisting on greater attention to their own values, their own cultural history, and even their own linguistic patterns. (There is, today, more than a little pathos in such aspects of this movement as would teach Arabic and Swahili as part of their heritage; for Swahili was never spoken in West Africa, from which the American Negroes came, and both these tongues were notoriously used by the slave traders.) But destructive revolutionists, of whatever type, are never long on history; and the necessity for a myth may give it at least a temporary emotional validity. And so it is also with the varieties of non-standard English spoken by Negroes in urban slums. There are those who would reject "standard English" altogether, as a vehicle of white oppression, and insist on the recognition of something called "Black English" as the language of Negro communities.

This is not the place to argue on the feasibility of such a gesture, or on whether there really is such a thing as "Black English" in the United States. My own suspicion is that most of its features are shared by non-standard Southern American white dialects, and are traceable to the folk speech of the British Isles. However many disagreements I have with James Sledd of Texas, I agree with him that solving the problem of the origins of these dialects of Negro Americans will call for the mastery — synchronically, diachronically, and diatopically — of a far more extensive linguistic armamentarium than anyone is likely to boast in this century. Nevertheless, the pattern of racial settlement in the urban North — so that the only language one is likely to hear for miles is nonstandard English of Southern origin, spoken by Negroes — is such as to foster the notion among Northern whites of a discrete "Negro speech", since this is the only type of Southern speech most of them hear from day to day. And that the speech of white Southerners may be racially misidentified by Chicagoans of various complexions (and I have evidence out of

my own traumata that this misidentification may befall even those
with some degree of education) simply lends another ironic twist to
the jest. That black Americans should resent the downgrading of
the language they learn as children is comprehensible; and it is good
that other cultural groups are beginning to see something worthy in
this pride of speech (or in that of the Spanish-Americans, even if
some of these go all the other way and define "bilingual education"
as education solely by means of Spanish). It remains to be seen
whether this ethnic consciousness, and acceptance of it among other
groups, will be emulated by the Americans of Slavic, Scandinavian
and German descent. And I am skeptical as to whether this new acceptance would be extended to the speech of poor whites of Southern
origin, should they claim the privilege of cultural autonomy. For experiences of the past few years have shown that the ostentatiously
liberal white Northerner looks upon the white Southerner as something subhumanoid, as something to be blamed for the urban troubles
the North is unable to solve.

Nevertheless, the new ethnic consciousness is not the only
force creating new dialectal divisions in our cities. There is always
a tendency for the most recently acculturated to resent the pressure
of the incoming group. In the early Nineteenth Century, Boston parks
bore signs saying "Dogs and Irish not allowed". As the Irish put the
pig out of the parlor and hung up lace curtains, they felt the pressure
of the Italians and Slavs; these now feel the threat of the Negroes,
who again in some communities resent the later intrusion of Spanish-
Americans. One speculates on what will happen when the next wave,
the Southern poor whites, reaches all the Northern cities in sizeable
numbers.

The disadvantage of the automobile is here particularly
manifest. The automobile is useful to introduce one to scenes and
people at a distance; but in urban areas its chief effect is to isolate
the driver — and his passengers, if any — from the rest of humanity.
One who never has the opportunity to speak to his fellow man between
his home and his job — even if only to say "please" or "excuse me"
— is reducing his awareness of the speechways of others and his
sympathy with them. Furthermore, the automobile accelerates a
trend toward segregated residence, not only by race but by age and
income. Some suburbs are designed specifically for young business-
men, with small families; when they are promoted and their families

grow larger, their companies practically force them to move to more
luxurious environments, with another limited range of human contacts.

Nor have the labor unions or the schools shown the responsibility they might have. Negroes justifiably blame the unions for helping block their way to economic advancement; but here again the critic often overlooks history. In many Northern cities — as in the Chicago packing houses — Negroes were first introduced in large numbers
as strikebreakers. And union leaders — many raised in the Central
European tradition of social democracy — have borne this grudge for
a long time, even if often unconsciously. And in the schools, from
kindergarten to university, few teachers indeed have been adequately
trained in the nature of language and in the causes of linguistic diversity. Often themselves of the most recently risen group, anxious
to demonstrate their own linguistic chastity, with a simple dichotomy
of right and wrong, they have too frequently insisted on unrealistic
and even false standards. A friend of mine, an anthropologist of
Cherokee descent and Oklahoma boyhood, found himself put in a
course in corrective speech when he moved to Detroit — simply because he had a sort of Southern accent. A California school classed
as speech defectives the children of a colleague who had moved out
from Connecticut, simply because they had no constriction of postvocalic /-r/. And it was a long time before I convinced some of my
Northern colleagues that my natural way of speaking fell within the
limits of standard English (barely a year ago, at a conference on language variety, a young businessman expressed his incredulity at the
thought). It is thus apparent that not only is Standard American English difficult to define, but that in attempting to teach a standard the
schools often do not take advantage of what knowledge is available.
No wonder their efforts are sometimes resented.

*

As the struggle between centripetal and centrifugal forces
goes on, hardly any two American cities have the same situation.
Just as the population of each of the original settlements was one of
linguistic — or at least dialectal — diversity, with no two alike, so
it is with our cities, and with the interactions of their population
groups. We might end with descriptions of a few communities, on the
basis of evidence that is becoming available.

Washington, D.C., for a long time a basically Southern community, has been swamped by two kinds of migration — one of poor Negroes from the South, the other of unmarried government workers from all parts of America. As the latter marry and rise in rank, they tend to move out into the suburbs. The population of the city is more than half black; that of the public schools approaches 95 per cent, with white families usually sending their children to private schools. The old middle-class Negro neighborhood, near Howard University, has felt the dialectal impact of the new migration, which has replaced the speech pattern of the older generation with something more clearly Southern and definitely non-standard. White speech in the suburbs is losing its Southern flavor, but no new characteristic pattern seems to have emerged (at least it has not been described).

In New York City the heavy early Nineteenth Century immigration of Germans and Irish was followed by three other heavy migrations — of Italians and Russian Jews at the turn of the century, of Southern Negroes beginning with the first World War, and of Puerto Ricans from 1940 on. The public school population (private and parochial schools are an old New York City tradition) is about a third white, a third Negro, and a third Puerto Rican. Many of the older New York speechways are disappearing, such as the [ɜɪ] diphthong in bird and the like. The neutralization of /ɜ/ and /ɔi/ — as in Earl and oil — whether ultimately as [ɜɪɫ] or [ɔɪɫ], has rarely been found in educated speech in the past three decades, and is seldom heard from any of the younger generation. Postvocalic /-r/ seems to be returning to the speech of New York, at least among the middle-class whites; the practices of the upper class are not clear, since the most recent study, by W. Labov, did not sample that group. Interestingly, though local whites are turning away from traditional New York speech patterns, some Negroes are turning to them as a change from their Southern ways; yet other Negroes are reemphasizing the Southern patterns, as a part of their racial consciousness. There seems to be little new data from the rapidly swelling suburbs, where population movements are very complicated — with New Yorkers moving out of the city proper and outsiders being drawn to the metropolitan area.

Phoenix, Arizona, has also been studied by Labov. He reports that the white population seems to be losing the phonemic

opposition between /a/ and /ɔ/, as between cot and caught — a neutralization common in much of the Rocky Mountain area — but that
the contrast is retained among Negroes. Since Negroes are relatively recent arrivals in this relatively recently urbanized area, one
can only speculate on future developments. If the experience of
other Northern and Western cities may be used, there may be a dialectal cleavage along racial lines. And yet the recency of the Negro
migration to Phoenix — at a time when discrimination is breaking
down — may give this community a different history.

Through R. Shuy's investigations, Detroit has provided the
most massive quantities of evidence that we have on the speech patterns of any American city. But, as with Labov in New York, the
sampling procedures were such as to exclude all speakers above the
middle class. There does seem to be the familiar development — of
a growing divergence of Negro speech from the local white norms;
the disparity is less as one moves up the social scale. In an experiment involving reactions to speech samples from taped interviews,
Detroit respondents identified the race of the speakers eighty per
cent of the time; but there were no representatives of Southern white
migrant speech on the sample tape, though there are at least a quarter of a million of this group in the Detroit metropolitan area. The
upper-middle-class Negroes were hardest to place — a conclusion
borne out by experiments with my own students. Detroit respondents
were less successful in identifying social class than they were with
race; interestingly, they tended to upgrade the class of the whites
and downgrade that of the Negroes. There must be many other conclusions to be drawn about the speech of other ethnic groups in Detroit, notably the Polish community, but Shuy has not yet published
his evidence.

Chicago I can speak of in somewhat more detail — as a resident, as a participant in several projects involving local social dialects, and as the husband of a professor whose students (in a teacher-
training institution) are intimately concerned with social dialects in
the daily exercise of their profession. As I have mentioned before,
in Chicago — as elsewhere — there seems to be awareness of something which is popularly known as "Negro speech", though most of its
linguistic characteristics — I am less sure of the paralinguistic ones
— are shared by Southern whites as well. Racial divergence in

speech is relatively small among the best educated; among the oldest,
also, there is very little — the evidence being that Chicago-born
Negroes over 70 differ more among themselves in speech practices
than they do from their white contemporaries. The younger generation, however, tend to lack postvocalic /-r/, to preserve the Southern
contrast of /ɔ/ and /o/ before /-r/ and its reflexes (so that morning and mourning contrast), and to have /-z-/ in greasy. Furthermore there seem to be differences between the white speech of the
city and that of the outer ring of suburbs, particularly in the pronunciation of hog, fog and Chicago. For these words there is the Inland
Northern /a/ in the outlying areas, but the Midland /ɔ/ in the city.
In the few integrated neighborhoods, such as the one we live in,
racial identification of speech is very difficult. I have even mistaken
for my youngest son's speech that of one of his second-generation
Japanese American, or Nisei, playmates (or perhaps third generation, Sansei, is here more accurate). I look forward to further evidence from the investigations by my students, both in the racially
polarized satellite city of Gary and in "East Side", a somewhat isolated white community, which has retained for nearly four generations its flavor as an ethnically mixed working-class neighborhood.

There is less detailed evidence, as yet, from Southern
cities, but there are suggestions that their developments are somewhat different from what one Finds in Detroit or Chicago. In a transition belt in northern Georgia, Lee Pederson finds that the racial differences in speech simply reflect the differences between plantation
and hill culture. In the southernmost communities investigated, the
poor whites had many features of hill speech; in the northernmost,
the Negroes had many speech-traits of the plantation country. It is
likely that similar differences between the speech of poor blacks and
poor whites will be found in a metropolitan area like Atlanta. In a
smaller industrial community like Greenville, South Carolina, where
— as suggested before — the segregated society of the cotton-mill
workers became a de facto third race, town Negroes and whites in
my boyhood shared phonological features not found in the mill villages,
but poor whites — including mill workers — and poor Negroes shared
the same non-standard grammatical features. The integration of the
three groups in one school system is too recent to allow one to draw
conclusions; but the fact that it was accomplished with a minimum of
publicity and strife suggests a recognition that in small Southern

cities the educational problem — basically a linguistic one — cuts
across racial lines.

Two features formerly associated with Southern poor white
speech seem to have become a part of the regional standard, though
not yet used by all standard speakers. One is the constricted postvocalic /-r/ ; the other is the monophthongal [a:] for /ai/ before
voiceless consonants, as in the shibboleth <u>nice white rice</u>. The first
development, the expanding use of constricted /-r/, has been attributed by outsiders to the spread of a "national norm", under the influence of radio and television. But this would not explain the second.
I would suggest a more economical explanation — that as groups
hitherto disadvantaged rise in the social scale, through better economic and educational opportunities, they bring some of their speech
habits with them, and modify the standard. This has happened so often elsewhere in the world that we should not be surprised when it
occurs in the American South.

For one of the most interesting American cities, Charleston,
South Carolina, the evidence will be based on my student Raymond
O'Cain's dissertation. It is clear that the winds of linguistic change
are disturbing even this most traditionally oriented of American
cities. Many of its speech characteristics — ingliding diphthongs
for /e/ and /o/, centered beginning of the diphthongs /ai/ and /au/,
neutralization of front vowels before reflexes of /-r/ so that <u>ear</u> and
<u>air</u> are homonymous— are suffering attrition, at different rates
among different social groups. Younger Negroes seem to be acquiring
constricted /-r/, while their white contemporaries lack it. Despite
all kinds of leveling influences, it seems likely that for decades to
come there will be greater diversity in Charleston speech than in that
of Detroit.

All of the recent evidence suggests that the urbanization of
American English, far from producing linguistic uniformity, may be
creating a new kind of linguistic diversity. This poses a challenge to
the schools and to society at large.[1]

NOTE

[1]Since other linguists frequently assume the prophetic role
outside their professional competence, perhaps I may assume it within mine.

1. One of the first suggestions I would make to American
educators is that all students be required to take some language different from their own, beginning no later than the third grade (approximately eight years old). This would put speakers of standard and
non-standard varieties of the language on the same level, and should
induce in the former a feeling of sympathy for the student who is required to master in school the linguistic system of a dialect different
from what he uses at home.

2. Whatever the status of a student's home language may be,
it should be respected as a viable linguistic system in its own right,
capable of expressing the full range of human experience and — given
the transmutation by an artist — of becoming the vehicle of the finest
literature.

3. The standard language should be conceived of, not as
monolithic and immutable but as multivalent and subject to change.
For language is the most characteristic of human activities, and it is
the activities of human beings in their manifold interrelationships
that determine what is the standard for a given time and place.

8 | Prejudice and Pride: Linguistic Acceptability in South Carolina

In Collaboration with Raymond K. O'Cain

Those who have examined human speech have frequently commented on the differences between what people think they ought to say and what they actually say.[1] However these differences are phrased, they exist; and no amount of theoretical prestidigitation can remove them from our attention. It is for this reason that there have been numerous surveys of actual usage and of attitudes toward usage (Mencken 1963: 512-521; Creswell 1975). These surveys reveal that the Platonic ideals enunciated by the guardians of linguistic chastity are seldom justified by the usage of those who should be the best models for the generality; even the American Heritage Dictionary (1969) is more relaxed in its editorial comments than would seem warranted by its highly publicized Usage Panel — an apparent attempt to create an American analogue to the Immortals of the French Academy.

A realization of these differences between what people say and what they think they ought to say guided Hans Kurath in his design of the methodology for the Linguistic Atlas of the United States and Canada. Though careful to incorporate the best from traditional European dialect geography, Kurath unhesitatingly introduced modifications where American conditions required them; indeed, he transformed dialect geography by insisting that a systematic investigation of the speech of the folk, those least affected by standardizing forces, was insufficient. In every community a second informant should be interviewed, a representative of a contrasting cultural level, using what Kurath called popular or common speech. Such informants were more intensely subject to standardizing influences, education in particular, and were generally younger as well. Kurath's methodology also specified that in about one-fifth of the communities investigated, a speaker of the local prestige dialect be interviewed. Such cultivated

informants might be alumni of reputable colleges and universities in
their region, though for about half those on the Atlantic Seaboard,
community opinion of their family rank more than compensated for
any lack of formal higher education. [2]

Included as an essential adjunct to the phonetic record of
the Linguistic Atlas of New England (Kurath et al. 1939-1943) and subsequent regional atlases were the observations of the field workers
concerning the currency and social status of linguistic forms, whether phonological, lexical or grammatical. In addition to recording the
forms obtained by questioning, the field workers were instructed to
pay particular attention to recording variants from the informant's
unguarded conversation — a task simplified for contemporary field
workers by the tape recorder. The field workers were also instructed to denote forms (1) offered as spontaneous corrections, (2) accompanied by indications of doubt, (3) evoking expressions of amuse-
ment, (4) elicited only after repeated questioning, (5) offered hesi-
tatingly, (6) repeated at the request of the field worker, (7) pronounced by the informant after being suggested — only as a last resort — by the field worker, or (8) offered by another local resident
who happened to be present during the interview. Though such observations serve chiefly to indicate the attitude of the informant toward a particular form, they are a fruitful source of indications about
the status of forms, perhaps that a topic and its terminology are unfamiliar or even taboo.

The explicit statements of informants about the currency or
status of forms were denoted by the field workers as (9) heard, i.e.,
current, but not actually used by the informant himself, (10) old-
fashioned or obsolete or replaced in the speech of the informant by
a newer form and (11) modern, recently introduced, used only by
younger persons or adopted only later by the informant. [3] Furthermore, not only do a number of the logical combinations of the designations (1) - (11) appear in the field records, but sometimes detailed
elaborations of them as well. All forms recorded outside the context of a direct reply to some elicitation frame are labelled on the
LANE maps, and significant elaborations by the informants are re-
produced, sometimes verbatim, sometimes in summary, in separate
commentaries to the maps.

It should surprise no one that the judgments of the LANE informants were sometimes in sharp contrast to actual usage, whether of informants themselves or of social groups or regions. Yet to date no investigator has attempted to correlate the LANE informants' judgments with the status of the forms actually used[4] in their communities, even though LANE is the only American survey for which the full phonetic record is available.[5] Regrettably, the most egregious disregard of Linguistic Atlas materials, published and unpublished, has been on the part of scholars in the emerging discipline of sociolinguistics; their judgments on language and society would seem to demand an examination of this evidence, at least as a starting point (cf. McDavid and O'Cain, 1977).[6]

It is for this reason that the two authors have decided to examine a small part of the evidence from the Linguistic Atlas of the Middle and South Atlantic States. The sociolinguistic judgments of the 32 cultivated informants interviewed in South Carolina will be compared not only with the actual status among the cultivated of the forms they judged but also with the actual status and the ascribed status of the same forms among the 112 uncultivated informants interviewed in South Carolina. The authors have limited themselves to South Carolina for several reasons, perhaps advantageous to the validity of their findings: (1) each is a native speaker of one of the varieties of cultivated English indigenous to South Carolina;[7] that they learned their respective varieties a generation apart adds breadth to their common perspective; (2) each has had extensive field experience with the varieties of English spoken in South Carolina;[8] that these experiences were nearly a generation apart likewise enhances their common perspective; (3) as South Carolinians they can speak there more confidently of social class than they might in other regions; (4) social class distinctions are relatively sharper and more persistent in South Carolina than in many other regions; and (5) in the South Carolina field records[9] there are more sociolinguistic judgments[10] on the part of informants than in almost any other state, and there are likewise more forms recorded from free conversation.

The copiousness of both the forms recorded from free conversation and the sociolinguistic judgments required several arbitrary limitations. Comparison of the usage and judgments of the informants on an individual basis would admit fewer comparisons, for

not every informant judged the same forms (cf. McDavid 1974). We
chose to examine the usage of South Carolinians as a group in just
those cases where there is quantitative, and even some qualitative,
convergence of sociolinguistic judgment; as a further limitation, we
shall define the specific items singled out for detailed comparisons
in terms of the number of judgments obtained from cultivated informants. The forms judged by the cultivated are those which do not
have unequivocal status as Standard English but are, at least potentially, socially marked — broadly speaking, they are disputable usages in the opinion of those who define Standard English, not by their
usage alone, but by their attitudes as well.

   To survey the judgments of the informants and the actual
usage to which they correspond in South Carolina, then, the first step
was to systematically search the field book of each cultivated informant for forms about which judgments were made. Such forms and
the judgment given were copied on index cards and filed by their linguistic categories: (1) lexical, (2) phonological, or (3) grammatical.
Excluded from (1) were judgments about the meaning of terms, e.g.,
that a piazza is larger than a porch or stoop; included in (3) were
both morphological and syntactic items. In a number of instances
more than one card was filed for an informant for a single item in the
Atlas work sheets (questionnaire), e.g., for the stressed vowel of
yellow an informant might judge /ɪ/ as old-fashioned and /æ/ as
modern. However, combined judgments, particularly common with
forms characterized as heard, were treated as single judgments.

   Table 1 displays the number of judgments and items judged
in each of the three categories for each cultivated informant. Map 1
shows, designated by their LAMSAS serial numbers, the locations
of the communities investigated in South Carolina. Underscorings
denote the location and number of cultivated informants; numbers
followed by n denote communities where Negro informants were interviewed.

   Nearly all the cultivated judgments fall into the categories
(9) heard, (10) old-fashioned or (11) modern, from above, and are
often further specified as typical of a particular social group or region. Less frequently, terms may be characterized as jocular, correct or incorrect, informal, restricted to use in very limited

Table 1. Judgments and items per category per informant

	Lexicon		Phonology		Grammar	
Informant	Judgments	Items	Judgments	Items	Judgments	Items
3c	29	28	10	10	8	8
5c	17	17	9	8	3	3
6c	30	28	3	3	3	2
7c	20	20	0	0	0	0
7d	12	11	7	7	0	0
9c	13	13	10	10	6	5
9d	14	12	2	2	0	0
10b	6	6	1	1	0	0
10c	10	10	2	2	0	0
11g	34	33	9	7	1	1
2N11	32	27	11	10	4	4
11h	28	26	19	18	5	5
11i	33	30	24	21	15	13
11j	161	116	59	42	28	14
14b	37	31	6	6	4	4
18c	50	36	20	19	6	4
19d	1	1	3	3	0	0
20d	9	8	1	1	0	0
22b	15	13	4	4	2	2
22c	20	19	11	10	1	1
23e	19	16	3	2	0	0
24d	6	6	1	1	0	0
25c	13	12	2	2	0	0
26b	18	18	3	3	0	0
30c	48	42	13	10	5	4
36d	6	6	12	8	0	0
38c	8	6	5	5	0	0
38d	35	33	22	20	6	5
42b	22	19	9	9	0	0
42c	52	44	9	8	6	6
42d	13	13	13	12	4	4
42e	25	23	4	3	6	4

contexts, etc. Several informants seem to favor certain designations for forms they do not use themselves, e.g., 18c favors poor white, and 42c favors rural; no informant seemed expecially prone to designate usages as exclusively Negro; and though a large majority of the forms were associated with Negro usage by at least one informant, only infrequently is it the consensus of the cultivated that a usage is Negro. In a number of instances, mostly from among informants living along the coast, an informant characterizes a form as not being the dominant form among the cultivated, yet in the next breath says that, nevertheless, he uses it, e.g. /ɛt/ as the preterite of <u>eat</u>.

It is evident that some cultivated informants have offered many more judgments than others; in some cases the paucity of judgments is related to the incompleteness of the field record; on the other hand, some informants are more inclined to offer their opinions — it comes as no surprise to the authors that the greatest number of judgments comes from a Charlestonian, and that all the Charlestonians are relatively willing to offer opinions, for the self-assurance of Charleston is a well-advertised fact.[11] Notice, too, that as the number of judgments increases, the size of the gap between judgments and items generally increases; as informants become more interested in the language, they become increasingly discriminating, though judgment should be reserved on the question of accuracy.

After the figures for Table 1 were compiled, the cards were sorted according to the order of the appearance of each item in the LAMSAS work sheets. The number of cultivated judgments for each item was tallied and an arbitrary cut-off point was taken for each category. Not included in the following treatment of the individual items were lexical items for which fewer than 7 judgments were obtained, phonological items with fewer than 5 judgments and grammatical items with fewer than 4 judgments; left for consideration were 19 lexical items, 18 phonological items, and 8 grammatical items.

In the treatment of individual items there is a summary tabulation of the number of informants using each of the principal variants of an item. There is also a second tabulation, the number of informants attesting that there is some <u>restriction</u> (cf. Creswell 1975) on one or more of the variants; this figure is preceded by <u>r</u>.

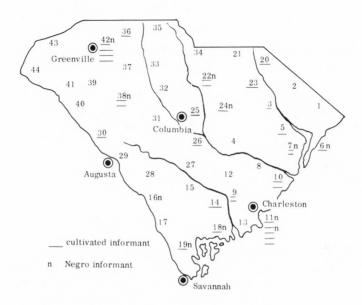

Map 1. LAMSAS communities in South Carolina

     Whereas the unmarked forms indicate the natural, even con-
versational, usage of the informants, the restricted forms are those
not only explicitly judged by informants but also those whose naturalness is subject to question. Restrictions include the entire range of
observations (1) - (11) above noted by the field workers. Suggested
forms were not tabulated as unrestricted unless explicitly accepted
as natural by the informants. For this reason, the number of restrictions will usually exceed the first judgment per item tally for
the cultivated informants. This original tally may be still further increased by a number of inferential judgments; for example, if an informant characterized <u>groundnuts</u> as his natural usage during childhood, it is inferred that <u>peanuts</u> is a modern or newer term, even
though not so characterized explicitly. Accordingly, there is not always an exact correspondence between the judgments cited in the
tables of usage and the summaries of the items analyzed.

    For the purpose of comparing judgments to actual usage the
informants were divided into four groups: the cultivated informants,

the Negro informants exclusive of the cultivated Negro informant, who
is in a group by himself, and, taken together, the users of folk speech
and common or popular speech. While no judgments indicated that
the two latter groups need be separated, the numerous judgments that
can be interpreted as 'not used in cultivated English' or 'not predominant in cultivated English' point to a cultivated-uncultivated dichotomy;[12] and, naturally, the comparison of cultivated usage and cultivated judgment is of interest. The separation of the ten Negro folk informants is occasioned by the frequent opinion that a usage is characteristic of them, but their tabulations can be considered jointly with
those of the other uncultivated informants as well. Likewise the usage of the lone cultivated Negro informant, a member of Charleston's
Negro elite, is tallied separately.

In the following summaries of usage and judgments (the latter marked r), the principal variants of each item are listed, and the
number of occurrences of each is given. The usage of the folk and
middle class are in the column headed I, II, and the columns headed
N, 2N11, and III designate, respectively, the usage of the Negro folk
informants, the cultivated Negro informant and the cultivated white
informants. The lexical items are presented first, followed in order
by the phonological and grammatical items. Within each category,
the order of items corresponds to the order in the LAMSAS work
sheets; numbers in parentheses refer to the pages in the work sheets.

LEXICON[13]

(2) afternoon

	I, II[14]	N	2N11	III
afternoon	60 r13	5	1	19 r4
evening	77 r2	6	1	10 r6
no response	3	2		4

The cultivated informants judged evening as heard (1), heard frequently (2)[15] or old (2); afternoon was judged new (2) or correct (1)
and heard (1). The collective judgment that afternoon is (slowly) re-
placing evening as the term for the part of the day after midday is
borne out by the facts of usage.[16] Though mixed usage is frequent,

it is somewhat more prevalent in the middle class, for exclusive use
of evening is usually characteristic of the oldest, least-cultivated informants, and exclusive use of afternoon is indicative of greater cul-
tivation and youth. Finally, the judgments of the uncultivated are
most often that afternoon is new or correct.

(3) sunrise

	I, II	N	2N11	III
sunup	61 r9	3 r1	1	8 r7
no response	14	4		13

The judgment of the cultivated is that sunup is a heard term; though
it does occur in cultivated speech, only one cultivated informant did
not offer sunrise as well. Though sunup is used by over half the uncultivated, only a third of the total use it exclusively, i.e., reject
sunrise. The judgments of the uncultivated are evenly divided as to
which term is predominant.

(7) living room

	I, II	N	2N11	III
living room	55 r8	2 r2	1	18 r4
parlor	55 r12	5	r1	17 r13
sitting room	53 r2	9		15 r6
front room	15 r2	2	r1	1 r3
drawing room	3		1	4 r4
hall	6 r6			1 r3
company room	5 r2			r1

The judgments of the cultivated indicate that living room is new (4) or
natural (2); all the other terms are generally judged old in about half
the cases and heard or less frequent in the other half. The uncultured
judge parlor and the variants of hall as old-fashioned somewhat more
decisively, in about two-thirds of the cases; they judge living room
as a modern term unanimously. The three leading variants are not
only of the same frequency, but there is no apparent geographical
distribution of the terms; only rarely does each of the three fail to
show up in any particular community, and there is no social distribution worthy of comment.

(8) andirons

	I, II	N	2N11	III
andirons	36 r9	5		18 r4
fire dogs	57 r13	2		9 r11
fire irons	5 r1			
dog irons	22 r3	6	r1	7 r3
dogs	8 r3			3 r2
irons	5	1		
no response	5	1		2

The cultured judge the prevailing folk term fire dogs as heard (7) or
old (2); like judgments are given for the other folk terms. Andirons
is considered new (3) or probably correct and appears to be the established usage among the cultivated, for alternate terms are almost
always described as heard or old. Andirons does appear to be at
least moderately well established in the cities, and when it does appear among the uncultured is almost always paired with other terms.
The uncultured generally characterize andirons as a new term.

(9) kitchen

	I, II	N	2N11	III
cook house,	18 r7	1 r1		3 r7
~ shed, ~ room				
stove room	9 r2	r2		r3

All the variants of universally used kitchen were characterized as
heard by the cultivated, though with the additional specification rural
(3) or poor white (1) at times. The only striking contrast with the
judgment of the folk was that kitchen was called old (2) or paired with
a variant that was considered new (3).

(10) porch

	I, II	N	2N11	III
porch	75 r11	7 r2	r1	26 r6
piazza	72 r25	10	1	20 r7
no response	2			

The cultivated, in about equal numbers, consider porch modern,
piazza old-fashioned or piazza the usual term. The uncultived almost

unanimously characterize porch as modern and piazza as old-fashioned.[17]

(17) frying pan

	I, II	N	2N11	III
spider	73 r14	8 r3		14 r11
skillet	56 r11	7 r1	1	17 r6

Though frying pan is universal, spider is an older term that still en-
joys wider currency than skillet. The cultivated usually consider
spider old-fashioned (8); opinion is divided on skillet, which is somewhat more common in the usage of the cultivated and in urban areas,
though the two terms are both found in nearly every community. The
uncultured who offer judgments characterize frying pan as modern,
or more often, pair it with a term they consider older.

(19. 6) paper bag

	I, II	N	2N11	III
poke	13 r20	r1		1 r8
no response				5

Paper bag is universal, and the cultivated informants judged poke for
the most part as heard but also old-fashioned (1) or not characteristic of their area (2). Poke is a Midland term (Kurath 1949: Fig. 70)
and both the uses of poke and the cultivated judgments are from informants in communities above or near the fall line[18] in most cases.
The folk[19] judge poke largely as a heard term, though occasionally
as old.

(19. 7) crocus sack

	I, II	N	2N11	III
burlap	24 r5	2	1	8 r5
gunny	5 r5		1	1 r4
guano	23 r5	3 r1		3 r1
tow	13 r3	1		2 r2
jute	12 r3			2 r1
no response				5

The consensus of the cultivated is that gunny sack is heard but uncommon and that burlap sack is new (2) or proper (1). Crocus sack,
or less commonly croker sack, is all but universal, a fact the cultivated recognize (5). Crocus sack is judged most often as new (4) by
the uncultured; less often the same opinion is given of the other variants, except for jute sack, burlap sack, gunny sack, and guano sack
which are heard or rarer terms in the judgment of the folk. Guano
sack is in a majority of cases the usage of the older, less cultivated
informant in the communities in which it appears, generally those below the fall line, or if above the fall line, usually in communities
nearer North Carolina. Burlap sack, the preferred variant of the
cultured, is concentrated in the tidewater though also found above the
fall line; among the uncultured, burlap sack is rare in the usage of
the oldest, least cultured informants.[20]

(24) kerosene

	I, II	N	2N11	III
kerosene oil	25	3		8
coal oil	13 r23	r1		5 r7
lamp oil	9 r4	3		r1
oil	8 r1	1		5
no response	3	3		

The cultivated judged coal oil as heard (3) or as a rare or occasional
term, and lamp oil was judged old. The folk judges reported coal oil
as heard in a large majority of the cases, as not local (3) — specifically, Northern (2) — and old, Negro or new (1 each). Lamp oil
was reported as heard (3) or old. Kerosene is in general usage, and
kerosene oil, though less usual, is evenly distributed geographically.
Coal oil is generally found above the fall line along the upper reaches
of the Savannah River or in communities relatively near the North
Carolina border. In the Low Country, coal oil is associated with cultivated speakers in coastal communities

(27.2) vest

	I, II	N	2N11	III
waistcoat	15 r23	1 r1		9 r14
jacket	23 r8	r2		3
no response	3	2		1

Waistcoat is characterized as a heard (9) or old (3) term by the cultivated. The folk are evenly divided between heard and old for waistcoat, but a large majority consider jacket old. Vest is predominant
everywhere, and jacket is usually found above the fall line — when it
appears below the fall line it is found only well away from the coast.
Waistcoat is most often found in the Low Country — excluding the Pee
Dee — where it is associated with the cultured and with the least cultured, but not with the middle class; above the fall line waistcoat is
associated with the cultured or middle class and not with the least
cultivated.

(27.3) trousers

	I, II	N	2N11	III
breeches	65 r17	6 r5	r1	15 r9
no response	3			1

Pants and trousers are virtually universal, and when judged are considered new or natural as a rule; frequently one or both occur with
jeans or breeches, which are judged older. The cultured judge
breeches generally as heard (6) or jocular (2). About half the folk
judges considered breeches old, with the remainder about equally divided between jocular, frequent and rare.

(45) doughnut

	I, II	N	2N11	III
doughnut	52 r27	7 r1	1	16 r8
no response	18	2		6

The cultured informants judged doughnut as rare (3), not native (3)
or new. Half the folk who offered opinions characterized doughnut as
rare, and the remainder were about evenly divided between not native (6) and new (4). Though typical of cultivated usage, and found in
every community, in nearly half the communities — mostly near or
below the fall line — at least one informant failed to affirm doughnut
as either familiar or natural.

(48) food

	I, II	N	2N11	III
vittles	35 r21	5 r2	1	8 r10
no response	5	3		5

The consensus of the cultivated is that vittles is a heard term (5),
sometimes further detailed as Negro usage (2), old (2) or jocular.
The Negro folk informants characterize vittles as old or rural. The
white folk consider vittles as Negro usage (5), heard (6), not correct
(4), old (3) or rural (3). Vittles is rather evenly distributed geographically in South Carolina; socially it is most typical of the least
cultivated informants and everywhere competes with the general food
and the only slightly more common rations. Only occasionally judged,
rations has a geographical distribution like that of vittles, and in the
Up Country has a similar social distribution as well. In the Low Country, however, rations is more likely to be found in the speech of
somewhat more cultivated informants, though it is significantly absent in the speech of Charleston.

(54) peanut

	I, II	N	2N11	III
peanut	r9			r8
pinder	66 r19	4 r2	1	11 r6
goober	35 r12	2 r1	r1	6 r4
groundpea	11 r6	3		
groundnut	22 r7	4		13 r3
no response	5	2		8

Peanut is usually characterized as new (5) by the cultivated; the other
variants are judged heard or old as a rule, though pinder is sometimes judged natural (3). The majority of the uncultured judge peanut
as new or rare, groundnut and pinder as old, and goober and groundpea as heard. Though peanut is almost universal, it has strong competition. Goober, except along the coast, is not common below the
fall line, especially in the Pee Dee (cf. Kurath and McDavid 1961;
Map 118); pinder is common everywhere. Groundnut is concentrated
along the coast and is rare above the fall line; groundpea is common
only above the fall line, with several scattered instances near the coast.

(79) casket

	I, II	N	2N11	III
casket	43 r21	2 r4	1	11 r6
box	20 r12	4 r1		7 r6
pinto	r4	2r2		1
no response	12	2		6

Casket is judged by the cultivated most often as new (4), but genteel
and fancier also suggest newness. Box is equally judged as Negro and old-fashioned, and coffin, the general term, is once judged
old. The folk informants nearly unanimously judge casket as new and
coffin as the older term; like the cultivated informants, they are
equally divided in their opinions on box as old or a Negroism. And
unlike the cultivated, they report pinto as a Negroism, reported by
2N11 as old. Casket is found in all but a few scattered communities,
with no apparent social distribution. Box is widespread in the Low
Country, though not concentrated, and notably rare in Charleston;
box is more common in the Up Country than in the Pee Dee, but with
no appreciable frequency.

(93) Merry Christmas

	I, II	N	2N11	III
Christmas gift, ~ treat	57 r20	4 r2	r1	6 r8
no response	11	4		12

Christmas gift (occasionally Christmas treat) is most often reported
as heard (4) by the cultivated; other judgments are Negroism (2), old
(2) and jocular. The uncultured are about evenly divided in their
judgments of Christmas gift as old, heard or formerly heard from
Negroes. Only occasionally is Christmas gift not paired with Merry
Christmas (19), and the reverse is true about as often (18).

(98) lug

	I, II	N	2N11	III
tote	25 r10			4 r8
no response	8			9

Tote is reported by the cultivated as a heard (4) term; it also has
other judgments which can be summarized as informal (3). The
judgments of the uncultured are heard (3), frequent (3), Negroism (2)
and informal (2). Tote is found all along the North Carolina border
and along the coast.

(100) <u>address</u> (the letter)[21]

	I, II	N	2N11	III
back	47 r28	5	1	1 r8
no response	21	5		15

The cultured informants consider <u>back</u> a Negroism (5) or a heard
term (2).   Three-quarters of the folk judgments are equally divided
between Negroism, heard and old; the remaining quarter is evenly
divided between <u>back</u> as laughable and <u>address</u> as a new term.   <u>Back</u>
is the exclusive term of 11 informants, mostly below the fall line;
socially they are the least cultivated informants in their communities as a rule; <u>back</u> is the sole term of two of the Negro folk informants.

PHONOLOGY[22]

(8. 2) <u>hearth</u>

	I, II	N	2N11	III
/æ/	12 r10	2		r3
/ɜ/	29 r19	3 r2	1	4r9
/a/	r1	1		
no response	1			1

Cultivated informants report that /ɜ/ is old (4), heard and humorous
(2), new or affected (2) or simply heard; /æ/ is considered a Negroism (2) or heard.   The uncultivated informants characterize /ɜ/ principally as heard (10) and, in equal but smaller proportions, as old,
new or correct.   Likewise in even proportions they characterize /æ/
as heard or old.   While /a ᷉ ɒ/ is regular, notably in cultivated
speech, /ɜ/ is also widespread below the fall line, including the cultivated speech of the coast; it is also found above the fall line in communities near the North Carolina border.   /æ/ is considerably less
common and is found principally in the Low Country above the tidewater.

(8.7) <u>soot</u>

	I, II	N	2N11	III
/ʌ/	36 r7	9	1	11 r6
[ɣ]	40 r3	3		9
/ʊ/	12			8
/u/	3 r2		r1	2 r3
/ɨ/	7			
no response				2

Cultivated informants are divided on /ʌ/ as heard and usual; they
agree that /u/ is not general. The folk judgments are inconclusive,
though they are not inclined to accept /ʌ/ . [ɣ] a diaphone of /ʌ/,
is common except near the coast, and it does not occur in cultivated
coastal speech. /ʌ/ , which is common in coastal cultivated speech,
is rare above the fall line. Most instances of /ʊ/ and /u/ occur
in cultivated or urban speech.

(17) <u>vase</u>

	I, II	N	2N11	III
/vɑz ~ vɒz/	r3			r5
/vez/	r1	1		6 r2
/væz/	r1			1 r1
no response	29	3		5

The cultivated consider /vɑz ~ vɒz/   affected, or judge it a heard
form. /vez/ is a heard form; /væz/ is affirmed as natural, and
still another informant says there are many pronunciations of <u>vase</u>.
Strikingly, the standard /ves/ is almost universal in folk speech; of
the few variants, all found along the coast, only one is not from a
cultivated speaker.

(24) <u>kerosene</u>

	I, II	N	2N11	III
/æ/	47 r3	5		10 r5
/a/				r1
/ɪ/	1	1		1
no response	3	3		

All the cultivated judgments of the pronunciation of <u>kerosene</u> were
from Low Country informants, usually that /æ/ was a heard form (3)

or a Negroism or in uneducated speech. /a/ was also cited as heard, but no examples occurred in actual usage. /æ/ is found in cultivated speech in all areas of the state and notably in the principal cities; it is more common below the fall line, where all three examples of /ɪ/ were recorded as well.

(26) <u>apron</u>

	I, II	N	2N11	III
/epən/	30	8		4 r5
no response	5			2

Judgments about the status of /epən/ — always that it was old-fashioned — were recorded only from cultivated informants of the lower coastal region (Charleston and Beaufort[18, 19]). Two of these pronunciations in cultivated speech were recorded in the upper coastal region (Georgetown[6, 7]), and the other two were from near the coast. /epən/ is found in all areas of South Carolina, though somewhat more often below the fall line; in about one-third of the communities it represents the usage of the least cultivated informant.

(30) <u>creek</u>

	I, II	N	2N11	III
/ɪ/	13 r3	5 r1	r1	2 r10
no response	6			4

In the Up Country, the two cultivated informants who judged <u>creek</u> associated /ɪ/ with Charleston or Negroes. The opinion of the Low Country judges was that /ɪ/ was heard (5) or old. The two cultivated uses of /ɪ/ were from rural areas around Charleston; the only use of /ɪ/ outside the immediate coastal region was from a Low Country Negro informant.

(35) <u>tusks</u>

	I, II	N	2N11	III
/tʌʃɨz/	60 r8	8 r2	r1	5 r6
no response	5	1		7

One cultivated informant found /tʌʃɨz/ humorous; the remainder judged it heard, additionally qualified as Negro (1) or old (1). For most uncultivated judges /tʌs(ks)/ has prestige, for they consider it new or correct or consider /tʌʃɨz/ as old-fashioned or as a heard form. /tʌs(ks)/ is the dominant form in cultivated speech and is also the exclusive form of about one-quarter of the uncultivated, most of whom are from below the fall line. Only a small minority use both forms. Aside from cultivated usage, no striking social distribution of the two forms is apparent in the usage of whites, though /tʌʃɨz/ prevails among the Negro folk speakers.

(45.6) yeast

	I, II	N	2N11	III
/ist/	68 r4	7		7 r6
/jist/	33	3	1	23
no response	5	2		4

One cultivated judge reports /jist/ is correct; another feels both pronunciations are natural; the remainder are equally divided between old and heard for /ist/. The folk judgments follow the same pattern as those of the cultivated. /jist/ prevails among the cultivated; its exclusive use by the uncultured is evenly distributed geographically, but socially is more characteristic of better-educated informants.

(45.7) yolk

	I, II	N	2N11	III
/jɛlk/	13 r2	3		2 r4
/jɜlk/	9			9 r2
/jok/	34			12
/jolk/	15 r2		1	6
no response	27	5		5

For the cultured judges /jolk/ is correct (1) and other forms are evenly divided between heard and old. The uncultured judges agree that /jolk/ is correct, or of /jɛlk/ that it is heard or natural. /jo(l)k/, the majority form in cultivated speech, is current in all areas. It competes with /jɛlk/ in the upper Savannah River watershed, and in fall line communities, where it prevails in cultivated speech; along the coast it is largely found in the speech of the least cultured. /jɜlk/ though in cultivated speech along and above the fall

line, is not very common in those areas; in the Low Country it is concentrated in and above — inland and coastwise — Charleston. The
least common forms, [ʌ ~ ɪ ~ e ~ ɣ ~ a ~ ɵ ~ ʊ ~ ɒ] are also concentrated near the coast, generally in the speech of the uncultivated.

(45. 8) yellow[23]

	I, II	N	2N11	III
[æ]	41 r16	8		8 r7
[a ~ ɑ]	11 r1			
[ʊ ~ ɒ ~ ɔ]	9 r3			3
[e ~ ʌ]	21	4		4
[ɪ ~ ɨ]	23 r2	2		r2
no response	4	1		3

The cultivated judge [æ] as old (2), new, correct and heard (3), the
latter amplified as Negro, rural and incorrect. [ɜ] and [ʊ] are termed
natural, and [ɨ] is termed old. The uncultural judge [æ] about equally
old or heard but also natural (1) or Negro (2). [a] and [ɔ] are judged
old, though the latter is also termed new, and [ɪ] is considered natural. Though its phonemic status is doubtful (Kurath and McDavid
1961: 134), [ɜ] is by far the most common form, and it frequently al-
ternated with [ɛ]; in cultivated speech the two occur twice as frequently as all other variants combined. In cultivated speech [ʌ] is confined
to Beaufort (18, 19) and Greenville; [ɒ] is most likely to be found in
Charleston. [ɛ] and [ɜ] are also the most common variants in common speech, but [æ] is missing from few communities, mostly concentrated in the Low Country. [ɪ] and [ɨ] are distinctly less common
and are also most characteristic of the Low Country. [ɔ] and the low
vowels are most characteristic of the Pee Dee and the uppermost
section of the state, though they do occur along the coast in the Low
Country. [ʌ] and [e] are absent only in a rather wide band of communities near the fall line.

(48) vittles

	I, II	N	2N11	III
[β]	2 r2	1		r1
[b]	2 r7	r1		r4

Phones other than [v] initially in <u>vittles</u> are judged as Negro by the
cultivated, all from the coast but one, who further specifies coastal
Negro usage. The uncultivated informants, also all in the coastal
region, say these are Negro forms. The Charleston Negro folk informant specifies [b] as rural. The two whites who say [β] say the
stop is the Negro form.

(50) <u>chew</u>

	I, II	N	2N11	III
/ɔ/	8 r23	1 r1	r1	1 r12
no response	5	1		5

Half the cultivated judges state that /ɔ/ in <u>chew</u> is used only in the
expression <u>chew of tobacco</u>; the remainder give it as a heard form,
with the additional specification of rural (4) or old (1). The folk informants say this form is restricted to tobacco (7), generally speci-
fying it as old as well. /ɔ/ is also cited as a heard form (6) or rural
(3) or humorous (3). Most of the instances of /ɔ/ are found in the
Pee Dee, but it occurs above the fall line as well.

(55) <u>tomato</u>

	I, II	N	2N11	III
/ɒ ~ ɔ/	3 r20	1	1	4 r1
/ɑ/	r3			2 r1
/æ/	5 r11			7 r8
no response	4			1

Cultured informants in the Low Country say that /æ/ is an old form,
but some continue to use it. The Up Country informants report the
variants as heard, /ɒ/ being further characterized as rural or
Charlestonian, /æ/ as Negro. The folk judges consider /æ/ old (10)
as a rule but also as heard, Negro or humorous. Old is also the
general characterization of /ɒ/ , and heard is general as well, but
humorous and Negro are also applied. /e/, of course, is virtually
universal, and cultivated variants are found only on the coast. Though
/ɒ ~ ɔ/ and /æ/ are widely reported in the Up Country, they are seldom found there.

(77.3) deaf

	I, II	N	2N11	III
/ɪ/	7 r3	1		r1
/i/	27 r27	4	r1	r5
no response	13	3		8

The cultivated opinion, all from the Low Country, is that the variants /i/ and /ɪ/ are heard forms and rural (1) or rare (1). For about two-thirds of the folk judges, these are heard forms, and half the remainder characterize them as old. Occasionally the forms are said by the folk to be Negroisms (4). /i/ and /ɪ/ , though not especially common, are rather evenly dispersed over the state.

(77.5) boil 'furuncle'

	I, II	N	2N11	III
/ai/	7 r7	3		r5
no response	28	3		13

/ai/ in boil is considered by the cultured judges as heard but also old (2). A similar consensus exists among the folk judges, though they also characterize /ai/ as Negro usage (2) or more natural (1). /ai/ occurs most frequently in the Pee Dee but is also found elsewhere; it is generally the usage of the least cultured informants.[24]

(90) haunt (ed)

	I, II	N	2N11	III
/æ/	70 r16	5	1 r1	6 r13
/e/	6 r2			
no response	16	4		11

Half the cultured informants report /æ/ as heard; the remainder are equally divided between Negro, old and humorous. Most of the uncultured cite this as a heard form as well, though about half say it is heard from Negroes. /e/ is cited as old or Negro. Though not prevailing in cultivated speech, /æ/ is not lacking there either and is rather general among other speakers. /e/ is scattered in the Pee Dee and above the fall line.

(97) stamp

	I, II	N	2N11	III
/ɔ/	85 r5	5	1	5 r8
/æ/	3 r4		1	5 r5
no response	17	5		6

The cultivated informants judge /ɔ/ in stamp as a heard form (5)
and elaborate to deny the use of it (3) or to point out that /æ/ is correct (2). The judgments of the uncultured are generally divided between heard, or that one or the other of the forms was correct. /ɔ/
is universal in the speech of the uncultured — even those few who say
/æ/ have both forms. Exclusive use of the latter is confined to cultivated informants.

(104) hoist

	I, II	N	2N11	III
/ai/	35 r13	5		2 r8
no response	31	4		6

The general opinion of the cultivated on /ai/ in hoist is that it is a
heard form; they elaborate to specify that it is a Negroism (2), rural
or what a dog does with his hind leg. The latter is also the opinion of
the uncultured (5) or that /haist/ is what a boil does; somewhat more
commonly it is a heard term (6), elaborated as old (2), Negro or
rural; and finally, it is said to be incorrect (3). /haist/ is found in
all areas of the state, especially among the most rustic informants.

GRAMMAR[25]

(3) rise (preterite)

	I, II	N	2N11	III
/rɪz/	14 r10	r1	r1	r4
/raiz/	3	r1		
/raizd/	4	3		
no response	22	5		11

For the cultivated informants, /rɪz/ is a heard form, also further
described as Negro (1) or predominantly Negro (1). The majority of

the folk who judged <u>rise</u> were relatively more cultivated. The opinion of the folk, as a rule, is that /rɪz/ is a heard form, especially
Negro (2) or rural; a minority characterize the form as incorrect
(3). The zero preterite was considered old-fashioned. /rɪz/ is
most common in the Pee Dee and along the fall line but absent only in
the lower coastal region.

(12.4) <u>ain't</u> stressed, (12.5) <u>ain't</u> unstressed 'have'

	I, II	N	2N11	III
<u>ain't</u> not recorded	19		1	22 r4
no response	5	2		3

<u>Ain't</u>[26] is reported as a heard form by the cultivated, though two of
them use it in informal contexts. <u>Ain't</u> is general among the uncultivated, except for those with social aspirations.

(25.3) <u>I ain't,</u> (25.4) <u>ain't I</u>? 'be'

	I, II	N	2N11	III
<u>ain't</u> not recorded	10 r2			4 r9
no response	4	2		13

The judgments of the cultivated are varied: taught to avoid <u>ain't</u> (2),
informal (2), old, common, rare, careless and heard frequently.
The spouse of one informant who avoids <u>ain't</u> uses it regularly, as
does one informant taught to avoid it. One uncultured judge gives
<u>ain't</u> as heard; the other admits to occasional use of it. The most
striking fact about <u>ain't</u> 'be' is that it is rejected much less often than
<u>ain't</u> 'have,' especially by the cultivated informants. Furthermore,
the judgments of the cultivated are much less emphatic.

(27) <u>shrink</u> (preterite)

	I, II	N	2N11	III
shrunk	61	3	1	23 r3
shrank	8 r3			7 r1
shrink	5 r1	4		
shrinkt	9 r5	4		r1
no response	22	4		3

The opinion of the cultivated informants is that shrank is correct,
though one declares shrunk is natural; shrinkt is reported as a frequently heard form. On the latter form, the uncultured informants
offer the judgment heard (4), with the additional qualification that it
is a Negroism (2) or old-fashioned. The uncultured find shrank less
natural, and the zero form is reported as heard. Shrunk is the predominant form in cultivated speech in South Carolina, as it is throughout the Atlantic Seaboard (Atwood 1953: 21). The weak preterites are
found in uncultured speech below the fall line, as are the majority of
the zero preterites.[27]

(48) eat (preterite)

	I, II	N	2N11	III
eat	51 r2	5		1 r1
et	38 r6	4	r1	9 r5
no response	3	2		3

The judgment of the cultured is that et is heard (4) or old (3), though
it is also characterized as natural. Eat is also a heard form. The
uncultured characterize et as heard or old or ignorant, and eat is
termed old. Ate is a heard term for one cultivated informant who
states et is natural; the uncultivated judge ate as new (1) or proper
(1). Ate is the form preferred by most of the better-educated informants; et is found in cultivated speech only below the fall line, and it
is always paired with participial eaten. There is considerable mixed
usage in all communities, though eat is somewhat more rustic in the
Low Country and appreciably more rustic in the Up Country, where et
occurs less often. The participial eaten is a much better touchstone
of social acceptability than the preterite.

(95) dive (preterite)

	I, II	N	2N11	III
dived	53 r1	1 r1	1	11 r2
dove	14 r4	1 r1		14 r2
div	15 r5	1 r1		r1
dive	8	4	1	
no response	17	4		8

The cultivated judged all forms as heard; both dived and dove, however, are cited as correct by two of the cultivated. The prevailing

judgment of the uncultured was that all the variants were heard forms, though div was cited as Negro, old and incorrect. A form not attested in usage, /duv/, was once cited as a Negroism. Dived is current everywhere, but dove is chiefly a Low Country form (cf. Atwood 1953, Fig. 6); div is current everywhere but in the tidewater. Though dived is the commonest form, dove is slightly more used by the cultivated. Dive and div are chiefly found in the speech of the least cultivated.

(96) climb (preterite)

	I, II	N	2N11	III
/klʌm/	20 r8		r1	r6
/klæm/	3 r3			
/klɪm/	7 r5			r1
/klom/	3 r2			
no response	16	4		9

The cultivated judged all forms as heard, though /klʌm/ is further identified as old (1) or Negro (1). /klɪm/ and /klʌm/ are characterized as heard forms, though the latter is also identified as old-fashioned, natural and incorrect. /klom/ is identified as old-fashioned, uneducated usage, and /klæm/ was judged a Negroism (2) or old. /klæmd/ was also judged heard, but no examples were found in actual usage. Climbed is the only form used by the cultivated and predominates in the speech of better-educated or urban informants. All other forms were found in rural communities below the fall line except two instances of /klɪm/ in the northwest corner of the state and one /klʌmd/ just above the fall line.

(104) fight (preterite)

	I, II	N	2N11	III
/faut/	12 r14	1 r1		r3
/fɪt/	5 r9	1		r2
/fait/	1 r1	2		
no response	9	5		5

The cultivated informants reported only heard judgments; for /faut/ the judges were from the Low Country, for /fɪt/ they were from the Up Country. The uncultured judged the former as heard (10), sometimes old (3) as well. Half the uncultivated judgments of /fɪt/ were

that it was old-fashioned; the remaining attributions were equally divided between Negro and poor white. /fɔt/ was judged as correct or
less natural (2), and the zero preterite was judged as Negro and rustic by the same informant. /fɔt/ is predominant at all social levels
in all parts of the state; the other forms are confined to the speech of
the least educated, with /faut/ being found only below the fall line.

Conclusion

The 144 South Carolina field records for the <u>Linguistic Atlas of the Middle and South Atlantic States</u> were systematically examined for the currency and generally ascribed status of 45 items
about which a significant number of the 32 cultivated informants had
offered judgments of acceptability.

Judgments were made most frequently where there were a
large number of competing forms, e. g., synonyms for (54) <u>peanut</u>
and (7) <u>living room</u>, or the pronunciations of (45. 7) <u>yolk</u> and (45. 8)
<u>yellow</u>; yet a large number of judgments does not necessarily indi-
cate either a large number of variants or a frequently occurring
variant, e. g., the pronunciations of (48) <u>vittles</u> and (17) <u>vase</u>. Lexical variants reflecting cultural change are usually accurately evalu-
ated, e. g., the innovations (7) <u>living room,</u> (8) <u>andirons,</u> (45) <u>dough-
nut</u> and (79) <u>casket,</u> or the older (3) <u>sunup,</u> (8) <u>fire dogs,</u> (17) <u>spider,</u>
or (27. 3) <u>breeches.</u> There is somewhat less accuracy in judgments on
pronunciation, especially with (24) <u>kerosene.</u> For grammatical items,
the most striking fact is the scarcity of comments on uninflected
preterites, among the clearest touchstones of non-standard usage.[28]

Since the informants' attitudes were obtained indirectly, the
number of judgments varied greatly from one interview to another.
Moreover, the indirect approach often evoked such judgments as (1)
two or more forms may be equally acceptable; (2) certain forms may
be judged as unnatural or affected, as well as old-fashioned or rustic; and (3) even though an alternate form may be widely current or
generally held to be correct, informants often prefer their own usage
to the dictates of external standards.

With respect to the number of judgments on a given item,
the uncultivated informants, like the cultivated, most often judge

lexical items and least often judge grammatical items. Still, a large number of cultivated judgments does not necessarily predict a large number of uncultivated judgments. One direction further research should take is the determination of items which the uncultivated find most interesting, but which excite little or no interest in the cultivated. As for the quality of the judgments, it is hardly rare for the uncultivated to be at least as perceptive as the cultivated, particularly for lexical items. Finally, of particular interest to scholars concerned with intercultural relations, forms are rarely labelled unequivocally as Negroisms — by informants of any class or region in South Carolina. Those forms that are labelled Negroisms are not infrequently widely distributed in white speech and are not necessarily predominant among Negroes.

The evidence from the regional linguistic atlases — both recorded forms and judgments — thus constitutes a useful supplement to other studies of acceptability. Even though language and usage continually change, it may not be safe to assume that attitudes change at the same rate, cf. (27) shrank. Atlas evidence can be used to establish benchmarks from which change can be measured.

Conclusions about usage are best drawn from systematically executed surveys of actual usage, of whatever design. The future researcher cannot be too skeptical of preconceived notions, whether those of his informants or his own.

NOTES

[1]We gratefully acknowledge the permission of the American Council of Learned Societies to quote from the unpublished archives of the Linguistic Atlas of the United States and Canada, which has enjoyed since its inception the good offices of the Council. We also acknowledge the continuing support of our respective institutions, the University of Chicago and the University of South Carolina, for the editing and publication of the Linguistic Atlas of the Middle and South Atlantic States.

[2]Informants were life-long residents of their respective communities. In the longest-settled regions, their families had been resident two or more generations, sometimes six or more; cf. Kurath

and R. McDavid 1961 (23-27). In more recently settled regions, informants with two or more generations of family residence would be atypical, if not impossible to find; cf. Allen 1973-76.

In locating informants and ascertaining their social rank, field workers paid close attention to the opinions of local contacts familiar with the class structure of their communities and to the position of individuals within the class structure. The informants' vitae take note not only of these comments but the educational and occupational histories, membership in churches and other organizations, social contacts, intellectual pursuits and the like of the informants, and, where available, of their immediate and more remote ancestors; salient points of the character of the informants are also noted. In the course of eight hours face-to-face contact during a typical interview, normally in the informant's home, there was ample opportunity to revise and refine preliminary judgments about social rank.

Though aware that no single factor is an adequate indicator of social rank, linguistic geographers have paid close attention to education since it deals specifically with usage and attitudes towards usage, often fostering usages and attitudes towards usage contrary to the oral traditions. Correspondingly, the folk informants are typically minimally educated, the cultivated of generally superior education, and users of common or popular speech represent a distinctly intermediate level of education. Still, the three types are more or less rough classifications; for the study of social differences in speech, Kurath has always insisted that the vitae be consulted (Kurath et al. 1939: 44; cf. McDavid and O'Cain 1973).

[3]Field workers varied in their practices: some were more interested in the temporal succession of forms, some were more attentive to careful distinctions in various semantic fields, etc. The character and temperament of the informant himself and the interplay between informant and field worker are significant as well (Kurath et al. 1939: 46-47, 143-145).

[4]Kurath et al. (1939: 48): "The views of the informants must be accepted with caution, but they are significant even when they are wrong."

[5]The North American surveys comprising the Linguistic Atlas of the United States and Canada are a group of autonomous regional surveys sharing a common methodology, though modified as local conditions and resources dictate. In addition to the full phonetic presentation of LANE (Kurath et al. 1939-1943), there exists

a full treatment in normal orthography of the lexicon and grammar of
the Upper Midwest (Allen 1973, 1975); for pronunciation, Allen (1976)
is analogous to Kurath and McDavid (1961). There are also summary
volumes for the entire Atlantic Seaboard, Kurath (1949), Atwood
(1953), and Kurath and McDavid (1961). V. McDavid (1956) is analogous to Atwood for the North Central States and the Upper Midwest.
Similar summary volumes for the North-Central States are being prepared (Payne, forthcoming). For the Middle and South Atlantic
States (Kurath, R. McDavid, and O'Cain 1978-) the full phonetic
record will be published in list manuscripts. Lee A. Pederson expects
to publish the transcribed Gulf States field records on microfiche. The
transcription of the responses is considered merely a protocol of the
basic records, all tape recorded (Pederson [1976]).

[6]Kurath et al. (1939-1943) and Allen (1973-76) contain lists
of significant comments by the informants for each item as well as
conventional designations for the status of forms in the general pre-
sentations.

No scholar has ever been denied access to the regional collections in our custody, and we know of no restrictions on the use of
the other LAUSC collections.

[7]McDavid was interviewed for LAMSAS by Bernard Bloch in
1937. For the judgments in the record see McDavid (1974).

[8]McDavid made 119 field records for LAMSAS in South Carolina alone and over 500 for various regional surveys. O'Cain made
20 records (each about three times the length of a typical Atlas interview) in South Carolina for Cassidy (forthcoming), as well as 100
brief records for his survey of Charleston (O'Cain 1972).

[9]There are 145 field records from South Carolina. Guy S.
Lowman, Jr. made 19 (1933-1934, 1937); Bloch, 1 (1937); Lee A.
Pederson, 5 (1965); O'Cain, 2 (1967); and McDavid, 119 (1941, 1946-
48, 1964). The records by Pederson and O'Cain were tape recorded
and were re-transcribed by McDavid to minimize field worker differences in LAMSAS, for which fewer than one percent of the records
were transcribed by workers other than Lowman or McDavid.

[10]Even some incomplete records have rather substantial numbers of judgments, e.g., 24e, 38c.

[11]According to Albert H. Marckwardt, Marjorie Daunt summarized a report on the teaching of English in the United States by
saying that there were three possible attitudes toward grammar and
usage: indifference, assurance and anxiety. No Americans were

indifferent, and the only assured ones were two maiden ladies from Charleston.

[12]Historical and sociological evidence aside, there are ample indications in Kurath (1949), Atwood (1953) and Kurath and McDavid (1961) that this approach is reasonable. We have excluded any marginal cases from group III.

[13]Kurath (1949) was completed before the McDavid records became available and is based on the 20 records by Lowman and Bloch. Of the items treated herein, numbers 2, 3, 9, 27.3, 48, 54, 79, 98 and 100 are not treated by Kurath. Cultivated and cultured are used interchangeably with no difference in sense; folk is likewise interchangeable with uncultured or uncultivated.

[14]There are 102 uncultivated white informants, 10 uncultivated Negro informants, 1 cultivated Negro informant and 31 cultivated white informants.

[15]Numbers following judgment labels in parentheses give the number of judgments. Where there are no numbers the figures are derivable or of no particular significance.

[16]Statements about the social and geographical distribution of forms are strictly limited to those forms actually current in the speech of the informants.

[17]Stoop has some currency in the Savannah River valley but is quite marginal elsewhere.

[18]The fall line is the head of navigation on the rivers and sets off the Low Country from the Up Country (Piedmont). Communities 21, 22, 25 and 29 are situated more or less on the fall line. The Pee Dee, a separate cultural subdivision of South Carolina (cf. Kurath 1949: Fig. 3), is set off from the Low Country by the river of that name, which empties near communities 6 and 7. The tidewater extends from the mouth of the Pee Dee southward and includes the lands within about 30 miles of the coast.

[19]Folk is used in a somewhat broader sense than heretofore to mean all the uncultured informants, groups I, II and N.

[20]There are also 24 occurrences of other terms, all of which are distinctly minor variants, few occurring more than once. In several of the items there are minor variants that resist summary treatment, and about which expressions of opinion are non-existent or insignificant.

[21]Matter following a single parenthesis gives the context in which a form was elicited or instructions to the field worker.

[22]Phonetic details are of necessity greatly abridged; phonemic transcriptions are consistent with Kurath and McDavid (1961). Items 24, 26 and 48 are not treated by Kurath and McDavid (1961).

[23]Additional phones of the stressed vowel in yellow were taken from pages (56) yellow corn, (60) yellow bellied cooter, (60A) yellow jacket and (79) yellow jaundice.

[24](46) boiled egg, (24) oil, and (89) joined, from another etymological source than (77.5) and (104) hoist, also very rarely have /ai/; the distribution of /ai/ in the former does not alter the conclusions about the latter.

[25]The number of grammatical items treated is smaller for two reasons: the judgments were less frequent because the items were recorded from free conversation and the number of grammatical items in the work sheets is proportionately smaller.

[26]Ain't, even more than other grammatical items, is best recorded from free conversation. The principle is that by which one never asks a stranger if he is from Virginia: if he is, one will learn within ten minutes; if he isn't, one should avoid embarrassing him.

[27]Interestingly, there was no commentary on the incidence of /ʃr-/ and /sr-/; the latter is dominant in South Carolina.

[28]Surprisingly, the multiple plurals (54) /mætəsɨz/ 'tomatoes' and (64) /tʃɪlənz/ 'children', and such double comparatives as (26) more prettier pass without comment.

REFERENCES

Allen, H. (1973-76), Linguistic Atlas of the Upper Midwest. Minneapolis, University of Minnesota.

American Heritage Dictionary (1969), Boston, American Heritage Publishing Co. & Houghton Mifflin Co.

Atwood, E. B. (1953), A Survey of Verb Forms in the Eastern United States. Ann Arbor, University of Michigan.

Cassidy, F. G. (in progress), Dictionary of American Regional English.

Creswell, T. J. (1975), 'Usage in dictionaries and dictionaries of usage'. Publication of the American Dialect Society, 63-64.

Kurath, H. (1949), A Word Geography of the Eastern United States. Ann Arbor, University of Michigan.

Kurath, H., et al. (1939), Handbook of the Linguistic Geography of
    New England. Providence, Rhode Island, American Coun-
    cil of Learned Societies. [2nd ed. 1973. New York, AMS
    Press]
_____ (1939-1943), Linguistic Atlas of New England. Providence,
    Rhode Island, American Council of Learned Societies. [Re-
    printed 1972, New York, AMS Press]
Kurath, H., and McDavid, R. I., Jr. (1961), The Pronunciation of
    English in the Atlantic States. Ann Arbor, University of
    Michigan.
Kurath, H., McDavid, Jr., R. I. and O'Cain, R. K. (1978-), Lin-
    guistic Atlas of the Middle and South Atlantic States. Chi-
    cago, University of Chicago.
McDavid, R. I., Jr. (1974), 'The failure of intuition'. Unpublished
    paper delivered before the Henry Lee Smith, Jr., Memorial
    Symposium, Buffalo, New York.
McDavid, R. I., Jr., and O'Cain, R. K. (1977), Review of Wolfram
    and Fasold, The Study of Social Dialects in American Eng-
    lish (1974), American Anthropologist 79.947-48.
_____ (1973), 'Sociolinguistics and linguistic geography', Kansas
    Journal of Sociology, 9, pp. 137-156.
McDavid, V. G. (1956), 'Verb forms in the north-central states and
    upper midwest'. University of Minnesota dissertation.
    [Microfilm]
Mencken, H. L. (1963), The American Language. [One-volume
    abridged edition; 4th ed. & 2 supplements, edited with new
    material by R. I. McDavid, Jr. with assistance of D. W.
    Maurer] New York, Alfred A. Knopf.
O'Cain, R. K. (1972), 'A social dialect survey of Charleston, South
    Carolina'. University of Chicago dissertation. [Microfilm]
Payne, R. C. (forthcoming), 'The Linguistic Atlas of the North Cen-
    tral States: Plans and Prospects', American Speech.
Pederson, L. (1974 [1976]), 'Tape/Text and Analogues', American
    Speech 49, pp. 5-23.

9 | Social Differences in White Speech

I

This paper summarizes the information available on social differences in the language of whites who are speakers of English, principally but not exclusively in the United States. It is based on identifiable utterances of identifiable informants; the evidence is available to other scholars who may wish to refute or replicate the findings. Essentially the evidence consists of: (1) published surveys, such as Joseph Wright's English Dialect Grammar (1905) and English Dialect Dictionary (1898-1905), Harold Orton's Survey of English Dialects (1962-71), Hans Kurath's Linguistic Atlas of New England (1939-43), and Harold Allen's Linguistic Atlas of the Upper Midwest (1973-76); (2) the accessible if yet unpublished materials of the Linguistic Atlas of the Middle and South Atlantic States, the Linguistic Atlas of the North-Central States, and related collections; (3) independent investigations such as Harold Paddock's thesis (1966) on the speech of Carbonear, Newfoundland; (4) derivative studies based on systematic investigations, notably the regional linguistic surveys in North America. [1]

II

This paper is deliberately restricted to Caucasoids who are native speakers of English in English-speaking communities, contrary to the emphasis of American sociolinguistics in the past decade. Mission-oriented and at least partially sponsored by educational administrators, most of that research is concerned with the language of blacks and Spanish speakers in Northern and Western cities; almost no attention is given to the speech of the largest disadvantaged group, the native whites, or to previous regional surveys.[2] Since most of the investigators were Northerners, there was almost no attention to regional differences in educated speech. Furthermore, most of these investigators have not only avoided reference to upper-class speech, even in the North, but have set up research designs that exclude speakers of upper-class varieties of English.[3] As a result there has been a disproportionate attention to so-called "Black English," though it has not been defined, and though its existence has been challenged, especially by linguistically sophisticated Southerners of African descent.[4] As a Southern Caucasoid I do not feel that I should meddle in these matters. I am prepared to recognize a de facto Black English in Chicago, if not in Charleston, much as we can recognize a separate Ukrainian language in North America if not necessarily in Europe. I concede to my more brilliant colleague James H. Sledd the role of Ralph Nader to the Black English industry.

III

In evaluating social differences in language we have moved a considerable distance from the polar opposition between "correct" and "incorrect."[5] We now recognize that the status of any linguistic form involves a complicated set of interlocking dimensions: the medium (speech or writing), the degree of formality, the relationship between the speaker and the auditor, the attitudes of both parties, the identification of the speaker with his community or parts of it.[6] Even more important are the dimensions of history, geography and social position; geographic or social isolation from cultural foci is likely to prosper the retention of archaisms and inhibit the spread of local innovations.[7]

IV

There are, finally, two complications resulting from the worldwide dissemination of English (that such complications would be multiplied enormously if the varieties in India, Pakistan, Bangladesh, Nigeria, the Philippines and the West Indies were included is sufficient justification for limiting the scope of this paper).

At least in North America, where we have the largest amount of comparable evidence, it is impossible to trace any

regional or local variety of English to any single regional dialect in
the British Isles. Even in the educated speech of the Atlantic Seaboard, which has been influenced by educated London English since
the beginnings of settlement, no community follows London practice
in every detail.

Second is the problem of determining the standard against
which other varieties are to be judged. Although class distinctions
in the British Isles have become somewhat abraded with the simultaneous development of the Welfare State and new concentrations of
wealth and power, Received Standard is still the prevailing model,
with some concessions to Scots in the Northern Kingdom (an independent Irish standard seems as remote as unification of the island).
In smaller units of the Commonwealth, such as the Falklands or
Tristan da Cunha, where no substantial local elite has arisen, Received Standard is perforce still the approved model. In Australia,
Canada, and New Zealand, however, its preeminence is less generally conceded, though in each country there is a vocal minority
("Brits" the Canadians call them, in humorous disparagement) who
consider it the only legitimate mode of speaking. [8] Counterparts of
the "Brits" also exist in various neighborhoods, communities and
occupations in the United States — including some proper Charlestonians (South Carolina) who still openly bemoan the success of the
American Revolution.

Competition with Received Standard varies from country to
country. Little is known about varieties of educated New Zealand
speech; in Australia there are supposedly no significant regional
variants, except possibly in Tasmania; in Canada, as in the United
States, there are marked geographical differences, and local standards have been recognized and encouraged by the Canadian Broad-
casting Corporation.

The situation in the United States is fluid. Each major colonial center developed its own prestigious speechways, more or less
independent of the others. Though some of these have lost their lus-
ter or have been engulfed in metropolitan agglomerations, others have
persisted and new ones have arisen as the nation moved westward.
Since no one can fairly claim superiority, it would seem logical that
all the local varieties of educated American English should be

recognized as equal. But in Orwellian terms, some are apparently
more equal than others. During the presidency of Lyndon Johnson,
for instance, it was common practice for Easterners to deride foreign policy as discussed in a "cornpone accent," and at the opening
of the Watergate it was piously observed that Southern senators
couldn't possibly conduct an adequate investigation. On the other
hand, Albert H. Marckwardt reported from Kentucky a contrast felt
between the coldness of John F. Kennedy's speech, and the human
warmth of Lyndon Johnson's. Since other varieties from the Atlantic Seaboard, notably those of eastern New England, were suspect in
the American heartland for being too much like British English, there
arose the myth of a "General American" — a myth that now survives
despite the demonstration that regional varieties exist in the Middle
West. Under other labels — such as "network English" and "consensus English" — it has received much favorable comment from sociolinguists, particularly those wishing to provide what they considered
a standard to those unfortunate enough to be poor and speak in Southern accents. Informally, I had personally noticed only one genuine
speaker of "network English," Richard Nixon, though the pulpit style
of Billy Graham came close to qualifying before events of 1973 made
him revert toward his native North Carolinian. However, that "network English" exists became dramatically evident as the media displayed the accents of Kalmbach, Strachan, Segretti, Chapin, Dean
Haldeman and Ehrlichman.[9] Perhaps a side benefit of Watergate will
be a distrust of homogenized speech, and greater respect for those
who reveal their regional origins as they talk. It seems apparent
that Jimmy Carter has become a particular beneficiary of that attitude.

V

An ideal model for describing social and regional differences
in speech would follow Austin 1972 and include all the phenomena of
communication — proxemics, haptics, kinesics, suprasegmentals,
phonology, morphology, syntax and vocabulary.[10] But in our imperfect world we are far from achieving this model. Systematic work in
proxemics, haptics, kinesics and paralanguage is at best a quarter-
century old; the most comprehensive study of one communication
situation — The Natural History of an Interview (McQuown 1970) —
took fifteen years to complete. We have no generally accepted

notation, and almost no comparative studies in depth. Of course we can make certain general statements, principally of an anecdotal order. As the Watergate hearings progressed, my manual and facial gestures were frequently compared to those of Senator Ervin; and years ago the entomologist Henry Townes, a sometime neighbor of mine, had remarked that some of these manual gestures are apparently restricted to the Carolina uplands. But more specific statements are few.

For suprasegmentals there is also little comparative work. Despite suggestions in Pike 1945, there has been little questioning of the notions of four levels of pitch, let alone descriptions of how such levels function in particular varieties of English. For stress we have little more to go on; for the transitional and terminal phenomena, grouped together in Trager and Smith 1951 as "junctures," we have much less. Again, we can make impressionistic and anecdotal statements; for instance, the difference between highest and lowest pitches, between strongest and weakest stresses, seems to be greater in Received Standard and in Southern and South Midland American than in Great Lakes American — and these impressions may be dramatically confirmed, as in a 1957 confrontation between Joos and Sledd (in Trageremic terms Sledd's nón + sénse was interpreted by Joos as nón-sénse; my speech follows Sledd's). But the details are still to be worked out. By way of exception is the placement of primary stress in particular words, which is to be discussed along with other matters of phonemic incidence.

Systematic treatments of English syntax are rare. A decade and a half of transformational rule-writing has produced nothing more waterproof than we had before; in fact, the transformationalist's disparagement of data has discouraged objective comparative work. Some comparative work has been done by sociolinguists, but largely with selected items. The treatment here is similarly restricted, though the body of comparable data is somewhat larger and better controlled.

Attempts to structure the lexicon have so far been futile; even such heroic operations as Cassidy's Dictionary of American Regional English touch only a part of it. So far as the social significance of vocabulary items is concerned, there seem to be two conclusions: (1) the better educated tend to use national terms rather than regional ones — mantel(piece) rather than fireboard, cottage cheese rather than curd(s); (2) on the other hand, upper-class speakers strongly identified with a community will use the regional or local term with those they consider their social peers, while the newly risen and other peripherals, those concerned with external norms, will avoid local terms, using them rarely and often denying their existence.[11]

Our observations then are restricted:

I. Phonology[12]

    A. Differences in the system of phonemes
    B. Differences in the phonetic shape of the phonemes.
    C. Differences in the incidence of the phonemes.

II. Morphology[13]

    A. Differences in the system of inflections.
    B. Differences in the phonemic structure of inflections.
    C. Differences in the incidence of inflections.

III. Syntax: Selected Features

We will also dismiss the medium of writing from our discussion. Within the English-speaking world, standard writing is highly uniform, differing only in vocabulary, a few local spelling conventions (e.g., center and centre, labor and labour), and an occasional principal part of a verb. For the United States, and probably by implication elsewhere, the differences between standard and nonstandard were pretty well covered by Fries 1940. A generation later we need only add a few amendments:[14]

(1) The population of educational institutions at all levels has swollen tremendously. It is still possible for an inmate, almost anywhere, to get something like a good education, but this is rarely inevitable. Ill-prepared for the new constituencies that began flooding the schools in the 1920's, the educational bureaucracy has taken

refuge behind such clichés as social promotion, life adjustment, peer group identity and recognition of life styles, to the disparagement of academic values. Today, even a college diploma is no guarantee of a mastery of reading, writing, and ciphering — the traditional curriculum of the elementary schools. [15]

(2) Although misspellings have heretofore normally reflected confusion between the sound system of the writer and the conventions of English orthography, new word-recognition schools of reading instruction have produced new kinds of misspellings, based on confusion of the visual shapes of words. And the disparagement of rote-learning by "liberals" and "conservatives" alike has reduced the emphasis on spelling that might correct misspellings, of whatever origin. The fact that, in the past, large numbers of speakers of English, of various sociolinguistic status and dialect backgrounds, have mastered the conventions of the written mode — reading and spelling alike — suggests that a part of the problem may be a failure of will on the part of the schools.

VI

I. A. Socially significant differences in the system of phonemes are few:

1. The absence of an /h/ phoneme, as in many of the folk dialects of Southern England. Vestiges of this absence occur in other lands, including Cornish settlements in the American Middle West.

2. Lack of a contrast between /θ,ð/ and /f, v; t, d; s, z/: thin, fin, tin, sin; then, Venn, den, Zen. [16] In various forms, the loss of this contrast is manifest in urban proletarians of English or Irish origin, to say nothing of many blacks and speakers with various foreign-language backgrounds.

3. Lack of a contrast between /v/ and /w/: vile, wile. Traditionally associated with Cockney, it also appears in the folk speech of the South Atlantic States, but does not seem to be systematic there.

4. Lack of contrast between /ɔi/ and /ɜ/: <u>oil</u>, <u>earl</u>.[17]
This feature, like the up-gliding diphthong [ɜɨ] for /ɜ/, seems to
be of North American origin, since it is not found in any dialect records in the British Isles. It is traditionally associated with lower-
class New York speech, but is far less common than it used to be.[18]

5. Preservation of the contrasts between reflexes of Middle
English /æ:/ as in <u>male</u> and /æi/ as in <u>mail</u>. This feature is most
common in folk speech of Southern England, if not limited to it
(Kurath-Lowman 1969).

I. B. Differences in the phonic quality of the phonemes.
These are usually of local significance.

1. The centralized beginning of long vowels and diphthongs
is associated in Britain with Cockney, lower-class London speech.
In Australia, however, it is hardly stigmatized at all; "Broad Australian," of which highly centralized beginnings are characteristic,
is simply one variety of standard Australian, and to many ears sounds
more masculine than the "cultivated" or "modified" alternatives,
more or less influenced by Received Standard (Mitchell-Delbridge
1965).

2. Raised and lengthened varieties of /æ/ and /ɔ/, often
with in-glides, are associated with semi-educated speakers in American cities of the Middle Atlantic Seaboard, and a few urban areas of
the Middle West.

3. Dentalization of the alveolar consonants /t, d, n, s, z, r, l/
is especially associated with the semi-cultivated of New York City.
It may ultimately be due to foreign-language backgrounds.

4. Raised beginnings of /au/ and backed beginnings of / ai/
occur in various communities, but are more likely to provoke ami-
able humor than social stigmatization. The monophthongization of
Southern /ai/ is often misinterpreted (and even mis-heard) in other
regions, but carries no social significance at present.[19]

I. C. Since phonemic incidence typically involves single
words, representative examples will suffice.

1. Omission of weak-stressed syllables before the primary stress: 'fessor for professor, 'merican for American, 'sho-unce for insurance (Fisher-R. McDavid 1973).

2. Generalization of the Germanic pattern of initial stress to words of Romance derivation: ró-mance, pó-lice, ée-ficiency.[20]

3. Heavy stress on what are normally weak-stressed final syllables, perhaps reflecting older patterns in borrowings from Romance: presidént, elemént.[21]

4. Such isolated words as Italian with initial /ái-/ and April with final /-áil/. Those pronunciations are generally old-fashioned, and may once have been standard, such as bal-cóny instead of the present bál-cony. The pronunciation /ái+táɪ jən/ by Carter became a minor campaign issue in 1976.

II.A. Systematic features of inflection.

1. Some non-standard dialects, notably in Newfoundland, formally distinguish a present, with zero inflection (I think, he think) and a timeless non-past (I thinks, he thinks). It is possible that this aspectual difference occurs in some varieties of Irish English.[22]

2. A number of non-standard dialects have either preserved the older distinction between singular and plural in the second person pronoun, as in the west country of England, or have developed new second person plurals. In the United States one finds /ɟɨz/ in urban communities (less often in rural), you-uns in the South Midland, and mongst-ye on Chesapeake Bay. The distinction also appears in standard informal Southern and South Midland you-all.

3. The -ing of the present participle, the -d/-ed of the preterite and the past participle, may be lacking; speakers are rarely consistent.

II.B. Differences in the shape of the morphemes.

1. In pronouns:

a. The generalization of the /-n/ of <u>mine</u> for other abso-
lute genitives: <u>ourn</u>, <u>yourn</u>, <u>hisn</u>, <u>hern</u>, <u>theirn</u>. Absolute <u>its</u> is so
rare that I hope I may be pardoned for not having found *<u>itsn</u>.

b. Leveling of the pattern of the compound reflexive-inten-
sives, so that <u>hisself</u>, <u>theirself</u>, <u>theirselves</u> replace <u>himself</u>, <u>them-
selves</u>.

2. In adjectives:

a. Inflectional rather than periphrastic comparison of participles and long adjectives: <u>lovinger</u>, <u>beautifullest</u>.

b. Double comparison of adjectives: <u>more prettier</u>, <u>most
ugliest</u>.

3. There are divergent shapes of the plural morpheme for
nouns, usually in the direction of regularity: <u>oxes</u>, <u>houses</u> (with
/-s-/). Several nouns have been regularized in standard usage, or
at least regular forms appear alongside traditional irregular ones.
Since the Walt Disney movie, <u>dwarfs</u> has been common in American
usage. [23]

4. Verbs.

a. Occasional survival, notably in Southern England, of
historical /-θ/ in the third singular present: <u>he rideth</u>.

b. Variant forms in the past tense and the past participle.
These may be survivals of older forms, such as <u>clumb</u> or <u>clome</u> for
the regular form <u>climbed</u>. On the other hand, they may be regulari-
zations not yet accepted as standard, such as <u>blowed</u>, <u>drawed</u>, for
<u>blew</u>, <u>drew</u> (Atwood 1953, V. McDavid 1956, Mencken 1963). [24]

II.C. Incidence of inflections. Most non-standard varieties
of English distribute inflections somewhat differently than the standard, though the inflectional categories seem to be present. At least
in the United States, no community or speaker is fully consistent.

1. Nouns sometimes lack the plural inflection (<u>two boy</u>) or
the genitive (<u>Mr. Brown hat</u>). [25]

2. Verbs may lack the third singular -s inflection or generalize it for all person-number forms: he do, we does. Mixed usage is very common. [26]

3. The present of the verb to be may vacillate among am, is, are, and be, with certain alternations especially frequent in particular communities.

4. The preterite of to be may vary between was and were. Mixed usage is common. [27]

III. Syntax. Most of the socially significant features of syntax involve verb forms; they are most significant in formal styles of discourse, especially in writing. Many of them occur in cultivated informal speech in some regions or communities.

A. Omission of the auxiliary have in statements, especially in the third singular, before past participles.

B. Omission of the copula to be, especially the third singular is, in statements before adjectives, predicate nominatives, present participles, past participles.

C. For to and for as infinitive markers.

D. Ain't and hain't (the latter being more stigmatized) as negative forms of have/has and am/is/are. [28]

E. Multiple negation, which may be mere double negatives like he ain't done nothing, or structures as complicated as there ain't nobody never makes no pound cake no more.

VII

The inventory is probably incomplete, since regional surveys have been undertaken for only small parts of the English-speaking world, and intensive surveys of particular communities are even rarer. [29] But the evidence in hand suggests that a description of present-day English is bound to be complicated, and that within the body of Caucasoid Anglophonic discourse there is much to be explored before scholars can justifiably dichotomize on the basis of race or ethnic antecedents.

NOTES

[1] The insistence on observed field data, rather than intuition, is based on repeated observations of experienced fieldworkers that informants have the human quality of susceptibility to self-bamboozlement, especially when a linguistic form seems to be a social marker. In the South, informants of some education have often denied the existence in Caucasoid speech of forms that are widely distributed in the region and that they even use themselves. Nor should one take too seriously sentences self-generated in an effort to test grammaticality. Students of American Indian languages will recall Sapir's attempt to ascertain the existence of a certain verb form. Suggesting it to the informant he asked, "Can you say it?" "Yes." "What does it mean?" "It don't mean nothing."

For my own part, I remember that when Charles C. Fries suggested, early in 1952, that three-object sentences (with indirect object, direct object, and object complement) might simply not occur in English, I vainly tried to produce a counter-example. However, a year later, in a telephone conversation I caught myself saying, "We've elected us Ike president, and now we're stuck with him."

[2] A notable exception to the neglect of the speech of poor whites is the work of Lawrence M. Davis with Appalachian migrants and their descendants in Chicago's Uptown, on the North Side (Davis (1971). The Rev. Jesse Jackson, an outspoken black leader, concedes that 80% of the American poor are English-speaking whites.

Shuy, Wolfram, and Riley 1968 and Wolfram 1969 made no use of the collections for the Linguistic Atlas of the North-Central States, which included a dozen interviews from Detroit and its environs.

[3] E.g., Labov 1966, Shuy, Wolfram and Riley 1968. The only intensive investigation of American upper-class metropolitan speech, and how it differs from the upper middle class, is Uskup 1974.

[4]E. g., Williamson 1967, 1970. A black Southerner, teaching in a Southern metropolitan area, Miss Williamson — with the aid of her students — is in a unique position for observing Southern informal speech of both races and all classes; perhaps for that very reason her work is rarely cited and almost never taken seriously by the magnates of the sociolinguistics industry.

[5]Joos 1962 a, b; Allen 1964; R. McDavid 1967.

[6]Labov 1972. Observers differ in what they consider the community norm. Labov apparently takes as his the adolescent street gangs; without any less sympathy for the individual, other observers, such as David W. Maurer (Mencken 1963, Ch. 11), might well consider such groups parasitic.

[7]R. McDavid 1967. The archaisms and innovations in question may be of various origins, including aboriginal or immigrant languages.

[8]Orkin 1970 sets up an opposition between "standard English" and "General American," with Canadian usage somewhere nervously in the middle. By "standard English" Orkin apparently means the upper reaches of Received Standard, confined to the English hereditary landed aristocrary. Orkin shows little familiarity with the diversity of educated speech in the United States (R. McDavid 1969).

[9]The term Watergate English, apparently coined by Aitken Pyles, appeared in the Chicago Sun-Times, August 19, 1973.

[10]For these terms and others, see Austin 1972.

[11]My first cues as to the effects of racial segregation on language behavior came from vocabulary checklists distributed to students at the University of Illinois in the spring of 1950. Almost without exception, blacks native to Chicago used the Southern terms crocus sack, croker sack to designate a burlap bag, rather than one of the more common Middle Western terms, such as gunny sack.

[12]This analysis follows Kurath-McDavid 1961.

[13]A full treatment of morphology would also include bases and derivational suffixes; regrettably, comparable evidence is scarce.

[14]Fries's evidence is of World War I vintage — letters to the U. S. Government about personal problems, which would probably put the writers on their best linguistic behavior.

[15]There is no need to rehearse the statistical horrors, including the fact that in some urban school systems the average high school inmate performs at least two years below the normal

expectations of his grade. Demands for the same kind (if not degree)
of accountability demanded of baseball managers and football coaches
have generally been brushed aside or disparaged as reactionary, as
have been attempts to enrich the elementary curriculum with larger
doses of elementary subject matter. Subject matter, in fact, is a
dirty word to many of our most advanced educational theorists.

[16]For many Southern cultivated speakers, especially males,
/θ/ and /ð/ often become /t/ and /d/ in informal conversation
with their peers.

[17]Folklore would have New Yorkers reversing the incidence
of the phonemes, giving earl boiner instead of oil burner; this is a
characteristic reaction when a speaker lacks a contrast that exists
in a hearer's speech. At one time the lack of contrast even appeared
in the usage of some upper-class New Yorkers.

[18]The up-gliding diphthong in bird, and the like is also found
in some varieties of Southern speech; however, the contrast with
Boyd seems to be maintained in the South, and the up-gliding diphthong in bird is without social significance.

As for other neutralizations: however exotic they may seem
to those who lack them, there is only regional significance (and that
sometimes declining) in the lack of contrast between pin and pen, between cot and caught, between horse and hoarse.

[19]At one time, monophthongal /ai/ before voiceless consonants was considered non-standard in the South (except for the
Charleston region, Southerners generally had it finally and before
voiced consonants), but the broadening of economic and educational
opportunities has removed the stigma.

[20]For some of these words, the stress may vary with position in the phrase or sentence, e.g., hotél but hótèl swítchbòard.

[21]Such syllables were stressed in Chaucer's verse.

[22]In the United States, an aspectual difference in the use of
the copula has been noted in the speech of many urban blacks: no
copula in the present, be/bees in the non-past. But there is nothing
like the systematic difference in the entire body of verbs as reported
in Paddock 1966.

[23]Non-standard speakers often have disyllabic plurals of
nouns in /-sp/, /-st/, /-sk/, sometimes with the final stop lost,
sometimes with it retained. A clear regional patterning in England
is shown in the evidence in Orton 1962-71, as well as in the records
from Southern England in the Archives of the Linguistic Atlas. See
R. and V. McDavid 1979.

[24]The use of -in instead of /-ing/ in the present participle
is a matter of region and style, and does not necessarily have social
significance. In fact, it is often deliberately used by upper-class
speakers (especially the British landed aristocracy and their analogues in the American South) in conversation with their peers.

[25]Zero plurals of nouns of measure — two mile, three ton,
five year, six foot, ten pound — are widespread, and may even occur
in formal writing (two mile on Michigan highway signs, load three ton
on a sign on the University of Chicago campus; R. and V. McDavid
1964). For what the information is worth, many uninflected plurals,
of various categories of nouns, have been observed in the campaign
speeches of Governor George C. Wallace of Alabama.

[26]The zero third person is common in the South of England,
with the disappearance of older /-θ/. Generalized -s has been
characteristic of northern British usage since 1300, as evident in the
Cursor Mundi. That many speakers of American English say he do
but they thinks probably reflects the facts of dialect mixture rather
than any hypercorrection.

[27]Some writers in eighteenth century England used you was
as a singular and you were as a plural.

[28]Hain't is always considered more old-fashioned or rustic
than ain't: Atwood 1953, V. McDavid 1956, Mencken 1963. An ill-
conceived press release about the 1961 Webster's Third New International Dictionary evoked such a hurricane of hostility (R. McDavid
1971) that James Sledd (1964: 473) observed sardonically that apparently any redblooded American would prefer incest to ain't. However, there is solid evidence that ain't is often used informally by
upper-class speakers among their peers, chiefly but not exclusively
in the American South.

[29]As Kurath 1968 pointed out, the orderly development of
sociolinguistics would have started with stable small communities in
the middle of clearly defined dialect areas, rather than with megalo-
politan agglomerations.

REFERENCES

Allen, Harold B. 1964. Introduction: linguistics and usage. Read-
        ings in applied English linguistics, ed. Harold B. Allen, 2nd
        ed., 271-74. New York: Appleton-Century-Crofts.

Allen, Harold B. 1973-76. Linguistic atlas of the Upper Midwest.
    3 vols. Minneapolis: University of Minnesota Press.
Atwood, E. Bagby. 1953. A survey of verb forms in the eastern
    United States. Ann Arbor: University of Michigan Press.
Austin, William M. 1972. The behavioral components of a two-way
    conversation. Studies in linguistics in honor of Raven I.
    McDavid., Jr., ed. Lawrence M. Davis, 231-37. Univer-
    sity, Alabama: University of Alabama Press.
Baubkus, Lutz, and Wolfgang Viereck. 1973. Recent American stud-
    ies in sociolinguistics. Archivum linguisticum NS 4.103-11.
Davis, Lawrence M. 1971. A study of Appalachian speech in an ur-
    ban setting. Final report. Project O-E-142. Washington:
    U.S. Department of Health, Education and Welfare.
Fisher, Lawrence E., and Raven I. McDavid, Jr. 1973. Aphaeresis
    in New England. American Speech 48.246-49.
Fries, Charles C. 1940. American English grammar. New York:
    Appleton-Century-Crofts.
Joos, Martin. 1962a. The five clocks. International Journal of
    American Linguistics 28.2.
_____. 1962b. Homeostasis in English usage. College Composi-
    tion and Communication 13.4.18-22 (Oct.).
Kurath, Hans, et al. 1939. Handbook of the linguistic geography of
    New England. Providence, Rhode Island: American Council
    of Learned Societies. 2nd ed., revised, 1973. New York:
    AMS Press.
_____. 1939-43. Linguistic atlas of New England. 3 vols. bound
    as 6. Providence, Rhode Island: American Council of
    Learned Societies. Reprinted 1972, 3 vols. New York:
    AMS Press.
_____. 1968. The study of urban speech. Publication of the
    American Dialect Society 49.3-12.
_____, and Guy S. Lowman, Jr. 1969. The dialect structure of
    southern England. Publication of the American Dialect So-
    ciety 54.
_____, and Raven I. McDavid, Jr. 1961. The pronunciation of
    English in the Atlantic States. Ann Arbor: University of
    Michigan Press.
Labov, William. 1966. The social stratification of English in New
    York City. Washington: Center for Applied Linguistics.

Labov, William. 1972. Language in the inner city: studies in the black English vernacular. Philadelphia: University of Pennsylvania Press.

McDavid, Raven I., Jr. 1967. Historical, regional and social variation. Journal of English Linguistics 1. 25-40.

_____. 1969. Review of Speaking Canadian English, by Mark M. Orkin. American Speech 46. 287-89.

_____. 1971. False scents and cold trails: the prepublication criticism of the Merriam Third. Journal of English Linguistics 5. 101-21.

_____, and Virginia G. McDavid. 1964. Plurals of nouns of measure in the United States. Studies in languages and linguistics in honor of Charles C. Fries, ed. Albert H. Marckwardt, 271-301. Ann Arbor: The English Language Institute, University of Michigan.

_____ 1979. Intuitive rules and factual evidence: /-sp, -st, -sk/ plus {-Z}. Linguistic and literary studies in honor of Archibald A. Hill, ed. M. A. Jazayery, E. C. Polomé, and W. Winter. The Hague: Mouton. Vol. 2: Descriptive linguistics, 72-90.

McDavid, Virginia G. 1956. Verb forms in the North-Central States and Upper Midwest. Dissertation, University of Minnesota.

McQuown, Norman A. 1970. The natural history of an interview. Manuscripts in Cultural Anthropology 15. Chicago: The Joseph Regenstein Library, University of Chicago.

Mencken, H. L. 1963. The American language: one-volume abridged edition with new material, ed. Raven I. McDavid, Jr., with the assistance of David W. Maurer. New York: Alfred A. Knopf.

Mitchell, A. G., and Arthur Delbridge. 1965. The speech of Australian adolescents. Sydney: Angus and Robertson.

Orkin, Mark M. 1970. Speaking Canadian English. Toronto: General Publishing Company, Ltd.

Orton, Harold, et al. 1962-71. Survey of English dialects. Introduction, 4 vols., each in 3 parts. Leeds: E. J. Arnold and Son, Ltd.

Paddock, Harold. 1966. A dialect survey of Carbonear, Newfoundland. MA thesis, Memorial University of Newfoundland.

Pike, Kenneth L. 1945. The intonation of American English. Ann Arbor: University of Michigan Press.

Shuy, Roger, Walter A. Wolfram, and William K. Riley. 1968.
    Field procedures in an urban language study. Washington:
    Center for Applied Linguistics.
Sledd, James H. 1964. Review of A linguistic introduction to the
    history of English, by Morton Bloomfield and Leonard New-
    mark. Language 40. 465-83.
Trager, George L., and Henry Lee Smith, Jr. 1951. An outline of
    English structure. Studies in Linguistics, Occasional Pa-
    per 3.
Uskup, Frances L. 1974. Social markers in urban speech: a study
    of Chicago elites. Dissertation, Illinois Institute of Tech-
    nology.
Williamson, Juanita V. 1967. A phonological and morphological
    study of the speech of the Negro of Memphis, Tennessee.
    Publication of the American Dialect Society 50.
_____. 1970. Selected features of speech: black and white. Col-
    lege Language Association Journal 13. 419-33.
Wolfram, Walter A. 1969. A sociolinguistic description of Detroit
    Negro speech. Washington: Center of Applied Linguistics.
Wright, Joseph. 1898-1905. The English dialect dictionary. 6 vols.
    Oxford: Henry Frowde.
_____. 1905. The English dialect grammar. Oxford: Henry
    Frowde.

Part II. Sociolinguistics and Dialectology

10 | The Sociology of Language

Introduction

The Concept of a Linguistic Standard

Much of the problem of developing a language program for the schools grows out of a widespread acceptance of the assumption that there is a standard variety of the language which for various reasons has become a model of usage. Unfortunately, however, this assumption is not always based on an examination of the facts of usage; indeed, many of those who discuss the need for a standard do not understand the rationale from which standard languages have developed, consciously and otherwise.

In a tribal society, without literacy and the need to preserve permanent religious or commercial or literary records, there is little overt reason for a generally recognized standard. Its need is fulfilled, if at all, in two ways: first, by the attempt to preserve intact, in oral tradition, texts of cultural importance, even though over a period of time there arises considerable divergence between the language of the texts and that of everyday use; second, by the recognition by the tribe, in a situation of linguistic free trade, that certain of its members — usually those vested with roles of some traditional importance — are better models of usage than their fellow tribesmen. Neither of these situations need happen; in some speech communities, various bands or tribal groupings may dispute vociferously about which variety of their language is correct. Those who have worked with the Ojibwa-Ottawa of the Great Lakes, or with the various peoples of Malaita in the Solomons, report all kinds of dialectal prejudices arising from the relative power of groups whose language is mutually intelligible or out of the history of blood feuds and civil wars. Still, within a particular tribe, one of these two developments will probably occur.

The situations described above continued with the development of writing and of more highly structured political units. Writing was at first the possession of a tiny minority (even today, less than half the population of India is literate); it was devised for what the culture considered practical ends — maintenance of commercial records and preservation of sacred texts. It would naturally be established on the basis of the most prestigious form of the language, and its use for religious texts would make this form even more prestigious. (We will leave to others the problem of a writing system's becoming outdated in terms of the current state of the language). As states became wealthier, there was increasing need for a standard language by which the more important business of the community could be transacted. Increasing literacy tended to increase the demand for a standard; the development of printing — and of other media for providing identical copies of a text in large numbers at low cost — made it more useful to have a linguistic frame of reference generally recognized as standard; the rise of technology made uniformity of vocabulary and syntax more desirable to prevent misunderstanding.

The prestige of literary models, too, has strengthened the appeal of a standard language, though not in all respects. For, as anyone knows, many of the most prestigious works, in whatever language, do not reflect current usage. The Homeric poems were recited in Periclean Athens in an archaic variety of Greek; the idiom of Chaucer or of Shakespeare is not that of twentieth-century America; and many of our contemporaries feel that the only legitimate text of the Bible is the King James Version completed in 1611, archaic even then in grammatical practice, and in some details (such as the use of the second-person pronouns) more archaic than the fourteenth-century language of Chaucer. As Charles C. Fries (1940) was wont to say, while it is true that such writers as Chaucer and Shakespeare helped to give cultural prestige to London English, it is also true that they wrote in London English because it was already the most prestigious variety of the language. In general, then, a variety of the language becomes the standard because it is used by the people who make the important decisions for the speech community, and over the years it will change not only with the ineluctable passage of time but also with changes in the membership of the group of decision-makers.

There is no intrinsic reason why the standard language must be an everyday spoken language of the territory in which it is used. There are numerous examples of contrary situations in the past. In Asia Minor, circa 1000 B.C., Akkadian — the language of Assyria — was widely used in countries where other languages were spoken. The conquests of Alexander the Great spread Greek as an administrative language into Egypt and as far east as India; it retained this status in much of this area until the Islamic conquests, while Latin — once a local Italic dialect — was established in the western half of the Roman Empire. Similarly, with the Islamic conquests, the classical Arabic of the Koran became the standard for the Caliphate and its successor states. And even today, despite the liquidation of colonial empires, English and French are languages of higher education and of much intercommunication in parts of Asia and Africa where local languages are numerous and of minimum mutual intelligibility.

Nor does the standard language have to be a contemporaneous spoken tongue; it may represent the usage of a bygone era. Hieroglyphic Egyptian, used as late as the period of Greek domination, was an archaic variety, considerably removed from the popular Demotic. Among practicing Moslems, there is a widespread feeling that the only standard for the language is the seventh-century variety in which the Koran is written; all twentieth-century varieties of Arabic, no matter how widely spread, are adjudged as no language at all (Joos 1962). And in present-day Greece, there is a powerful movement to value usage good to the extent that it rejects contemporary practice and "purifies" itself according to ancient models.

Sometimes what has become the standard language (even though not consciously archaic) is sharply different from the everyday language of affairs. The literary Latin we study in schools today was probably pronounced much the same way as the everyday Latin of Caesar's time, and it seems to have had the same system of inflections of noun and verb and other parts of speech; but because it was consciously shaped by rhetoricians according to the models of Greek excellence, its syntax was not that of everyday use, and its vocabulary was strikingly different. For instance, the everyday word for "horse" was caballus, from which descended all the present-day Romance designations for the animal; but in literary Latin it was equus.

As we have suggested before, most of the standard languages of today have arisen by the process of trial and error — by the establishment of the prestigious speech of one community or area that had, itself, already established commercial or political leadership over other communities in which varieties of the language were spoken. Latin followed the march of the Roman legions — first throughout Italy and then over Western Europe — and later the paths of the Christian missionaries. The standard varieties of Italian, French, Spanish, Russian, and British English reflect the cultural and economic preeminence — of various kinds — won by Rome and Florence, Paris, Toledo, Moscow, and London. And though the German-speaking community had been atomized politically for more than six centuries before the founding of the Second Reich in 1870, the prestige of the Saxon Chancellery, between imperial Austria to the South and the Hansa League to the North, was such that its variety of German became accepted as a written standard, which Luther used for his translation of Scripture.

In recent years, however, there has been some conscious thought as to the shape a national tongue might take. In Norway, after the personal union under the Swedish crown was substituted in 1814 for the Danish sovereignty that had endured since the fourteenth century, champions of cultural autonomy — and later of independence — felt that the national tongue should bear a closer relationship to the speech of the people than did the slightly modified Danish, or Dano-Norwegian, that had served so long as a standard. Led by a group of folklorists, a movement arose to establish a Landsmål, based on the folk dialects; a countermovement naturally developed toward keeping the older standard or Riksmål, though modifying it somewhat in the direction of everyday speech. The debate continued until, in effect, the two varieties of Norwegian — now known as Nynorsk and Bokmål respectively — were both recognized as standard, though each has since been modified in the direction of the other, and the industrialization

and urbanization of Norway has given <u>Bokmål</u> a heavy preponderance
of present-day speakers. In Prague, after the liberation of Czechoslovakia in World War I, Czech linguists took an active part in determining the directions the standard language — the first standard
variety of modern Czech — would take. More spectacular have been
some of the instances of deliberate language engineering after World
War II, in the new nations of Africa and Asia. Practical decisions
have often been made in terms of establishing a standard tongue that
would be intelligible to the greatest number of speakers of the various dialects. And at least one decision, in Indonesia, was based on
political considerations: It was desirable to have, as a national language, a variety of Malay that was equally intelligible to speakers of
Javanese and Sumatran dialects; it was also desirable — in view of
the long rivalry between the two major islands — to base the new
standard on a dialect that was neither Javanese nor Sumatran. The
result was the selection of a dialect spoken by relatively few people,
a dialect without political connotations, and therefore generally accepted throughout the republic. Now, thanks to a centrally directed
educational system, it is well on its way to general use, and native
speakers of the new standard are appearing, since it is encouraged
in the homes of the educated.

     As standard varieties of language have become established,
a demand has arisen for some sort of arbiter which should strive to
keep the standard pure and free from the contaminations of unbridled
change. Usually the demand has been for an academy of the élite,
the authority of whose judgment might be thought to outweigh the
taste of the uneducated masses. The first of the important academies
was the Accademia della Crusca, of Florence; more famous, probably, has been l'Académie francaise, established by Cardinal Riche-
lieu. Its forty "Immortals," meeting once a week, work through a
small segment of the alphabet at each session, and a word they do
not recognize is supposedly consigned to linguistic limbo until its
turn comes up again, some thirty or forty years later. Other countries, such as Spain and the Soviet Union, have their academies, too;
all are charged with the awful responsibility of resisting the dele-
terious effects of uncontrolled linguistic change. In practice, we
learn, their influence has been far less than their creators expected; words come and go, and meanings change, regardless of official
decisions. And in fact the academies themselves may take a liberal

(or at least a realistic) attitude toward the problems of linguistic change.

The English-speaking peoples, so far, have never established such an academy. During the Restoration period (1660-1685), there was a strong feeling that an English academy might be desirable; but even among those who wished for it, there was so strong a rivalry as to who would be the presiding officer that it was impossible to agree on the articles of incorporation. Later, it was felt that Dr. Johnson, through his Dictionary, had fulfilled the aims of an academy. But even the authority of this work waned with the passing of time, and the English settled down to adjudging the acceptability of language on an unspoken consensus of the educated and well-bred.

The American search for a standard was almost schizoid in its beginnings. On the one hand, with the national feelings of a newly independent country, there was a desire to establish an American standard, independent of British models; on the other, the awareness of national immaturity encouraged an almost slavish deference to British opinion. There were several movements toward an academy, all unsuccessful. Noah Webster, the prototype of American free enterprise, sought to set himself up as linguistic arbiter. As many observers have noted, he rejected British authority, not because he rejected the notion of authority but because he wished to establish his own. Yet, he did succeed in convincing Americans that models of good usage must be sought among themselves and not in Britain. With national maturity, it became evident (a) that American standard English must be based on American practice, (b) that there was a healthy variety on the standard level, since each region was bound to select its model from those whom it considered the most prestigious speakers and writers, and (c) that linguistic changes — both obsolescence and innovation — were not only inevitable but also healthy, responding to the inexorable passage of time. Still, there was always a minority who sought to arrest the inevitable, such as the editorial writer for the late Saturday Evening Post who in 1946 called for an authoritarian lexicographer who would purge the language of the superfluous words created by frontier wits and saloon columnists. And the ordeal of the Merriam Webster's Third New International Dictionary, following its publication in 1961, suggests that American authoritarianism is more vigorous than many of us would like to think.

Yet academies, in the long run, have relatively little influence on the course of a language. French purists may deplore the corruption of their language by the inundation of Americanisms; but if an American term is useful in the everyday business of Parisians, they are not going to wait until its next alphabetical turn before the Immortals of the Académie, nor are scientists and technicians likely to be constrained in their invention of new terms. A language, after all, must respond to the needs of the people who use it. If the lack of a guiding authority is likely to encourage an uncontrolled efflorescence of vocabulary and syntactic structures, each innovation still has to prove itself in the marketplace; the test of its fitness is the practical one of whether or not people are willing to use it.

In fact, one should worry less about inadequate control than about too much. We have a striking example of the latter in the fate of Latin as a language of international communication. During the Middle Ages it had proved vigorous and adaptable, capable of taking in new words to deal with new concepts — however inelegant it might have been by Ciceronian standards. Then, in the Renaissance, more elegant models of Latinity were provided, and an author's Latin — regardless of his message — came to be deplored if it failed to measure up to classical excellence. Latin was no longer a working language, adaptable to any number of practical situations; it was a social ornament, with a standard of excellence that could be achieved only by a tiny minority. And despairing of achieving a satisfactory standard of Latinity, scholars and scientists gradually turned to the vernaculars, where there was no Cicero against whom the style, if not the content, of their message would be measured. Meanwhile, other forces — the growing wealth of the middle classes, the extension of education, and the Protestant movement to make the Scriptures available in the vernacular — had already ended, to some extent, the traditional domination of Latin; but the ossification of Latin style did nothing to delay the disuse of the language.

The Standard and Actual Usage

It should go without saying that — except for highly codified situations, such as communications between aircraft and ground installations — there is considerable variety in the way a standard language is used by its speakers; and the larger the speech community, the greater the amount of variety possible. In some instances striking differences in pronunciation, in vocabulary, and even in grammar — especially in the spoken variety of the language — may be permissible as the subject of discourse becomes more homely and intimate. But in all standard languages there will be variety, and there will be change with the passing of time. To take British Standard English as an example, since the eighteenth century there have been important changes in the pronunciation system (notably the loss of post-vocalic /-r/ in <u>barn</u>, <u>beard</u>, <u>board</u>, and the like); in the incidence of particular sounds, such as the "broad <u>a</u>" /a/; and in the development of new syntactic structures, such as the progressive passive <u>a new house is being built on our street</u> — to say nothing of changes in the vocabulary and in the meanings of words.

Attitudes toward usage vary widely in a speech community. In the more traditional societies with rather clearly defined classes, the aristocratic tradition prevails that a person has the right, even the obligation, to shift according to his social situation; a person will be suspect if he is too conspicuously "correct" in situations demanding informal usage. But where there is social mobility, it is the wont of the newly risen to become very rigid in their attitudes, especially toward the informal usage of the group from which they have risen. In communities settled heavily by immigrants with a foreign-language background, the English is likely to be more formal and bookish than where there is a native English colloquial tradition.

Public-school teachers are likely to be more rigid in their attitudes than graduate professors, and newspaper columnists are likely to be even more rigid; the editors of women's magazines are most rigid of all. In all these instances, there is likely to be a limited training in the actual structure and history of the language, a reliance on such older artifacts as the "Blue Back Speller" and on such newer ones as lists of common grammatical errors and words most commonly mispronounced. Moreover, there is a tradition in America that the English teacher has an obligation to impose a rigid standard on his students, so that the revelation of one's professional identity in a social situation is likely to curdle the conversation with such remarks — not always in jest — that the others had better watch their grammar. This tendency, to be sure, is also reinforced by the fact that most English teachers — indeed, most teachers — are drawn from the newly risen lower-middle class, the group most unsure of their own status and therefore most concerned with imposing a rigid standard. But many of the laymen — chiefly, also, of lower-middle-class origins despite their current prosperity — are even more restrictive in their attitudes; they feel that all those who have to do with the language professionally have not only the right but also the duty to impose rigid standards on everyone else. It is amusing that in the controversy over the "lowered standards" of the Merriam Third (1961-64), editorial writers, newspaper columnists, and casual critics-at-large were the most violent in their condemnation; litterateurs and teachers in the schools were often perturbed, but the professional students of the language generally accepted the principles upon which the new dictionary had been constructed, even though they were not always happy about the way these principles had been put into practice.

It is not surprising that most people are not fully aware of their own usage. It is a commonplace for a field investigator to have an informant deny that a given word is used in the community — only to hear it five minutes later, or to have an informant sternly condemn a grammatical construction he habitually uses in his own unguarded conversation. In the controversy over the Merriam Third, The New York Times editorially condemned President Kennedy for using the verb finalize, which the Third had recognized as standard, only to have it revealed that some of the citations upon which the acceptance of the word had been based were found in the columns of the Times. And in casual reading, early in 1969, I encountered in the Times — zealously guarded by Theodore Bernstein, one of the most scrupulous of word-watchers — a half-dozen examples of the confusion of who and whom, nonstandard agreement of subject and verb, and other deviations from the purist's canon of good usage.

Social Dialect and Social Class

Dialect and Class Membership

As we have pointed out, the prestigious social dialect originates in the upper-class usage of a culturally important part of the speech community. In various ways, differing from one speech community to another, a number of the features of this standard language will spread from its original focus to the upper classes in satellite communities. Then, as new groups rise in the social scale, they will assimilate these models of good usage. But even members of lower-class groups may assimilate the prestigious variety of the language, at least for situations in which they come in contact with the public. It is notorious in England that butlers and club stewards are among the most meticulous speakers of British Received Pronunciation. And in the older South, no one could speak the standard variety of English more elegantly than Negro house servants ministering at a formal dinner.

What seems to be the case is that a person's habitual social contacts will provide him an opportunity to develop a range of linguistic behavior. The wider the range of contacts, the greater the social assurance, the sharper the intelligence and powers of observation of a speaker, the greater the likelihood of his being able to switch not only from one degree of formality to another, but from standard to nonstandard language as well.

And, of course, if individuals rise from one social class to another, they will take with them some of their language practices, even while they are assimilating the practices of their new environment. In this way, upper-class usage escapes petrification and continues to express the range of experience of those who make the important decisions in the speech community.

Social and Regional Differences, and Other Modes of Variation

In many language communities, where a more or less rigid standard is established (or at least assumed), the word dialect is pejorative, describing a form of the language that an educated person would never condescend to use. In others, it is applied to the speech of quaint old people in out-of-the-way places. In still others, it describes the funny way everybody talks but me and those I grew up with. Scientifically, a dialect is simply a habitual variety of a language — regional or social or both — set off from other such habitual varieties by a complex of features of grammar and pronunciation and vocabulary. But despite the attempts of linguists to provide adequate definitions and descriptions, the term dialect is still too often used pejoratively, and some of the best-known materials devised for coping with striking social differences in language still set up an opposition between standard language and "local dialect." For this reason, as Haugen has suggested, it is probably best to drop the term dialect altogether and confine oneself to a discussion of regional and social variations in language (Haugen 1966).

Regional varieties, however exotic from one's personal point of view, are not corruptions of primordial excellence. Rather, each regional and local variety, on whatever level, has its own history, and is the result of a complex of forces such as (a) settlement history, (b) routes of migration and communication, (c) prestige or isolation of the community, and (d) its social structure and educational system. In the United States, every local variety of English — to say nothing of the more important regional ones — has developed from a mixture of various British dialects, plus foreign-language settlements, plus varying degrees of contact with the Standard English of the British Isles and with other varieties of American English. In each area, thanks to the tradition of cultural and political autonomy of the various colonies and states, a prestige group developed. And one might say that in each community the standard variety of speech is essentially a modification of the basic local type of speech by the tradition of Standard English. This influence of Standard English, as has already been pointed out, is such that the vocabulary of the most formal varieties of discourse, oral and written (especially the vocabularies of science and technology), is fairly uniform throughout the English of the Western Hemisphere, indeed throughout the English-speaking world. And grammar is pretty much the same among educated speakers, especially in formal writing. There are very few tags — one of them being woken as a participle, where Americans would use woke or waked — that tell us a book is by a Briton and not a North American. In educated informal usage there are a few more touchstones — Britons will say have you any ? whereas Americans will say do you have any ? — but even these are not numerous. Nor do we find many grammatical differences, on the standard level, among the various regional types of American English. In pronunciation, however, and in the more familiar parts of the vocabulary, these differences are much more numerous.

Social differences, on the other hand, are rather striking so
far as the extent of the vocabulary is concerned, simply because the
less educated have a narrower cultural experience. These differences are not likely to be reflected per se in the humble part of the
vocabulary; a Southerner of whatever degree of education is likely to
know a dragon fly as a snake doctor or mosquito hawk, if he comes
from an environment where the insect is seen in everyday life. As
far as pronunciation is concerned, all classes of speakers in a given
community — with few exceptions — are likely to have the same system of vowels and vowels of the same phonetic quality, but there may
be social differences in the way these vowels occur in different
words. Thus, in eastern Massachusetts or in the Pittsburgh area,
such pairs of words as cot and caught, collar and caller, are homonyms on all levels of usage, and in most of the upland South all speakers dipthongize the /æ/ of can't — when they do not replace it with
/e/ so that it rhymes with paint. But in New York City the homonymy of coil and curl is a feature of old-fashioned speech, and in
such words as bad and dog a lower variety of the vowel is felt to be
more elegant than a higher. Everywhere the substitution of the /ai/
diphthong for /ɔi/ , as in boil, joint and join, is felt to be a bit
quaint, despite the fact that it is hallowed by the rhymes of Alexander
Pope.

Differences in the consonants have been studied less inten-
sively than those in the vowels, but it is possible that some of these
differences may be of greater social significance. Certainly, the
lack of /θð/ as distinct from /t d, f v, s z/ is a clear social marker, and the omission of intervocalic /-r-/ in such words as barrel
and tomorrow is likely to be, as is the use of a bilabial variety of
/f v/ instead of the usual labiodental kind. (This last feature, like
the equally stigmatizing dentalization of /t d n s z r l/, is usually
associated with the imperfectly acculturated speaker from a home in
which a foreign language is spoken.) Yet the homonymy of Hugh and
you, or of whales and wails, is a matter of indifference.

But differences in grammar are the clearest indices of social difference. Various lists have been provided (one of the most
useful is that published by the Southeastern Educational Laboratory,
of Atlanta). It is sufficient to indicate a few of the types of grammatical differences:

1. Absence of inflectional endings for noun plurals, noun
   genitives, third-singular present indicative, past tense,
   present participle, past participle.
2. Analogical forms such as <u>hisself</u>, <u>theirselves</u> and the
   absolute genitives <u>ourn</u>, <u>yourn</u>, <u>hisn</u>, <u>hern</u>, and <u>theirn</u>.
3. Double comparatives and superlatives, such as <u>more
   prettier</u>, <u>most lovingest</u>.
4. Omission of the copula <u>be</u> with predicate nouns, predicate adjectives, present and past participles.
5. <u>Be</u> as a finite verb.
6. Differences in the principal parts of verbs, such as
   <u>growed</u>, <u>drawed</u>, <u>taken</u> as a past tense, <u>rid</u> as the past
   participle of <u>ride</u>, <u>clum</u> or <u>clim</u> as the past tense or past
   participle of <u>climb</u>.

The ways in which social varieties of a language differ are
essentially the same as those which distinguish regional varieties.
The difference is that in one instance certain linguistic forms are
shared by an entire area or region, regardless of class, and in the
other, forms are shared by the users of the standard language, regardless of region. For standard usage is much more uniform than
nonstandard.

Since we are all more or less ethnocentric, and since the
pronunciation of such a community as Charleston, South Carolina,
may seem as strange as the idiom of Hell's Kitchen, we can be pardoned our occasional assumption that Charlestonians do not speak
good English. To one who knows the self-assuredness of the proper
Charlestonian, however, such an assumption is ludicrous on the
face of it. It is necessary to be sure of the class of the speaker, in
relation to the traditions of his community, before judging his language.

Clearly, social varieties of a language, like regional ones,
are not deviations from a uniform and pristine standard. Each has
its own history. Cockney, a nonstandard variety of London English,
has a long history, developing parallel with standard London speech,
occasionally giving words and usages, occasionally taking them. The
same is true of the rural uneducated speech of the Southern Appalachians, alongside Southern upland standard, or of any local

nonstandard variety of the language alongside its standard counterpart. Neither is a corruption or derivative of the other; though they
have undoubtedly influenced each other, each is a legitimate variety
of the language in its own right.

It is also important to distinguish social varieties of language, in their habitual sense, from other kinds of language variation. Formal language is not necessarily better than informal; in
fact, as J. S. Kenyon and others have pointed out, there is a formal
substandard, marked by the use of such hyperforms as I have went
instead of the more informal I done gone. Slang is a matter of vogue,
not of social class. And though the pungent argot of lower-class
teen-age gangs is sometimes described as a class idiom, it is the
same kind of phenomenon one finds in any closely knit group with a
common set of interests, whether safe-crackers, model-railroad
fans, or Anglo-Catholic clergy. And the most important features
that set off nonstandard usage from standard are often very old in the
language, though (like the features of standard usage) they often appear in new combinations.

Methods of Investigation

One should expect the techniques of investigating social varieties of language to have grown from those developed for investigating regional varieties. In fact, one is justified in saying that
some serious work with regional varieties of language is necessary
if one is to interpret social varieties intelligently. The first linguistic atlases — those of Germany and France (and those modeled on
them) — were really studies of regional differences in substandard
usage, with the standard language everywhere taken as a given norm:
only the "characteristic local dialect" was sought by these projects.
Not until the Atlas of Italy and Southern Switzerland was there any
attempt to assay social differences, and then only for the larger communities.

In the United States, the first two systematic studies of social differences in usage were American English Grammar, by Fries
(1940), and the Linguistic Atlas of New England, by Kurath and his
associates (1939-43). Fries's study involved the analysis of a large

body of correspondence directed to a government bureau during
World War I. Since the letters dealt with personal or family hard-
ships, one could assume that each writer was on good linguistic behavior, attempting to achieve his notions of proper style. Furthermore, since the dossiers provided a great deal of biographical information about each writer, it was possible to classify them on extralinguistic evidence as written by users of Standard, Common or Vulgar English (or as unclassifiable). Those that were classifiable were
then examined for their grammatical practices, so that it was possi-
bile to state objectively what were the actual differences between
standard and vulgar usage. Though some of the details of the study
may be out of date (after all, the body of users of Standard American English is quite different from what it was fifty years ago), it remains a model. Furthermore, its statement of the obligations of the
schools in the matter of teaching standard usage is still one of the
clearest, most precise, and most emphatic.

    The Linguistic Atlas of New England was the first study of
its kind to investigate systematically the social variations in a speech
community (the other regional atlases, still unpublished but in various stages of completion, have been modeled on the New England
study). Instead of seeking speakers of "the local dialect," Kurath
sought three local cultural types who were alike only in naturalness
of utterance and in identification with their community for at least
two generations and for as many more as possible:

> 1. In every community, an attempt was made to interview
> a representative of the oldest living native generation with
> a minimum of formal education, travel, and other outside
> interference.
> 2. In every community, likewise, an attempt was made to
> interview a middle-aged speaker with about a high school
> education, and somewhat greater reading, travel, and gen-
> eral sophistication.
> 3. Finally, in about one community of every five, the field
> workers interviewed a cultivated speaker, who was usually
> a college graduate and a member of one of the oldest fami-
> lies — presumably a representative of the best local cul-
> tural traditions.

Although any student of social structure would concede that
every community probably has more than three social classes, this
selection of informants does provide an opportunity to examine the
differences between cultivated speech and the extreme uneducated
types, and (by including the intermediate group) to suggest the probable direction of change. Traditionally, the sharpest break in such
democratic communities as the small towns of the Middle West has
been found between the first and second groups; in such communities
as those in the Old South, where the existence of an elite has been
taken for granted, the break occurs between the middle group and the
cultivated. However, changes in the economic and social structure
of a community may produce changes in values: With the spread of
higher education and industrialization in the South, the new decision-
makers are increasingly drawn from outside the traditional elite, and
new models of language prestige are arising alongside the old. Conversely, in northern cities, massive immigration of lower-class
speakers from outside the region — whether from foreign countries
or from other regions of the United States — may have created sharper social distinctions in language. Nevertheless, the framework provided by studies on the Atlas model makes it possible to interpret recent changes in the social status of language varieties, however the
structure of the community may have changed.

Outside of drawing conclusions from the existing body of
Atlas data, as in McDavid (1946, 1948), there have been various
modifications of method; Pederson's study of pronunciation in Chicago (1965) involved a closer network of informants, with attention to
descendants of the ethnic minorities that have settled in the metropolitan area. Some younger informants — high school students — were
interviewed with an abbreviated questionnaire to permit a more accurate judgment on the possibility of increasing linguistic cleavage
between Negroes and whites, but, like the primary informants, all
these were natives of the metropolitan area. Pederson also introduced a more complicated socioeconomic classification of informants,
by which one can determine more easily where or whether linguistic
fault-lines are developing in a speech community. The follow-up study
(McDavid and Austin 1966) sought to polarize the distinctions between
standard and nonstandard speech in the Chicago area by concentrating on the two extremes and eliminating the middle group. Since the
problems of the schools had been aggravated by recent immigration

from other sections, the design of this project included recent arrivals as well as natives. It was noted in both of these surveys that
there were no appreciable differences between middle-class Negroes
and middle-class whites; furthermore, the oldest generation of Chicago-born Negroes, of whatever class, differed more among themselves than they did from their white contemporaries. However, with
the patterns of residential segregation and decreasing economic opportunity (through the phasing-out of the unskilled jobs on which earlier immigrants had always counted for getting a leg up), the speech
of the younger generation of Chicago-born Negroes often differed
very sharply from the Middle Western speech norms of younger Chicago-born whites, (a) in the tendency to lose post-vocalic /-r/, (b)
in such structural contrasts as that between such pairs as <u>morning</u>
and <u>mourning</u>, (c) in phonemic incidence, as /-z-/ in <u>greasy</u> rather
than the characteristic Chicago /-s-/, and (d) in the use of a number
of nonstandard verb forms that are practically unknown in the Middle
West. Furthermore, by an accompanying instrument designed to
evaluate the status of pronunciations, it was revealed that, in Chicago, Southern varieties of pronunciation — regardless of the race
or education of the speaker — were usually characterized as rural,
uneducated, and Negro.

The studies of William Labov, of Columbia University, have
concentrated on a smaller number of linguistic features but have
used a relatively large number of informants, a variety of styles, and
judgments about the social status of the speakers (1963). A pilot
study of the diphthongs /ai au/, as in <u>ride</u> and <u>cloud</u>, on Martha's
Vineyard disclosed a tendency for the centering beginning of the diphthongs (which had been recorded in the New England <u>Atlas</u>), to be lost
to the degree that a speaker was oriented away from the island; that
is, it was likely to be lost among those of the younger generation who
had most of their contacts with off-island people and who intended to
make their careers on the mainland. Conversely, it was retained
among those who had identified themselves with the island and intended to remain.

In his study of the Lower East Side of New York (1966),
Labov concentrated on five linguistic variables: postvocalic /-r/,
the initial consonants /θ ð/ of <u>think</u> and <u>then</u>, the vowels /æ ɔ/ of <u>bad</u>
and <u>dog</u>. A range of formality was sought, from the reading of

potentially homonymous pairs of words to accounts of children's
games or of an incident in which the narrator thought he might be
killed. Since the informants were selected more or less at random,
in the follow-up of a previous sociological analysis of the neighborhood, Labov was able to include such ethnic groups as Negroes,
Italians, and Jews, whose families had arrived too recently to be considered for the Atlas investigations of New York (conversely, by Atlas standards he included no cultivated speakers, and the older white
Protestant stock of New York was not represented). His conclusions
were: (a) that postvocalic /-r/ was being reestablished in New York,
(b) that the substitution of affricates or stops for the spirants /θ ð/
was particularly characteristic of lower-class speech, and (c) that
in bad and dog, lower vowels had more prestige than higher ones.
These conclusions were reached both on the basis of the characteristic utterances of each social class and on the basis of formality, it
being assumed that the more careful the style of utterance, the greater the likelihood that the reader would approach the real or fancied
linguistic norm of the community. Furthermore, New York respondents tended to value styles of speech in terms of this scale, and to
attribute to their own speech a higher ranking on this scale than it
actually had. Whether or not speakers in other communities are so
much aware of a scale of values as New Yorkers seem to be, let
alone of the same scale, Labov has clearly introduced an interesting
new dimension into the evaluation of social differences in language.

The study of Detroit by Shuy and his associates (1966) com-
bines the techniques of the Linguistic Atlas and those of Labov with
a careful demographic investigation beforehand and a sophisticated
computer program afterward. Employing a selection of elementary
schools, public and parochial (by census tracts, with special care
that no major ethnic group was slighted), his team of investigators
completed more than 700 hour-and-a-half interviews in one summer,
including a generous sample of free conversation and responses to a
selection of the most significant items from the questionnaire for
the Linguistic Atlas of the North-Central States. For each household
selected, there were interviews with an upper-grade student and a
parent; and, whenever the situation permitted, there were interviews
with an older sibling, a grandparent, or both. Although the process-
ing of the data has not been completed, preliminary examination suggests that social differences are more a matter of incidence than of

fundamental typology; that is, social groups differ in the frequency
with which they use certain linguistic forms rather than in the structure of their varieties of language. For instance, though the less educated Negroes — thanks to historical forces — seem to show the
sharpest divergence from the local standard, there seem to be no
forms used exclusively by Negroes or whites. Again, there were attempts to elicit evaluations of the race and social class of selected
speakers; Detroiters seem to judge race correctly some 80 percent
of the time (there were, however, no specimens of Southern poor-
white speech on the tapes used for this purpose, though the group is
an important numerical fraction in metropolitan Detroit), with the
greatest number of inaccuracies in the evaluations of the educated
Negroes. Social class was judged less accurately; there was some
tendency to downgrade the class of Negroes and upgrade that of
whites. Modifications of Shuy's approach have been introduced in
other projects, notably by Pederson and his students in metropolitan
Atlanta and in other Georgia communities.

Since Linguistic Atlas techniques have concentrated on
short-answer questions, they provide a less satisfactory body of evidence for syntax, stress, intonation, and paralanguage than they do
for vocabulary, vowels and consonants, and inflections. Even the
modifications by Labov are not completely satisfactory in these respects; Shuy's are somewhat better. Since syntactic differences
create some of the most painful classroom difficulties for Negroes,
there have been several recent investigations designed to provide
extensive corpora of connected discourse which could be analyzed.
Perhaps the most important of these in print is Conversations in a
Negro American Dialect (Loman 1967), a by-product of the Urban
Language Study of the District of Columbia. The study reveals —
as does almost every study of a similar population — striking differences between the syntax of lower-class urban Negro adolescents
and that of middle-class Midwestern white adults.

What is yet unanswered, however, is the question as to
whether these differences are really typological or — as Shuy suggested in Detroit — merely statistical; informal observation of the
unguarded speech of Southern whites (even highly educated ones) suggests that at least some of these differences may be due to a greater
difference in the South, among all social groups, between formal and

informal speech than one finds elsewhere. The current study of adolescent white speech in Cullman County, Alabama — an area almost
without Negroes — may provide some of the clues; yet there is a
possibility that the rural life-style may not be as conducive to the
kind of highly verbal juvenile gang-life that one encounters in cities.
Perhaps what is necessary is the simultaneous study, with identical
techniques, of Negro and Southern white groups under similar conditions of translation to a northern industrial environment, such as one
might find in Akron or Detroit or Cincinnati. Perhaps some of the
answers will be suggested in Dunlap's study (1974) of the syntax of a
hundred fifth-grade students in Atlanta. In any event, the studies recently made and those in progress show the need for dropping rigid
dogmas about language standards and for examining the speech of
many communities and social groups on their own merits.

Two other kinds of studies might be mentioned — the British investigations by David Abercrombie of Edinburgh and by Basil
Bernstein of London. As we have observed, in addition to being a
superb descriptive and instrumental phonetician, Abercrombie has
made a number of shrewd observations on the relative status of various British "accents," or patterns of pronunciation. Upper-class
London pronunciation, or RP, is accepted everywhere, though in
Edinburgh or Dublin it may have no edge on cultivated Scots or Anglo-
Irish. What constitutes this upper-class standard, however, is as
subject to change as any other standard; with the rise of the welfare
state and the current prestige of such figures as Harold Wilson,
Twiggy, and the Rolling Stones, it is difficult to imagine that the older speech values of country estates and gentleman's clubs will survive intact, and with the expansion of higher education and economic
opportunities, there may be changes analogous to those that have
taken place in the prestigious speech of New York City or the American South.

Bernstein has shown less interest in the taxonomy of linguistic forms than in cognitive styles. In a series of articles he has
pointed out that the differences in such styles reflect the essential
differences in world outlook between the middle classes and the working classes, the former being more verbal and more inclined to reason, the latter being more inclined to simple answers or physical responses. The cognitive styles of the two groups he labels respectively

as an <u>elaborated code</u> and a <u>simple code</u> with the former susceptible
to more variations in style and more amenable to abstract thinking.
This division is a plausible one; to some extent it replicates the conclusions of Fries in his <u>American English Grammar</u> (1940) that the essential difference between Standard English and vulgar English is
less in the details of usage than in the greater richness of the former
— in vocabulary, in sentence patterns, and in the variety of conjunc-
tions and prepositions. But there are exceptions: we can all recall
the prosperous citizen — and literature is full of such characters as
Fielding's Squire Western — who despite all kinds of outward advantages seems able to discourse on only a limited range of topics, such
as farming, hunting, or finance. And as every college teacher knows,
the ability to use abstractions glibly is not necessarily accompanied
by any depth of understanding.

Not all aspects of social differences in communication have
been adequately studied; there is nothing sensible we can say about
stress, intonation, and paralanguage until the long-overdue regional
comparisons have been made. But in the generation since Fries's
pioneering study we have accumulated a generous amount of data and
an understanding of the psychological and sociological correlates.
And — unlike such findings in the past — a great deal of this information is already beginning to appear in materials for the schools.

Implications for the Schools

The Nature of Language Differences

What we have found out about language differences, regional
and social, should keep us from repeating some of the old cliches
about the degeneration of language in the mouths of the people. If
the speaker of nonstandard varieties of the language generally has a
smaller vocabulary than his more highly educated neighbor, he has
far more than the five hundred words that were once alleged to be
the limits of peasant speech. What is more important is the realization that all habitual varieties of language are learned in the same
way — through contacts with other speakers. The differences between standard and nonstandard varieties can be explained, not in
terms of intellectual or moral differences, but simply in terms of

differences in social and cultural experience. An awareness of this fact should be the foundation of any program in the language arts. Furthermore, since any educational program is subject to external pressures, it is the responsibility of the teacher of the language, especially the university scholar, to communicate the nature of language differences to parent-teacher associations, school administrations, citizens' boards, newspapers, and the other instrumentalities by which public opinion is formed on educational issues.

The same message might well be used in the classroom, so that dialect differences, whether regional or social, become a source of enrichment of the curriculum. After all, a person's language is one of his most intimate possessions, something that he associates with his family and friends and neighborhood. As such, it is to be respected by all who encounter it — especially in those situations in which a student may be called on to supplement his native variety of the language with another form of discourse for public occasions. So long as the situation is handled with respect for every person's speech-ways, there is no reason why one should not use the varieties of grammar, pronunciation, and vocabulary found in the classroom population to show that language, the most characteristic feature of human behavior, can come in a wide range of patterns. For by the time any child enters the first grade, he has already achieved his most important feat of learning; though he is not yet in control of all the details, he has a tolerable mastery of a variety of his native language — nearly all of the pronunciation features, most of the inflectional patterns (such as they are), and a large number of syntactic structures. What happens thenceforth depends on the opportunities he is given. And whatever the variety of the language, as a simple instrument of intercommunication it is as good as any other variety, and — in the hands of a literary artist — it is capable of expressing all the knowledge and emotions, all the inmost experience of humanity.

From Nonstandard to Standard

But if this is true, why should children be expected to master the standard language, whatever it is? Again, the fact is that some varieties of the language are "more equal" than others. Most of the exchange of public information on which the functioning of our

society depends — including almost all of what is found in print —
is through the standard language. The extension of one's education,
the functioning on the job, the handling of one's affairs with the ever
expanding governmental bureaucracy, the coping with leases and in-
stallment contracts — all these activities demand an ability to understand the formal variety of the standard language, especially in writing. If one's job involves writing, a productive command of it is
necessary as well. And if one's job involves meeting all kinds of citizens, this command must extend to the spoken mode. It is all very
well to argue that a minority group — any minority group — has the
right to its own form of speech; but the argument is hollow if restriction to a single given form of speech shuts this minority off from the
economic and educational opportunities they seek. Here the minority
group as a whole is often wiser than its self-appointed spokesmen;
parents in such groups are the most insistent that the schools teach
their children the kinds of language behavior that will better enable
them to cope with the demands of society.

But what is important is that the schools get rid of the notion that a home dialect — regional or social — is something loath-
some, from which the children must be purged, so that a new kind of
speech (and writing) may be imposed upon them. Not merely the poor
(of whatever race), but all those who differ linguistically from the
model the teachers have set up as a rigid standard of perfection, have
suffered in the past from this attitude. Many Americans, of excellent family and superior educational background, have been ridiculed
and patronized by those who would provide them with an allegedly better kind of English — so that the English teacher becomes not merely
a busybody but also a sadist. Psychologists as well as linguists have
taught us better; we no more have to destroy the home idiom to teach
the standard one (itself with many varieties) than we have to forbid
playing football to those who are trying to learn tennis. The end, in
the long run, is greater fluency, facility, and versatility; our world
is not homogeneous, and no student should be expected to use a single
kind of discourse in coping with all kinds of problems. In this sense,
language education is the work of a lifetime; we should at least hope
that those who direct the language programs in the schools should not
inhibit students from exploiting the resources of the language.

REFERENCES

Dunlap, Howard G. "The Syntax of Fifth-Grade Schoolchildren in
    Atlanta." Publication of the American Dialect Society, Nos.
    61-2, 1974.
Fries, Charles C. American English Grammar. New York: Apple-
    ton-Century-Crofts, 1940.
Haugen, Einar. "Dialect, Language, Nation," American Anthropolo-
    gist, 68 (1966), 922-35.
Joos, Martin. "Homeostasis in English Usage," College Composition
    and Communication, 13 (October, 1962), 18-22.
Kurath, Hans, et al. Linguistic Atlas of New England. 3 vols. (6
    parts) and Handbook. Providence, R.I.: American Council
    of Learned Societies, 1939-43.
Labov, William. "The Social Motivation of a Sound Change," Word,
    19 (1963), 273-309.
_____ The Social Stratification of English in New York City. Wash-
    ington: Center of Applied Linguistics, 1966.
Loman, Bengt A. (ed.) Conversations in a Negro American Dialect.
    Washington: Center for Applied Linguistics, 1967.
McDavid, Raven I., Jr. "Dialect Geography and Social Science
    Problems," Social Forces, 25 (1946), 168-72.
_____ "Postvocalic /-r/ in South Carolina: A Social Analysis,"
    American Speech, 23 (1948), 194-203.
McDavid, Raven I., Jr., and Austin, William M. Communication
    Barriers to the Culturally Deprived. Final Report, Cooper-
    ative Research Project 2107, U.S. Office of Education, 1966.
Pederson, Lee A. The Pronunciation of English in Chicago: Conso-
    nants and Vowels. Publication of the American Dialect So-
    ciety, No. 44, 1965.
Shuy, Roger W., Wolfram, Walter A., and Riley, William K. Lin-
    guistic Correlates of Social Stratification in Detroit Speech.
    Final Report, Cooperative Research Project 6-1347, U.S.
    Office of Education, 1966.

11 | Two Studies of Dialects of English

In Honor of Harold Orton

I

Forty years ago, no variety of the English language had been surveyed by the modern techniques of dialect investigation. Now, at least the first stage of data gathering has been completed for England and the United States, and some of the evidence has been published; a respectable beginning has been made in Scotland; in Canada there are modest first steps towards a national survey, and one has been proposed for Australia. Since there are some interesting differences in objective and method as well as fundamental similarities between the two projects furthest along, the English and the American, it is fitting to compare them in some detail, particularly in a volume dedicated to one of the directors.

Each of these surveys has been designed, essentially, by one person — by Harold Orton in England and by Hans Kurath in the United States. Each director has had experience in the field; Orton, however, did not do any of the actual interviewing for the English survey, while Kurath contributed fifteen field records to the Linguistic Atlas of New England. Both are thorough gentlemen — energetic, generous, and devoted to their work.

There have been several differences in administrative practices. Orton has kept control of the Survey of English Dialects pretty firmly in his own kands, even in retirement. At the outset of the American project, Kurath was aided by an unusually strong advisory committee of distinguished scholars; furthermore, he shared responsibilities and credit with his staff, several of whom — for example, Bernard Bloch, Lee Hultzén and Martin Joos — went on to distinguished careers in their own right. When the archives for the Atlantic Seaboard were transferred to Chicago, and editorial responsibility was assumed by Alva L. Davis and myself, he gave us free rein; although he has been readily available for consultation (and we have been happy to draw freely on his knowledge and experience), he has never sought to impose his ideas upon us. In fact, as early as 1938 he was glad to decentralize the work of the American Atlas project, since it was apparent that to organize and direct field work and editing for the entire United States and Canada was beyond the capacity of a single scholar, even if adequate funds were available — and they were not.

It thus developed that each of the regional surveys beyond the Atlantic Seaboard — the North-Central States under Albert H. Marckwardt and myself, the Upper Midwest under Harold B. Allen, Texas under Bagby Atwood and Rudy Troike, Colorado under Marjorie Kimmerle, California and Nevada under David Reed, and Nova Scotia under H. Rex Wilson — has been autonomous, though there have naturally been informal consultations among the regional directors and with Kurath. In other words, though the original plans called for a Linguistic Atlas of the United States and Canada, and though Kurath has been titular director of that project since 1930, for the past 30 years he has really been primus inter pares, and no one will succeed to his title. The considerable uniformity that one finds among the various regional surveys is due not to the hand of a single director, but to the fact that Kurath's principles have been pretty well accepted by the others, and that the more successful of Kurath's fieldworkers have helped to train the investigators for other regions. Thus, at various times, Kurath, Bloch and Guy S. Lowman, Jr. have helped to supervise the training of Marckwardt, Allen, Raven and Virginia McDavid, A. L. Davis, Carroll Reed and Atwood, who in turn have trained others.

The two surveys have come at different places in the careers of the directors. For Orton his Survey is the culmination of a distinguished record as a student of the English language, with a steady interest in dialects, particularly those of the north of England. The project encountered innumerable difficulties, especially at the beginning, because learned Britons could not see that English dialects needed to be investigated by the new techniques developed on

the Continent; after all, a great deal of evidence — more than enough
in the eyes of many — had been provided in the fifth volume of A. J.
Ellis's Early English Pronunciation (1889) and in Joseph Wright's
English Dialect Dictionary (1898-1905). In the planning days, funds
were no less difficult to secure than was the support of the academic
community. However, once the field work was done, editing and publishing proceeded so rapidly that all the Basic Material — the part
most interesting, or at least most useful, to scholars — was published by 1971.

        Kurath's career has been more varied; in fact, his work
with the American Atlas has occupied only part of his time since the
beginning of World War II. Under forty when the American Council
of Learned Societies launched the project in 1929, he had begun as a
Germanicist and general Indo-Europeanist, but — out of his teaching
experience — had already begun to modify older views about the dialect divisions in American English and the causes of those divisions.[1]
With an uncommon genius for organizing and directing research, he
developed a team of field workers that in two years (1931-33) completed the interviewing for New England. Then, despite the retrench-
ments that all academic projects suffered under the Depression, he
not only edited and published the Linguistic Atlas of New England
(1939-43) but kept Lowman in the field until 1941, when he died in an
automobile collision on a back road in Upstate New York; then Kurath
brought me into the project to complete the field work for the Atlantic Seaboard (1945-49). Although editing came to a halt during World
War II and Kurath's commitments as editor of the Middle English
Dictionary (another project which profited from his skill at organization) took up most of his time and energy from 1946 till his retirement, he never lost sight of the aims of the Atlas project. In fact,
one might say that he has had his deepest influence on dialectology
during the post-war period, by helping to train a new generation of
scholars and by encouraging them to develop new techniques for dealing with the linguistic phenomena of the areas of secondary and tertiary settlement.

        But where Orton found his project hard to launch but rela-
tively easy to keep going, Kurath's experience has been just the opposite. There was no difficulty at the beginning in getting approval
from the scholarly community, or — by the standards of the time —

rather generous financial support. But despite the expansion of
American linguistics during and after World War II, there has been
little money for the Atlas or for other projects in dialectology. Volatile in linguistics as in other fields, American taste has favored the
newer activities of the profession rather than the traditional ones.
To promising beginners of the last two decades, new methods in sec-
ond-language teaching, structuralism, generative theories and computer linguistics have all seemed more exciting than dialect investigations. Perhaps also these new developments have been less demanding (1) in terms of personal relationships with live informants
in a diversity of situations and (2) in terms of the stubbornness of
massive bodies of data. [2] Only with the urban crises of this decade
has there come a fresh realization that divergent patterns of language
behavior must be studied against a background such as the Atlas provides; the first generous institutional support in many years has been
my arrangement with the University of Chicago for released time to
spend on editing.

II

As Kurath has often remarked, the presentation of facts postulates an underlying theory, though the converse is not necessarily
true. In comparing the English and American surveys, one must
first notice the definitions of "dialect" with which the investigators
worked. Although neither project is a "pure" example of a particular
point of view, there are basic differences.

No linguistic survey is designed to record the whole language
of all kinds of speakers in all kinds of situations; the purpose is,
rather, to provide a framework within which other studies may be
more effectively designed. It is interesting to know the full range of
language variety in such a rapidly growing community as Fresno,
California; but to understand that complex situation — to appreciate
the dynamics of variety and change — it is necessary to have a record of the usage of old-stock native Fresnonians of various age and
educational and social groups, and of similar informants from surrounding communities, some of which have not changed as much as
Fresno.

Consequently, a first-stage general survey of a wide area
is bound to stress the older and more stable elements in the

population, and the more traditional elements in the language system. To young Turks, impatient to grapple with the language problems of seething urban multitudes, such an emphasis may seem quaint or "ruralistic," but it is a necessary background for their investigations — and of course it has its uses in other kinds of linguistic work, notably in reconstructing the past stages of the language.

The English survey tacitly assumed a basic opposition between dialect and standard language, between the uncorrupted folk speech of a given locality and that entity which bears the name of Received Standard. Actually, Received Standard was more or less of a fiction, even before the rise of Harold Wilson and Twiggy and the Beatles; but it was a useful fiction, as suggesting a single ideal model of linguistic excellence, such as would befit a compact country with a single, overwhelmingly prestigious cultural focus. Since Received Standard has been well described, it made sense to confine the English investigations to what one would feel are the purest local types of speech. True, the interesting intermediate types — the everyday speech of urban centers and the smaller county towns — would be overlooked, but they could be the subject of another kind of investigation.

The North American survey started from other assumptions, arising from a different cultural situation. There is no single standard of cultivated American English; neither in Canada nor in the United States is there a community whose natural educated speech is considered worthy of emulation everywhere else. Rather, in every community of consequence (and consequence does not depend on size alone) it is assumed that educated local usage is as good as any to be found in the English-speaking world — even though in other communities it may sound a little grotesque.

For this reason, in addition to the usual folk informants — the oldest and least sophisticated local types — the American investigators have interviewed educated speakers in all parts of the United States and Canada, and an intermediate group between the two extremes, whose responses serve to indicate the direction of linguistic change. Furthermore, since "dialect" is a vague term and often misunderstood (and besides, from the earliest settlements there has been a constant process of dialect mixture in all American communities, even without taking account of the influence of foreign-language groups), informants are sought by non-linguistic criteria, such as age and education and travel.

Of course, neither Orton nor Kurath has felt that dialect investigations should cease once their surveys are completed.[3] In fact, there is a need for a new investigation every generation, to see what time and cultural change have done to local speech. Already, in New England a group of scholars from the University of Massachusetts, under the direction of Professor Audrey Duckert, have replicated the Atlas investigations of selected communities and noted the changes since 1933.[4] Furthermore, in both England and the United States there have been interesting studies of the speech of urban areas, many of them by investigators for the wider-meshed surveys, and all making use of what those surveys have revealed. As different as are the interests of William Labov from those of the Atlas, he admits that his study of New York City speech[5] would have been impossible without the records which Lowman made in 1940-41. The study of dialects, like any other study of human behavior, is cumulative and continuing, with each investigation building on its predecessors.

III

With such different attitudes toward dialect phenomena, it is not surprising that there are differences in the research design, even though both projects have built upon the principles of field investigation as set forth by Jules Gilliéron for the <u>Atlas linguistique de la France</u> (1902-10):

1. A network of selected communities.
2. Representative local informants in each community.
3. A questionnaire of selected items.
4. Interviewing by trained investigators.
5. Interviewing in a conversational situation.
6. Recording of responses in finely graded impressionistic phonetics.

In the application of each of these principles the two surveys differ from each other, and often both differ from Gilliéron's actual practice.

1. The English network, 311 communities, is about the same density as that of Gilliéron, whose fieldworker, Edmond Edmont, recorded the usage of some 600 French communities. The American network is much denser: over 200 communities in New England alone. However, as Kurath points out,[6] Orton was primarily interested in rural and village speech, and New England of 1930 was far less urban than England of 1950; if one applies to the two surveys the same kind of weighting of urban and rural population (the latter being proportionately more heavily represented by the criteria of both surveys), the two networks end up with about the same density.

Where the networks differ most strikingly is in the kinds of communities investigated. Despite a few urban exceptions — York, Leeds, Sheffield, Hackney (London) — most of the English communities are villages, as were all the communities in Gilliéron's survey of France. In North America, by contrast, there is every kind of settled community — from metropolitan complexes such as New York and Philadelphia to crossroads villages like Rushford, New York, and Mountville, South Carolina — to say nothing of informants living on isolated farmsteads. Cultural foci and backwaters, growing and declining towns, are all represented. In addition, since the settlement of North America is so relatively recent, there is a deliberate effort to sample what were originally compact settlements of peculiar ethnic groups: Germans in most states, Dutch in New York and Michigan, Scandinavians in Wisconsin, Finns in Minnesota; there is no parallel situation in England (at least not since the Middle Ages), and no need to worry about ethnic representation.

There are further differences in the distribution of communities. Within each American survey there has been an attempt to space the communities evenly, with some attention to population density and time of settlement. Thus in New York State only one county[7] was not investigated; in South Carolina, only 7 of 46. In the areas of secondary settlement, in the Middle West and the Rockies, there have been from 20 to 35 counties per state, depending on the density of population. In England, however, there are wide variations: 13

communities were investigated in Norfolk, 5 in Suffolk, 15 in Essex. Perhaps there is a reason for this discrepancy, but it is not apparent in Orton's Introduction, a volume roughly comparable to Kurath's Handbook of the Linguistic Geography of New England.

2. In Gilliéron's design, each community was represented by a single field record, from a single representative speaker of the local dialect. As we have indicated, the American fieldworkers interview informants of three basic types:

a. In every community, a minimally educated representative of the oldest living native generation.
b. In every community, a middle-aged speaker with formal education to about 16.
c. In about a fifth of the communities, at least one cultivated speaker, highly educated[8] and representative of the best local cultural traditions.

Furthermore, in larger and more complicated communities there are even more interviews — 25 in New York City, 10 in Charleston, S. C. , 8 in Philadelphia. Each field record typically represents the usage of a single informant, though responses from auxiliary and supplementary informants sometimes appear.[9]

The practice of the English survey is somewhere between the French and the American. There is a single field record from each community — Great Snoring and Leeds alike — but the field record rarely represents the usage of a single informant and sometimes includes responses from as many as seven. From the start it was felt necessary to share out the interviewing, both to save the fieldworkers' time and to assure expert testimony on each of the fields of the vocabulary represented in the questionnaire. All of these informants, of course, were supposed to be of the same cultural level and to represent the local traditions of folk speech; even so, dividing up the questionnaire in this fashion poses many problems in ascertaining the structure of the local dialect.[10]

3. The questionnaires of both projects are designed to sample pronunciation, grammar and vocabulary. The American questionnaire is concerned with both relics and innovations, including

the pronunciations of <u>library</u>, <u>postoffice</u>, <u>hotel</u>, <u>theater</u>, <u>hospital</u>,
and the various names for the baby carriage ("perambulator") and
kerosene ("paraffin"); whether these terms are "dialectal" or not is
a matter of one's personal definition, though they show clear regional
and social variations in North America. But even in the domain of un-
questioned folk speech there are omissions in the English questionnaire that keep students from making as effective comparisons as
they might between English and American usage. Among the items
not recorded in England are the names for the <u>earthworm</u> and the
<u>dragon fly</u>, the past tenses of <u>climb</u> and <u>dive</u> and <u>rise</u>, the pronuncia-
tions of <u>January</u> and <u>February</u>, of the verb <u>to grease</u> and the adjective <u>greasy</u>. That such items have significant variants in English
folk speech is shown not only by their distribution in the primary
areas of American settlement but also by the English field records
made by Lowman in 1937-38, to say nothing of occasional responses
recorded by the English investigators. Undoubtedly there were sound
reasons behind Orton's decisions; but the English data would have
been far more useful, both synchronically and diachronically, had
the American questionnaires — accessible since the 1930s — been
replicated in more detail on items of common experience (see Maps
1-3).

The English questionnaire follows Gilliéron's ideal of uniformity throughout the area under investigation — though, since interesting new items keep turning up, Gilliéron himself observed that
the perfect questionnaire cannot be devised until after all the field
work has been completed. In the United States, on the other hand,
despite a substantial common core, the questionnaires vary from
one region to another, in response to differences in topography,
ecology, culture and ethnic composition.[11]

In length, the English questionnaire is considerably greater
— nearly 1,100 items to about 750 for the longer form of the American one (Kurath's shorter version, the basis of most of the regional
questionnaires used away from the Atlantic Seaboard, has about 520).
Orton estimates a minimum of 18 hours for a complete interview,
which seems a little long by American experience; here, a practiced
fieldworker could comfortably complete the long questionnaire in 8
hours, the short one in 6.[12] The difference is perhaps accounted for
by the more rigid structure of the English questionnaire, in which

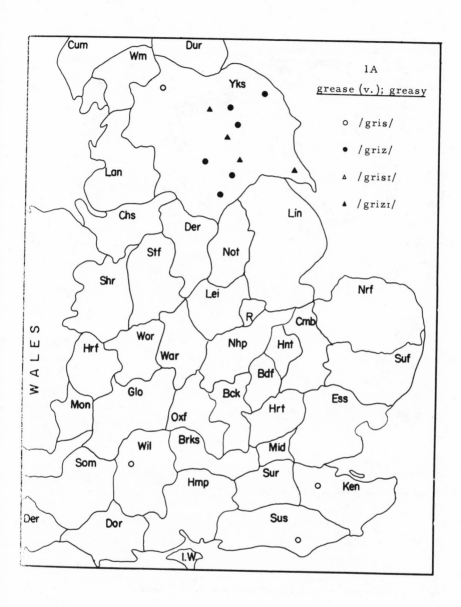

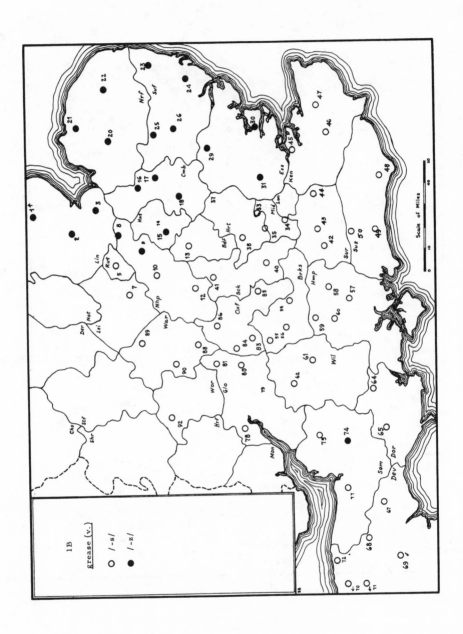

1B

grease (v.)

○ /-s/

● /-z/

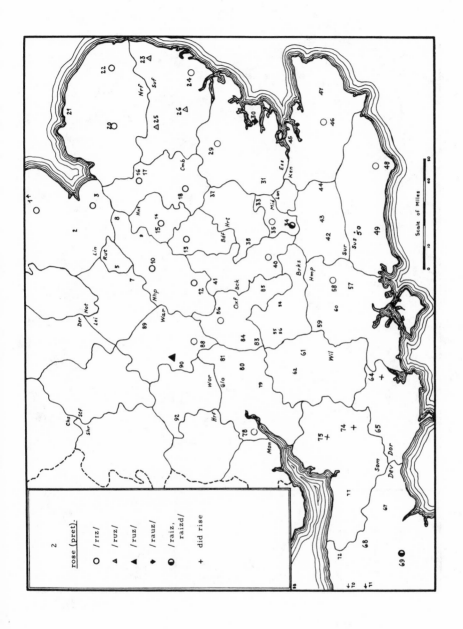

2

rose (pret).

○ /rɪz/

△ /ruz/

▲ /ruz/

✦ /rauz/

◉ /raiz, raizd/

+ did rise

Scale of Miles

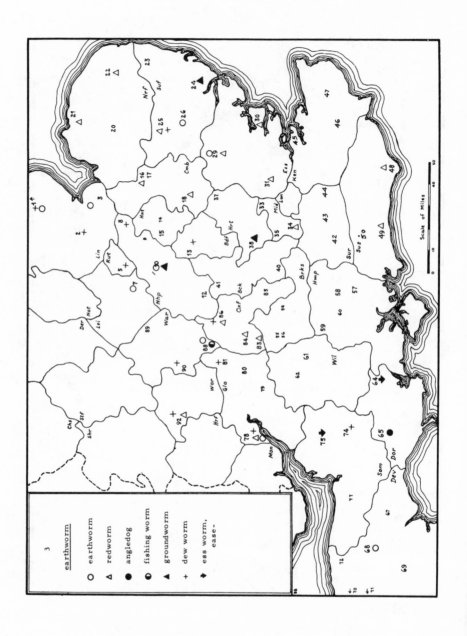

each response was sought by a specific question, with deviations in
procedure being discouraged. The American investigators, in contrast — though they shared their most successful frames for eliciting
responses — were encouraged to use their ingenuity as the situation
suggested; some of them were able to get up to half of the responses
from the informant's unguarded free conversation. Whether uniformity in procedure is as important as naturalness in usage is a problem
for each student to appraise. [13]

    4. As an interesting coincidence, the field work for the Eng-
lish Survey and that for the Linguistic Atlas of New England were
each shared by 9 investigators. [14] In each, one investigator — Stanley
Ellis for Orton, Lowman for Kurath — did nearly 40% of the interviews, 118 and 158 respectively. Scholars are naturally interested
in how the various investigators for a given survey measure up
against each other, since everyone has his strengths and weaknesses
in an interviewing situation. For the English survey there is no explicit comparison of the fieldworkers; [15] on the other hand, the New
England Handbook (52-53) rates Kurath's investigators on 9 scales.
Although Kurath, Lowman and Bloch showed general superiority, on
some scales they were not as high as some of their colleagues. [16]
Probably, with the more rigid form of eliciting questions in the Eng-
survey, these detailed ratings, though informative for the reader,
would be less important than in the American situation where the investigators were more on their own. [17] In any event, the person examining either set of data is better off than in consulting the French
Atlas, where a single fieldworker was used, whose strengths and
weaknesses are not only unknown but impossible to reconstruct.

    5. Since every interview is an independent exercise in in-
terpersonal relationships, some interview situations will inevitably
be more relaxed than others. We can probably assume for both surveys that some interviewers were more successful than others in
adapting to various kinds of personality, and that those who continued
to do field work over a period of years were among the most successful.

    6. The transcriptions for the English survey are in the un-
modified International Phonetic Alphabet; those for the American atlases are in a modified form developed by Kurath — including

differentiation of low-central and low-back unrounded vowels. With the
IPA as a given referent, Orton offers no discussion of variations in
practice among the field workers; Kurath provides a full chapter in the
New England <u>Handbook</u> in explanation of the phonetic alphabet and
other symbols, and of variations among the field workers, particularly in handling the low-central and low-back range. [18]

   Both projects have supplemented the field records with electronic recordings. At the end of the New England field work, several
dozen aluminum disc records of the natural speech of informants
were made by the associate director, Miles L. Hanley. These have
not yet been made available to the public, nor was anything like
Hanley's project attempted for the Middle and South Atlantic States.
With the advent of lightweight tape recorders, several of the regional
directors began to supplement field interviews with tapes; in fact,
some fieldworkers have taped their entire interviews. [19] None of
these American regional surveys, however, has provided an archive
of recordings. [20] The English fieldworkers, in contrast, not only
have made supplementary recordings of many of their informants but
plan to issue phonograph records as part of their publication program.

                               IV

   Gilliéron's <u>Atlas Linguistique de la France</u> and the subsequent <u>Sprach- und Sachatlas Italiens und der Südschweiz</u> (1928-40)
presented their basic information in cartographic form, with the responses of each informant for a given item overprinted in full phonetic detail on a base map, by lithoprinting from hand lettering. The
<u>Linguistic Altas of New England</u> was published in an analogous format,
and preliminary drafting was done for some of the materials from the
South Atlantic States. However, even before he gave up active editing, Kurath decided to publish the evidence from the Middle and South
Atlantic States in tables, probably printed by photo-offset from typed
copy. [21] Conceding that the cartographic presentation of the data is
more impressive, he found three compelling arguments against it:

   a. The giant folio volumes required for cartographic presentation are not only unhandy to shelve but cumbersome to
   use.

b. With the rise in draftsmen's wages, the cost of preparing the overprints would far exceed that of field work and
editing.

c. In preparing interpretative charts, it is easier to work
from tables than from maps. This is especially true when,
as in the American atlases, a community is normally represented by at least two informants, and may be represented
by a dozen or more.

For the Middle and South Atlantic States the presentation
will be essentially that of the New England Atlas, with each item preceded by a brief commentary; but the data will appear in tables instead of maps. A similar format is tentatively proposed for the
North-Central States. For the Upper Midwest, where evidence gathered in the field has been supplemented by correspondence checklists, [22] Allen has utilized a format somewhere between simple presentation of data and interpretative studies. In other regions editorial plans are still pending.

Orton's Basic Material — four regional volumes, each in
three parts — is comparable to the Linguistic Atlas of New England
and the forthcoming Linguistic Atlas of the Middle and South Atlantic States. The phonetic data for each item are presented in tabular
form, paragraphed by English counties. The only obvious objections
are trivial: one might have preferred larger pages, so that the Survey could have been shelved with analogous works; perhaps, also,
the number of special explanatory symbols could have been reduced,
or a key — something like the pronunciation line in a dictionary —
could have been printed at the foot of alternate pages. [23] But the
severest critics concede that the Basic Material volumes are very
easy to use.

From Gilliéron on it has been customary to provide a guide
to a linguistic atlas, so that it can be consulted effectively. This purpose is served by Kurath's Handbook of the Linguistic Geography of
New England and by Orton's Introduction. [24] A comparison of these
guides reveals some striking differences, which may reflect the tem-
peraments of the two directors or the financial resources available
to them.

With larger pages and more than twice as many of them, the
Handbook offers at least four times as much information as the Introduction. When it is further noted that nearly two-thirds of the latter
is taken up with Orton's questionnaire, while the New England work-
sheets (including a more detailed explanation of sources, rationale
and use than Orton provides) account for only 5% of the Handbook, the
difference is even more striking. In addition to the ranking of the
fieldworkers and the greater detail on communities and informants, [25]
the Handbook provides the following kinds of information that are
lacking in the Introduction or elsewhere in the Survey:

    a. A summary of dialect areas and a discussion of their
    origins.
    b. A bibliography of linguistic geography.
    c. A summary of settlement history and population move-
    ments, with attention to geological features of importance.
    d. A bibliography of regional history (in addition to the bib-
    liographical information on particular communities).

In short, there is much more material in the Handbook to help the
scholar interpret the recorded linguistic data. It is possible that the
education of the average British linguist (or other potential user of
the Survey) would include so deep an immersion in topography, communications, demography and local history that he could do without
this help; but his American counterpart could not, even in dealing
with the dialects of his own region. And without some such leads he
would not even know where to begin. Still, since Orton's financial
support has always been limited, it is understandable that the Introduction might not have such copious information as one would like.
One would hope that, once the Basic Material is published, the additional information will be provided, either in a separate publication
or in one of the interpretative studies.

    All linguistic atlases have allowed for such interpretative
studies, for generalizations from the field data. One might say, in
fact, that Wrede's Deutscher Sprachatlas (1926-56) is really an interpretative work, since it involves generalizing from the data contained in 44,251 responses to Georg Wenker's original questionnaire.
Of the American surveys, only one so far has presented its findings
solely in an interpretative study — Atwood's The Regional Vocabulary

of Texas (1962).[26] For the Atlantic Seaboard there are three summaries for parts of the data:

> Kurath, A Word Geography of the Eastern United States
> (1949).[27]
> Atwood, A Survey of Verb Forms in the Eastern United
> States (1953).[28]
> Kurath and McDavid, The Pronunciation of English in the
> Atlantic States (1961).

These volumes are not intended as substitutes for the regional atlases, nor are they part of the official publication program. Rather,
they were designed both to summarize some of the evidence and to
interpret it, in terms of geographical, demographic and social forces,
for the benefit of the reader who is not a professional dialectologist.
The Pronunciation, for instance, is concerned not only with the various phonic qualities of the phonemes in particular environments but
with phonemic incidence and with differences in the phonemic system.

For the English Survey it is proposed to have a Linguistic
Atlas of England in addition to the Basic Material. As yet there is
no published statement about its plan and content. If, however, one
may draw inferences from the Phonological Atlas of the Northern
Region (1966) by Eduard Kolb, one of Orton's associates, one could
still be looking for the broad-gauge interpretation the more general
reader desires and needs. Essentially, the Phonological Atlas merely reproduces in elaborate and expensive cartographic form the phonic evidence already available in the Basic Material. Its emphasis is
phonic, not phonemic; it is arranged by Middle English ancestral
sounds rather than by present-day significant sound-types; and on the
differences between the phonemic systems of the various dialects it
is silent. For instance, the Basic Material indicates that in several
communities the contrast between /o/ and /ɔ/ has been lost before
postvocalic /-r/ and its counterparts, as in horse and hoarse. This
neutralization is also found in British Received Pronunciation and in
many varieties of North American English.[29] But though hoarse is
an item in Orton's questionnaire, Kolb has not included it in his
study, much less the comparison with horse; nor does he touch the
similar neutralization of the vowels of four and forty. One would
like to suggest that Orton's proposed Linguistic Atlas of England be

modeled more closely on Kurath's Word Geography, that if anything
Orton should provide fuller detail about topography, communications
and population history. If he must choose between this background
information and elaborate cartography, he would well dispense with
the latter. For the purpose of interpretative volumes is to lead the
readers to investigate intelligently on their own the greater riches of
the Basic Material.

V

Although this comparison has so far been concerned with
evaluating Orton's Survey as objectively as possible against analogous studies, it would be unfortunate to leave the impression that it
is not a significant work. It is, indeed, a monumental contribution to
knowledge.

First of all, it is the first investigation of English dialects
to be built upon field investigations on the spot by trained investigators using a uniform questionnaire. However we may argue about
their procedures and what they found, there are indubitable recordings of identifiable informants in specific localities, and they will be
indispensable for generations of students of the English language.

Second, where the data can be checked against other field
investigations, similar patterns are found (Maps 4-5). This is especially true for the loss of postvocalic /-r/ in barn, in Southern
England. For the lack of contrast between horse and hoarse the
greater number of informants in the Survey and perhaps the increasing influence of Received Pronunciation may explain the higher frequency of this neutralization.

Finally, neither study pretends to have said the last word;
each provides a framework within which other scholars may conduct
more intensive investigations. It is interesting that the new attention
to urban problems has provoked similar responses from dialectologists on both sides of the Atlantic. If the responses in the United
States have come earlier and on a larger scale, it not merely that the
problems are more acute, but that more evidence has been available
for a longer time. What has been undertaken in the United States so

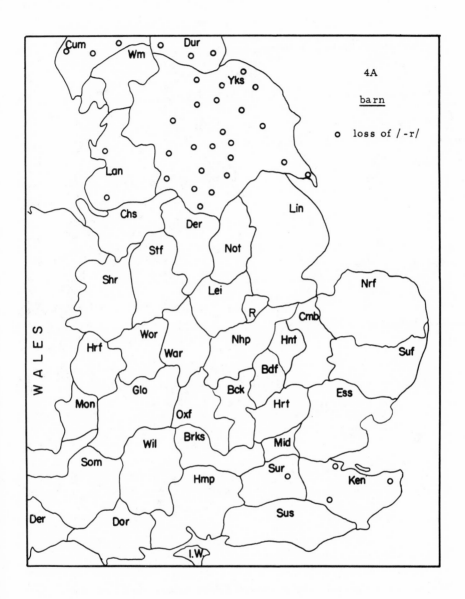

4A

barn

o loss of /-r/

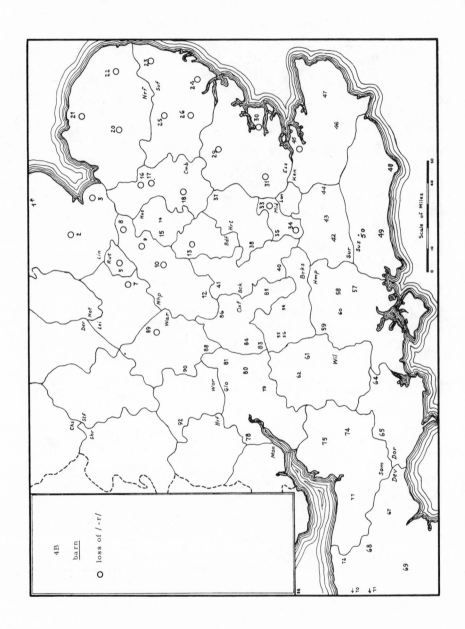

4B

bärn

○ loss of /-r/

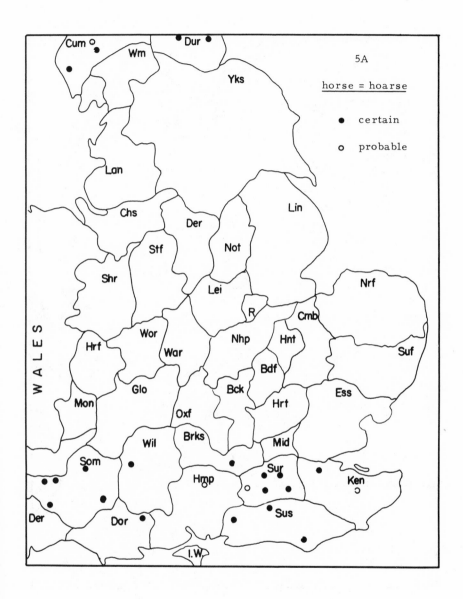

5A

horse = hoarse

● certain

○ probable

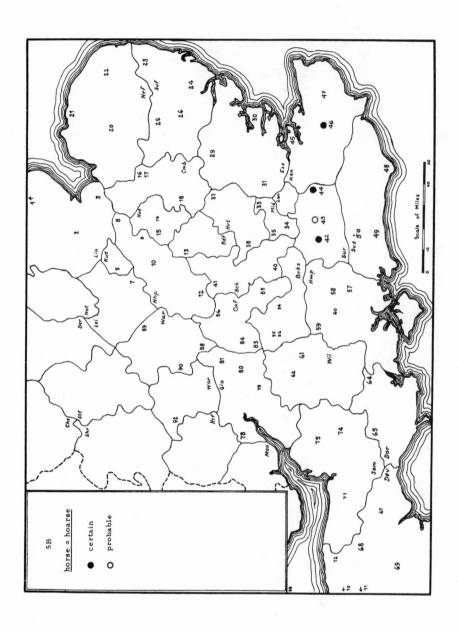

5B

horse = hoarse

● certain

○ probable

far by Frank, Hubbell, DeCamp, Sawyer, Howren, Pederson, Labov, Shuy and Udell[30] is now being essayed in Britain by Stanley Ellis and his colleagues. These new studies — which could never have been undertaken without the framework provided by the American regional atlases and Orton's Survey — not only should provide us with the means for more sensitive and effective teaching of English in the schools, but should lead us to a deeper understanding of human behavior, through a greater appreciation of man's most characteristic activity, the use of language.

NOTES

For statements about the American atlases I am naturally indebted to long association with Kurath, Marckwardt, Allen and others, as well as to the American Council of Learned Societies, which sponsored the project and has contributed generously to its support. Maps 1A, 4A, 5A are based on what has been published of Orton's Basic Material. Maps 1B, 2, 3, 4B, 5B are based on the unpublished field records from southern England, made by Lowman in 1937-38. For an analysis of the grammatical and lexical evidence in the Lowman records, see Wolfgang Viereck, Lexikalische und Grammatische Ergebnisse des Lowman-Survey von Mittel- und Südengland, 2 vol., München: Wilhelm Fink Verlag, 1975.

[1] "The Origin of Dialectal Differences in American English," Modern Philology, XXV (1927-28), 385-95; "American Pronunciation," SPE Tract XXX (1928), 279-97.

[2] The possible applications of linguistics to the needs of Cold War diplomacy and defense technology have resulted in generous government support for several kinds of research in some of the newer aspects of linguistics; for example, much of the work of Noam Chomsky and his transformational disciples has been subsidized by the military establishment.

[3] It is hard to convince both the learned and the laity that the study of speech is a continuing business. As we mentioned above, the mere existence of the work of Ellis and Wright — however outdated their methods — for a long time stood in the way of Orton's project. And every field investigator encounters the notion that amateur studies or regional novels have said everything. I recall the incredulity of a county official in Milledgeville, Georgia: "Isn't all that in Gone with the Wind ?"

[4]For example, Mrs. Ruth Schell Porter, "A Dialect Study in Dartmouth, Massachusetts," Pub. Am. Dial. Soc., XLIII (1965), 1-43. Professor Duckert herself has revisited Plymouth, Mass., and by good fortune has been able to interview one of the original informants for the New England Atlas. A report of her investigation was presented to the Linguistic Society of America, Dec. 29, 1968.

[5]The Social Stratification of English in New York City, Washington, D.C., Center for Applied Linguistics, 1966.

[6]Review of the Survey of English Dialects: Introduction and The Basic Material, Vol. 1, in American Speech, XXXVIII (1963), 124-29.

[7]Rockland, the southernmost county on the west bank of the Hudson. For Atlas purposes, the county is the basic community for all regions except New England, where the smaller township is the more effective unit of local government.

[8]A cultivated informant is usually a graduate of one of the more prestigious colleges, but there are exceptions — members of old families who were educated by private tutors. One of these was a Pulitzer Prize journalist, another an internationally known water colorist.

[9]An "auxiliary informant" is a husband, wife, other kinsman or long-time friend who is present during parts of the interview and offers his responses (sometimes when the principal informant is unable to answer, sometimes when he disagrees with a response the principal informant has made). A "supplementary informant" is someone with a background similar to that of the principal informant, who completes the interview when the principal informant cannot.

[10]The New England Handbook provides much more information than Orton offers about the communities and informants. Typically, Julia Bloch, a member of Kurath's editorial staff, provides a brief history of the community with population changes, the names of local histories if any, a biographical sketch of each informant, and notes on his speech characteristics, whether apparently idiosyncratic or typical of a wider area. The character sketches are often quite vivid.

[11]A compilation of atlas questionnaires for field work (or "work sheets," as Kurath prefers to call them), edited by Virginia and Raven McDavid, was published in 1951. A second edition of this compilation, with Davis as a third editor, was published by the Uni-

versity of Chicago Press in 1969. Some 1500 interviews had been completed for the various American surveys before Orton began his investigations.

Some 1500 interviews had been completed for the various American surveys before Orton began his investigations.

[12]I have actually completed a long interview in about four hours, a short one in two. But this demanded extraordinary rapport with the informant.

[13]In the American cultural situation, conversational responses are especially valuable for grammatical evidence. Even illiterates have confused notions about "correctness" when they are confronted with a choice of grammatical forms — though their notions are probably no more inaccurate than those of the educated, if we examine the hostile reactions to Webster's Third New International Dictionary (1961). Under direct questioning an informant is not only likely to give the "standard" form (or what he thinks is "standard") but to deny using non-standard forms that the fieldworker has noted as common in his unguarded speech. As James H. Sledd put it, "Any red-blooded American would prefer incest to ain't, " Language, XL (1964), 473.

[14]Lowman and I did most of the field work for the Middle and South Atlantic States. In the North-Central States I did over half the interviewing, though thirty others participated; in the Upper Midwest Allen did the greater part, with six others helping.

[15]One may of course draw certain conclusions, as from the apparent ability of fieldworkers to elicit non-standard grammatical forms.

[16]For other regions, there have been informal comparisons. A field record which Bloch made of my speech in 1937 is useful in appraising his transcriptions, since I have subsequently made a tape of the responses he recorded. What is particularly interesting is the consistency of the transcriptions made by fieldworkers with comparable training. There are only minute differences between my records and those of my wife and Davis; all of us were trained by Bloch.

[17]Unfortunately, in some American surveys there are striking differences where the fieldworkers have not been given a period of common training or the opportunity to do practice interviews under the supervision of experienced investigators. This is regretably true of most of the field records from Indiana.

[18]This area of the vowel quadrangle is very important in
North America, since a number of American dialects (including
most of Canada) lack a contrast between /a/ and /ɔ/, as between
cot and caught. For certain other dialects, as those of east Texas,
this contrast is lacking before /-r/ or its counterparts, as in card
and cord.

[19]In fact, some fieldworkers have conducted interviews without transcribing on the spot and have later transcribed (or had others
transcribe)from the tapes. For a discussion of this procedure see
my "Tape Recording in Dialect Geography: a Cautionary Note,"
Journal of the Canadian Linguistic Association, III (1957-58), 3-8.

[20]However, a parallel project, Recordings of Standard English, directed by Davis, has provided a wide sampling of cultivated
American speech.

[21]The development of interchangeable shuttles for electric
typewriters has made available an almost unlimited variety of phonetic characters. Several reference works with difficult typography,
notably the Middle English Dictionary, have been published in this
fashion.

[22]The Deutscher Sprachatlas of Wenker and Wrede was prepared from data collected by correspondence; the atlases of Norway
and the Netherlands have also relied on correspondence. After
Gilliéron — and Romance dialectologists in general — pointed out
that the German method was notoriously ineffective in achieving its
primary aim, the collection of phonological data, the correspondence
method fell into disrepute. However, in his dissertation, A Word
Atlas of the Great Lakes Region (Michigan, microfilm, 1949), Davis
showed that a carefully prepared multiple-choice questionnaire could
yield a great deal of reliable vocabulary evidence. Since then, collection of vocabulary evidence by correspondence questionnaires (or
"checklists," as distinguished from the "work sheets" used for field
interviewing) has been a part of the program of the regional surveys
in the Upper Midwest, the Rocky Mountains, and the Pacific States.
For the Gulf States it has provided the only evidence available till
recently. This method has also been used in the Linguistic Atlas of
Scotland, ed. Mather and Speitel (1975-).

[23]Since there are only 311 interviews, one might also prefer
to have all the evidence for a given item in one place, rather than divided among four volumes. Orton, however, justifiably felt that publication of the northern materials would bring both critical approval

and financial support that would make possible the early publication of his other material.

[24] A Handbook was published as the first part of Vol. 1 of Harold B. Allen, Linguistic Atlas of the Upper Midwest, 3 vol. Minneapolis: University of Minnesota Press, 1973-6. Similar Handbooks are being edited for other regional surveys.

[25] A minor irritation: the two maps in the Introduction — the national network and the localities recorded by each fieldworker — are so small that the symbols are hard to distinguish, and the symbols for the various fieldworkers are not distinctive enough.

[26] Atwood's data, vocabulary and some verb forms, were gathered by students as class assignments, over several years.

[27] The Word Geography went to press before the completion of field work in South Carolina, eastern Georgia, and upstate New York. For these regions it is partially supplemented by two articles of mine: "The Folk Vocabulary of New York State," NYFQ, VII (1951), 173-92, and "The Position of the Charleston Dialect," Pub. Am. Dial. Soc., XXIII (1955), 35-53.

[28] Further data are found in Virginia McDavid, Verb Forms in the North-Central States and Upper Midwest, and in her grammatical study for the Atlas of the North-Central States.

[29] Along the Atlantic Seaboard, homonymy prevails in all classes of speakers in Metropolitan New York, the Hudson Valley, and most of Pennsylvania. It is spreading in the area of New England settlement and prevails west of the Appalachians and in most of Canada.

[30] In addition to works already mentioned, there are Yakira H. Frank, The Speech of New York City, diss., University of Michigan, 1948; Allan F. Hubbell, The Pronunciation of English in New York City: Consonants and Vowels, New York, 1950; David DeCamp, "The Pronunciation of English in San Francisco," Orbis, VII (1958), 372-91, VIII (1959), 54-77; Janet B. Sawyer, A Dialect Study of San Antonio, Texas: a Bilingual Community, diss., University of Texas, 1957; Robert R. Howren, The Speech of Louisville, Ky., diss., Indiana University, 1958; Lee Pederson, The Pronunciation of English in Chicago: Consonants and Vowels, Pub. Am. Dial. Soc., XLIV (1965); Roger W. Shuy, Walter A. Wolfram, William K. Riley, Field Techniques in an Urban Language Study, Urban Language Series 3, Washington, D.C., 1968; Gerald Udell, The Speech of Akron, Ohio, diss., University of Chicago, 1966.

12 | Planning the Grid

Some time ago, Hans Kurath observed that every selection of facts postulates a theory — though the converse is not necessarily true.[1] In discussing the planning of a grid for a linguistic survey, the same observation can be made: whether the survey involves regional or social dialects, the theoretical interests of the investigators will determine the kind of grid — of communities and informants — selected for investigation.[2]

I

The bias of this paper derives from the problems encountered in editing the Linguistic Atlas of the Middle and South Atlantic States (LAMSAS).[3] The archives consist of approximately 1200 field records; the area in which they were made extends over a thousand miles from Martintown, Ontario, on the St. Lawrence (roughly opposite the boundary between New York State and the province of Québec) to Gainesville, Florida, and some four hundred miles from the eastern tip of Long Island to Ironton, Ohio, at the confluence of the Ohio and the Big Sandy. The basic questionnaire contains about eight hundred items, though for various reasons not every item was recorded in every record.[4] For each item a list manuscript must be prepared, with the full phonetic record for each informant's responses, including synonyms and forms known but not personally used, and any comments by the informant or observations by the fieldworker on the informant's reactions. The simple listing of the responses for an item takes from five to twelve hours, depending on its complexity, which cannot be predicted in advance.[5] After each list manuscript is prepared, it must be checked by at least one other editor, and a headnote and commentary provided. The list manuscript is then typed on a special

phonetic typewriter, for reproduction by photo-offset, and proofread
once more before going to the printer. [6]

This paper will thus have as an underlying concern the relationship between the amount of data gathered and the amount of time
required to make it available to those who can profit by it. Even the
best-laid plans gang aft agley: no one was more realistic than Hans
Kurath, but he never succeeded in getting funds to edit and publish
the materials from the Middle and South Atlantic States. Consequently, many recent studies in sociolinguistics have commented adversely
about the regional linguistic atlases of the United States and Canada,
including this one, without the critics examining a single page of field
data. [7]

Editors must also face, and try to resist, academic Parkin-
sonianism. Even if unlimited funds permitted increasing the number
of editorial workers, the increase would create new problems, not
only in maintaining the quality of work but in providing adequate supervision and review. [8] Mechanical aids are, so far, of little help; in
fact, they may create additional problems. The tape recorder may
make it possible to dispense with full phonetic transcription on the
spot (though even crude phonetic notations are extremely useful to
the ultimate transcriber), but it does not materially shorten the time
required to interview an informant; and even the most experienced
phonetician requires three to four hours to transcribe and put in order
the responses on an hour of tape. [9] The computer — an electronic
moron with an infinite capacity for the rapid replication of mistakes
— is of no help until the full phonetic record is edited and encoded,
and as yet there are no financially feasible provisions for computer
input and output of fine phonetic data.

II

There is, thus, no single canonical method for constructing
a grid; if Gilliéron could observe that each word has its own history,
we may observe that each speech community (in the broad or the nar-
row sense) has not only its own history but its own social structure,
which must be taken into account along with the interests of the investigators. Where criteria from one investigation are applied more or

less mechanically to another, the results are likely to be unsatis-
factory. Some of the less satisfactory results of some of the recent
work in American social dialects have derived from this mechanical
extrapolation.

It is best, then, to examine some of the more important
projects that have been undertaken, beginning with the classics of
European dialectology. For these we must remember that the investigators could assume with some accuracy a polar opposition between
folk speech and the standard language, and a basic uniformity in the
latter as a sort of platonic ideal, however imperfectly realized in
practice. "Pure dialect" was thought to be the possession of rural
and village life; the everyday speech of townsmen, uneducated or
partially educated, was largely ignored until recently, except for
such interesting and inescapable aberrations as London Cockney.

The Deutscher Sprachatlas of Wrede, appearing in fascicles
over a quarter-century, from 1926, was a development out of an inquiry initiated by Georg Wenker in the 1870s. Using a correspondence questionnaire, Wenker sought to get information on local folk
speech from every German village with a school; cities were not so-
licited. The final archive consisted of 44,251 questionnaires from
40,736 communities. A similar technique was used by Walther
Mitzka, in 1938, for gathering data for his Wortatlas; he obtained
evidence from 48,069 communities; both projects came close to the
ideal of obtaining total coverage of European German. Whether or
not the parallel between Wenker's investigations and Mitzka's needed
to be so close is another matter; in his review of the Wortatlas (Language, 34, 1958, 428-39) Kurath observed that by the time Mitzka
began his investigations the dialect areas of German were so well de-
lineated, in such fine detail, that it might have been desirable to
have a wider-meshed network and a longer questionnaire. (On the
other hand, even with the authority of an authoritarian state behind
the investigation, there are limits to the amount of time local informants and agents can devote to correspondence materials.) In a
paper presented at the Linguistic Institute of 1941, Kurath advocated
a relatively wide-meshed network for any proposed dictionary of the
regional vocabulary of American English — a proposal that, in effect,
Frederic G. Cassidy has adopted for his Dictionary of American Regional English (DARE).[10]

For the Atlas linguistique de la France (ALF, 1902-10),
Jules Gilliéron had a network of 639 communities, more or less
mechanically spaced — again eschewing cities. The influence of
Paris, say, as a focal area can be deduced from what is recorded in
the villages around the capital; nevertheless, there is no way of
finding out from the ALF the actual usage of the Parisian working
class at the time the survey was conducted. The network was perhaps too widely spaced, if one thinks of an ideal arrangement; but it
made possible the use of a single field investigator, the redoubtable
Edmond Edmont, and a long questionnaire, and the completion of the
field work in five years. The publication of Gilliéron's Atlas was essentially complete before the first fascicles of the German investigation appeared.

The Sprach- und Sachatlas Italiens und der Südschweiz (AIS,
1928-40), by Karl Jaberg and Jakob Jud, was the first survey to
weight the distribution of communities. Of some four hundred places
investigated, three-fourths are located in the old Papal States and
northward, eighty in southern Italy and Sicily, twenty in Sardinia. [11]
Possibly the coverage of southern Italy was scanted by the need of
the Swiss scholars to complete the survey of the peninsula when Italian scholars would not adopt comparable methods. [12] Nevertheless,
the weighted distribution finds justification in the facts of Italian
history. The kingdom of the two Sicilies (however affiliated with
foreign interests) had been a political unit almost continually since
the middle of the fifteenth century, and before that from the establishment of the Norman hegemony to the fall of the Hohenstaufens;
for a long time it had had no cultural centers competing with Naples.
In contrast, north of Rome there were many competing cultural centers of various sizes — Turin, Milan, Bologna, Padua, Venice,
Florence, Genoa, and Pisa, to name the most obvious. Such centers
were not ignored by the fieldworkers for the AIS; they investigated
cities as well as villages, and in some places conducted more than
one interview.

The Atlante Linguistico Italiano (ALI), launched by Bartoli
and Bertoni in 1925, was conceived on an imperial scale. It had a
questionnaire of 7500 items; its proposed network included a thousand
communities, of three types — "large," "middle-sized," and "villages" — spaced fifteen to thirty kilometers apart and generally not

selected in advance. Reverting to Gilliéron's practice, the ALI en-
trusted the field work to a single investigator, Ugo Pellis. Predict-
ably if regrettably, he did not live to complete his herculean labors.
At his death, 18 July 1943, he had investigated 727 localities, with
the record incomplete for 31.[13] Only fragments have been published.

The linguistic atlas of the Slavic languages — not to be confused with the atlases for particular languages and areas — returns
to the principles of the German and French investigations, with a concentration on folk speech, on the villages rather than larger communities. A grid is laid out to provide for communities at set intervals, and the field investigator chooses the village nearest to the
intersection of the coordinates.

Little has been published about the network for the survey of
Scotland, which has attempted to combine correspondence materials,
principally for vocabulary, and field investigation for pronunciation.[14]
Questionnaire booklets were sent out, like Wenker's questionnaire,
to be filled in under the supervision of local schoolmasters and other
interested local persons. However, returns were not as good in
Scotland as in the Second and Third Reichs, because no central authority could press for local cooperation; there was a sharp drop-off
in the returns for the second postal questionnaire, and no further
ones were attempted.

The Survey of English Dialects by Harold Orton and his associates (1962-71) investigated 311 communities. With a primary interest in folk speech and in the survivals of older forms, Orton preferred "agricultural communities that had had a fairly stable population of about five hundred for a century or so" (Introduction, p. 15).
But there were exceptions: Hackney in northeast London, Harmonds-
worth in Middlesex, and the cities of York, Leeds, and Sheffield in
Yorkshire. (Why not also Liverpool, Manchester, Bristol, and
Plymouth ? Perhaps the fact that the Survey was conducted out of the
University of Leeds was responsible for the inclusion of the Yorkshire cities.) Local history was not studied as an aid to the selection,
which was left to the investigator. The density of the network varies
from shire to shire: thirteen communities in Norfolk to six in Suffolk, two in Cambridgeshire to six in Oxfordshire, without explanation.[15]

III

European investigations have dealt with long-settled populations, however urbanized by the industrial revolution and two world
wars. The situation in English-speaking North America is strikingly
different. Permanent settlement began only in the seventeenth century. It was 1733 before there was a continuous belt of settlement
along the Atlantic Seaboard, from the Spanish colony of Florida to the
Gulf of St. Lawrence; four more decades elapsed before there was a
permanent settlement west of the Appalachians. Settlement had just
reached the edge of the Great Plains by the Mexican War (1846); then
it leapfrogged to the Pacific Coast, with the intervening areas filling
up as transportation improved. But the settlement spread unevenly;
in a state as long settled as New York, some areas did not have permanent communities till the end of the nineteenth century. And everywhere one encounters — or at least can read about — not only communities that failed to grow, but once-prosperous ones that stagnated,
declined, and were even abandoned.

To plan a network for investigating the regional English of
North America, then, one must allow for the continuous interaction
of a number of forces in a way unparalleled elsewhere: [16]

1. In every community on the Atlantic Seaboard, there was
a mixture of dialects from all parts of the British Isles. As settlement spread westward, the process of dialect mixture continued, except that the elements for secondary and tertiary settlement were
the older forms of American regional English, first those of the Atlantic Seaboard and then those of the Middle West.

2. Everywhere, though in varying proportions in different
communities, there was a continuing leaven of speakers of other languages. The most widely disseminated group, regionally and socially,
were the Germans, but most familiar tongues — and some unfamiliar
at the time, like the languages of West Africa — made their contributions.

3. There has been geographic mobility, with Americans always on the move, from older communities to new, and back again.
The proportion of the population who moved has varied little from

decade to decade, and everywhere those already established have
felt newcomers a disturbing influence, even though the newcomers
may have followed by only a few years.

4. There has been social mobility, with each group gradually rising and contributing its share to those who make the decisions.

5. One consequence of industrialization has been the disappearance of words associated with folk crafts. For example, dairy-
ing and butchery, once a part of the work of every homestead, are
now primarily commercial enterprises.

6. Urbanization has accelerated the process of dialect mixture and has eliminated local peculiarities, especially in pronunciation.

7. A commitment to general education has spread standard
grammatical forms at the expense of their folk counterparts.

In reckoning with these forces — and a failure to reckon
with them would have ignored the realities of American English —
Kurath adopted a policy of weighted selection of his communities,
drawing on information provided by historians, notably Carl Briden-
baugh and Marcus L. Hansen. There were two basic principles: rural
communities would be represented more heavily than urban ones; and
older areas of settlement would be represented more heavily than
more recent ones. This means that in the Atlantic seaboard areas the
network is finer meshed along the coast than inland; in New England,
the coastal communities were about fifteen miles apart. There was also
the need to complete the investigation within a practicable time-limit.
With nine field workers participating (though only Lowman worked full
time) and a questionnaire of about eight hundred items, 416 interviews in 213 communities were completed within two years; in consequence, editing was largely complete before World War II curtailed
activity.

A similar plan was adopted for the Middle and South Atlantic
states, with a few modifications:

1. Because the funds for fieldwork were limited, Kurath worked with a single investigator — Lowman till his death in 1941, R. McDavid afterward. [17]

2. Since detailed studies of local history were not as plentiful for the South Atlantic states, Kurath initiated a wide-meshed preliminary survey (1933-34) before drawing up the final grid. This preliminary survey also provided an opportunity to test an adaptation of the questionnaire to the different geographical, economic, and social conditions of the Old South. The questionnaire was further modified for the Middle Atlantic states on the basis of early interviews in New Jersey and Pennsylvania.

3. The network was adjusted to a different definition of what constituted a community. In New England the township — locally known as a town, however rural it may be — originally organized around a village, is the traditional unit of local government, with the larger county relatively unimportant. Further south and west, the county was the functioning unit of local government from the beginning, with the township of minor significance if it existed at all. [18]

In general, though, the density of coverage was about the same as in New England, taking into account that New England was more densely populated; the projected schedule of fieldwork was also about the same. That there are somewhat more interviews in Georgia than were originally planned results from the development of the tape recorder, so that student interviews could be transcribed by experienced phoneticians.

IV

For the Linguistic Atlas of the North-Central States (LANCS) Albert H. Marckwardt extended Kurath's principles to an area of secondary settlement, again using a preliminary survey; his questionnaire was about two-thirds the length of those employed along the Atlantic Coast. He settled upon approximately 25-30 communities for each state, so that with the shorter questionnaire a fieldworker might cover a state in six months, which could be two academic summer vacations. This density was generally maintained, with a few additions and other modifications to deal with special circumstances. [19]

However, the wider network required somewhat more explicitly detailed principles of selection than those used along the Atlantic Seaboard, and several types of communities, some not previously taken
into account, had to be chosen:

     1. Earliest settlements: e.g., Marietta, Ohio.
     2. Important way stations along transportation routes: e.g.,
Maysville, Kentucky.
     3. Communities settled primarily by cohesive ethnic groups:
e.g., Albion, Illinois, directly from England. [20]
     4. Cultural and economic foci: e.g., Cincinnati.
     5. Backwaters of settlement, more or less isolated: e.g.,
Calhoun County, Illinois.
     6. Communities of declining importance: e.g., Shawnee-
town, Illinois. [21]

     Marckwardt's principles have been generally followed in
later regional investigations, though the general use of checklists in
such surveys, for gathering vocabulary data by correspondence, has
provided an additional network, with somewhat finer intervals than it
would have been possible to achieve with the funds available for fieldwork. [22] There are slight variations in the regional surveys, each of
which is an autonomous project. [23]

                        V

     Since there have been differences in the principles by which
scholars have planned the networks for studies in regional dialects,
there should be no surprise at finding as least as many differences in
the planning of networks for studies in social dialects. The latter not
only have the various kinds of appeal to a scholar's curiosity, but also have potential immediate application to the practical needs of society.

     One cannot reiterate too often the fact that the Linguistic
Atlas of the United States and Canada, as conceived by Kurath, was
the first regional survey to recognize a social dimension. The scholars who undertook the investigations in Germany, France, Italy, and
England could assume a polar opposition between local dialects and

a monolithic standard language. But the development of North American English had been decentralized, with a number of cultural centers
from the beginning, each one developing its own prestigious variety
of the language. Consequently it was necessary to assume, and investigate, regional varieties of cultivated speech, as well as of folk
speech, in any North American survey; and to assess the effect of the
social forces already discussed — forces operating differently in each
community — it was necessary to interview an intermediate group.
Thus it has been possible to use the Atlas evidence to make certain
general statements about social differences and the direction of change,
for the nation as a whole and for particular areas. And for some individual communities, the Atlas collections make possible fairly detailed studies, such as Yakira Frank's analysis of New York City. [24]

But if one must reiterate the fact that the Atlas project pio-
neered in recognizing the social dimension in accounts of regional
speech, the corollary is that one must reiterate with equal force that
no one associated with the project has ever asserted that the Atlas
project could provide a full sociolinguistic study of American English.
For one thing, there are likely to be more than three social classes
in almost any community, however small, to say nothing of age differences and the caste differences created by race and ethnic origins.
For another, by insisting on natives of the communities investigated,
with families of long-term residence (as any study of authentic regional varieties is bound to do), the Atlas could not sample the recent
immigrant stock or those of older groups who have changed their community of residence. By its nature the Atlas network merely estab-
lishes benchmarks for more detailed local investigations, and to some
extent suggests which communities might be most profitably investigated in detail. Actually, the study of any community could provide
interesting evidence, if it appealed to an investigator.

If the study of American social dialects could have proceeded
without external distractions, there might have been an orderly progression from small communities clearly within dialect areas, through
medium-sized communities and those situated on or near dialect
boundaries, to the large metropolitan agglomerations. [25] What was
learned at each stage would have provided cues to the next step, and
the materials already gathered in the study of regional dialects would
have been used continuously.

Such an orderly progression, however, was rendered impossible by the very circumstances that promoted the development of social dialectology in the United States. Under the presidency of Lyndon Johnson, attention was drawn as never before to problems of the large number of the poorly educated and low skilled, displaced from rural areas as agriculture became industrialized, and drawn to the big cities. It became apparent that the differences between the speech of the migrants (usually nonstandard Southern) and the local varieties of the standard constituted one of the obstacles to the employment of the new arrivals and success in school for their children. Consequently, metropolitan school systems sought and often obtained large sums for the study of speech differences, in the hope of improving teaching materials and methods of instruction. Although, from the point of view of research in sociolinguistics, the first grants might have been better allocated to such communities as Bamberg, South Carolina, and Hyden, Kentucky, such communities could not dramatize their case nearly as effectively as could the mayor of New York City, nor did they have local universities with traditions of social research and officers trained in the art of soliciting funds for it. As it was, so much money was allocated through urban school boards, and so few were the scholars with competence in field research in language variety, that it was often necessary to use inexperienced investigators and try new methods, some more successful than others. Since these experiments were burgeoning at the time somewhat more traditional studies were being completed, we should examine a few studies of each kind, to discover the differences among them, particularly in the relationships between their materials and those of the regional atlases.

"The Pronunciation of English in Akron, Ohio," by Gerald Udell (diss. Univ. of Chicago 1966) is a study of a rapidly growing industrial community, near a major dialect boundary, that between the North and the Midland. The community itself had not been previously investigated, but was ringed by communities in the LAMSAS and LANCS networks. Furthermore, both Kurath's Word Geography and the Kurath-McDavid Pronunciation had utilized some of these communities and had helped to establish the boundary. The informants were selected to represent both older and more recent ethnic stocks but all were natives. As a by-product of his study, Udell first established the elusiveness of the recent migrants from the Southern uplands;

although this group is by far the largest group of the American "disadvantaged," it is difficult to identify in metropolitan areas — partly
because it is not as physically or linguistically visible as some others,
partly because it is reluctant to cut its ties with its place of origin. In
Akron, it was found, the migrants from West Virginia tend to retain
citizenship and franchise at home and some claim to property, in the
hope of returning to the farm; so numerous are they, that in one year
both gubernatorial candidates for West Virginia thought it advisable to
make campaign speeches in Akron. But this same attachment to their
home means that it takes a special effort to seek them out in the cities.
A recent investigation of the Kentuckians in the Uptown area of Chicago has been more successful; in the past decade they have become
more vocal, and the investigator — Lawrence M. Davis, of the Illinois Institute of Technology — not only made use of the Atlas materials
from eastern Kentucky but conducted supplementary field investigations there and a follow-up study in detail of the speech of Breathitt
County.

The various studies of the speech of Chicago, in which Lee
Pederson is the key figure, represent successive stages of building
on previous foundations. Some half-dozen field records had been
made in the Chicago metropolitan area, and both LANCS and Shuy's
dissertation on the Northern-Midland boundary in Illinois (PADS,
38, 1962) had provided the evidence on the surrounding area before
Pederson wrote his dissertation, The Pronunciation of English in
Chicago: Consonants and Vowels (PADS, 44, 1965). To these he
added thirty-eight full-length field records, using an expanded version of the LANCS questionnaire; his additions included words and
pronunciations that he had reason to suspect were characteristic of
Chicago, or of particular social groups within the city; here, as in
the choice of informants, he drew on histories and demographies of
the city, as well as on his experience as a Chicagoan with first-hand
knowledge of the local political organization. Finally he used an
abridged questionnaire to interview some eighty supplementary informants of various age groups, including many high-school students,
in order to provide additional evidence on the fate of items that seemed
to be characteristic of Chicago. An effort was made, with both principal and supplementary informants, to reflect the ethnic and social
complexities of the metropolitan area, but all informants except one
were natives.

A follow-up study, Communication Barriers to the Culturally Deprived, found Pederson collaborating with R. McDavid, William M. Austin, and A. L. Davis; their purpose was to gauge the adaptation to standard Chicago speechways of speakers with other backgrounds, notably lower-class black migrants from the South. Two groups of the latter were included (along with middle-class blacks, and middle- and lower-class whites, all natives of Chicago): one of blacks resident in the Chicago area a decade or more, the other of arrivals within two or three years before the study. As with Pederson's dissertation, informants were selected through personal contacts in the community.

A special adaptation of Atlas methods is Juanita V. Williamson's A Phonological and Morphological Study of the Speech of the Negro of Memphis, Tennessee (PADS, no. 50, 1968). Begun in the early 1950s, Williamson's study did not have the advantage of a regional atlas to provide a framework; however, she had examined the Atlas materials from the Old South, including the records from Negro informants, and was aware of Lorenzo Turner's studies of the survivals of Africanisms in Gullah. Since she is a Memphis-born Negro herself and selected her informants from working within the Negro community, her dissertation should be one of the principal works consulted by those concerned with the speech of Negroes elsewhere. However, the situation is the opposite; she is rarely mentioned, and almost never accurately cited, by the authors and editors of the more popular treatments. In Black-White Speech Relationships, edited by Wolfram and Clarke (Washington: Center for Applied Linguistics, 1971), her contribution is discussed only in an appendix to an article by Virginia and Raven McDavid; in Language, Society and Education: A Profile of Black English, edited by Johanna S. DeStefano (Worthington, Ohio: Charles A. Jones, 1973), her name does not appear in the index.

One of the most influential studies of urban language is William Labov's The Social Stratification of English in New York City (Washington: Center for Applied Linguistics, 1966), a third-generation study. The LAMSAS interviews had provided a more systematic picture than the observations in nineteenth-century studies; but to do what LAMSAS was designed to do, the investigator could not touch the speech of newcomers, whether from other countries or from other parts of the United States. The dissertations of Frank and Hubbell, as well as the various articles of the late C. K. Thomas, had dealt with the speech of natives and principally or entirely with the older resident stock. Labov wished to see what was happening as newer groups came into the city.

To find a suitable microcosm, Labov concentrated on an area of high mobility, the Lower East Side of Manhattan, between Fourteenth Street and the Brooklyn Bridge. His starting point was a previous sociological study of the same area, in which approximately a thousand residents had been interviewed from some thirty thousand "residential units"; social class had been assigned more or less mechanically on the basis of traditional sociological indices. From the respondents for the original survey, Labov eliminated three groups: those who had moved after the earlier survey, those who were not native speakers of English, and those born in other countries who had come to the Lower East Side after their eighth birthday. Weighting the percentages to be interviewed for each ethnic and social group, he found himself with 195 potential informants, of whom he interviewed 122 directly, in a situation considerably abridged from that of an Atlas interview, and 33 (still more briefly) over the telephone in what purported to be an inquiry about television programs. The LAMSAS records, through Frank's dissertation and the Kurath-McDavid Pronunciation, served as a baseline. However, although Labov suggests that drastic changes have taken place in New York pronunciation since the LAMSAS interviews were completed in 1941, comparison is not a simple matter. [26] As Kurath has remarked, the Lower East Side is not likely to be typical of Metropolitan New York. The English and Scotch Protestant representation is low, as is the Irish and German; only eight of 83 white natives of New York City in Labov's survey are not Jewish or Italian. The established upper class is not represented; in fact, none of Labov's informants could be classed as "cultured" by the Atlas standards. But this study admirably complements the Atlas investigations and reminds other scholars that the speech of New York, indeed that of any living community, is never a closed book.

Almost as influential as Labov's study, has been the investigation of Detroit speech by Roger Shuy and his associates, though as with Labov's materials the primary evidence is not in a shape in

which the conclusions can be tested by outsiders. Sponsored by the
Detroit school system and Michigan State University, a team of eleven
investigators completed more than seven hundred interviews, each an
hour and a half long, in the summer of 1966. Since the investigation
was designed to describe the varieties of language encountered in the
classroom, a decision was made to work through the schools in establishing the network. Through a process of ostensibly random
sampling, a selection was made of the public and Roman Catholic elementary schools in Detroit and the two enclaves of Highland Park and
Hamtramck; this sampling was supplemented by an "ethnic sample"
to include groups that the original sampling did not reach. For each
school, interviews were arranged with families of a more or less
random sampling of students in the upper elementary grades. There
would always be interviews with the student and a parent; if possible
there would be interviews with such other members of the household
as older siblings, grandparents, and occasionally great-grandparents.
Conceding the magnitude of Shuy's accomplishment, one must still
raise some questions about his network:

   1. As with Labov's study in New York, there was no sampling of upper-class speech. Members of this class either live in the
outer suburbs, send their children to non-Roman Catholic private
schools, or do both. [27]

   2. The large migration of Southern poor whites, dating
from World War I, and by now amounting to half a million persons in
metropolitan Detroit, is inadequately represented. As in Akron, they
are not physically conspicuous; and most of them live outside the city
limits. But like the upper class, they are an important part of the
economic system.

   3. Other ethnic groups may have been overlooked, or their
representation skewed, by failure to consult the latest demographic
studies.

   4. There was no use of the evidence from the regional atlases. The Michigan and Ontario and Ohio records from LANCS, including several from Detroit, would have provided a regional framework for interpreting Shuy's data from the point of view of the local
schools. The records from the South Atlantic states, of blacks and
upland whites, would have given some idea of the baselines from which
the migrants have come.

In all fairness, however, one is compelled to pay Shuy a
tribute for basic honesty. He himself presents the evidence by which
his methods can be criticized, in the most ruthlessly frank description for any survey since Kurath's Handbook of the Linguistic Geography of New England (1939; 2d ed., 1973).[28]

One of the most recent projects is Raymond K. O'Cain's
"Social Dialect Survey of Charleston, South Carolina" (diss. Univ.
of Chicago 1972). Like Labov's investigation in New York City, this
is a third-generation study. Charleston speech had been described
by Sylvester Primer in the 1880s; for the Atlas, Lowman and
McDavid had completed more interviews in Charleston than in any
other Atlantic Seaboard community except New York City, and
McDavid had not only summarized the characteristics of Charleston
speech but had indicated its relationship to other American dialects.[29]
In addition to distinctive and well-studied speech characteristics,
Charleston has an interesting history and social structure. The dominant mercantile center of the lower South Atlantic coast before the
Confederate War, it had lapsed into a kind of cultural backwater,
with a declining population until the 1930s. With the New Deal, the
economic and population trend was reversed; during World War II,
Charleston became an important military base, a role which it has
since enjoyed, along with new importance as a commercial port. The
population has expanded rapidly, with most of the increase coming
from the uplands of the Carolinas and Georgia, with speechways
sharply different from those of the coastal plain. Finally, the social
structure is distinctive: a small inside group of the descendants of
old merchant and planter families, not necessarily affluent, is still
sharply set off from the newer — and sometimes more wealthy —
middle class. The black subordinate caste also has its class divisions; its proportion of the total population has declined with the
black migration northward. Charleston also serves as a center for
urbanizing black migrants from rural South Carolina and the Sea Islands; often these latter are speakers of Gullah, a creolized language
long of interest to dialectologists, and described in particular by
Lorenzo D. Turner in Africanisms in the Gullah Dialect (Chicago:
Univ. of Chicago Press, 1949).

Since the studies of Primer and others had shown that
Charleston speech was strikingly divergent from other American

dialects, O'Cain restricted himself to informants who considered themselves native Charlestonians, even though they may have spent some time away. That is, unlike Labov, he was concerned with what happened to Charleston English and not simply to English in Charleston. He tried to include the full range of both races, both sexes, social classes, ethnic groups, and age groups from the late teens up. This meant abandoning any pretense at random sampling. Furthermore, although the criteria of education, occupation, residence style, and wealth were not ignored, they were used only as instruments toward discovering the actual ranking by the community — by other informants and by people who knew them. Of some hundred informants interviewed by O'Cain, he finally used seventy-seven, for whom there was full agreement on social status. Every informant, whether those finally used or not, was personally known to some of the others and ranked by them, so that O'Cain achieved a true network of communicating relationships, of the kind that Leonard Bloomfield used to sketch. [30] For reasons beyond O'Cain's control, not every social group was represented as fully as he had wished; those omissions, however, are derived from the accidents of history and not from the basic design of the project. [31]

VI

It is apparent that the network for a dialect investigation can be drawn in various ways. Which way it is drawn will depend both on the personal interests and theoretical bias of the investigator and on the auspices under which the research is conducted. It also depends ultimately on the nature of the community being investigated; it is doubtful whether O'Cain's methods could have been adapted to Labov's situation on the Lower East Side, though they might still work in some parts of Staten Island; it would be at least as futile to apply Labov's procedures mechanically to Sylva, North Carolina. However conscientiously the investigator plans his network, it is not likely that it will satisfy every critic; but dissatisfaction can be kept to a minimum if the investigator follows certain elementary precautions: he should work with the latest and most accurate information about the population from which his informants are to be drawn, and he should provide as explicit information as possible about the principles upon which his network was planned.

NOTES

[1]The original version of this paper was presented at the conference on Methods in Dialectology, Charlottetown, Prince Edward Island, 19-26 July 1972. Much of the basic information, not otherwise acknowledged, is drawn from Sever Pop, La Dialectologie (Gembloux, Belgium: Duculot, 1950), and Hans Kurath, Studies in Area Linguistics (Bloomington: Indiana Univ. Press, 1973). The author also acknowledges his indebtedness to the University of Prince Edward Island and its President, Ronald Baker, and to H. Rex Wilson, of the University of Western Ontario, Chairman of the Conference.

[2]Planning the grid may also allow the investigators to start off without a predetermined selection of communities, so that the network may grow as the investigation develops. Such a procedure may be useful in an investigation like that of José Pedro Roma, in his search for the line of demarcation in Uruguay between "Spanish" and "Portuguese." His recommended procedure is like range-finding by bracketing a target with successive salvos. It would probably be very useful in the sociolinguistic study of a community. The judgments of informants as to each other's relative status would yield a more accurate picture of the social structure than would the mechanical use of such indices as education, income, and housing.

[3]The first fascicles of LAMSAS have just been submitted to the University of Chicago Press.

[4]Some interviews were broken off; some items were irrelevant or unprofitable in some areas, for example, terms for coasting in the lower South, designations for poor whites north of the Mason-Dixon Line or even in the Southern uplands. Some informants, especially younger ones in urbanized areas, did not know the vocabulary of farming; some could not be induced to utter taboo items.

[5]Somersault might be expected to be a relatively simple item, with variants chiefly in pronunciation. Actual editing, however, disclosed a number of lexical variants: somerset (fairly well known), tum(b)lesault, tum(b)leset, sum(b)lesault, sum(b)leset, sumberset.

[6]The editors must reckon with differences in the practices of the fieldworkers, both in transcription and in elicitation. In contrast with the Linguistic Atlas of New England (LANE, 1939-43), where there were nine fieldworkers with sometimes sharply divergent practices, all but eleven of the records for LAMSAS were transcribed by either Guy S. Lowman, Jr. (who did two-fifths of the

field work for <u>LANE</u>) or Raven I. McDavid, Jr., a student of Kurath
and Bernard Bloch (who did more than one-fifth of the New England
fieldwork and was assistant editor to Kurath). In addition to his own
305 field interviews, McDavid transcribed from tapes 61 interviews conducted by Gerald Udell, Lee Pederson, Raymond O'Cain and a number of
Pederson's students. Differences between Lowman's transcription
practices and McDavid's are of the order of those between Lowman's
and Bloch's; see <u>Handbook of the Linguistic Geography of New Eng-</u>
<u>land</u> (Providence, R.I.: Brown Univ., 1939; 2d ed., New York:
AMS, 1973). Differences in interviewing techniques tend to affect
the relationships between fieldworker and informant and the amount
and kinds of data recorded — the number of lexical variants, the
number of unguarded conversational responses, and comments about
other usages in the community or area. The interests of the fieldworker and the informant will have similar effects: no one is equally
familiar with all aspects of everyday human activity and able to talk
about them, or to ask questions to elicit information about them.
Fieldworkers grow more successful with experience, but even the
most experienced have their differences. One may be more interested
in foods, another in mental and physical states. It is the obligation of
the editor to point out how the fieldworkers differ. To reduce the differences between the practices of fieldworkers, especially inexperienced ones, it has been proposed that each item of the questionnaire
be framed in a canonical form that must be asked exactly as stated.
This has been the practice both of Orton's <u>Survey of English Dialects</u>
and of Cassidy's <u>Dictionary of American Regional English</u>. However,
this procedure is not without its disadvantages; mechanically adhered
to, it prevents the skillful fieldworker from exploring openings in the
conversation; it hinders the gathering of synonyms; it discourages
the recording of unguarded responses from free conversation; it does
not prevent personal boundaries between fieldworkers, because personality — the indefinable quality of rapport — creates such boundaries as much as do the ways in which the questions are framed. Such
boundaries are not absent in the basic data from Orton's <u>Survey</u>,
though no one has as yet undertaken a detailed examination of them.
          [7]Some of the evidence is encapsulated in such summaries as
Kurath's <u>Word Geography of the Eastern United States</u> (Ann Arbor:
Univ. of Michigan Press, 1949), Kurath and Raven McDavid's <u>Pro-</u>
<u>nunciation of English in the Atlantic States</u> (Ann Arbor: Univ. of
Michigan Press, 1961), or Yakira H. Frank's "The Speech of New

York City" (Diss. Univ. of Michigan, 1949). However, these present only selections and summaries. Although the archives have always been accessible to reputable scholars, they were not consulted by William Labov for The Social Stratification of English in New York City (Washington: Center for Applied Linguistics, 1966), nor were the North-Central records examined by Walter Wolfram for his Sociolinguistic Description of Detroit Negro Speech (Washington: Center for Applied Linguistics, 1969). Although Joey Dillard's Black English (New York: Random, 1972) is loud in its denunciations of the high crimes and misdemeanors of linguistic geographers, it does not even mention Kurath in its index.

[8]Robert W. Burchfield, editor of the new Supplement to the Oxford English Dictionary (1972) insists that his staff should not be so large that he cannot know them all personally and properly evaluate their work.

[9]The latest discussion of the effective use of the tape recorder is W. R. Van Riper, "Shortening the Long Conversational Dialect Interview," Studies in Linguistics in Honor of Raven I. McDavid, Jr., ed. Lawrence M. Davis (University, Ala.: Univ. of Alabama Press, 1972), pp. 177-83. Experienced American fieldworkers, such as Kurath and Bloch, advocated from the beginning the gathering of high-frequency grammatical items in conversation, especially nonstandard forms with an aura of social taboo. (James H. Sledd has observed sardonically that any red-blooded American would prefer incest to ain't; this insecurity is particularly true of the rising lower-middle class, though not of long-established "old families.") In experimental taped interviews on Prince Edward Island in the summer of 1972, H. Rex Wilson found that some 90 percent of the grammatical items in his questionnaire would show up in about half of an interview.

[10]Cassidy has a thousand interviews for the fifty states; LAMSAS has 155 from Pennsylvania alone. But Cassidy's questionnaire is perhaps half again as long and is supplemented by correspondence materials and the systematic reading of regional and local novels, magazines, newspapers, and the like.

[11]Again in contrast to the ALF, the AIS employed three field investigators: Paul Scheuermeier in the north, Gerhard Rohlfs in the south, Max Leopold Wagner in Sardinia. Furthermore, in contrast with Edmont — an excellent practical phonetician and an amateur historian, but not a trained linguist — all three went on to distinguished academic careers. Because he feared that philological

knowledge might prejudice the investigation, Gilliéron described the ideal fieldworker as an animated transcribing machine.

[12]Jaberg and Jud had originally intended to study only northern Italy and the adjacent portions of Romance Switzerland, leaving central and southern Italy and the islands to the Italians.

[13]The eighteen years Pellis spent in the field is the longest consecutive full-time stint for any investigator, though others (for example, R. I. McDavid, Jr., in the United States and H. R. Wilson in Canada) have worked over longer periods. Lowman was in the field nearly ten years consecutively, before his death in 1941. Even the most experienced and durable investigators, when working full time, find it necessary to alternate periods of intense field activity — a month to six weeks at most — with interludes for recovery and for planning the next expedition. It is the extraordinary investigator who can maintain his interest, let alone his professional skills, over a long period.

[14]See Angus McIntosh, Introduction to a Survey of Scottish Dialects (Edinburgh: Nelson, 1953).

[15]During his visiting professorship at the University of Tennessee, Orton proposed a dialect survey of the state, concentrating on elderly uneducated farmers. He proposed to select six communities in each of the state's 95 counties and conduct one interview in each community (whether he would adopt the policy of splitting the interviews among several informants, as was the usual practice in England, was not specified); he would thus have almost twice as many interviews as in his English survey, for perhaps a tenth the population. To those familiar with the Southern scene, it is questionable whether either Davidson County (Nashville) or Shelby County (Memphis) would provide so many communities unaffected by urbanization, or whether such predominantly rural counties of low population as Houston, Moore, Pickett, and Van Buren really have so many distinctive communities. A study of settlement history and present-day population distribution might be in order before plans go further.

[16]In Europe the industrial revolution imposed new urban centers on already settled areas; in North America, urban centers were coeval with settlement. By the time of the American Revolution, despite the amount of unsettled land even east of the Appalachians, Philadelphia and Boston were the second and third most important cities under the British Crown.

[17]Unanticipated, of course, was the interruption of fieldwork by World War II.

[18]Some counties have clear cultural divisions and are studied as two communities. On the other hand, the planning of the network took into account the fact that in some states several counties have been divided to help dominant political factions retain control of at least one house of the state legislature. Since such divisions rarely reflected older cultural divisions, they were rarely reflected in the network. Sometimes, too, a metropolitan community has spread over two or more counties, which have been grouped together, such as DeKalb and Fulton counties in Georgia, which make up the Atlanta metropolitan area.

[19]After Roger Shuy completed his dissertation (PADS, no.38, 1962) on the boundary between the North and the Midland in Illinois, his field records were added to the North-Central archives.

[20]A number of communities, beginning with the Hudson valley Dutch, were originally settled by speakers of other languages than English: Germans, Scandinavians, and the like. Half of the communities investigated in Wisconsin were selected precisely because they had been settled by such groups. Naturally, for the regional linguistic atlases of American English every informant must be a native speaker of English, regardless of what other languages he speaks as a native.

[21]Since most of rural Kentucky shows stationary or declining population and many communities are still relatively isolated, it was proposed that it might be desirable to expand the network and in nearly half the communities interview only the oldest and least sophisticated informants. Although it was not necessary in Kentucky, such a policy might be desirable in Arkansas or Tennessee if adequate geographical coverage cannot otherwise be achieved.

[22]The validity of checklist evidence was demonstrated in A.L. Davis, "A Word Atlas of the Great Lakes Region" (Diss. Univ. of Michigan 1949). The first regional atlas incorporating checklist evidence is Harold B. Allen's Linguistic Atlas of the Upper Midwest (Minneapolis: Univ. of Minnesota Press, 1973-6). The first survey of the Gulf states region, by Gordon R. Wood, used checklist evidence alone.

[23]The evidence for E. Bagby Atwood's The Regional Vocabulary of Texas (Austin: Univ. of Texas Press, 1962) was gathered by student field investigators; the network was limited by the origins of the students and by their local contacts. David W. Reed, director of the

Linguistic Atlas of California and Nevada, conducted an investigation on the scale of a Cecil B. DeMille spectacular — three hundred field records and a thousand checklists, in an area of comparatively recent English-speaking settlement and very heavy recent accretions of population. As with the ALI, the sheer bulk of the evidence has complicated the editorial process. The one major publication resulting from it is Elizabeth Bright's Word Geography of California and Nevada (Berkeley: Univ. of California Press, 1971).

[24] Contemporaneous with Frank's dissertation is Allan F. Hubbell, The Pronunciation of English in New York City: Consonants and Vowels (New York: King's Crown Press, 1950), which used some of the Atlas records as well as independent interviews, mechanically recorded. The late C. K. Thomas also did extensive studies of New York City speech, using tape recordings of college students.

[25] Here I am indebted to Hans Kurath, The Investigation of Urban Speech, PADS, no. 49 (1970).

[26] As already pointed out, Labov did not consult the primary Atlas evidence, but only the statements in the derivative studies of Frank and Kurath-McDavid. Nor have any of his later studies of New York made use of contacts with the old upper-class population.

[27] The first study of such a group in a metropolitan area is Frances Uskup's, Social markers in urban speech: a study of elites in Chicago; Diss., Illinois Institute of Technology, 1974. She finds differences between upper-class and upper-middle class speech in both pronunciation and vocabulary.

[28] Roger W. Shuy, Walter A. Wolfram, and William K. Riley, Field Techniques in an Urban Language Study (Washington: Center for Applied Linguistics, 1968). For many of the criticisms I am indebted to the students in my courses in sociolinguistics, 1968-72.

[29] "The Position of the Charleston Dialect," PADS, no. 23 (1955), 35-49.

[30] That informants should evaluate their social status with respect to each other is one of the techniques for the study of social class recommended by my colleagues McKim Marriott and Julian Pitt-Rivers. That there should be disagreement on some informants (the data, of course, being otherwise useful, if not in this study) is not surprising. See for example C. C. Fries, American English Grammar (New York: Appleton, 1940).

[31] A strike of service personnel in one of the local hospitals restricted O'Cain's contacts with the lower-class black population, especially the younger group.

13 | New Directions in American Dialectology

Forty years have passed since I was introduced to dialectology as a demonstration informant in Bernard Bloch's seminar in field methods at the Ann Arbor Linguistic Institute of 1937. As my postscript indicates, this experience changed the direction of my career. It also sets up a time frame within which to survey the development of the field. If my emphasis here is on the aspects of dialectology with which I have been most closely concerned, it does not imply derogation of other kinds of inquiries. The vineyard is large enough for workers of assorted vocations; even the failures are significant in revealing the complexity of the problems investigated.

Reviewing a field in which one has actively participated for some time raises the question of how to differentiate between the professional and the personal — of avoiding both arrogance and false modesty. The solution I have followed is to use the third person when dealing with matters of record, the first person when treating matters of yet unrecorded personal experience.

I

Interest in the study of American dialects is now greater and more knowledgeable than at any time in the past. Government support, once concentrated on applications, has recently shifted to basic research, to the benefit of several of the regional surveys and Cassidy's Dictionary of American Regional English (1978-). The ten numbers of the Urban Language Series of the Center for Applied Linguistics (Shuy 1966-) have publicized some of the implications of dialect research, as have various projects initiated by members of the Center;

other sociolinguistic investigations, more closely tied to traditional
dialect studies, continue at such other institutions as Chicago, Emory,
Massachusetts, and South Carolina. Two anthologies (Allen and
Underwood 1971, Williamson and Burke 1971) indicate the various in-
terests of dialectologists. The second edition (1977) of Carroll Reed's
Dialects of American English (1967) is an excellent introductory over-
view by a scholar who has investigated dialects of English and German
(C. Reed and Seifert 1954).

Much of this interest is due to a renewal of energy in the
American Dialect Society, sadly moribund in 1937. Founded in 1889
with the aim of preparing an American Dialect Dictionary comparable
to The English Dialect Dictionary of Joseph Wright (1898-1905), the
Society, never large, nearly succumbed to the great depression of the
1930's, publishing only six volumes of Dialect Notes in five decades. [1]
Since 1942 it has gradually enlarged its membership and raised the
standard of its publications. Its new series, Publications of the
American Dialect Society [PADS], has included many significant contributions, e.g. Shuy 1962, Pederson 1965a, Kurath and Lowman
1970, Creswell 1975. With the Society assuming responsibility for
the more general publication American Speech, PADS has become a
supplementary monograph series; both AS and PADS, once three
years behind schedule, have made up their time lag — a testimony to
the heroic efforts of their editors, notably John Algeo of Georgia,
editor of AS since 1970. [2] With the Society alone there are better opportunities than ever for students of American dialects — and not
merely dialects of English — to see their work in print in a reasonable time.

II

The largest-scale project for the study of American dialects
has been the Linguistic Atlas of the United States and Canada, conceived in 1929 under the sponsorship of the American Council of
Learned Societies and the directorship of Hans Kurath, after several
distinguished linguists — notably Charles C. Fries, Edgar Sturtevant,
and Edward Sapir — had observed that the time was ripe for a survey
of Western Hemisphere English comparable to that of French under
Jules Gilliéron (1902-10) and that of Italian under Karl Jaberg and
Jakob Jud (1928-40). New England was chosen for the pilot project

of a survey whose completion was envisaged within a decade. However, the launching of the Atlas coincided with the onset of the Depression. Though field work in New England was completed in two years (1931-33) and publication by 1943 (Kurath et al. 1939, 1939-43), sources of funds had dried up meanwhile, so that only one investigator, Guy S. Lowman, Jr., could be kept in the field in other regions. On Lowman's death in 1941, and the involvement of the United States in World War II later that year, field work along the Atlantic Seaboard came to a halt. Meanwhile, Kurath had decided that managing a survey of two nations was beyond his foreseeable resources; he advocated a series of regional projects west of the Appalachians, retaining jurisdiction only over the New England project, nearing completion, and the proposed regional atlases of the Middle and South Atlantic States, for which Lowman had completed two-thirds of the projected interviews.

The war also interfered with the distribution and criticism of the Linguistic Atlas of New England [LANE] (Kurath et al. 1939-43), printed in an edition of only three hundred copies. The continental European universities, where dialectology had arisen, were cut off from communication with North America; wartime austerity and the effects of the Depression restricted sales in both the British Commonwealth and the United States. The result has been that a generation of scholars has grown up with little first-hand exposure to the actual findings in New England; and their students in turn — knowing this work largely by hearsay — frequently misunderstand its purpose and accomplishment. Some of this ignorance, fortunately, has been dissipated by the reprinting of the New England Atlas and a new edition of its accompanying Handbook of the Linguistic Geography of New England (Kurath et al. 1939), the last with an inventory of the contents of its maps and a word index of all forms recorded. [3]

III

With postwar grants from the Linguistics Fund of the ACLS, Kurath was able to manage the completion of the field work along the Atlantic Seaboard, but was never able to secure funds for editing and publication. Some of this difficulty stemmed from the fact that he moved to the University of Michigan in 1946, as editor-in-chief of

the Middle English Dictionary, and thenceforth had to regard the Linguistic Atlas project as a spare-time activity. Upon his retirement
the Atlantic Seaboard archives were transferred to the University of
Chicago and the Illinois Institute of Technology, and editing was resumed. In 1974 they were transferred again, this time to the University of South Carolina, which has provided not only comfortable
quarters for editorial work and housing of the archives but money and
manpower to keep editorial operations under way.[4] By now, the first
fascicles of the Linguistic Atlas of the Middle and South Atlantic
States [LAMSAS] are in the hands of the publisher, the University of
Chicago Press (Kurath, McDavid, O'Cain and Dorrill 1979-); editing and composition for printing are both proceeding rapidly.

        Kurath had already decided that there would be a single Lin-
guistic Atlas of the Middle and South Atlantic States, embracing the
area from southern Ontario through northeastern Florida. Because
of the size of the area and the number of the interviews, some 1200,
presentation of the data on maps would be difficult. There were also
two practical considerations: (1) draftsmen's wages, for preparing
the phonetic overlay for base maps, have risen far more than academic salaries, as has the cost of binding large volumes; (2) the size
and weight of the New England volumes, with slightly more than four
hundred interviews in a far smaller territory, have created difficulties in shelving in libraries and in handling by students. The
LAMSAS is being printed in tables, somewhat like those in Harold
Orton's Survey of English Dialects (1962-71), but on a somewhat
larger page, that of the Oxford English Dictionary and analogous
works. Each volume — the number of volumes cannot yet be estimated — has prefatory maps indicating the principal topographic features and major cities and the communities investigated. Publication
is by photo offset, less expensive than set type and eliminating a stage
of proofreading.[5]

                                    IV

        In the meantime, derivative and supplementary studies have
made some of the findings for the Atlantic Seaboard accessible to an
audience wider than that which has a copy of the Atlas of New England
in the reference room of their library, let alone those who can travel
to where the unedited archives are housed. Kurath himself made

available the data on a selection of vocabulary items in his Word Geography of the Eastern United States (1949); E. Bagby Atwood summarized the largest group of grammatical items in his Survey of Verb
Forms in the Eastern United States (1953); Kurath and R. McDavid
provided a phonological summary in their Pronunciation of English in
the Atlantic States (1961). Two articles by R. McDavid, "The Folk
Vocabulary of New York State" (1951), and "The Position of the
Charleston Dialect" (1955), present vocabulary evidence that was not
available when the Word Geography went to press. Three of Kurath's
students — Walter S. Avis (1955), Thomas Wetmore (1956), and W.
R. Van Riper (1958) — have discussed in detail in their dissertations
the Atlantic Seaboard evidence on the mid-front and mid-back vowels,
the low-central and low-back vowels, and postvocalic /-r/. The
first was published in part in Language (1961), the second in PADS 32
(1959).

V

The progress of the autonomous regional surveys has been
uneven, depending on the presence of an energetic director, the
availability of competent field workers, and financial support — the
last usually meaning a long-term commitment by a major university.
But these surveys have seen two innovations in the gathering of data:
(1) the revival of the correspondence questionnaire; (2) the introduction of the tape recorder.

Correspondence questionnaires are old in dialect study. They
were used in gathering data for the Deutscher Sprachatlas of Wenker
and Wrede (Wrede, Mitzka, and Martin 1926-56), for Mitzka's complementary Wortatlas (1951-73), and for the surveys in Norway and
the Netherlands. But they came under severe criticism from such
scholars as Gilliéron and Jaberg, on the ground that there were too
many personal variations in transcription. As Albert H. Marckwardt
got his Atlas of the North-Central States under way (Marckwardt,
R. McDavid, et al., 1978-), he was wont to suggest to his seminars
at the University of Michigan that the problem was not in the correspondence technique but in the use to which it had been put; that a multiple-choice check list, restricted to items without social taboo,
would at least serve as a preliminary investigative instrument, and
could provide useful evidence supplementing what was obtained in the

field. These hopes were confirmed in the dissertation of A. L. Davis,
A Word Atlas of the Great Lakes Region (1949). Marckwardt did not
incorporate the check list in his own survey, but investigators in Ohio,
Indiana and Illinois have utilized it for special studies, or just as a
means of familiarizing students with the methods and aims of linguistic geography. In other regions, notably the Upper Midwest and California, it has been an integral part of the survey.

     The tape recorder, a by-product of electronic research dur-
ing World War II, has been used in many investigations, including
some of the last interviews for Marckwardt. It has a number of advantages: it provides a permanent record; it makes possible the division of the task of data-gathering between a skilled interviewer and
an expert transcriber; and above all, it permits the gathering of copious conversational data, especially grammatical forms (about which
even the least literate informant may be on guard), on a scale which
cannot be matched by the best interviewer transcribing in the field.
But it has its disadvantages: it is another object which the field worker has to watch; it may give out at critical moments in the interview; its greatest advantage, the garnering of unguarded responses,
must be weighed against the need for very close listening for as much
as four times the length of the original interview. Most dangerous,
its presence sometimes tricks the interviewer into believing that it
will materially shorten the interview, so that he often hurries through
and forces or skips items that might be of considerable interest, or
fails to explore the possibility of variants (but cf. Van Riper 1972).
It is worth knowing that the earliest field records in Indiana, using
the tape recorder, provide far less grammatical evidence than those
in Michigan and Ohio,where the older techniques were employed. If
a survey depends on tape recorders for gathering data, the interviewer must not only be trained in the operation and maintenance of
the machine, but must be given particular instruction in conducting
the interview and getting all the questions answered, in other words,
in handling the interview as if the machine were not present. Except
for close attention to conversational items, the transcriber in turn
should make his notations as if he were working with a live informant,
and avoid tormenting himself by repeated playings-back in an effort
to record ever finer phonetic shadings. [6]

     The Linguistic Atlas of the North-Central States was begun
by Marckwardt in 1938, in an effort to discover whether there was

indeed a highly uniform "General American" in the old Northwest Territory (R. McDavid 1976). When preliminary investigations revealed that the Great Lakes Basin and the Ohio Valley differ strikingly in vocabulary and pronunciation and even in some details of grammar, he proposed a survey with a network somewhat coarser than that for the Atlantic Seaboard (Marckwardt 1957). Of the states in the survey, only Wisconsin was completed before the United States entered World War II, and it was after 1970 that the last communities were investigated. Since most of the work was locally financed, principally by the state universities (the University of Michigan was by far the most generous), there have been over thirty field workers, with many divergences in their practices. However, as in New England, one interviewer did the greatest part of the work, and since he was the most experienced it is possible to calibrate against his practices those of the others in the same or adjacent communities. [7]

Editorial work on the North-Central materials lagged for a decade after the field work was essentially complete: Marckwardt was in constant demand by committees, government bureaus and professional associations; and R. McDavid, who had worked most closely with him, had inherited in 1964 the responsibility for the Middle and South Atlantic States. A small conference in 1974 led to a larger one the next June, at which Marckwardt outlined his editorial plan and assigned tasks to various colleagues; these plans continue in effect after his death, with one major change. Since the division of editorial responsibilities among several institutions demanded several copies of the field records, they have been published in their entirety, in microfilm and Xerox, by the Joseph Regenstein Library of the University of Chicago. Where tapes have been retranscribed, the original transcription will also be available, as will the tapes (Marckwardt, R. McDavid, and Payne 1976-78). For the first time in the history of linguistic geography, it is possible for scholars, without leaving their own institutions, to go behind a published atlas to the primary data from which it is derived — field records, retranscriptions, and tapes. Thus the data of general interest can appear in summary volumes like those for the Atlantic Seaboard. The published Atlas — editing is well under way — will contain treatments of grammar, pronunciation and vocabulary, as well as interpretive apparatus like that contained in the New England Handbook.

The Linguistic Atlas of the Upper Midwest, the second
American regional survey to be published (Allen 1973-76; Allen 1958
and Allen 1964 are early studies), was begun in 1947 by Harold B.
Allen of Minnesota, a lifelong friend of Marckwardt as well as one of
his original field workers and a former colleague at Michigan. Allen
did the lion's share of the field work and almost all of the editing;
three of his investigators had received training under Kurath and
Bloch, of the original New England staff. The chief complications
arose in Iowa, where inexperienced students took on the interviewing
and divided the state along an east-west line, so that there is sometimes a problem of separating regional from personal boundaries.
With check list data supplementing field records, Allen faced the
problem of interpreting two kinds of evidence; the check list findings
are normally presented as graphs with percentages, rather than by
individual plottings or isoglosses on maps. As a by-product, one of
Allen's field workers, Virginia McDavid, completed a dissertation
on Verb Forms in the North-Central States and the Upper Midwest
(1956), a major supplement to Atwood's Survey for the Atlantic Seaboard. It provided the kernel of Allen's grammatical volume (1975)
and will serve a similar function for Mrs. McDavid's grammatical
volume on the North-Central States.

The Atlas of the Rocky Mountain States was begun ambitious-
ly in 1950, by Marjorie Kimmerle of the University of Colorado.
With assistance from her university and other local institutions, she
completed the Colorado field work in a year (cf. Kimmerle, R.
McDavid, and V. McDavid 1951). But elsewhere there was little
support for field workers, and of those, none ever completed a state.
Since Miss Kimmerle's death (1963) the project has lagged. Two dissertations have been derived from the Colorado materials, by
Elizabeth Jackson (1956) and Clyde Hankey; the latter has appeared
in PADS (1960). But otherwise the only published account of a survey, and that in microfilm, is of eastern Montana by Thomas O'Hare
(1964), a student under Atwood at Texas.

Little more has appeared from the Pacific Coast. While at
the University of Washington, Carroll Reed — one of Kurath's students and co-author of a Linguistic Atlas of Pennsylvania German
(1954) — completed field work in Washington, with a few interviews
in Idaho and Montana; nothing was done in Oregon, nor have his

materials been edited. In California and Nevada, David W. Reed, one of Marckwardt's students, secured from the University at Berkeley the most generous institutional support an American survey has had — enough to complete in a short time three hundred field records and a thousand check lists (D. Reed 1954). But again editing has lagged, though the summary of the vocabulary evidence from the field records in Elizabeth Bright's Word Geography of California and Nevada (1971) whets a reader's appetite.

In the interior of the United States, the field work for Oklahoma was completed by Van Riper in 1957-63, that for Missouri by Gerald Udell in 1965-68. Both sets of records are slowly being edited; the death of Van Riper in 1977 has caused a revision of plans, but the completion of editing is assured. In 1970, Gary Underwood, one of Allen's students, began to organize a survey of Arkansas, more as a series of local sociolinguistic projects than in the tradition of linguistic geography (cf. Underwood 1972). For the latter type of investigation, Arkansas was incorporated in Pederson's survey of the Gulf States. In Kansas, several scholars have attempted to launch a statewide survey; James Hartman of the state university, associated with Cassidy on the Dictionary of American Regional English, promises to complete field investigations. The late C. M. Wise of Louisiana State provided seventeen field records toward a linguistic atlas of Hawaii; but they have not been edited, and recent interest in Hawaiian speech continues to concentrate on the complex area of creoles and pidgins.

The newest regional investigation in the United States, and in several respects on the largest scale, is the Linguistic Atlas of the Gulf States, directed by Lee Pederson of Emory University (cf. Pederson 1969). Until recently the difficulty in coordinating and funding work in the region was all too reminiscent of the difficulties the late Confederacy experienced in waging war in that territory. Funds were lacking; institutional and personal rivalries prevented any concerted effort, and there was no one strong and energetic enough to be director. Texas, with the most extensive linguistic operations of any American university, did not provide adequate support for such a distinguished scholar as Atwood. His survey of the lexicon, conducted on a shoestring with student investigators, produced a remarkable Regional Vocabulary of Texas (1962); but after

his death in 1963 no one completed his complementary survey of pronunciation. In Louisiana, Wise's students conducted more than a
hundred interviews with the long Atlas work sheets, but Wise never
considered them a substitute for field work with trained investigators,
and neither he nor his successors were able to organize such a survey. For the rest of the region, from central Georgia to the Mississippi, there was only the check list survey by Gordon Wood, utilized
in two early studies (Wood 1960, 1961) and published as Vocabulary
Change (1971).

A new situation developed when Pederson arrived at Emory
in 1966. A student under R. McDavid and a former colleague of
Allen, he brought to the Gulf States the same energy that had characterized his earlier study of Chicago (Pederson 1965b, 1970b). To
help the public schools of Atlanta understand the varieties of language
spoken by students newly arrived in the city, he organized a survey
of rural Georgia (Pederson 1975), using a short questionnaire to interview four informants, two black and two white, in each quadrangle
of a finely meshed grid covering the state. From 1968 he has developed the regional atlas. After several small grants for pilot
studies, including one for the investigation of East Tennessee (the
last pre-Revolutionary settlements to be studied)[8], he obtained generous and continuing support from the National Endowment for the
Humanities. The Gulf States survey extends from Georgia to central
Texas, with a more extensive coverage of urban areas than in any of
its predecessors (cf. Pederson 1971a). All interviews are recorded
on tape and transcribed later; the tape is considered the field record,
the transcription being the protocol. Publication will be in various
forms: protocols on microfiche, a Handbook, summary volumes,
and ultimately a regional dictionary including all recorded utterances.

In Canada the greatest activity so far has been in the Maritimes, where Lowman made several interviews in New Brunswick for
the New England Atlas (border communities in Canada were also investigated for the Atlases of the Middle and South Atlantic States, the
North-Central States, and the Upper Midwest). Early attempts by
Henry Alexander, of Queens University, to provide more extensive
coverage of the Maritimes ran afoul of military suspicion during
World War II. Two local surveys — by H. Rex Wilson in the sometime German settlement of Lunenburg County (1958) and by Murray

Wanamaker in the Annapolis Valley (1965) — have been supplemented by later field work to the point where an atlas of southern Nova Scotia is in the editing stage.[9] Murray Kinloch, of the University of New Brunswick, has resumed field work in that province. There have been three conferences on methods in dialectology (Prince Edward Island 1972, 1975; the University of Western Ontario 1978), to stimulate Canadian interest. In Newfoundland the interest has been chiefly in dialect lexicography, but there has also been active study of phonology and grammar.[10] In 1970 the Canadian Council of Teachers of English launched a national survey of usage (Scargill 1974, Scargill and Warkentyne 1972, Warkentyne 1971), conducted principally by check lists distributed in schoolrooms; though not a substitute for field interviewing, it provides — like Wood's check list survey of the Gulf States — extensive coverage of a small number of items and should make it easier for scholars elsewhere in Canada to emulate the kind of work now going on in the Maritimes.

Although most of English-speaking North America has been surveyed for regional linguistic atlases, most of the findings remain as raw data in institutional files, with occasional articles on specific features. Atwood's study of the Texas vocabulary and Allen's Atlas of the Upper Midwest are the only large-scale studies to reach final publication since LANE. There are several reasons for the lag in publication. Editing demands not only patience and attention to detail but awareness that one's personal achievement is less important than the progress of the work. Furthermore, an editor-in-chief has different administrative problems from a dean or department head; and needs a different kind of institutional support, which is not always forthcoming. The glacial pace of editing is not without precedent in dialectology — although Wenker began the survey of German dialects in the 1870's, the first fascicle of Wrede's Deutscher Sprachatlas did not appear till 1926 — but it is often frustrating for those interested in interpretive studies. For this reason the publication of basic materials in microfilm or microfiche should be welcomed.

VI

All of the studies discussed so far have been in the tradition of Gilliéron and Jaberg and Jud, sometimes modified by the use of

check lists for studying the vocabulary. All of them, explicitly or
otherwise, recognize the traditional affiliations of linguistic geography with historical linguistics, as a means for tracing the relationships of various types of regional speech with each other and of helping to reconstruct the earlier states of the language. For this reason
there is a deliberate skewing in the direction of older and more traditional usage — through a somewhat heavier representation of rural
and small-town society, a larger selection of the oldest and least
educated segments of the population, and a more zealous search for
the old-fashioned elements of the vocabulary than current population
and usage might seem to justify on a purely statistical basis.[11] But
the peculiar linguistic situation in the United States and Canada, with
no single regional variety of speech having cultural preeminence, also made it advisable to include representative educated speakers in
a large number of communities, and in almost every community a
member of the intermediate group. From three basic types of informant — folk, common and cultivated — it has been possible to
make some judgments about social differences at the time the evidence was collected (cf. Pederson 1972), and about the indicated
direction of change at the time. No one involved in the Atlas project ever asserted that it could provide a definitive statement of sociolinguistic differences in a nation whose society has been characterized by movement and change; nevertheless, the evidence provides a
set of bench marks at a given period, against which the findings of
subsequent studies may be measured.

The number of community studies undertaken within the Atlas framework — that is, making use of the evidence gathered for the
regional surveys, at least as a starting point — is impressive. In
New England, Robert Parslow has restudied the speech of Boston
(1967); so has David Carlson (1973), using the evidence from
Cassidy's Dictionary of American Regional English. A number of the
students of Audrey Duckert (University of Massachusetts) have rein-
vestigated communities studied for the New England Atlas, occasionally (as Miss Duckert herself did in Plymouth) finding one of the original Atlas informants to start from (Duckert 1963). Yakira Frank
(1949) used the Atlas records for a study of New York City, as did
Allan Hubbell — supplemented by his own recordings (1950; also on
New York cf. Thomas 1947b and Bronstein 1962). Marckwardt's student Dennis Lebofsky has investigated the speech of Philadelphia

(1970). In North Carolina the sociolinguists Crockett and Levine
have studied the effects of increased education and affluence on the
speech of the small community of Hillsborough (Levine and Crockett
1966).[12] The independent oligarchy of Charleston, South Carolina,
has been studied afresh by Raymond O'Cain of the University of South
Carolina (1972); in turn, John Hopkins, one of his students, has investigated the rival principality of Savannah, Georgia (1975), and
others have examined smaller communities in the region (cf. Dorrill
1975 and Greibesland 1970). In the Middle West there have been numerous studies — Gerald Udell in Akron (1966), Pederson (1965b,
1971b) and Robin Herndobler (1977) in Chicago, Charles Billiard in
Fort Wayne (1969), Robert Howren in Louisville (1958), Robert
Weber in Minneapolis and St. Paul (1964), and Marvin Carmony in
Terre Haute (1965).[13] From the Pacific Coast we have the studies
of Fred Brengelman for the Puget Sound area (1957), David DeCamp
in Metropolitan San Francisco (1958-59), and Allan Metcalf (1971)
and others in Riverside. Utilizing Atlas methodology, but lacking a
regional frame of reference because no regional survey had been undertaken at the time, are such studies as those of Arthur Norman in
the southeast corner of Texas (1956) and Juanita Williamson among
the Negroes of Memphis (1968).[14]

VII

As yet there are no phonographic archives of American English comparable with those which Zwirñer et al. 1958- have established in Germany.[15] There is not even a satisfactory discography
— a list of language recordings with subject matter and dates. The
late C. K. Thomas accumulated several thousand tapes of a reading
passage, generally selecting his informants from the students at
teachers colleges, and out of his archives developed his successful
book on the phonetics of American English (1947a);[16] but since his
death his collection has not been accessible. More recently, as a
part of a project for preparing teachers of English in the state of
Illinois, Alva L. Davis and his associates at the Illinois Institute of
Technology developed a questionnaire for pronunciation alone, involving short responses, minimal pairs, a reading passage and free
conversation. With it they obtained some thirty specimens of cultivated speech in the United States and Canada, a diversity great

enough to shake the ethnocentricity of most teachers. Under the title of Recordings of Standard English, it has expanded its aims to the
sampling of as many varieties of English as possible, wherever spoken, and to exchanging tapes with scholars in other institutions
(A. Davis et al. IP). [17]

VIII

Dialect lexicography, we have noted, antedates dialect geography in English. Though the original aim of the American Dialect
Society — to make an American Dialect Dictionary comparable to
Wright's for England — was not immediately realized, the Society
never forgot its charge. Frederic G. Cassidy of Wisconsin, once a
student under Marckwardt, is now bringing it to completion. After
nearly two decades of preparation, including preparation and testing
of a new questionnaire of some 1500 items (originally it was used by
correspondence), a generous grant from the U.S. Office of Education
enabled him to launch the Dictionary of American Regional English
[DARE] in 1965. Within five years his operatives completed their
field investigations — 1002 interviews in all fifty states, representing
the same cultural spread that was achieved in the regional atlases;
others read extensively in regional novels, diaries, and local newspapers. With the aid of new technology, including computer storage
and printout, the DARE is in an advanced stage of editing. It was
Cassidy's plan to offer the DARE as a contribution to the national bi-
centennial of 1976, even as Walter Avis and his Canadian colleagues
made the Dictionary of Canadianisms (1967) an offering to the centennial of Confederation. The prophecy was fulfilled by the display of
specimen galleys in November 1976. Even in its unfinished state —
and publication is bound to take several years — DARE is a primary
source of material for regional and local studies. Its questionnaire
has also been used in independent studies, such as Saunders Walker's
dissertation on the speech of the eastern Alabama Negro (1957).

Outside of DARE, the most noteworthy venture into dialect
lexicography in English-speaking North America has been the Dictionary of Newfoundland English. For a long time a labor of love by
George Story, a member of one of the oldest Newfoundland families,
it has recently achieved outside support and is nearing completion
(Story et al. IP). Whatever comes to light about the speech of this

oldest and most isolated English-speaking community in the New
World is sure to be of interest on both sides of the Atlantic.

IX

"Dialect writing" has long been used as source material for
the study of regional and local speech. As evidence from field work
accumulates, the process gets turned around, so that scholars may
assess the authenticity with which local or regional speech is represented. Norman and Pederson and Curt Rulon (the last in greatest
detail) have made forays into Hannibal, Missouri, to discover the
baseline from which Mark Twain worked in Huckleberry Finn; apparently there is nowhere near as fine a discrimination in the novel
as is asserted in the preface (cf. Pederson 1965a, 1967; Rulon 1966).
Sumner Ives has analysed the dialect of the Uncle Remus stories
(1954, 1955), aided by the fact that Joel Chandler Harris's son
Julian was one of the Atlanta informants for LAMSAS. [18] More recently, Charles William Foster of Alabama has examined the works
of Charles W. Chesnutt (1971), utilizing the field records from Fay-
etteville and Greensboro, North Carolina. James W. Downer (1958)
has done a magnificent study of the representation of dialect in the
Biglow Papers — a study complicated by the fact that Lowell's Cambridge has been swallowed up in metropolitan Boston, so that the
speech of other communities, chiefly in southern New Hampshire,
had to be used to establish the baseline.

X

The best picture of bilingualism and non-English dialects in
North America can be obtained from the works of Einar Haugen, be-
ginning with The Norwegian Language in America (1953) and continuing
through successive versions of his Bilingualism in the Americas
(first published in 1956) to his summary in the tenth volume of
Sebeok's Current Trends in Linguistics (1973). The late Uriel
Weinreich has also contributed to the field, both through Languages
in Contact (1953) and through investigations of Yiddish dialects (1954;
Weinreich et al. IP); these last were largely conducted in New York
City because American investigators could not obtain access to informants in Eastern Europe (cf. Herzog 1965). There is a spate of

competent investigations of various languages transported to the
American scene, one of the most noteworthy being Janet Sawyer's
study of the bilingual community of San Antonio, Texas (1957; cf.
Sawyer 1959, 1964).[19] Joshua Fishman of Yeshiva University has
become a distinguished figure in this field, particularly for his emphasis on sociological method (Fishman et al. 1966). The current
emphasis on ethnic identity should lead to a new period of serious investigation of non-English dialects.

XI

As Jaberg 1936 indicated, conclusions about the social status
of linguistic forms can be drawn from geographical investigations,
even those — like the French and Italian atlases — that confine themselves to folk speech. The complexities of American life and language led Kurath to include in his design three general classes of informants — folk, common, and cultivated. This expanded coverage
permitted a finer-grained social analysis than was possible from the
records of previous atlases; it also suggested the direction of change
at the time of the interviewing. However, the Atlas records admittedly could not represent all classes in any community, let alone in all.
Moreover, the very rigor of the methods of linguistic geography, essential to its function as a part of historical linguistics — selecting
informants from the long-rooted and stable elements of the local
population — necessarily excluded some of the groups in which so-
ciologists have been most interested: the recently arrived in a community, whether from other lands or from other parts of the United
States. The Atlas records could — and did — provide benchmarks
for gauging the linguistic acculturation of the new arrivals, but they
said nothing about the speech of the new arrivals itself. For this,
new techniques were needed.

Kurath 1968 outlined a way in which the investigation of social
dialects might have developed under more relaxed circumstances:
starting with small homogeneous communities in the center of dialect areas, and proceeding to communities of greater complexity. In
this way, it would have been some time before investigations reached
the larger metropolitan areas, though the methods would have been
thoroughly tested en route. But circumstances ruled otherwise: if
something was lost in not proceeding in the orderly sequence from

small communities to great, much was gained in the increased attention to the importance of social differences in language, and in the development of linguistic theory.

The circumstances come from changes in American society, and in the educational systems of American cities. Beginning with the New Deal in 1933, there had been accelerated urbanization of American society. As agriculture became mechanized, blacks and poor whites and Spanish-Americans left the countryside and moved to metropolitan areas. Since government housing policies favored the development of new suburbs and neglected the rehabilitation of older neighborhoods, there was a steady flow of the more affluent out of the cities, leaving behind deteriorating areas into which the new arrivals swarmed. This replicated the earlier mass immigration of Irish, Italians, Germans, Scandinavians, Slavs and Jews, but with one important difference. The older immigrants were suspect for using a different language than that of the host communities; the new were suspect because, though generally speaking English, they had different cultural patterns. Moreover, the largest number were blacks, who were too conspicuous to fade into the neighborhoods and suburbs like their predecessors. [20]

It were futile to blame any community or region for the difficulty in assimilating the new groups. But a large share of the blame must go to two institutions — the labor unions and the public schools. The steady rise in the minimum wage has meant that employers, both agricultural and industrial, have periodically reexamined the role of unskilled labor. It has become economically feasible to invest in machinery for tasks like cotton picking, traditionally performed by hand. Tenant farmers and small landowners were displaced; they moved to the city, to compete with the other unskilled and unemployed, and their families swamped the already crowded schools.

The schools, meanwhile, had also undergone changes. In response to union pressures, to prevent competition from young people (not necessarily the poor) who heretofore had gone to work at 14 or 15, child labor laws were passed, and thousands were incarcerated in the schools longer than before. With good vocational training expensive, and traditional liberal arts education cheap, the newly enrolled were offered little to make them employable. Finally, in the

1930s, most schools adopted the practice of social promotion, by
which pupils were automatically advanced to the next grade, regardless of how little they had learned. [21]

The combination of these forces — social promotion, more
years of enforced enrollment, and the inundation of the schools with
new hordes of the impoverished — made teaching in urban schools
more difficult, a situation aggravated by the flight to the suburbs and
private schools of many who would have provided cultural models.
In almost every urban public school system there has been an alarm-
ing decline in academic performance, especially in reading and writing. Because linguists had been successful in teaching exotic foreign
languages — and teaching English to speakers of other languages —
in World War II and afterwards, they were summoned to deal with the
teaching of standard English to speakers of non-standard dialects
(cf. Labov 1970, Shuy and Fasold 1970). [22]

Unfortunately, there was nothing like the concerted effort
achieved by the American Council of Learned Societies in 1941-45;
each school system — and there are thousands of school systems in
the United States — approached the problem in its own way, often ig-
noring its neighbors; only by chance did any local program try to
make use of the massive amount of data collected or in the process of
being collected. One should not fault the local investigators but rather the traditional American urge to achieve instant solutions and to
ignore the past. No doubt a part of the blame must be shared by the
traditional dialectologists who were not as active as they might have
been in making their data generally available. Very rarely was any
of their evidence used by those who attempted to deal with the new
problems. [23] The strength and weakness of the new approach can be
found in the work of both of its best-known exemplars, William Labov
and Roger Shuy.

Labov first attracted attention through his investigation of
the diphthongs /ai, au/ on Martha's Vineyard (1963). He showed
that among the younger generation there were two competing tenden-
cies in the articulation of these diphthongs: those who identified
strongly with the island culture went against the historical trend and
favored centered beginnings [ə̆ɨ, əu]. A later study of the lower East
Side of Manhattan (Labov 1966) treated five linguistic variables:

postvocalic /-r/, affrication and stop-articulation of /θ,ð/ , tongue
height of /æ,ɔ/. Among the population studied, the more sophisticated favored constriction of /-r/, /θ,ð/ as fricatives, and lowest
tongue height of /æ,ɔ/ . More recently Labov has initiated a general
study of sound change in progress. The general thrust of his work is
presented in two collections, Labov 1972a, 1972c.

Shuy's principal achievement in social dialectology has been
the study of Detroit and the urban enclaves of Highland Park and Hamtramck, with the needs of the local school systems particularly in
mind (Shuy, Wolfram and Riley 1968). In the summer of 1966 a team
of investigators conducted over seven hundred interviews; working
with the public and Roman Catholic parochial school systems they interviewed on a more or less random basis a sample of pupils in the
upper elementary grades, parents, and (if available) older siblings
and grandparents. Although none of the basic evidence has yet been
published, the project has evoked a great deal of discussion and has
led to a number of derivative studies, e.g. Wolfram 1969, Wolfram
and Christian 1976.

XII

The increasing interest in the various implications of social
differences in language is more than scholars of the older traditions
could cope with. In the recent investigations much of the basic work
has been done by technicians, or by people drawn from other fields,
such as education. Even in linguistics, since Chomsky 1957 led to
an emphasis on 'theoretical insight' and to the decrying of data-orien-
tation, many students have not examined such a basic discussion of
linguistic geography as that in Bloomfield 1933; the insistence of linguistic geographers that generalizations be tested against the record
is taken as a threat. [24] Consequently, what should be cooperation is
too often felt as competition, with linguistic geographers labeled as
obstructionists in the way of more creative investigations.

Looking objectively, one should consider linguistic geography and sociolinguistics not as competing but as complementary; just
as linguistic geography starts from the findings of comparative and
historical linguistics and adds insights into linguistic history, so can
sociolinguistic studies start from linguistic geography and add new
insights to that field. The linguistic geographer cannot expect the

sociolinguist to replicate his previous findings, but he can expect his findings to be utilized when they deal with communities in question. The sociolinguist in turn cannot expect the linguistic geographer to use his methods, but he can expect a recognition that various aims and techniques are appropriate to various situations. Neither should let theoretical orientation stand in the way of the data.

Labov's study of the Lower East Side illustrates the complementarity of the two approaches. As Labov has repeatedly said, his work in New York would have been impossible without the Atlas evidence. The Lower East Side is a volatile area, through which successive waves of immigrants have spread into Greater New York. The Atlas records did not include Italians, Jews or blacks; Labov found no Dutch or English Protestants, and none of the older German immigration, and no informants who would qualify as cultivated by Atlas standards. The Atlas records present an over-all picture of the stable element in New York City speech before World War II; Labov shows how the picture is being modified by the more recent arrivals in a changing social situation.

Shuy's Detroit study does not show the same use of previously gathered evidence, and there are in addition some sociolinguistic problems that his survey does not reckon with. For a long time, city limits have not encompassed the full population of a major city; and some important elements of the population do not send their children to public or Roman Catholic schools. In the Detroit area, many of the Southern whites, who have been arriving since World War I — Marckwardt once estimated their numbers at about half a million — live outside the city where they can combine gardening and hog-raising with work in the automobile shops. The upper class and many of the upper middle class — the local models of prestigious speech — also tend to suburban living; or if they live in the city they send their children to what Australians call "non-Catholic independent schools" (Mitchell and Delbridge 1965).[25] Restriction of the survey to the city limits of Detroit and to a particular selection of the population introduces a skewing of the results. Yet one must remember that Shuy was working on a tight schedule with the interests of the Detroit school system in mind. One can only look forward to a more complete publication of the data than has yet been achieved, and to a supplementary study of prestigious speech analogous to Uskup 1974. Meanwhile the

Detroit study — which would have been impossible had it been de-
layed a year (the great riot occurred in 1967) — has garnered the
largest amount of data on the speech of the volatile population of a
major American city.[26]

The differences in aims between linguistic geography and sociolinguistic studies are reflected in two principal ways: the selection of informants and the presentation of the data. Since the regional
surveys are concerned with indigenous benchmark cultural groups,
their investigators rely on local intermediaries who know the community and its people; the assignment of social class is made tentatively on the judgment of the intermediaries, and refined after a long
period of interaction between field worker and informant. With the
interest in statistics common to the social sciences, sociolinguistic
studies try to employ objective techniques of selecting and classifying
informants. How successful they have been in achieving their goal of
a random sample is another matter, which can be judged by examining
such straightforward descriptions as Labov 1966 and Shuy, Wolfram
and Riley 1968.[27]

Linguistic geographers generally identify informants and
their responses; atlases like those for France, Italy and New England present the full phonetic record on maps; Orton's English survey and LAMSAS present it in lists; other studies use cartographic
or list devices for identifying classes of responses. In every instance the emphasis is on the informants as individuals. The sociolinguistic studies, emphasizing the usage of groups, generally sub-
merge the individual in statistical frequencies. Each type of presentation is legitimate for its particular purpose. As with other differences, each kind of investigation can learn from the other, and
both would probably benefit from a better knowledge of statistics.

XIII

Pardonably, much recent work in sociolinguistics has concentrated on the speech of blacks and of Spanish-Americans. Both of
these groups are conspicuous, by appearance or by surname; both
have inundated larger metropolitan areas during the last generation;
both have large numbers who have not achieved anything like full

participation in American society. Yet ironically the largest number
of the so-called 'disadvantaged' are white Protestant gentiles of colonial English-speaking stock; and in many ways this group —
especially those from the Southern uplands — have had more difficulty
than Southern blacks in coping with Northern metropolitan society
(L. Davis 1971). [28]

　　　With many of the sociolinguistic studies being pedagogically
oriented for Northern situations, and with blacks of Southern origin
conspicuous grammatically and phonologically, there has been a tendency to set up a dichotomy between 'Standard English' and 'black
English.' 'Standard English' is in turn identified with the outworn
label 'General American' or its more recent synonym 'network English'[29] — probably some variety of Great Lakes Basin upper middle
class suburban speech. As often used, 'Standard English' excludes
all Southerners, whatever their social credentials, though a half
century of research has demonstrated that in North America the standard may have many phonetic shapes.

　　　'Black English' is likewise discussed as if it were monolithic, though the speech of the black American comes in as many
varieties as that of the white American, [30] including all varieties of
the standard. This variety in black speech has been recognized by
Southerners for more than a century; it is slowly being accepted elsewhere — Shuy specifically restricts 'black English' to the Northern
metropolitan situation where there is a de facto contrast with prevailing white usage, unlike the Southern situation where there is generally
a continuum.

　　　The origins of the speech of American blacks have been de-
bated for generations. At one time it was fashionable to identify
everything in the speech of Southern blacks with Southern British regional rural dialects or with baby talk. Now the coin is reversed,
following serious study of Gullah (Turner 1949) and the growing interest in pidgins and creoles beginning with Hall 1943. The prevailing 'creolist' position is that all 'black English' results from a re-
lexification of a general 'plantation creole' spoken throughout the
South, with Gullah — the speech of blacks on the Sea Islands and necks
of the South Carolina and Georgia coast — being a relic of something
once far more extensive.

The truth, as usual, is somewhere in between. Gullah is clearly a creole (Kurath 1972b: 118-21); its perimeter has been contracting with the breakdown of geographical and cultural isolation, and many speakers of Gullah have migrated to Northeastern communities, where they mingle with other blacks, including native speakers of West Indian creoles. But Gullah was always atypical; the Southern plantation country was large and diverse, and often slow in developing — with stages when any original African or creole element was submerged through contacts with far more numerous whites. A century of emancipation, with a decrease in casual contacts between blacks and whites, has probably reduced the impact of white speech. The recent concentration of blacks in extensive Northern black belts has created a situation analogous to that in which the West Indian creoles arose. The de facto 'black English' in the Northern and Western cities may well represent a 'neo-creolization.' Meanwhile the accessibility of the new material on English folk speech (Orton 1962-71; Viereck 1975; cf. also Kurath 1970, 1972a) and on that of Newfoundland (e.g., Paddock 1966) provides further basis for comparison and the study of origins.

XIV

It is popular to draw up lists of stigmata for 'black English'; I myself have prepared a checklist of linguistic features with social significance (R. McDavid 1969), though not restricting it to any ethnic group — and found it necessary to abridge it with each revision. One of the best known lists, that of Fasold and Wolfram 1970, offers some fifty stigmata for 'Negro dialect.'

But of these, many are attested in the New England Atlas; observers have noted at least half in my natural speech, and almost every one has been found by Harold Paddock in Carbonear and other Newfoundland outports (cf. Paddock and R. McDavid 1971). To come down to specific cases, there is no reason to identify as peculiarly black a monophthongal pronunciation of /ai/ [a·], as in my eye, /ðez/ for there's (cf. R. McDavid and O'Cain 1977a), omission of the relative pronoun as subject of a relative clause, compound auxiliaries like might could and used to didn't, multiple negation extending across a principal clause and a subordinate clause (Ain't nobody never makes no pound cake no more; cf. Labov 1972b, Labov and R. McDavid IP),

disyllabic plurals of nouns in / -s̲p̲, -s̲t̲, -s̲k̲/, or omission of the
copula (we going, you a good boy, they all dead).

Much has been made of the aspectual difference in the 'black
English' copula: zero for present, be/bees for timeless non-past.
But Paddock 1966 shows that in Carbonear (as apparently in some
Irish dialects) every verb has a marked aspectual difference: present
I think, he think; timeless non-past I thinks, he thinks.

In attempting to identify the ethnic status of particular speech
forms, some linguists rely on informants' intuition. Nevertheless,
an experienced observer is wary of such identification: natural examples of allegedly ungrammatical structures are not always easy to
construct.[31] Most important, some forms are so thoroughly stigmatized that even an assured respondent is hesitant to admit them
(Sledd 1964: 473; R. McDavid and O'Cain 1977b).[32] Intuition is a
very poor substitute for recorded evidence. Yet until the findings of
the larger surveys become more accessible than they have been for
the past thirty years, misinterpretations are likely to continue.[33] In
the meantime it is to be hoped that linguistic geographers and sociolinguists can recognize the complementarity of their work and let the
polemics of the past fade away as old soldiers are wont to do. There
is enough variety in present-day American English, and tongues in-
teracting with it, to occupy several generations of linguists of all per-
suasions and interests.

XV

The development of American dialectology in the past few
decades reveals its unique qualities as a subdivision of linguistics.
It is a data-oriented discipline, in a land teeming with unrecorded
data. However fine the theoretical extrapolations one may wish to
make, the dialectologist's first duty is to present the data in such a
way that any reader can replicate the conclusions — or failing to replicate them, can show where the original statement went astray. However unfashionable this position may be at any given time, it is one in
which the dialectologist can take comfort. For sooner or later the
fashion will change, and data-oriented linguistics, like Sir Roger de
Coverly's coat, will again be in style. It is gratifying to know that

most Americans who work seriously in dialectology are following its traditional principles, albeit with new technical aids and in new situations.

NOTES

This paper was delivered at the Congress of the International Association of University Professors of English, in Istanbul, August 1971. It was published in its original form in Studia Anglia Posnaniensia [Poznan, Poland] 5.1-2.9-25 (1975); in revised form in English Studies Today 5.53-85 (1973). It was massively revised for my students at the University of South Carolina in the fall of 1976, and has been further revised for this volume. It cannot be either completely up to date or exhaustive: new works continue to appear, even as this last version is being typed. Nor can it be completely objective: each person properly emphasizes the kind of work he is most concerned with. It is hoped, however, that it will give some idea of the breadth and depth of the subject, and encourage readers to explore the topic for themselves.

[1] The health of the Society was not improved by the disappearance of its collections and the decision of its editor to devote most of the sixth volume of Dialect Notes to publishing the third part of Thornton's American Glossary (1931-39).

[2] As this is written, a committee of the Dialect Society has recommended a change of name to the American Language Society, with an accompanying change of PADS to PALS, and American Speech to American Language. The last change appropriately recognizes the influence of H. L. Mencken, the founder of AS (Mencken et al. 1945), whose American Language (1919), in various editions, has convinced "200% Americans that the study of their national tongue can be interesting, and more than interesting, important" (Mencken 1948).

The change of name does not symbolize a change of interest for the Society, one of the oldest learned bodies in America. But it may create a more favorable attitude in other disciplines. In many European countries dialect is a derogatory term — a variety of language an educated person had rather be found dead than speaking; in the United States, dialect has customarily been thought of as the property of "funny old people in out-of-the-way places" (Shuy 1967), and

'dialect collecting' has been identified with dilettantism; lately,
dialect has often been restricted to "the speech of poor black kids in
urban slums" (Griffith and Miner 1970).

[3] Audrey Duckert not only prepared the map inventory and
word index but chaperoned the new edition through the press. The
most detailed examination of LANE is O'Cain 1979.

[4] A 1977 grant from the National Endowment for the Humani-
ties has facilitated editorial operations. The commitment of South
Carolina to the Atlas was made possible by the interest of the late
John Welsh, Vice-President for Academic Affairs, of Milledge B.
Seigler, Senior Professor in the University, and of Kenneth Toombs,
Director of Libraries.

[5] For the phonetic transcriptions, the Atlas staff has designed
a special element for the IBM Selectric typewriter — Camwil 1873-M.

[6] As demonstrated with the last taped interviews in the North-
Central States, the best-conducted interviews are the most difficult to
transcribe adequately from the tape.

[7] Retranscriptions by R. McDavid, the principal investigator,
of taped interviews by many of the other field workers have aided in
the calibration of transcription practices.

[8] Students of American history will recall that frontiersmen
from what later became East Tennessee contributed heavily to the de-
cisive colonial victory at Kings Mountain, South Carolina.

[9] Wilson and his associates are exploring the use of computer
storage and retrieval in dialect geography, though there have been
previous experiments, notably by W. Nelson Francis with selected
forms recorded in Orton's Survey of English Dialects (1962-71).
Cassidy is making extensive use of the computer for his Dictionary of
American Regional English, which however does not have the phonetic
complexity of materials in linguistic atlases.

[10] The study of Newfoundland grammar is the particular concern of Harold Paddock, a Newfoundlander himself.

[11] Orton's English Survey is oriented far more toward the
past than are the American atlases, which include such cultural innovations as baby carriage and kerosene, and such urban institutions as
library and hotel. By traditional European standards these are not
'dialect' items, since they are not characteristic of old-fashioned
rural and village life; nevertheless, they show regional or social patterns of distribution in North America.

[12]Clearly there is an increase in /-r/ coloring among the younger educated informants, but explanations of this increase may differ. To a Southerner it seems less likely influenced by the radio than by two sets of sociolinguistic facts: (1) Hillsborough is near the intersection of four dialect areas — Albemarle Sound-Neuse, Pee Dee-Cape Fear, Western Carolina, and the Virginia Piedmont — of which only the last has shown loss of /-r/ among all social classes; (2) since 1930 there has been in the South a dramatic extension of education and affluence to groups, predominantly /-r/ retaining, who had hitherto been outside the mainstream of Southern society.

[13]Pederson participated in the sociolinguistic projects initiated by the University of Chicago and the Illinois Institute of Technology; some of his findings appear in Shuy 1965.

[14]Because Miss Williamson is herself a Negro American, her findings are of importance in assessments of the relationship between the speech of blacks and that of whites. Regrettably, those who push the case for fundamental divergence often deliberately ignore her work; nothing of hers was included in Wolfram and Clarke 1971.

[15]Efforts to provide a discography for the National Council of Teachers of English have come to naught; several institutions are assembling collections of recordings, but there is no coordinated effort. Clearly the making of a discography is a necessary first step, which probably calls for the sponsorship of several organizations, such as was given the Biographical Dictionary of the Phonetic Sciences (Bronstein et al. 1977).

[16]Thomas's two chief interests are the low-back vowels before intervocalic /-r-/ and the phonetic quality of that phoneme.

[17]For a description of the project, including the questionnaire, see the Newsletter of the American Dialect Society 1.3.14-17 (1969).

At the Poznan Congress of the International Association of University Professors of English (1977) the project received informal endorsement from the Association and from the local representative of the British Council. The project is now under the supervision of Mackie Blanton, a junior colleague.

[18]Ives 1950, "A Theory of Literary Dialect," is one of the basic studies; it is matched only by the introduction to Downer 1958, which is available as yet only in microfilm and Xerox.

[19]Mrs. Sawyer and Daniel Cárdenas have combined to make Long Bearh (California) State University one of the most important centers for the study of Spanish-American bilingualism. Baird 1977 probes further into the complexities of San Antonio speech.

[20]'Urban speech' and 'inner city speech' have become de facto euphemisms for black speech.

[21]Demands for some kind of accountability on the part of the schools are resisted violently by various liberal groups. Most notorious is a resolution of the College Conference on Composition and Communication on students' right to their own language — a resolution widely disseminated by the CCCC parent body, the National Council of Teachers of English. It is an ironic 'right' that would not only cut the students off from that part of their cultural heritage that represents the best that has been thought and said in the world, but would reinforce the notion that blacks and other minorities are incapable of learning.

[22]Contrariwise, such pundits at large as Dwight Macdonald and Edwin Newman blame the 'permissiveness' of the linguists for the 'deterioration' of the English language — a charge familiar since the belletristic hue-and-cry against the Merriam Third New International (R. McDavid 1971). Since writing is taught by products of university English departments — bodies not given to sympathy to either linguistics or the teaching of writing — the charge is absurd; but absurdity has never limited the spread of misconceptions.

An attempt to disseminate a more rational attitude was made at the Chicago Conference on Language Variety (April 1977); a selection of the papers offered at this conference is on its way to publication.

[23]Exceptional is Labov's use of Linguistic Atlas of New England, of Kurath and R. McDavid 1961, and of Frank 1949.

[24]As Kurath has frequently observed, the presentation of data postulates an underlying theory, but the reverse is not always true.

[25]What is true of Detroit is even more true of the older cities along the Atlantic Seaboard, where the public schools were long considered institutions designed for paupers. In Brooklyn Heights, well before the influx of blacks and Puerto Ricans, it was rare for the children of the educated and well-to-do to attend public schools.

[26]The problems in conducting the survey are set forth in Shuy, Wolfram and Riley 1968. Though one may question many details of the operation, one can only applaud the honesty of presentation, and the fact that the investigation was completed on schedule.

[27]Because O'Cain was concerned with the continuity of Charleston speech, not simply with the speech of those who happened to be living in Charleston at the time, he used personal contacts in

locating his informants. For assignment to social class he relied on
his own judgment (as one who had been intimately associated with the
community), on the judgments of his intermediaries, and on the judgments of other informants. Only if all judgments agreed was an interview considered for his study, though it would be useful for other
purposes (cf. Fries 1940).

[28]One who began his teaching career in a fairly prestigious
all-white Southern college learned early that white students with some
advantages may have difficulties in mastering the grammatical conventions of written English.

[29]The ideal of a deregionalized 'network English' has been
achieved by few Americans, notably Richard Nixon and Barbara
Walters. Some would add Billy Graham; but during the Watergate
hearings it was observed that Graham's speech was reverting to its
North Carolina origins. Nor is it without significance that most of
Nixon's Watergate playmates were speakers of faceless deregionalized English, while the members of the prosecuting committee —
notably the senior senator from North Carolina — spoke unabashedly
in their native idiom.

[30]There are many bibliographies of black English; the most
comprehensive is I. and W. Brasch 1974, but see also McMillan 1971.

[31]Fries 1952 (197) observes that ". . .'indirect objects' and
'object complements' never, so far as I know, occur in the same sentence." Attempts to construct a natural contrary example failed; however, about a year later I caught myself saying, "We've elected us
Ike President, and now we're stuck with him." Subsequently I found
several other examples, but they are not common.

[32]R. McDavid and O'Cain 1977b was prompted by the discovery that my own judgments, when I was interviewed by Bloch in 1937,
were frequently at variance with the facts. Eastern Virginians often
asserted to Lowman that forms widely spread in local white usage,
like the preterite clim, were restricted to blacks. So far, no one
has examined the validity of the judgments of informants interviewed
for the Linguistic Atlas of New England.

[33]Part of the misinterpretation has been caused by the changing emphasis in graduate studies since World War II. Graduate programs in English rarely require the serious study of the language
that was expected in the 1930s, and many programs in linguistics
openly decry the 'dull cataloguer of data.' Most of those who attribute peculiar ethnicity to forms like we tells have never examined
closely a Middle English text like the Cursor Mundi.

REFERENCES

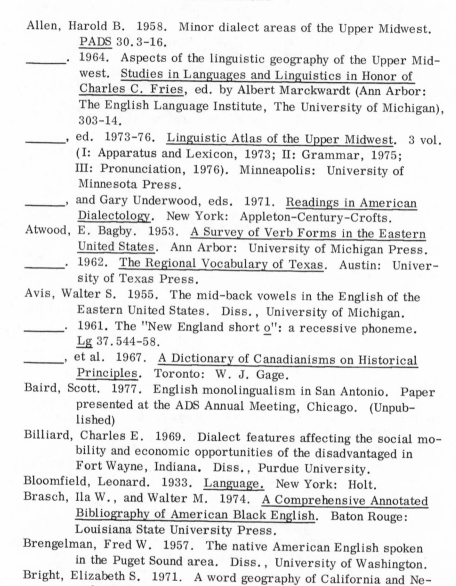

Allen, Harold B. 1958. Minor dialect areas of the Upper Midwest.
    PADS 30.3-16.
_____. 1964. Aspects of the linguistic geography of the Upper Mid-
    west. Studies in Languages and Linguistics in Honor of
    Charles C. Fries, ed. by Albert Marckwardt (Ann Arbor:
    The English Language Institute, The University of Michigan),
    303-14.
_____, ed. 1973-76. Linguistic Atlas of the Upper Midwest. 3 vol.
    (I: Apparatus and Lexicon, 1973; II: Grammar, 1975;
    III: Pronunciation, 1976). Minneapolis: University of
    Minnesota Press.
_____, and Gary Underwood, eds. 1971. Readings in American
    Dialectology. New York: Appleton-Century-Crofts.
Atwood, E. Bagby. 1953. A Survey of Verb Forms in the Eastern
    United States. Ann Arbor: University of Michigan Press.
_____. 1962. The Regional Vocabulary of Texas. Austin: Univer-
    sity of Texas Press.
Avis, Walter S. 1955. The mid-back vowels in the English of the
    Eastern United States. Diss., University of Michigan.
_____. 1961. The "New England short o̱": a recessive phoneme.
    Lg 37.544-58.
_____, et al. 1967. A Dictionary of Canadianisms on Historical
    Principles. Toronto: W. J. Gage.
Baird, Scott. 1977. English monolingualism in San Antonio. Paper
    presented at the ADS Annual Meeting, Chicago. (Unpub-
    lished)
Billiard, Charles E. 1969. Dialect features affecting the social mo-
    bility and economic opportunities of the disadvantaged in
    Fort Wayne, Indiana. Diss., Purdue University.
Bloomfield, Leonard. 1933. Language. New York: Holt.
Brasch, Ila W., and Walter M. 1974. A Comprehensive Annotated
    Bibliography of American Black English. Baton Rouge:
    Louisiana State University Press.
Brengelman, Fred W. 1957. The native American English spoken
    in the Puget Sound area. Diss., University of Washington.
Bright, Elizabeth S. 1971. A word geography of California and Ne-
    vada. University of California Publications in Linguistics, 69.

Bronstein, Arthur J. 1962. Let's take another look at New York
    City speech. AS 37.13-26.
_____, et al. 1977. A Biographical Dictionary of the Phonetic
    Sciences. New York: The Press of Lehman College.
Carlson, David B. 1973. The common speech of Boston. Diss.,
    University of Massachusetts.
Carmony, Marvin D. 1965. The speech of Terre Haute: a Hoosier
    dialect study. Diss., Indiana University.
Cassidy, Frederic G., et al. 1978-. Dictionary of American Re-
    gional English. Cambridge, Massachusetts: Belknap
    Press.
Chomsky, Noam. 1957. Syntactic Structures. The Hague: Mouton.
Creswell, Thomas J. 1975. Usage in dictionaries and dictionaries
    of usage. PADS 63-64.
Davis, Alva L. 1949. A word atlas of the Great Lakes region.
    Diss., University of Michigan.
_____, et al. IP. Recordings of Standard English.
Davis, Lawrence M. 1971. A study of Appalachian speech in a
    Northern urban setting. Final Report, Project no. OE-142.
    Washington: USOE, HEW.
DeCamp, David. 1958-59. The pronunciation of English in San Fran-
    cisco. Orbis 7.372-91; 8.54-77.
Dorrill, George T. 1975. A comparison of Negro and White speech
    in Central South Carolina. M.A. thesis, University of
    South Carolina.
Downer, James. W. 1958. Features of New England rustic pronun-
    ciation in James Russell Lowell's Biglow Papers. Diss.,
    University of Michigan.
Duckert, Audrey R. 1963. The Linguistic Atlas of New England
    revisited. PADS 39.8-15.
Fasold, Ralph W., and Walter A. Wolfram. 1970. Some linguistic
    features of Negro dialect. Teaching Standard English in the
    Inner City, ed. by Roger W. Shuy and Ralph W. Fasold
    (Washington: Center for Applied Linguistics), 41-86.
Fishman, Joshua, et al. 1966. Language Loyalty in the United
    States. The Hague: Mouton.
Foster, Charles W. 1971. The phonology of the conjure tales of
    Charles W. Chesnutt. PADS 55.
Frank, Yakira H. 1949. The speech of New York City. Diss., Uni-
    versity of Michigan.

Fries, Charles C. 1940. American English Grammar. New York:
    Appleton-Century-Crofts.
_____. 1952. The Structure of English. New York: Harcourt,
    Brace.
Gilliéron, Jules, and Edmond Edmont. 1902-10. Atlas linguistique
    de la France. Paris: H. Champion.
Greibesland, Solveig C. 1970. A comparison of uncultivated Black
    and White speech in the Upper South. M.A. thesis, Univer-
    sity of Chicago.
Griffith, Jerry, and L. E. Miner, eds. 1970. The Second and Third
    Lincolnland Conferences on Dialectology. University, Ala-
    bama: University of Alabama Press.
Hall, Robert A., Jr. 1943. Melanesian Pidgin English: Grammar,
    Texts, Vocabulary. Baltimore: Linguistic Society of America.
Hankey, Clyde T. 1960. A Colorado word geography. PADS 34.
Haugen, Einar. 1953. The Norwegian Language in America. 2 vol.
    Philadelphia: University of Pennsylvania Press.
_____. 1956. Bilingualism in the Americas: A bibliography and
    research guide. PADS 26.
_____. 1973. Bilingualism, language contact, and immigrant lan-
    guages in the United States: a research report 1956-1970.
    Current Trends in Linguistics, Vol. 10, ed. by Thomas A.
    Sebeok et al. (The Hague: Mouton), 1.2.505-91.
Herndobler, Robin. 1977. White working-class speech: the East
    Side of Chicago. Diss., University of Chicago.
Herzog, Marvin I. 1965. The Yiddish language in Northern Poland.
    IJAL 31.2 (Part 3).
Hopkins, John. 1975. The white middle-class speech of Savannah,
    Georgia: a phonological analysis. Diss., University of
    South Carolina.
Howren, Robert R., Jr. 1958. The speech of Louisville, Kentucky.
    Diss., Indiana University.
Hubbell, Allan F. 1950. The Pronunciation of English in New York
    City: Consonants and Vowels. New York: King's Crown
    Press.
Ives, Sumner. 1950. A theory of literary dialect. Tulane Studies
    in English 2.137-82.
_____. 1954. The phonology of the Uncle Remus stories. PADS 22.
_____. 1955. Dialect differentiation in the stories of Joel Chandler
    Harris. American Literature 27.88-96.

Jaberg, Karl. 1936. Aspects géographiques du language. Paris: E. Droz.

_____, and Jakob Jud. 1928-40. Sprach- und Sachatlas Italiens und der Südschweiz. Zofingen: Ringier.

Jackson, Elizabeth H. 1956. An analysis of Colorado Atlas vocabulary records with regard to settlement history and other factors. Diss., University of Colorado.

Kimmerle, Marjorie, Raven I. McDavid, Jr., and Virginia McDavid. 1951. Problems of linguistic geography in the Rocky Mountain area. Western Humanities Review 5.249-64.

Kurath, Hans. 1949. A Word Geography of the Eastern United States. Ann Arbor: University of Michigan Press.

_____. 1968. The investigation of urban speech. PADS 49.1-7.

_____. 1970. English sources of some American regional words and verb forms. AS 45.60-68.

_____. 1972a. Relics of English folk speech in American English. Studies in Linguistics in Honor of Raven I. McDavid, Jr., ed. by Lawrence M. Davis (University: University of Alabama Press), 367-75.

_____. 1972b. Studies in Area Linguistics. Bloomington: Indiana University Press.

_____, and Guy S. Lowman, Jr. 1970. The dialectal structure of Southern England: phonological evidence. PADS 54.

_____, and Raven I. McDavid, Jr. 1961. The Pronunciation of English in the Atlantic States. Ann Arbor: University of Michigan Press.

_____, et al. 1939. Handbook of the Linguistic Geography of New England. Providence: American Council of Learned Societies. 2nd ed., with addenda by Audrey R. Duckert and Raven I. McDavid, Jr. (New York: AMS Press, 1973).

_____, et al. 1939-43. Linguistic Atlas of New England. 3 vol. in 6 pts. Providence: American Council of Learned Societies. Repr., 3 vol. (New York: AMS Press, 1972).

_____, Raven I. McDavid, Jr., Raymond O'Cain, and George T. Dorrill. 1979- . Linguistic Atlas of the Middle and South Atlantic States. Chicago: University of Chicago Press.

Labov, William. 1963. The social motivation of a sound change. Word 19.273-309.

_____. 1966. The Social Stratification of English in New York City. Washington: Center for Applied Linguistics.

Labov, William. 1970. The Study of Non-Standard English. Urbana:
       NCTE.
———. 1972a. Language in the Inner City. Philadelphia: Univer-
       sity of Pennsylvania Press.
———. 1972b. Negative attraction and negative concord in English
       grammar. Lg 48.773-818.
———. 1972c. Sociolinguistic Patterns. Philadelphia: University
       of Pennsylvania Press.
———, and Raven I. McDavid, Jr. IP. Affirmative anymore.
Lebofsky, Dennis S. 1970. The lexicon of the Philadelphia metro-
       politan area. Diss., Princeton University.
Levine, Lewis, and Harry J. Crockett, Jr. 1966. Speech variation
       in a Piedmont community: postvocalic r. Sociological In-
       quiry 36.204-26.
McDavid, Raven I., Jr. 1951. The folk vocabulary of New York
       State. New York Folklore Quarterly 7.173-92.
———. 1955. The position of the Charleston dialect. PADS 23.35-49.
———. 1969. A checklist of significant features for discriminating
       social dialects. American Dialects for English Teachers,
       USOE Project HE-145, SS-12-32-67, ed. by Alva L. Davis
       (Urbana: Illinois Statewide Curriculum Study Center in the
       Preparation of Secondary School English Teachers), 62-66.
———. 1971. False scents and cold trails: the pre-publication
       criticism of the Merriam Third. Journal of English Lin-
       guistics 5.101-21.
———. 1976. In memoriam: Albert H. Marckwardt (1903-1975)
       and the Linguistic Atlas of the North-Central States. A
       memorial. Orbis 25.176-86.
———, and Raymond O'Cain. 1977a. Existential there and it: an
       essay on method and interpretation of data. James B.
       McMillan: Essays in Linguistics by his Friends and Col-
       leagues, ed. by I. Willis Russell and James Raymond (Uni-
       versity, Alabama: University of Alabama Press), 29-40.
———, and Raymond O'Cain. 1977b. Prejudice and pride: linguis-
       tic acceptability in South Carolina. Acceptability in Lan-
       guage, ed. by Sidney Greenbaum (The Hague: Mouton), 103-
       32.
McDavid, Virginia. 1956. Verb forms in the North Central states
       and Upper Midwest. Diss., University of Minnesota.
McMillan, James B. 1971. Annotated Bibliography of Southern Amer-
       ican English. Coral Gables: University of Miami Press.

Marckwardt, Albert H. 1957. Principal and subsidiary dialect areas of the North-Central states. PADS 27.3-15.

_____, Raven I. McDavid, Jr., and Richard C. Payne. 1976-78. Linguistic Atlas of the North-Central States: Basic Materials. Manuscripts on Cultural Anthropology, Series 38, nos. 200-208. Chicago: Joseph Regenstein Library, University of Chicago.

_____, Raven I. McDavid, Jr., et al. 1978- . Linguistic Atlas of the North-Central States.

Mencken, H. L. 1919. The American Language. New York: Knopf. 4th ed., 1936.

_____. 1948. Letter to Raven I. McDavid, Jr. (Presently in possession of the Newberry Library)

_____, et al. 1945. American Speech: the founders look back. AS 20.241-46.

Metcalf, Allan A. 1971. Riverside English. ED 071-464. Bethesda, Maryland: ERIC Document Reproduction Service.

Mitchell, A. G., and Arthur Delbridge. 1965. The Speech of Australian Adolescents. Sydney: Angus and Robertson.

Mitzka, Walther, and L. E. Schmitt. 1951-73. Deutscher Wortatlas. 20 vol. Giessen: W. Schmitz.

Norman, Arthur M. Z. 1956. A southeast Texas dialect study. Orbis 5.61-79.

O'Cain, Raymond K. 1972. A social dialect survey of Charleston, South Carolina. Diss., University of Chicago.

_____. 1979. The Linguistic Atlas of New England: a review article. AS 54.

O'Hare, Thomas. 1964. The linguistic geography of Eastern Montana. Diss., University of Texas.

Orton, Harold, et al. 1962-71. Survey of English Dialects: Basic Material. Introduction; 4 vol., each in 3 pts. Leeds: E.J. Arnold.

Paddock, Harold J. 1966. A dialect survey of Carbonear, Newfoundland. M.A. thesis, Memorial University of Newfoundland.

_____, and Raven I. McDavid, Jr. 1971. "Black English" in Newfoundland? Paper presented at the Annual Meeting of the Canadian Linguistic Association, St. John's, Newfoundland.

Parslow, Robert L. 1967. The pronunciation of English in Boston, Massachusetts: vowels and consonants. Diss., University of Michigan.

Pederson, Lee A. 1965a. Negro speech in the <u>Adventures of Huckle-berry Finn</u>. <u>Mark Twain Journal</u> 13. 1-4.

_____. 1965b. The pronunciation of English in metropolitan Chicago. <u>PADS</u> 44.

_____. 1967. Mark Twain's Missouri dialects: Marion County phonemics. <u>AS</u> 42. 261-78.

_____. 1969. The Linguistic Atlas of the Gulf States: an interim report. <u>AS</u> 44. 279-86.

_____. 1971a. An approach to urban word geography. <u>AS</u> 46. 73-86.

_____. 1971b. Chicago words: the regional vocabulary. <u>AS</u> 46. 163-92.

_____. 1972. Black speech, white speech, and the Al Smith syndrome. <u>Studies in Honor of Raven I. McDavid, Jr.</u>, ed. by Lawrence M. Davis (University, Alabama: University of Alabama Press), 123-34.

_____. 1975. The plan for a dialect survey of rural Georgia. <u>Orbis</u> 24. 38-44.

Reed, Carroll E. 1967. <u>Dialects of American English</u>. Cleveland: World. 1977, 2nd ed., rev., Amherst, Massachusetts: University of Massachusetts Press.

_____, and Lester W. Seifert. 1954. <u>A Linguistic Atlas of Pennsyl-vania German.</u> Marburg/Lahn: W. J. Becker.

Reed, David W. 1954. Eastern dialect words in California. <u>PADS</u> 21. 3-15.

Rulon, Curt M. 1966. Geographical delimitation of the dialect areas in <u>The Adventures of Huckleberry Finn</u>. <u>Mark Twain Jour-nal</u> 14. 9-12.

Sawyer, Janet B. 1957. A dialect study of San Antonio, Texas, a bilingual community. Diss., University of Texas.

_____. 1959. Aloofness from Spanish influence in Texas English. <u>Word</u> 15. 270-81.

_____. 1964. Social aspects of bilingualism in San Antonio, Texas. <u>PADS</u> 41. 7-15.

Scargill, M. H. 1974. <u>Modern Canadian Usage</u>. Toronto: McClel-land and Stewart.

_____, and H. J. Warkentyne. 1972. The survey of Canadian Eng-lish: a report. <u>The English Quarterly</u> 5. 3.

Shuy, Roger W. 1962. The Northern-Midland dialect boundary in Illinois. <u>PADS</u> 38.

Shuy, Roger W., ed. 1965. Social Dialects and Language Learning. Urbana: National Council of Teachers of English.
_____, gen. ed. 1966-. Urban Language Series. Washington and Arlington: Center for Applied Linguistics.
_____, ed. 1967. Discovering American Dialects. Urbana: NCTE.
_____, and Ralph W. Fasold, eds. 1970. Teaching Standard English in the Inner City. Washington: Center for Applied Linguistics.
_____, Walter A. Wolfram, and William K. Riley. 1968. Field Techniques in an Urban Language Study. Washington: Center for Applied Linguistics.
Sledd, James. 1964. Review of Bloomfield, Morton, and Leonard Newmark, A Linguistic Introduction to the History of English. Lg 40.465-83.
Story, George, et al. IP. Dictionary of Newfoundland English.
Thomas, Charles K. 1947a. Introduction to the Phonetics of American English. New York: Ronald Press. 2nd ed., 1958.
_____. 1947b. The place of New York City in American linguistic geography. Quarterly Journal of Speech 33.314-20.
Thornton, Richard H. 1912. The American Glossary. Pts. I and II. London: Francis and Co.
_____. 1931-39. The American Glossary. Pt. III. Dialect Notes 6.101-216, 238-80, 286-312, 336-52, 368-84, 392-416, 424-48, 456-80, 488-512, 528-76, 600-16, 644-708, 711-42.
Turner, Lorenzo D. 1949. Africanisms in the Gullah Dialect. Chicago: University of Chicago Press.
Udell, Gerald. 1966. The speech of Akron, Ohio. Diss., University of Chicago.
Underwood, Gary. 1972, The research methods of the Arkansas language survey. AS 47.211-20.
Uskup, Frances L. 1974. Social markers of urban speech: a study of elites in Chicago. Diss., Illinois Institute of Technology.
Van Riper, W. R. 1958. The loss of postvocalic /-r/ in the Eastern United States. Diss., University of Michigan.
_____. 1972. Shortening the long conversational dialect interview. Studies in Linguistics in Honor of Raven I. McDavid, Jr., ed. by Lawrence M. Davis (University, Alabama: University of Alabama Press), 177-83.
_____. IP. Linguistic Atlas of Oklahoma.

Viereck, Wolfgang. 1975. Lexicalische und Grammatische Ergeb-
    niss des Lowman-Survey von Mittel- und Südengland. Mu-
    nich: Wilhelm Fink.
Walker, Saunders A. 1957. A dictionary of the folk speech of the
    East Alabama Negro. Diss., Western Reserve University.
Wanamaker, Murray. 1965. The speech of Kings County, Nova
    Scotia. Diss., University of Michigan.
Warkentyne, H. J. 1971. Contemporary Canadian English: a re-
    port of the survey of Canadian English. AS 46. 193-99.
Weber, Robert H. 1964. A comparative study of regional terms com-
    mon to the Twin Cities and the Eastern United States. Diss.,
    University of Minnesota.
Weinreich, Uriel. 1953. Languages in Contact. Publications of the
    Linguistic Circle of New York, 1.
_____. 1954. The Field of Yiddish. Publications of the Linguistic
    Circle of New York, 3. 2nd collection, The Hague: Mouton,
    1965. 3rd collection, The Hague: Mouton, 1969.
_____, et al. IP. Language and Culture Atlas of Ashkenazic Jewry.
Wetmore, Thomas H. 1959. The low-central and low-back vowels in
    the English of the Eastern United States. PADS 32.
Williamson, Juanita V. 1968. A phonological and morphological
    study of the speech of the Negro of Memphis, Tennessee.
    PADS 50.
_____, and Virginia M. Burke, eds. 1971. A Various Language.
    New York: Holt, Rinehart, Winston.
Wilson, H. Rex. 1958. The dialect of Lunenburg County, Nova Sco-
    tia. Diss., University of Michigan.
Wolfram, Walter A. 1969. A Sociolinguistic Description of Detroit
    Negro Speech. Washington: Center for Applied Linguistics.
_____, and Donna Christian. 1976. Appalachian Speech. Arling-
    ton: Center for Applied Linguistics.
_____, and Nona H. Clarke, eds. 1971. Black-White Speech Re-
    lationships. Washington: Center for Applied Linguistics.
Wood, Gordon R. 1960. An atlas survey of the interior South. Orbis
    9. 7-12.
_____. 1961. Word distribution in the interior South. PADS 35. 1-
    16.
_____. 1971. Vocabulary Change. Carbondale: Southern Illinois
    University Press.

Wrede, Ferdinand, Walther Mitzka, and Bernhard Martin. 1926-56.
    Deutscher Sprachatlas. Marburg/Lahn: N. G. Elwert.
Wright, Joseph. 1898-1905. The English Dialect Dictionary. 6 vol.
    Oxford: H. Frowde.
_____. 1905. The English Dialect Grammar. Oxford: H. Frowde.
Zwirner, Eberhard, et al. 1958-. Lautbibliothek der Deutschen
    Mundarten. Göttingen: Vandenhoeck and Ruprecht. (texts
    and recordings)

Part III. Lexicographic and Onomastic Studies

14 | The Social Role of the Dictionary

When Philip Gove, born a New Hampshire colonial, moved to the Mother State of Massachusetts and entered upon his career of professional lexicography, he soon rediscovered (if he had ever forgotten) the New England institution of the <u>vendue</u> or household auction. Such an auction takes place, most characteristically, when a farmer discovers that no one else in the family wants to continue the struggle against upheaved (or uphoven) rocks, drought, frost, pests, and the Federal Government. As he made the rounds, it became apparent very early that most rural estates, be they ever so humble, boasted a dictionary; and as a professional maker of dictionaries he began to watch what happened to them. It was also noticeable that no dictionary, of whatever imprint, editorship, or age, ever went unsold; moreover, as a canny Yankee himself, and as one generally aware of the going price for second-hand dictionaries, Gove soon discovered that tight-fisted New Englanders were often willing to pay for second-hand dictionaries on sale at a farm — regardless of age or condition— much more than the same book would sell for on the second-hand market, and indeed often much more than a more recent dictionary would have cost had the buyers taken the trouble to visit a bookstore or to respond to the advertisements appearing in the public prints. Clearly, dictionaries are in demand, and play an important role in American society — a society that is not notorious for the purchasing of books.

At one time — in the dear, dead days we might wish to recall — a dictionary, of a specific quality and size — one of the so-called 'collegiate' dictionaries — was the single book most likely to be required of college freshmen, and they carried it with them through the baccalaureate and on into graduate school, and even used it to set

up housekeeping. That in later years it became a book more ven-
erated than used — like that only more successful best-seller, the
Holy Scriptures — mattered little. A literate household without a
dictionary (and it mattered not what dictionary) was as badly exposed
as a shoe salesman without his pants. And even though the new cults
of creative expression, which deem conventional spelling an oppres-
sive instrument of exploitative capitalism, have largely succeeded
in eliminating the requirement that a student own a dictionary, the
demand is still there. While there were in the 1930s, when I was
first professing English, only three 'collegiate' size dictionaries —
Merriam, Funk & Wagnalls, and Winston — we now have at least
five: Merriam, Funk & Wagnalls, Random House, American Heritage, and World, to give them order of seniority of their current editions. [Since this paper was delivered, others have appeared.] This
of course excludes the sondri companye of the Barnhart enterprises,
and various reprints — modestly updated with an ostensibly glamorous
title — with which most students of the English language have had
some involvement in their careers. And what Karl Dykema once said
(1954) about current college dictionaries[1] is still true: that taken all
in all, they are very good buys, however little they differ from each
other, and however much any of them might profit from a shot of innovation.

Or we may look at the experiences many of us have had in
investigating the speech of live Americans. It doesn't take a lot of
field interviews for one to report that he has met someone who was
reluctant to offer his natural usage unless he had at hand his own dictionary to verify it, regardless of what that dictionary might be.

And on the larger scene, we have positive evidence, in newspaper accounts that anyone can examine, of the wide public concern
with dictionaries. In 1961 there was far more newspaper concern,
editorial and otherwise, with the Merriam Webster's Third New International Dictionary than with American foreign policy toward Southeast Asia, and the good grey New York Times objected far more stren-
uously to the real or imagined defects of the Third than it did to
Mr. Kennedy's taking what turned out to be irretrievable commitments
to South Viet Nam. (They were far more perturbed over his use of
finalize.) The Merriam organization, for its part, felt it advisable
to commit to the Third what its then president described as the largest

advertising expenditure ever allocated to a single book. Since that
time, both the <u>Random House Dictionary</u> and the <u>American Heritage</u>
have become best sellers, and Barnhart's two-volume dictionary —
merchandised by Field Enterprises in connection with the <u>World Book</u>
— has clearly been profitable.

But the fact that a dictionary is a viable type of book, in wide
demand among a large number of people, does not satisfy the curiosity of those who are interested. It is important to examine the
social role of the dictionary that draws so much attention.

There are all kinds of dictionaries, from the twelve-volume
<u>Oxford</u> with supplement (and a new four-volume supplement in the
offing, with two volumes in print by 1977) to the paperbacks sold for
as low as a quarter on newsracks in every conceivable kind of location.
Size and popularity, however, do not justify a binary opposition between so-called 'scholarly' and so-called 'commercial' dictionaries.
The monumental <u>Oxford</u> by now has more than paid off the investment
of the Clarendon Press, and the <u>Thorndike-Barnhart Desk Dictionary</u>,
within its limits, is a thoroughly competent work that pays full attention to what linguistics has to offer a work of its size. What is of
more interest is the kind of things a dictionary is designed to do:

1. To scholars, in all probability, the most important function of a dictionary is that of a record of the language, whether a diachronic statement of the development of
words and their meanings from the earliest records to the
present, or the ordering of them in a contemporary context,
by frequency or centrality of meaning. To this type belong
the great historical dictionaries, from the <u>Oxford</u> to the new
historical Italian dictionary by Battaglia, of which nine volumes have already appeared. Granted, as James Sledd
pointed out in 1968, [2] that even the best historical lexicographers could use some of the more recent developments in
linguistic theory; it is also true that our most eloquent
theorists could profit by some exposure to the honest drudgery of evaluating words in context. For what distinguishes
dictionaries of this type from all others is their greater commitment to the principle of usage, to the practice of defining
words and their meanings in terms of identifiable citations,
in context.

2. Another function of a dictionary is that of acquainting a user with a language, or a variety of a language, other than his own. Here we have the bilingual dictionaries, sometimes highly specialized like William Card's proposed gourmet's dictionary of French, sometimes encompassing an entire language, like Liddell and Scott. In between we have, inter alia, medical dictionaries, dictionaries of slang, and even dictionaries of acronyms, to say nothing of something like Cassidy's Dictionary of American Regional English.

3. A third function is to supply incidental information, linguistic or otherwise, for the casual user. There are some English dictionaries, I have learned from the late James R. Hulbert, specifically designed to make it easier for the newspaper reader to work crossword puzzles. The encyclopedic appendices at the end of our 'college' dictionaries — weights and measures, colleges in the United States and Canada, common Christian names (for the harried and even desperate parent with a newborn infant), rhymes, and the like — fall into this category. So in fact do most of the occasions on which a bleary-eyed stenographer consults the office dictionary — to determine, say, whether jewelry has one l or two. The geographical and biographical information which most American dictionary users have come to expect in their dictionaries is not directly related to the history or structure of the language, or to the development or ordering of its semantic components.

4. Finally, there is the role of a conduct book, somewhere between Emily Post and Ann Landers, a guide to what one should do and especially to what one should not do. It represents a clear appeal to linguistic insecurity — or in Menckenian terms, an exploitation of the assumption that it is impossible to overestimate the gullibility of the American people. Yet even in this role a dictionary can be a respectable intellectual work, by indicating who uses what linguistic forms in what social situations and with what intent.

What all of these functions share is the need for evidence, evidence as objective as it is possible to gather. Sometimes the evidence is contained in excerpted citations; sometimes it is found in

equally well documented statements of attitude. When Miss Alice
Ravenel Huger Smith—a Charleston descendant of a colonial Carolina
landgrave — observed to me that "some people say tomahtoes and
some say tomaytoes, but I say tommattoes, because my grandmother
Huger always said tommattoes, and what my grandmother said is good
enough for me," it was clear that — whatever I might think in my Up
Country South Carolina ignorance — tommattoes (or her pronunciation
of yellow as yillow, rhyming with billow) was a part of super-U usage
in Charleston, one of the most class-conscious of American cities,
and that whoever sneered at that usage was simply betraying his own
crudity.

        Nor, indeed, are the purposes for which dictionaries are
used necessarily incompatible. A dictionary that indicates adequately
the historical development or the contemporary semantic ordering is
likely to provide better information to the person seeking to dispel his
ignorance, or to learn something about a new field. Its incidental information is likely to be more accurate, and its value as a guide to
conduct is likely to be greater.

        This, however, is not the way dictionaries are evaluated in
this great republic, or even how they are presented. As I have pointed
out, [3] the Third New International, long before the official date of publication, had won the implacable hostility of the professional defenders
of the good, the true, and the beautiful — on the strength of a publicity release, never made accessible to my eyes, but easily recon-
structed from the earliest news stories, such as those included in
Sledd and Ebbitt's Dictionaries and THAT Dictionary (Chicago, Scott,
Foresman, 1962). Both the release and the criticism were largely
concerned with the picking of nits, such as the names of those who
had furnished citations (notably the eminent practical sociologist
Madam Polly Adler), the novelties in the vocabulary, and a statement about ain't that misrepresented the actual usage note. There
was no recognition of the basic fact that the editors simply tried to
do better and more thoroughly what their predecessors had been doing
for a century, or that they had probably put in more time on better
treatments of long-known meanings of long-known words than they
had on new words and new meanings. Instead, the emphasis was all
on trivia, such as the inclusion of finalize (which had been listed in
the second edition of 1934, held up by critics hostile to the Third as

a model of linguistic propriety), on the reliance on contemporary
sources of quotations (though Samuel Johnson had drawn most of his
quotations from his own century), on the choice of 1755 — the date of
Johnson's dictionary — as a cutoff date for words except those found
in such major writers as Chaucer or Shakespeare. What is even
more amazing (or amusing), when the editors said that they would
await the judgment of scholars competent in lexicography and the English language (none of whom had been selected to write the reviews in
newspapers or popular magazines), and when those judgments, like
those of Sledd, proved in the main to be favorable, then there arose
a horrendous bleating of asses, to the effect that these scholars had
entered into a sinister conspiracy with the editorial staff at Merriam,
to defile and degrade the English language.

Of the Random House Dictionary, as criminis particeps, I
shall say little in the presence of its managing editor;[4] we had our
disagreements, as will appear later, but shed no blood in the process. Still, I confess I breathed easier when I learned that my introductory essay on usage had not drawn the attention of Dwight
Macdonald, the SMERSH of the New York Literary Establishment,
who had been shocked to discover, on a visit to Springfield, that the
editors of the Third were not attempting to impose their judgments
on the language, but were "recording like mad" the way the language
was actually used. For my essay contains, I think, a much more
overt recognition of the doctrine of usage than is found in the prefatory matter to the Third, or at least is in more readable English
than the prose uttered from the little red schoolhouse on Federal
Street. Perhaps the critics and pundits-at-large had exhausted themselves on the Third. But again, there was the same disregard for
professional competence in the choice of reviewers; The New York
Times assigned it to that eminent philologian, Kurt Vonnegut, Jr.,
who compared prescriptive dictionaries to honest cops, and praised
the Random House for returning to prescriptivism.

One of the most interesting phenomena in lexicography is
the American Heritage Dictionary, which won the rare distinction of
being reviewed in Time magazine (May 11, 1970) under "Marketing"
rather than under "Books" or "Education." From all indications, it
is a triumph of the huckster's art — a dictionary about as good as its
rivals being puffed into a best seller (not that any other dictionary

would reject such fortune). It was built, frankly, on the appeal to
backlash against the Third, so that it has been known at various
times as the Goldwater Dictionary, the George Wallace, and the Joe
McCarthy — and perhaps just the McCarthy would do, since some of
its advertising seeks to add the modishness of McCarthy II to the reactionary attitudes of McCarthy I (for example, a cut featuring a long-
haired young man bears a caption with the theme: "he doesn't like
your politics; why should he like your dictionary?"). Its publisher,
we must remember, sought to purchase the Merriam Company in
order to suppress the Third; and when the stockholders accepted
another offer, launched his own enterprise. Its editor, a popular
word columnist, had several times expressed hostility to the Third,
in language that suggests either malice or ignorance. [5] The prefatory
essays are more disjointed than most, and the appended index of Indo-
European roots is not only superfluous, but — in the words of the best
Indo-Europeanist of my acquaintance, the late William M. Austin —
sadly outdated. If Merriam's merchandising gimmick was a clumsy
appeal to novelty, this one's is an unabashed appeal to reaction — a
usage panel, who voted on the way certain items appealed to them
(fewer than three hundred, out of a vocabulary of something like a
hundred thousand), and who were apparently selected, for the most
part, from those who had disapproved of certain practices or entries
in the Third and were determined to take advantage of the opportunity
to vent their prejudices, regardless of the facts of usage. [6]

    The latest popular dictionary, the second college edition of
the Webster's New World, continues the tradition of its predecessor
for clean definitions and a simple pronunciation key. But it too has
its modest gimmickry, though less flagrant than those of some of its
competitors. With the assistance of Mitford Mathews, editor of the
Dictionary of Americanisms, it has marked with five-pointed stars
the words and meanings that seem to qualify as Americanisms, and
with a neo-Victorian squeamishness it has sought to eliminate all
epithets used in a derogatory way about ethnic groups. [7] Presumably
this is a resurgence of the old folk belief that a word doesn't exist
if you can't find it in a dictionary — though a carefully labeled dictionary would be more helpful to the unsuspecting stranger (the only
one who would look up such a word, anyhow) than the act of omission.

    What we have seen throughout all the lexicographical contro-
versy of the past decade is an emphasis on the trivial details of

manners, with the implicit assumption that the public needs to be told what is right. It is somewhat frightening to see how widespread this attitude is, and it is not limited to aspiring lintheads and hunkies or nervous black bourgeoisie. To name names, my distinguished colleague Wayne Booth, Pullman Professor of Rhetoric and sometime dean of the undergraduate college of the University of Chicago, has several times said that he wanted a dictionary that would show him the words he didn't use. As a non-rhetorician, I lose his reasoning (after all, there is nothing to keep him from reading through a dictionary and trying to mark the words and meanings outside his normal performance); but I find his attitude toward dictionaries shared by many, and extended to grammar, to the point where I seldom confess to a stranger that I teach English, lest he be afraid to talk. The functions of the dictionary as the historical record, or as the purveyor of the knowledge of something new, pale in the public eye beside its function as a molder of behavior.

But we should not think that there is anything new or strange in this attitude. Over the years, far more dictionaries have been produced — at least far more monolingual ones — as conduct models than as language records or as repositories of specialized knowledge.

To some extent, the emphasis on the dictionary as a conduct book is a tribute to the openness of a society of many classes. If there were no class differences in a language community, there would be no need of usage notes for native speakers, who would acquire the rules of lexical choice for particular situations as a part of the process of growing up (though of course the speaker of another language, whose rules of distribution might be class-ordered — or even if not, arranged differently except in a meaninglessly deep structure — would need them). If class lines were immutable, and every person's status fixed from birth, there would be no need to talk about usage, except perhaps as matters of style, because it wouldn't make any difference anyhow. One recalls that the county families of England, and their analogues in New England and the Old South, are the most relaxed in their usage in the presence of their social equals, so that the appearance of ain't in familiar conversation among proper Charlestonians is a token that the stranger has been accepted. It is the person who is moving to what he thinks is a superior station who fears that he will be stigmatized by the kind of language he learned

at home — and often is, though the stigmatizing forms aren't always
those he has been made to worry about; and it is the fact that the
lower middle class furnishes most of the teachers in our public
schools that makes the English classroom so often a torture chamber.

The earliest dictionaries — as Sledd and others have often
pointed out — were not the familiar monolingual ones that we now
usually think of when we talk of dictionaries. They were bilingual —
sometimes trilingual or more — and often not arranged alphabetically
but topically, like what we call a thesaurus. These works were designed as keys to Holy Writ, to the science and philosophy presented
in Latin or Greek, or — at a slightly later date — in the more prestigious continental languages, Italian and French. (It is to be remembered that the deficit theory of the vernacular is not a Twentieth Century invention.)[8] At the same time that the bilingual dictionaries
were developing, the need arose — or was felt, which amounts to the
same thing — for special works, such as dictionaries of mythology,
and various kinds of encyclopedic matter came to be included in the
general dictionaries. If one looks over the account of Renaissance
dictionaries by Starnes,[9] he will find that very little of the encyclopedic matter of modern dictionaries was overlooked; about all I can
think of is a table of Indo-European roots, because comparative linguistics was not yet an established discipline, and the tables of colleges and universities of the United States and Canada, because those
nations did not yet exist, and general education (let alone general
higher education) was not yet dreamed of.

The earliest dictionaries of English were dictionaries of
hard words, so that the reader would understand the new terms —
generally latinate — with which authors enriched their works and
through which science and technology in the vernacular had to be explained. But alongside these general dictionaries (though with a pro-
fusion of exotic words) one soon saw special monolingual dictionaries — on the one hand, dictionaries of law terms; on the other,
dictionaries of argot. As the bourgeoisie increased their wealth and
power, they began to wish to talk like their betters, and the seventeenth and eighteenth centuries prospered not only dictionary makers
but grammarians and teachers of speech (often Irish and Scots), with
a series of works, from The Knight of the Burning Pestle to The
Rivals, offering horrible or at least risible examples of those who

had imperfectly mastered their unaccustomed ornamentation. At the
same time the Academy movement (driven by the fear — still gnaw-
ing at the hearts of purists — of vocabulary run riot) sought to put
order and limits on the vernaculars, and the academies, especially
the French, produced dictionaries which were essentially social
registers of the lexicon. In this aim the academies have been very
successful; the latest version of the dictionary of the French Academy,
uttered shortly before World War II, is in two modest volumes, each
about the size of a pre-war Webster's Collegiate, though the live vocabulary of French must be in the hundreds of thousands of words.
But as Professor Forgue recently explained, [10] the Academy's dictionary is a joke — except to the Academy itself and to such purists
as Etiemble. [11]

  We are all aware that Samuel Johnson went into his harmless
lexicographical drudgery convinced that dictionaries might put a
bridle to linguistic change, and came out convinced that the task
could not be accomplished. We are also aware that — whether or not
Johnson wished it — his dictionary soon acquired in England the odor
of sanctity that the Academy dictionaries had sought on the continent.
We know, further, that Sheridan and Walker made dictionaries of
pronunciation, invading territory where Johnson had feared to tread,
and that this feature was adopted in the host of competent nineteenth-
century dictionaries in England, whether derived from Johnson or not.
It is also rather well known that in America Noah Webster's dictionaries were not universally applauded, even in his native New England,
because it was felt that he had untuned the string of the language by
offering an American standard rather than the more elegant British
model. Indeed, in many quarters the appeal of Joseph Worcester's
competing works was based on the fact that he showed more deference
than Webster to British practice. But both of these dictionaries were,
in their appeal, conduct books; for however much Old Noah might
exalt the language of the Yankee yeoman, he was far from accepting
that of the Virginia or Carolina gentleman.

  The Oxford English Dictionary is a massive achievement,
both in its own right and in its progeny of historical dictionaries of
more limited scope. But what is perhaps its most significant influence has been its effect on the general dictionaries, especially
those put out by Merriam. The Oxford was based on citations;

Merriam developed its own citation file, probably the largest in the
world. The Oxford arranged its senses historically; so did Merriam's
International of 1890 and its successors and their abridgments. If
other dictionaries chose other orders of senses — Funk & Wagnalls,
the ACD, Random House, and the American Heritage come to mind —
by and large their actual practice, like that of the Oxford, was to proceed from usage to judgment, and not the other way. And Vizetelly
of Funk & Wagnalls was a successful lexicographer before he became
a columnist for the late Literary Digest.

But the vocabulary keeps growing, and it became impossible
to contain it within the covers of a single volume. With the editing
of the Merriam Third the pressure became overwhelming — and the
knowledge that the ordinary American buyer of dictionaries doesn't
go for a two-volume work led the editorial staff (unholpen by outside
advisers) into a number of compromises. Company advertising had
traditionally emphasized "the supreme authority" of the Interna-
tionals; publicity for the Third suggested an "abdicating of authority"
in an effort to be folksy. Encyclopedic matter was left out; yet the
vocabulary, in an attempt to cover the ISV (international scientific
vocabulary, one of Gove's happier coinages) became to some extent
overloaded with technical terms. The same basis for respect was
there, resting as always on the fidelity with which the editors had
observed and recorded the language; yet somehow the respect was
not forthcoming. Perhaps, in addition to its disastrous publicity,
the Third tried to be too many things to too many people, to play too
many roles simultaneously. If more recent dictionaries have fared
better with the critics, perhaps they have attempted less, restricting
reach to grasp.

When the international conference Sledd has called for takes
place,[12] and when we finally see the establishment of the kind of re-
source center for dictionaries he and I have advocated in different
ways at different time (and foolish he who tries to score points by asserting priorities),[13] perhaps our dictionary publishers will rethink
some of their practices. The center will not conflict with what is
being established at Terre Haute, with the gift of the Cordell Collection, but will rather complement it. Where Indiana State University
will be a center for the study of lexicography, with an unparalleled
collection of dictionaries, the other center would be devoted to

organizing lexicographical raw materials for prospective editors and
critics — files of citations, files of recorded specimens of speech,
standard and otherwise, with ready access through computers. Citations will perhaps be collected by some sort of scanning,[14] so that
we will not find twenty for bump as a pelvic maneuver in burlesque
to one for bump as a surface irregularity or protuberance. We should
then have a more thorough history of the vocabulary than is yet possible; we should be able to allocate, with greater assuredness, the
more technical terms to specialized dictionaries; usage labels will
be more accurate, and not merchandised gimmicks — since any
statement can be checked by rivals or reviewers against the recorded
facts of the language. The editors will then be able to revert to their
proper function — of seeing who can best utilize and interpret what is
available to all. And perhaps we will have fewer extravagant claims,
less appeal to anxiety, and a public that makes more effective use of
the dictionaries in their hands. At least, we can dream.

NOTES

Delivered at the April 1971 conference to mark the dedication of the
Cordell collection of dictionaries at Indiana State University, Terre
Haute, Indiana.

[1]Review of Webster's New World Dictionary, College Edition, American Speech 39 (1954), 59-65.
[2]"Toward the First International Alvearie," paper presented
to English Group 13 (Present-Day English), MLA, December 1968.
[3]"False Scents and Cold Trails: The Prepublication Criticism of the Merriam Third," Journal of English Linguistics 5 (1971),
101-121. [In this volume, pp. 310-336.]
[4]Laurence Urdang was a participant in the Terre Haute conference.
[5]Mrs. Joan Teller has recently done a study of William
Morris's column "Words, Wit and Wisdom," in relation to the underlying philosophy of the American Heritage Dictionary. Its editor continues his merry ways in the Harper Dictionary of Contemporary
Usage (1975). For an appraisal, see the Journal of English Linguistics 11. 41-50 (1977).

⁶So far as I can determine, the panel contains only one person, Roy Copperud, who expressed approval of the Third. Eight of its members, at least — J. Donald Adams, Sheridan Baker, Lincoln Barnett, Jacques Barzun, Theodore M. Bernstein, Sydney Harris, Dwight Macdonald, Mario Pei — were members in good standing of the lynching posse that sought to make of the Third and its editor, Gove, the principal exhibits in an auto da fé. For an evaluation of the Usage Panel and related judgments, see Thomas J. Creswell, Usage in Dictionaries and Dictionaries of Usage, Publication of the American Dialect Society 63-4 (1975).

⁷In the discussion of this paper, David Guralnik, editor of Webster's New World Dictionary, defended this practice as removing from the dictionary the "true obscenities." A casual glance, however, reveals that the sensitivity of the editorial staff did not extend to the feelings of all ethnic stocks. In terms of my own cultural background, I note, inter alia, the inclusion of cracker, hillbilly, peckerwood, poor white and redneck, albeit with mild notes of caution (much milder than their designees would feel deserved). The highly offensive adjective common has no caveat whatever. But perhaps the World staff, like many other soi-disant "liberals," considered white Southerners subhumanoid.

⁸During the Renaissance it was repeatedly argued that the vernacular, particularly the English vernacular, was not copious or subtle enough to serve as the vehicle of science and philosophy. See, for example, Richard Foster Jones, The Triumph of the English Language (Stanford, Calif.: Stanford University Press, 1953).

⁹Dewitt T. Starnes, Medieval and Renaissance Dictionaries: English-Latin and Latin-English (Austin: University of Texas Press, 1954).

¹⁰Guy J. Forgue, Professor of American Studies in the New Sorbonne, and a participant in the Terre Haute conference. Editor of a selection of the letters of H. L. Mencken, and author of a biography — H. L. Mencken: l'homme, l'oeuvre, l'influence (Paris: Minard, 1967) — he has often crossed swords with his more reactionary colleagues.

¹¹René Etiemble, Parlez-vous franglais? (Paris: Gallimard, 1964). He avers that the French language has been irremediably corrupted by foreign loans, especially those from American English.

[12]As a result of Sledd's appeal to English 13 in 1968, a committee (Walter S. Avis, Frederic G. Cassidy, Audrey R. Duckert, Raven I. McDavid., Jr., and Allen Walker Read, with Laurence Urdang and H. Rex Wilson as recent collaborators) have developed plans for an international conference on lexicography in English, in New York City, June 5-7, 1972, under the sponsorship of the New York Academy of Sciences and the Center for Applied Linguistics. [The proceedings of this conference were published in Lexicography in English, Annals of the New York Academy of Sciences, 211, eds. Raven I. McDavid, Jr. and Audrey R. Duckert. New York: New York Academy of Sciences, 1973.]

[13]See, for example, H. L. Mencken, The American Language, one-volume abridged edition (New York: Knopf, 1963), pp. 423-424. Woodford Heflin of the Air University has made the first contribution to such a proposed center, with his collectanea on aviation and astronautics. [It has been set up at the University of Western Ontario.]

[14]Such devices have been used experimentally, but as yet they seem to be much more expensive than the traditional method. Still to be solved is the problem of getting citations for the most common words in the language without making the file impossibly bulky. The process of using mechanical means for getting citations from oral usage does not appear to have been even attempted.

15 | False Scents and Cold Trails: The Pre-Publication Criticism of the Merriam *Third*

The public reception of the Merriam Webster's Third New International Dictionary (Springfield, Massachusetts, 1961) is one of the most fantastic episodes in American literary history. The dictionary was in the best traditions of lexicography, exemplified not only by the record of the Merriam Company but by the great Century Dictionary and the incomparable Oxford. A wide-ranging reading program, enriching the company's magnificent citation file, provided more complete evidence on the English vocabulary than any recent competitor has had at its disposal — evidence not only on new words and new meanings but on the words and meanings that had been attested in earlier editions. A competent staff conscientiously worked to make the new dictionary the best possible record of mid-century usage. Nevertheless, well before September 28, 1961 — the official date of publication — the dictionary had won the hostility of a large and vocal proportion of newspaper editors, professional book-reviewers, and the miscellaneous pundits-at-large that are often described as the (New York) Literary Establishment.

Later, there were vigorous misrepresentations of the dictionary in such places as the Atlantic Monthly, the New Yorker, the Saturday Review, the American Scholar and Horizon.[1]

The journalistic assault on the Third, it must be noted, was not echoed by serious students of the English language, most of whom approved the principles on which the Third was constructed, even while indicating less than complete satisfaction with the ways in which these principles were put into practice. This reaction in the scholarly world led the opponents of the Third to a shrill assertion that American linguists — in particular,[2] the group known as structural linguists — had seized control of the editorial operations at Merriam as part of a sinister plot to degrade the English language.[3] The need to resume the battle over principles of evaluating usage — a battle which most linguists, structural or otherwise,[4] had assumed long won — diverted the attention of the students of the English language and its lexicography from a serious critical appraisal of the <u>Third</u>, though they offered a great deal of interesting incidental evidence on the history of dictionaries of the English language and the principles on which such dictionaries are constructed.

A number of the issues have been treated in three casebooks on lexicography,[5] but a full, documented history of the controversy is yet to be written.[6] If it is ever written, such a history not only will describe the various episodes in detail but will disclose the virtues and defects of the dictionary itself and the kinds of mistakes its editors and defenders have made in conducting their side of the debate.

This paper is a summary of the criticism between the appearance of the first prepublication release, for 6 September 1961, and the official date of publication, 28 September. In this period, as I have said, the tone of adverse popular criticism was set, and little has been added since.[7]

II

Space prevents a detailed presentation of the background of the <u>Third</u>. Nevertheless, since this generation is not aware of history as it might be, the recapitulation of a few details might put a number of arguments in better perspective.

1. Since Samuel Johnson's dictionary (1755) it has been a basic assumption of lexicographers that the function of a dictionary is to record and describe the language, not to direct it toward ideals of perfection. In his prospectus of 1747 Johnson had followed the Augustan tradition in proposing to fix the language for all time, but eight years of labor convinced him that the task could not be achieved. Most dictionaries have specifically indicated in their prefaces that their authority, including the value of their judgments on usage, rests on the accuracy with which they have reocrded the facts of the language. However, Merriam advertising, especially its slogan "The

Supreme Authority," conveyed another message to the American public — namely, that lexicographers, particularly those employed by
the Merriam Company, had the right and power to decide on their own
initiative whether a word was admissible to polite usage.

2. The reviews in major newspapers and popular magazines
were nearly always written by journalists, popularizers, or humanists
at large, rather than by professional lexicographers or by scholars
whose major field of competence was the English language.[8] That
many of these ad hoc reviewers were blown up into "authorities on
usage" is melancholy evidence in support of Mencken's observation
that the Americano is willing to follow authority with almost Russian
docility, but rejects the authority of knowledge and experience in
favor of the kind that presents novel and grandiose claims.[9]

3. The publication of dictionaries is a highly competitive
business, and for no company more so than for Merriam, which has
published almost nothing else for decades. The International series
of dictionaries — the so-called "unabridged" — with successive editions in 1890, 1909, 1934, and 1961,[10] has had no serious American
competition between the Funk and Wagnalls New Standard of 1913 and
the Random House Dictionary of 1966. The more profitable Collegiate
series had had little competition for a decade and a half until the appearance of the American College Dictionary in 1947.[11] In addition
to the attention that a new entry gets in a competitive market, and
the names of several of the linguists and other scholars who had participated in the work of the Army Language Section,[12] the ACD had
several features that would make it attractive. Not only was the page
larger, so that the type could be more readable, but it was more at-
tractively designed. The pronunciation key was simpler, and the
primary American pronunciation represented was Middle Western
rather than the Eastern New England variety that Merriam had traditionally used. The ACD used a single alphabet, including biographical and geographical names, in contrast with Merriam's separate
sections for these categories,[13] and presented meanings of words in
order of semantic frequency rather than the order of historical development traditional with Merriam.

The Merriam response to the ACD was the New Collegiate
of 1949, less a new edition than a resetting, in somewhat larger type,

of the Webster's Collegiate, fifth edition, of 1936; the failure to make
any significant changes in 1949 undoubtedly enhanced the shock effect
of the Third in 1961.[14]

In 1953 the appearance of the Webster's New World Dictionary
of the American Language, college edition, further intensified the competition. It also further disturbed the complacency of the Merriam organization — or at least of some of its public representatives —
because the publishers of the World had successfully contested the Merriam monopoly of the name Webster in the titles of American dictionaries.[15] Scholars in correspondence with the company noticed growing defensiveness about editorial practices, especially about the pronunciation key. Company advertising also took a hard-sell tone, again
with repercussions; for example, just before the appearance of the
Third, the Merriam Company received a cease-and-desist order from
the Federal Trade commission, for making unwarranted claims about
the New Collegiate.[16] In short, by 1961 there were many scholars,
and others, who were not only favorably disposed toward competing
dictionaries, but somewhat disillusioned about Merriam. Yet, in the
tradition of academic responsibility, it was these same scholars who
mounted the effective defense of the Third when it was attacked un-
fairly.

4. What constitutes standard American English has greatly
changed since 1934. The educated population is far larger. Many of
the speechways of the old elite now seem a little quaint, notably the
diphthong [əi] in heard and bird, once characteristic not only of upper-
class New York speech but of the speech of much of the plantation
class in the Deep South. A more relaxed mode of educated speech
and writing has developed, and the number of professional writers —
however unbeautiful the kind of letters they profess (notably sales
circulars and technical manuals) — has grown even more than the
college-educated population. One of the notable effects of technical
change has been the obsolescence of leather-lunged oratory of the
William Jennings Bryan school, in favor of the "fireside chat" of
Franklin Roosevelt; with electrical amplification, a speaker could
use conversational style and still be understood in a large auditorium.
Consequently the appropriate model for dictionary presentation is now
that of natural speech, with the relaxing of weak-stressed vowels;
the Third adopted this moadel and not the platform style favored by
its predecessors.

5. The lynching of Germanic studies in World War I upset
the academic balance so far as attitudes toward language and lexicography were concerned. [17] Those who went to college in the 1930s
and became the Literary Establishment of the 1960s had generally
been exposed to the prescriptive Romance tradition rather than the
descriptive Germanic one, and were predisposed to think of lexicography in terms of legislation rather than description. [18]

6. The typical English major and English teacher of the
past acquired little knowledge about the structure and variety of
modern English, even though they might have had a respectable background in Old and Middle English. Often fugitives from scientific
discipline, they tended to resist serious language description — and
their successors have followed suit. At many of the more prestigious
seminaries — Harvard, Yale and Berkeley, for example — it is possible to get at least a master's degree in English without any exposure
to the study of the language Americans use today.

7. The still prevalent sputnik-shock, following the successful launching of the first two Russian earth satellites and the failure
of the early American efforts, has made the literate American unduly
sensitive to charges (however unfounded) that responsible editors or
administrators are letting down educational standards.

8. The rise of descriptive linguistics, during and following
World War II, provoked the resentment of those who had dominated
foreign language teaching, except perhaps in German, and the bump-
tiousness of newly affluent linguists compounded the difficulty. [19]
Dictionary makers have utilized linguists in their operations for at
least a hundred years; for instance, the position of the Merriam
Company in American lexicography was largely consolidated by the
1864 edition, for which the German-trained linguist C.A.F. Mahn
drastically altered many of the practices of Noah Webster and completely revamped the etymologies. Thus it would have been strange
if the editors of the Third had not tried to enlist the services of American linguists, especially the structural school, which was then at the
height of its influence. In fact, several structuralists were consulted
about particular subjects. But the Company was unable to persuade
any leading American linguist, structural or otherwise, to assume
the role of editor-in-chief; [20] and despite some publicity releases

vaguely identifying the Third with structural linguistics, there is no
evidence that any linguist of this group had any policy-making position.

9. Unlike its predecessors and its recent competitor, the
Third did not utilize distinguished outside special editors on such
basic lexicographical matters as etymology, language history, usage,
synonymy, or pronunciation. It did not seriously consult outside language archives like those of the Linguistic Atlas, though such archives have always been accessible to reputable publishers. It was a
house dictionary, edited by house personnel, among whom there was
a relatively high turnover. [21]

10. The Merriam Company has always depended on extensive
advertising in what the trade refers to as "consumer magazines." As
publication date approached, Gordon J. Gallan, president of the Merriam Company, announced that the company was more than doubling
normal advertising expenditures — "the greatest concentration of
advertising ever used to promote a single book." [22] If simple publicity
was sought, the campaign was certainly successful. In 1961-62, few
American newspapers readers could have avoided hearing of the Third,
and Philip B. Gove, the taciturn Down-East Yankee who had risen
from the Merriam ranks to the position of editor-in-chief, suddenly
became the most widely known American lexicographer since Noah
Webster.

III

Apparently the first detailed announcement of the Third appeared in the Mason City, Iowa, Globe-Gazette, 6 September 1961.
Bearing a New York City dateline, attributed to no wire service or
newswriter, and somewhat longer than the other early news stories,
it is probably derived directly from the company release, described
elsewhere as a five-page mimeographed handout. [23] Unlike many of
the early stories, it does not mention Madam Polly Adler and her
sociological treatise A House Is Not a Home. It is not unsympathetic,
but its comments suggest the line of attack of the hostile reviewers:

1. The notion that the Third was designed "for average
families as well as scholars." (This was reiterated before publication date by the Buffalo News; the Pittsfield, Mass., Berkshire

Eagle; the Sioux City, Iowa, Morning Journal; the Lodi, California,
News Sentinel; the Santa Ana, California, Register; Office Appliances;
the NSOE Convention Scrapbook; and the National Stationer. Headlines in The New York Times read, "Third Edition has 200,000 Popular Quotations to Aid 'Average Families'; Classics Lose Ground.")

2. An emphasis on the novelty and unconventionality of the
sources of illustrative quotations: Ted Williams, Willie Mays, Ethel
Merman, Dinah Shore, Mickey Spillane.

3. An emphasis on the informality of present-day usage.

4. "Ain't gets official recognition at last as 'used orally in
most parts of the United States by cultivated speakers.'"

The emphasis is clearly on novelty. Illustrative citations
are described as novel, though they are centuries old in lexicography. [24] The single-phrase definition and the new pronunciation key
are presented as novelties, not as advantages. The labor of revision
is treated only in terms of catching up with the changing culture, of
catching new words and meanings; nothing is said about the labor of
getting better information about established meanings of established
words, and nothing except by very remote association about the fidelity of the Third to the central tradition of lexicography, including that
of the Company. There is little recognition of the editorial staff;
even Gove, the editor-in-chief, is barely mentioned. His name appears twice, almost as an afterthought, toward the end of the story;
Gallan, as company president, had been prominently mentioned four
times. Misunderstanding was inevitable, and misrepresentation soon
followed.

The next day, 7 September, the tone of the principal stories
indicated that the Third was going to get a working over. The New
York Times tipped its hand by the headline on the McCandlish Phillips
rewrite: "Webster Soups Up Its Big Dictionary" — one of the few
stories, incidentally, that featured Gove and ignored Gallan. Both
the AP and the UPI stories emphasized the shock effect by mentioning
ain't in the first paragraph and the terminal preposition in the second.
These early stories (*denotes stories of 7 Sept.) featured slang and
other novelties of the vocabulary, such as beatnik, goof and puff 'to
praise inordinately':

Mason City, Iowa, Globe-Gazette (6 Sept.):

A-bomb, astronaut, beatnik, den mother, fringe benefit, satellite, solar house, wage dividend, zen; ugrug, muu muu, veldt, poor boy ('submarine sandwich or grinder'); (living) roofdeck, breezeway, split-level, solar heating, expansion attic, flameware; (labor) fringe benefit, wage dividend, sit-in (also in civil rights sense); (TV) flutter, tape; (air age) skycoach, retro-rocket, airlift, deceleration, blip and dovap, no-show.

*Buffalo News (Chicago Tribune News Service): from A-bomb, astronaut, beatnik, den mother and fringe benefit, to satellite, solar house, wage dividend and zen.

*Chicago Sun-Times (UP):. . .from A-bomb, astronaut, beatnik, den mother and fringe benefit to satellite, solar house, wage dividend and zen.

*Chicago Daily News: A-bomb, astronaut, beatnik.

*New York Daily News:. . .ranging from A-bomb, astronaut, beatnik, den mother, fringe benefit to satellite, solar house, wage dividend, zen.

*New York Herald Tribune: A-bomb, astronaut, beatnik.

*Springfield Union:. . .from A-bomb, astronaut, beatnik, den mother, fringe benefit, to satellite, solar house, wage dividend, and zen; weekend, fabulous; (living) roofdeck, breezeway, split-level, flameware; (labor relations) fringe benefit, sit-in; (TV and recordings) tape, flutter, snow; (air age) sky-coach, airlift, blip and dovap, no-show.

Alice Hughes, "A Woman's New York" (syndicated column, 13 Sept.): finalize, systematized, prestissimo, go-go-go, dig, goof, astronaut, beatnik, satellite, zen, fringe benefit, cool, crazy.

Woonsocket Call (13 Sept.): (living) roofdeck, breezeway, split-level, solar heating, flameware; (TV) flutter, tape; (air travel) skycoach, retro-rocket, blip, no-show.

Life (15 Sept.): retro-rocket, sit-in, fringe benefit, split level, flutter, snow, muu muu, zen; drain (Ethel Merman), puff (Willie Mays), lexicographer (Samuel Johnson).

Watertown, N. Y., Daily Times (19 Sept.): shake, shakedown, shake off, shakeout, shake up; astronaut, beatnik, satellite, den mother.

Third Dimensions: Economic Profiles of Greater Springfield (Sept-Oct.): A-bomb, astronaut, beatnik, den mother, fringe benefit, satellite, solar house, wage dividend, zen.

These stories were equally attentive to such putatively unconventional sources of citations as the Police Gazette, the Maine Hunting and Trapping Code, and a TWA timetable.[25] There is some mention of the more decorous kinds of contemporaries from whom citations were obtained — President Kennedy, Roosevelt II, Churchill, Virginia Woolf, Hemingway — but more about figures of entertainment and sports: Madam Adler, Art Linkletter, Willie Mays, Ted Williams, Ethel Merman.

Mason City, Iowa, Globe-Gazette (6 Sept.): John F. Kennedy (jingoism), Dwight E. Eisenhower (goof), General Douglas MacArthur (shall), Winston Churchill (confront), Charles Goren, Ernest Hemingway, Ethel Merman (drain), Ted Williams (percentage), Dinah Shore, Mickey Spillane, Willie Mays (puff), Franklin D. Roosevelt (plain people), Somerset Maugham (pittance), Erle Stanley Gardner (pickup).

*UPI (Garry Gates): . . . selected quotations ranging in history from the Bible to the speeches of John F. Kennedy. . . . Besides Mr. Kennedy, former Presidents Dwight D. Eisenhower and Franklin D. Roosevelt, Dinah Shore, Winston Churchill, Gen. Douglas MacArthur (shall), Ethel Merman (drain), Ted Williams, Willie Mays (puff), Ernest Hemingway, Mickey Spillane and Polly Adler are among 14,000 contemporary notables whose words are quoted.

*Bethlehem, Pa., Globe-Times (Ruth Hutchison): General MacArthur (shall) to Mickey Spillane; Eisenhower (goof), Willie Mays (puff); Kenneth Roberts, Conrad Richter, The New York Times (all for shake).

*Boston Herald: President Kennedy, Dwight D. Eisenhower, General Douglas MacArthur, Winston Churchill, Charles Goren, Ernest Hemingway, Ethel Merman (drain), Ted Williams, Dinah Shore, Mickey Spillane.

*Buffalo, N. Y., News (Chicago Tribune News Service): (shake) Corey Ford, Polly Adler, Edna Ferber, Elmer Davis; (goof) Eisenhower, Harold Hobson, C. S. Palmer, Springfield Daily News, James T. Farrell, Calder Willingham, The Infantry Journal.

*Chicago Sun-Times (UPI): Ethel Merman (drain), TWA time-table (no-show), Polly Adler, Mickey Spillane.

*Chicago Tribune (UPI):. . .quotations ranging from the Bible to the speeches of John F. Kennedy. . . .among the modern figures quoted are Kennedy, former presidents Dwight D. Eisenhower and Franklin D. Roosevelt, Winston Churchill, General Douglas MacArthur, Ethel Merman, Ted Williams, Willie Mays, Ernest Hemingway, Polly Adler and Mickey Spillane.

*New York Daily News: (shake) Corey Ford, Polly Adler, Edna Ferber, Elmer Davis; (brainwash) Ed Sullivan.

*New York Herald Tribune: Kennedy (jingoism), Eisenhower (goof), Ethel Merman (drain).

*The New York Times (McCandlish Phillips): Ethel Merman (drain), Mickey Spillane, Corey Ford, newspapers and magazines, the Maine Hunting and Trapping Code, the Police Gazette, and even a Trans-World Airlines timetable; Polly Adler (shake).

*New York World-Telegram (John Ferris): Polly Adler, Tom Marvel, Virginia Woolf, Sinclair Lewis, Thomas Hardy, W. H. Hudson, Edna Ferber, Corey Ford — all from p. 2085 (shake); Willie Mays (puff); Dickens, Shakespeare, Deuteronomy, Police Detective, Publisher's Weekly, U. S. Navigation Code, Maine Hunting and Trapping Laws [sic], Mickey Spillane, President Kennedy, former President Dwight D. Eisenhower, Ted Williams, Dinah Shore, Wanda Neff, Ethel Merman (drain), N. Y. World-Telegram (snide), Inez Robb (spade), Samuel Lubell (infiltree).

*San Francisco Chronicle: Willie Mays (puff), President John F. Kennedy, Ernest Hemingway, Polly Adler, Mickey Spillane.

*Springfield Union: Presidents John F. Kennedy and Dwight D. Eisenhower, General MacArthur (shall), Winston Churchill, Charles Goren, Ernest Hemingway, Ethel Merman (drain), Ted Williams, Dinah Shore and Mickey Spillane; Willie Mays (puff).

Woonsocket Call (13 Sept.): President John F. Kennedy, Dinah Shore, Ethel Merman (drain), Willie Mays (puff), Dwight D. Eisenhower, Sir Winston Churchill, Ted Williams, Burl Ives, Billy Rose, Gene Tunney, Art Linkletter, James Cagney, Elsa Maxwell, General Douglas MacArthur, Earl Warren, Ernest Hemingway, Tennessee Williams.

Newsweek (18 Sept.): Polly Adler (shake), Shakespeare, Eisenhower (goof), Ethel Merman (goof), Kennedy (jingoism), Ted Williams (percentage), Mickey Spillane, Ernest Hemingway, T. S. Eliot, Art Linkletter (like).

Publisher's Weekly (18 Sept.): Presidents John F. Kennedy, Dwight D. Eisenhower; General Douglas MacArthur, Winston Churchill, Charles Goren, W. Somerset Maugham, Ernest Hemingway, Ethel Merman, Ted Williams, Dinah Shore, Mickey Spillane.

Watertown, N. Y., Times (Hiltburgh Overacker, 19 Sept.): Presidents John F. Kennedy, Dwight D. Eisenhower, General Douglas A. MacArthur, Sir Winston Churchill, Charles Goren, W. Somerset Maugham, Ernest Hemingway, Ethel Merman, Ted Williams, Mickey Spillane; (shake) Corey Ford, Edna Ferber, Mary McCarthy, Sinclair Lewis; Newsweek, The New York Times, Maine Hunting and Trapping Laws [sic], Book of Common Prayer.

Ain't, as the most unspeakable and unprintable four-letter word in English, is frequently cited, always in the abridged statement that appeared in the Globe-Gazette. The strong caveat of the actual usage note in the Third is never mentioned:

Webster's Third New International: . . .1 a are not. . .b is not. . .c am not. . . — though disapproved by many and more

common in less educated speech, used orally in most parts of the
U. S. by many cultivated speakers, esp. in the phrase ain't I? 2 sub-
stand a have not. . .b has not. . .

   Mason City, Iowa, Globe-Gazette (6 Sept.): "Ain't" gets official recognition at last, as "Used orally in most parts of the U. S.
[by] cultivated speakers."

   *Baltimore Morning Sun (AP): The new dictionary, Gordon
J. Gallan, President of G. and C. Merriam Company, said today,
"will say 'ain't' is used orally in most parts of the U. S. by cultivated
speakers."

   *Boston Herald (AP): The word "ain't" at long last has come
into its own. . . .The word "ain't," the new dictionary says, is "used
orally in most parts of the U. S. by cultivated speakers."

   *Chicago Sun-Times (UPI): "Ain't," according to the new
dictionary, is "used orally in most parts of the U. S. by cultivated
speakers."

   *Chicago Tribune (UPI): "Ain't," according to the new dic-
tionary, is "used orally in most parts of the U. S. by cultivated
speakers."

   *Iowa City Iowa Citizen (AP): The new dictionary, said
Gordon J. Gallan, President of G. and C. Merriam Co., will say
"'ain't' is used orally in most parts of the U. S. by cultivated
speakers."

   *New York Herald Tribune:. . .the new Webster's acknow-
ledges that "ain't" is now used in most parts of the U. S. by cultivated speakers." In 1934 the Merriam people branded "ain't" as
"dialectal" and "illiterate."

   *The New York Times (McCandlish Phillips): The use of
"ain't" is defended as "used orally in most parts of the U. S. by cultivated speakers."

   *San Francisco Chronicle (UPI): "Ain't" is "used orally in
most parts of the U. S. by cultivated speakers."

*UPI (Garry Gates): In settling the "ain't" question, the new dictionary calls it a word that is "used orally in most parts of the U. S. by cultivated speakers." [Five paragraphs on ain't, then two on the end preposition.]

*Springfield Union:. . .the official recognition, at last, of the word "ain't," which, the book says, is "used orally in most parts of the U. S. by cultivated speakers."

CBS Saturday News (Stuart Novins) (9 Sept.): For the first time it recognizes "ain't" as used orally in most parts of the U. S. by cultivated speakers.

Chicago Daily News (9 Sept.):. . .the lexicographers justify the word "ain't" on the ground that it is "used orally in most parts of the U.S. by cultivated speakers."

Woonsocket Call (13 Sept.): "Ain't" finally gets recognition as "used orally in most parts of the U. S. by cultivated speakers."

Life (15 Sept.): Even "ain't" is now conceded to be "used orally in most parts of the U. S. by many cultivated speakers."

Newsweek (18 Sept.): "Ain't". . .is now acknowledged to be "used orally in most parts of the U. S. by cultivated speakers."

Watertown, N. Y., Daily Times (Hiltburgh Overacker, 19 Sept.): "Ain't" gets official recognition as "used orally in most parts of the U. S. by cultivated speakers."

Third Dimensions: Economic Profiles of Greater Springfield (Sept.–Oct. 1961):. . .450,000 words, including "ain't" for the first time.

Even when rewrite desks buried ain't in the middle of the story, the headline writers often played it up:

*Baltimore Sun: Webster's Accepts Ain't as Cultivated

*Boston Herald: It Either Is or It Ain't

*Iowa City Press Citizen: "Ain't" Is Finally In the Dictionary

*New York Herald Tribune: New Webster OKs 'Ain't'

*Springfield Union: OK Now to Say Ain't; Used by Cultivated

*Toronto Star: Ain't Gonna Teach This New Kinda Talk

The impressions a reader would get from most of the early stories were that (1) the new dictionary had departed from the principles of its predecessors and had abdicated its authority; phrases to this effect appear far more frequently than chance would allow;[26] (2) illustrative citations were a novelty; (3) ain't was appearing in a dictionary for the first time, and this time with full approbation; (4) the dictionary was aimed at a mass audience rather than at its traditional scholarly readers. As for recognition of the editors, a rough count shows Gallan mentioned about six times as often as Gove. Atypical in several respects is the British Bookseller (9 Sept.), which mentions only Gove, concentrates on the scholarly labor behind the dictionary and ignores ain't, popular personalities, and vocabularly novelties. This striking difference foreshadowed an equally striking difference in the reviews in British popular publications.[27]

Other straws appeared in the wind. On 10 September The New York Times, the next day the Schenectady Gazette,[28] unveiled a new kind of criticism that later became very popular: passages stringing together "a few of the words which in the old Webster's Dictionary [the New International, second edition, 1934] were either classed as 'dialectal' or 'illiterate,' or did not exist, or had other meanings" — orientate, finalize (soon to become a cause celebre in American literary criticism),[29] upsurge, hipster, jazz as a noun of all work, and dig meaning "approve."

The apparent endorsement of ain't provoked an especially violent reaction from the defenders of the good, the true and the beautiful. On 8 September the Toronto Globe and Mail castigated the Third in an editorial, charging that it had unconditionally welcomed ain't into Standard English. On 17 September the columnist Charles McDowell, Jr., remarked sardonically about the hue-and-cry after the Third:

It is alleged that the new edition of the Merriam-Webster unabridged dictionary, entitled "Webster's Third New International Dictionary," includes in good standing the contraction "ain't." We say it is alleged, because we aren't sure of all the facts, and a man has to be careful about a matter this important.

We have not seen the new edition of the dictionary. What we have seen is a few news stories and many editorials discussing the inclusion of "ain't." None of them tells us exactly what the dictionary says about "ain't.". . .

. . .Let us end the discussion of "ain't," temporarily, by reporting that [of] a cross-section of 14 editorials on the subject, 11 were against "ain't," two were for it and one was on the fence and obviously very nervous about the whole thing. [30]

In the admittedly incomplete files at my disposal I have read some forty editorials about ain't that appeared before the publication date, 28 September — a dozen signed, some twenty unsigned, and eight separate appearances of what seems to be an unsigned bit of syndicated boiler-plate. This last begins urbanely with a reference to the clay-tablet dictionaries of Assyria, notes the problems of the lexicographer, snarls that the statement of the Third about ain't in cultivated speech could not be true unless one used cultivated in the sense of "loose or broken up," and concludes by conceding the justice of Johnson's comparison of dictionaries to watches. The first occurrence I have found is in the York, Pennsylvania, Dispatch of 12 September. [31] The next day it appeared in the Greenville, S. C., Piedmont (as a native of Greenville I know that the traditional local use of ain't is in accord with the usage note in the Third); on the 14th it was used by the Beverly, Massachusetts, Times, by the North Attleboro, Mass., Chronicle, and by the Lima, Ohio, Citizen. On the 22nd it appeared in the Jonesboro, Arkansas, Sun, on the 23rd in the Geneva, New York, Times.

The bobtailed statement on ain't provoked teacher-polls in Toronto, in Jacksonville, Florida, in Springfield, Massachusetts, and in Binghamton, New York — though in none of those towns had anyone seen what the dictionary actually had to say. (It is interesting that the Floridians seemed least perturbed; the superintendent of schools actually declared that if a word was in general use we might as well accept it.)

There were, of course, favorable and even understanding editorials and news columns, written by people with some knowledge of lexicography and the English language. Basil Hall, of the Charleston, S. C., Evening Post, aware that in his community ain't is a well established touchstone for upper-upper intimate speech, let out a joyous rebel yell:

> I ain't usually so exuberant, but this time I think maybe I've got to be.
>
> You see, for years now there's been a running battle between me and a rather stodgy set of schoolteachers, who've contended I'm undermining rhetoric in their English classes by my occasional use of "ain't" in this column.
>
> It's been my consistent view down the years that "ain't" — especially as it is used in the South — is a perfectly agreeable, acceptable word.
>
> So yesterday, it was with considerable delight that I read in the Post that the new Merriam-Webster Unabridged Dictionary — considered by scholars as the best published in the United States — lists "ain't" as a word that is "used orally in most parts of the United States by cultivated people."
>
> In case my foes again begin to carp over the phrase "used orally," let me say I've made a studied effort to write Keeping Posted in a chatty way that parallels my manner of speech.
>
> And by golly, if I've enjoyed even a modicum of success so far, I ain't thinkin' about changing at this late date. [32]

But the prevailing tone was hostile, and was clearly reflected in the flip headlines for the editorials. [33] Even the Episcopal cathedral in Springfield paid its respects to ain't and Merriam: "The inference was that the Soviets had 'discovered' what they had always suspected: That there 'ain't no heaven' (G & C Merriam please take note)." [34]

It was clear that the first press release, however contrived and by whom, had backfired. On 12 September there was another. Gove, hitherto almost ignored, became the public defender of the Third and explained the true history of ain't in the Merriam dictionaries: that it had been in the International series since 1890, but had never been unconditionally approved. Still, few newspapers or

columnists picked up the new release. Walter Winchell did, [35] and
the report in Life (Sept. 15) partially corrected the quotation of the
usage note. [36] But the damage had been done: Gove's equivocal position was noted, and his outward appearance of testiness under questioning provoked a new Albee-type game: getting Gove's goat. Tom
Malone, in the Wilmington, Delaware, News (Sept. 16), commented
that in the more recent release the Company's pain was "showing
through its typewriter." McDowell's column — already mentioned —
called attention to the discrepancy between Gove's statement and what
Gallan had said a few days earlier — a credibility gap before the
phrase became fashionable:

> Gordon J. Gallan, president of the publishers of the dic-
> tionary, was quoted as saying to reporters, "'Ain't' is used
> orally in most parts of the United States by cultivated
> speakers ...."
> Later, P. B. Gove, editor of the news [sic] dictionary,
> stepped into the controversy and seemed to contradict his
> publisher. Mr. Gove said, "The entry in the Third New In-
> ternational does not seem to us to constitute acceptance or
> approval of 'ain't.' Its frequent occurrence, in fact, is
> severely restricted to less educated speech, and when 'ain't'
> is the equivalent of have not is not, am not [sic], [37] it is
> clearly labeled substandard."
> This may or may not leave "ain't" in a more or less ac-
> ceptable position when it means "are not," although we still
> can't tell. Our own hope has always been that "ain't" would
> some day be accepted in the sense of "am I not," — that is,
> "ain't I?" which is at least better than "aren't I?"

In any event, as every professional politician knows, explanations and denials rate fewer headlines than attacks; the original
release, unmodified, was being used as the source of articles, reviews, and editorials into the spring of 1962. The initiative had
passed to those who knew what they would dislike in a book they had
not yet seen. [38]

IV

The repetitiousness of the statements about the Third in the
early news stories could not have come from chance; even some of

the most easily misinterpreted phrases recur so often that they must
have been found in the original release. If the aim of the release was
that of show business — to get people to talking, and to spell every
name correctly — it was a success. But if one looks at it from the
viewpoint of a linguist who has followed the progress of lexicography
from medieval glosses to the great historical dictionaries like the
Oxford, it was a disaster.

Not all of the innovations of the Third are improvements; one
may question the wisdom of the single-phrase definitions, the relative
paucity of status labels, the lack of a pronunciation line, and the typography — and still concede its real accomplishments. But this kind
of appraisal appeared in no American newspaper or popular magazine
in 1961-62. It was too easy to join the game of the moment and attack
what seemed to be a safe target. In turn, almost all of the scholars
in the field, who on balance would have given qualified approval but
indicated directions for improvement, were reduced to silence, to a
response to details, or to a monolithic defense, lest they seem to be-
tray their profession. Certainly, it is difficult to be coolly objective
in the face of hysterical attacks by those who should have known better. On both sides of the controversy there is ample cause for em-
barrassment. It is a lamentable state of affairs when the provost of
a great university announces that when the editorial board of a journal
discussed the possibility of reviewing the Third, no one on the board
had examined it but everyone knew what he wanted to say. [39] It is even
more lamentable to realize that the apparent tone of the press release
provoked reactions of this kind.

Nor has the effect ceased. The Random House Dictionary
(1966) has received unasked and undeserved praise from those who
think it marks a return to prescriptivism; [40] yet it has a more explicit statement of the doctrine of usage than one can find in the Third.
The American Heritage Dictionary (1969) was prepared under the
auspices of a publisher outspokenly hostile to the Third; its editor
frequently condemned the Third, in the public prints, through his
syndicated word column; and the panel of usage judges to whom
troublesom problems were referred — a merchandizing gimmick
used to promote the sales — is loaded with those who openly disapproved of what they fancied was the permissiveness of Gove's dictionary. [41] It will be a long time before the dust finally settles.

But who raised the dust? It seems inconceivable that it was anyone on the editorial staff; there is nothing like the sober drudgery of lexicography to make one wary of dramatic statements.[42] Nor could a simple ad-man have set up the release unaided; the sheer difficulty of finding detailed information in the Third, even when one knows what to look for, means that he must have had help on the inside. But to reach more specific conclusions one would need the help of professional investigators; and the woeful lack of objectivity which Nero Wolfe demonstrated, for example,[43] makes one suspect the disinterestedness of any detective.[44] Entertaining as this narrative is, in its own right and as a commentary on American society, there seems no reason to pursue it further. At Merriam there is a new staff, at work on new editions; like their predecessors, they will learn from scholarship and technology and experience. Since everyone — including competitors — can gain from better dictionaries, the time is at hand when scholars should seriously evaluate the real contributions of the Third and the ways in which it can be improved, without worrying about bright inaccuracies — even those perpertrated by the publishers themselves.

NOTES

This paper was presented under a slightly different title to the Present-Day English Group of the Modern Language Association at its meeting in New York City in December 1966.

     In "A Working Lexicographer Appraises Webster's Third New International Dictionary" [American Speech, 42 (1967), 202-10] Robert L. Chapman, of the Funk & Wagnalls Standard College Dictionary (1963) appraises the Third from a competitor's point of view. There are no consequential differences between his conclusions and those I reached.

     [1]Wilson Follett, "Sabotage in Springfield." The Atlantic, January, 1962, pp. 73-77; Dwight MacDonald, "The String Untuned," the New Yorker, 10 March 1962, pp. 130-34, 137-40, 143-50, 153-60; Mario Pei "The Dictionary as a Battlefront: English Teachers' Dilemma," Saturday Review, 21 July 1962, pp. 45ff.; Jacques Barzun, "What Is a Dictionary?" The American Scholar, Spring 1963, pp. 176-81; Lincoln Barnett, "Who Is Behind the Assault on English?" Horizon, 5 (July 1963), 33-48.

[2]See for example I. Willis Russell, The English Journal, 51, (May 1962), 331-34, 348; James H. Sledd, "The Lexicographer's Uneasy Chair," College English 25, (May 1962), 682-87.

[3]This charge is made, in particular, by MacDonald, Pei, and Barnett.

[4]In his American English Grammar (1940), Charles C. Fries pointed out that most judgments of usage had been subjective, a priori and ex cathedra, without attention to the actual structure or history of the language or to the social distribution of variants. By first determining the status of the writers of a large number of holograph letters and then analyzing their grammatical practices, Fries sought to discover, objectively, the differences between "Standard English" and "Vulgar English," and also the practices of the intermediate group. His method is still the model to be followed in such studies.

[5]James H. Sledd and Wilma R. Ebbitt, Dictionaries and THAT Dictionary, Chicago, 1962; Kenneth G. Wilson, R. H. Hendrickson, and Peter Alan Taylor, Harbrace Guide to Dictionaries, New York, 1963; Jack Gray, Words, Words and Words About Dictionaries, San Francisco, 1963. Philip B. Gove, The Role of the Dictionary, Indianapolis, 1967, is less comprehensive than the others; moreover, his association with the Third has inevitably (if pardonably) colored his judgment.

[6]A few years ago, The Encyclopedia Britannica, Inc., of which Merriam is now a subsidiary, asked me to evaluate the criticisms of the Third. In making my report I read thousands of public comments, but by no means everything. Except where the context clearly indicates otherwise, the evidence for this article is derived from those comments, which are accessible to any investigator — though the task would have been much harder had not the Britannica provided thermocopies for my use. Needless to say, my observations here are my own, and do not reflect the official position of either Merriam or the Britannica.

[7]A few serious articles have appeared in the last few years: Uriel Weinreich, "Webster's Third: A Critique of Its Semantics," International Journal of American Linguistics, 30 (1964), 405-09; John Dawkins, "Noun Attributives in Webster's Third New International Dictionary," American Speech, 29 (1964), 33-41; Raven I. McDavid, Jr., "Dialect Labels in the Merriam Third," Publication of the American Dialect Society, 47 (1967), 1-22.

⁸The only one which I have noticed is that by Sumner Ives, in the St. Louis Globe-Democrat, 24 Sept. 1961. Since Ives was also to publish a commissioned review in Word Study, the Merriam house organ (Dec. 1961), his opinions were inevitably discounted.

⁹The American Language, one-volume abridged edition, New York, 1963, p. 99.

¹⁰To publishers, unabridged simply means not cut down from any larger work. The American College Dictionary could be so described, as could the smaller Thorndike-Barnhart Desk Dictionary (1951). However, to the layman an "unabridged dictionary" suggests the inclusion of every word in the language, with all its meanings — or at least every reputable word and meaning. The manifest impossibility of producing such a dictionary has made little erosion in the folk belief.

¹¹For a long time, most American colleges have recommended, and many have required, that every freshman own a "college" dictionary — approximately the scope of the Webster's Collegiate.

¹²Clarence Barnhart, editor-in-chief of the ACD, had been active in organizing the military dictionary project of the Army Language Section. Among others involved in the ACD who had participated in the wartime programs were Bernard Bloch, Leonard Bloomfield, Charles C. Fries, Robert A. Hall, Jr., Mrs. Elizabeth J. Denning, William J. Gedney, Ralph Weiman, Charles F. Hockett, Martin Joos, Norman McQuown, William B. S. Smith, John Kepke, and George L. Trager.

¹³A small example: Arthur, king of Britain, appeared in the biographical section, since there is some historical evidence for a British Artorius of c. 500. But Lancelot and Guinevere, as literary characters, appeared only in the main vocabulary.

Like the Oxford English Dictionary, the Third has no separate biographical and geographical sections; furthermore it presents no proper names qua proper names (only God is capitalized). This was to figure prominently in the belletristic assault on the Third, but does not seem to have entered into the earliest criticism. Biographical and geographical sections continue to appear in the Merriam Seventh New Collegiate (1963).

¹⁴There was no attempt to revise the pronunciation key, which had drawn strong criticism from scholars; see Kemp Malone's account of the New International, second edition, in "Some Linguistic

Studies of 1933 and 1934," MLN, 50 (Dec. 1935) 515-18. Changes in
the word list and in definitions, from an early fifth edition Collegiate to a late New Collegiate are about what one would expect from
cumulative revisions in successive printings of the same edition.
Ironically, in view of later criticisms of the Third, one of the most
outspoken American structural linguists, Robert A. Hall, Jr., of
Cornell University, was an active consultant for the New Collegiate,
and his help is specifically acknowledged in the preface.

[15]It has been established for a generation that a company cannot legally assert proprietorship to a surname as part of a book title.
To be sure, Merriam had some traditional claim since it had bought
the rights to Noah Webster's dictionary; on the other hand, the Web-
ster-Mahn An American Dictionary of the English Language (1864)
was a drastically new edition, which left little of the original.

[16]As published in the Californian, September 1961, the paragraph about this decision was headed "You Can't Trust the Dictionary."

There was some bitterness among booksellers who asserted
that Merriam had continued to accept orders for the second edition up
to the announcement of the Third, but would not allow these over-
stocks to be returned for credit. See Publisher's Weekly, 18 Sept.
and 25 Sept. 1961. Later, the protestations of The New York Times
and other hostile critics made a freshly purchased copy of the second
edition a status symbol among genteel folk, and it was reported that
the leftover copies sold at a premium.

[17]To take one example, the Texas legislature abolished Germanic studies in all state institutions. In justification, it was alleged,
inter alia, that Eduard Prokosch, chairman of Germanics at the University of Texas, had identified English as a Low German dialect.

[18]The latent prescriptivism of American journalism was indicated in the Saturday Evening Post of 5 Oct. 1946, in an editorial
entitled "Is There a Lexicographer in the House?" It called for the
excision of all the casual words that had crept into the language and
referred to the editor's unabridged dictionary (almost certainly the
second edition of the New International) as "a big, fat fraud."

[19]Many of the best American linguists had been unable to get
permanent academic appointments in the 1930s. Now, hailed as
miracle workers and sometimes (as at Cornell) given special status,
they often deliberately antagonized literary scholars of the older tradition.

[20]W. Freeman Twaddell, of Brown, was offered the editorship and actually served for a year in Springfield, but decided not to

continue. Frederic G. Cassidy, of Wisconsin, and Albert H. Marckwardt, of Princeton (formerly of Michigan), also report receiving offers of the position.

[21]Curiously, no reviewer has called attention to the discrepancy between two statements in the early publicity: (1) that the Third
cost $3,500,000 to prepare; (2) that the "permanent staff" numbered
more than a hundred. If both statements were literally true, wages
would have been desperately low. Actually, as the front matter of
the Third reveals, only sixteen of the editorial and clerical staff
served through the ten years preceding publication.

[22]Business Week, 16 Sept. 1961.

[23]Binghamton, N. Y., Sun-Bulletin, 25 Sept.

[24]They had appeared in Johnson's dictionary and in many of
its continental predecessors; see James H. Sledd and Gwin J. Kolb,
Dr. Johnson's Dictionary (Chicago 1955), 41-43. They were the basis
of the Oxford and subsequent historical dictionaries, and had been
used in many commercial dictionaries, such as the second edition of
the New International.

[25]The editors of the Third had simply chosen, where they
found them in the file, citations that aptly illustrated particular meanings of particular words; for no-show, a passenger who makes a
reservation and does not use it, a timetable would be a most appropriate source. But many critics — at this stage, the Laporte, Ind.,
Herald-Argus, the Houston Chronicle and the Miami Herald — interpreted the selection of a citation as an approbation of literary quality.
This misinterpretation would have been averted by a clearer statement in the publicity release or by a pamphlet explaining the principles on which the dictionary had been prepared and the way it could
be most effectively used.

[26]McCandlish Phillips, The New York Times (7 Sept.): "radi-
cally altered in style."

New York Daily News (7 Sept.): "A new tradition-breaking
dictionary."

Buffalo News (7 Sept.): "A revolutionary tradition-breaking
dictionary."

Beaver, Pa., Times (16 Sept.): "The new dictionary liber-
ates the English language, to some extent, by recognizing the word
ain't for the first time."

Newsweek (18 Sept.): "Resigned acceptance of grammatical
error."

Burlington, Vt. , _Free Press_ (21 Sept.): ". . . might shock academicians, but which surely will please communicative people as a whole. . . . Unlike its earlier editions, this one is more concerned with describing a language in its present state than with dictating what is right in meaning and pronunciation. "

Kerrville, Texas, _Times_ (21 Sept.): "The new edition of the famous unabridged dictionary abrogates its right to prescribe correct usage. "

Fort Myers, Florida, _News-Press_ (21 Sept.): (head on Whitney Bolton column) "Dictionary Bastions Falling. "

Philadelphia _Bulletin_ (24 Sept.): (head) "New Dictionary Breaks Sharply with Tradition"; (text) "revolutionary break with tradition. "

Santa Ana, Calif. , _Chronicle_ (24 Sept.): (head) "Revolutionary New Dictionary to be Published by Merriam and Co. "

[27] Among British reviewers were Ivor Brown, the skillful popularizer; Robert W. Burchfield, editor of the Second Supplement to the _Oxford_; Alan S. C. Ross, who had written about the social status of words in British English; and Randolph Quirk, probably the finest British student of the English language since Henry Sweet.

[28] The most devastating was an editorial in The New York Times, 12 Oct. , beginning, "A passell of double-domes. . . . "

[29] In a news conference 29 Nov. , President Kennedy declared that his travel plans had not been _finalized._ His use of this word — cited by the _Third_ from Eisenhower's remarks, but known from World War I — provoked an inundation of splenetic editorials, often shamelessly lifted, without acknowledgment, by one newspaper from another. The New York Times expressed its editorial indignation as early as 30 Nov.

[30] "Capital Sidelights: Random Notes and Observations, " Los Angeles _Times_ (17 Sept.).

[31] The quip about "loose or broken up" was attributed to a local teacher by the Springfield, Mass. , _Union_ (11 Sept.). Barring further evidence, I would derive the _Union's_ remark from the syndicated comment and assume that the "local teacher" is a character of editorial fiction.

[32] 8 Sept.

[33] "Ain't Isn't, " Boston _Record_ (9 Sept.).

"Says Headline 'Ain't' OK, " People's Forum, Springfield, Mass. , _Union_ (9 Sept.).

"Ain't Ain't Cultivated," Boston Herald (10 Sept.). The ensuing editorial even deplores Fowler.

"Big Word Catalogue from Ain't to Zen," Life (15 Sept.).

"Merriam 'Ain't' Amused," Tom Malone, Wilmington, Delaware, News (16 Sept.).

"We Say It Ain't So," The Morgantown, West Va., Post (18 Sept.).

"'Ain't' Gains Respectability in New Family Dictionary," Dan Sullivan, St. Paul Dispatch (23 Sept.).

"'Ain't' Is a Couth Word, Webster Acknowledges," Connie Reese (verse editorial), the Newark Evening News, 23 Sept.

[34]The Cathedral Chronicle, Christ Church Cathedral, 29 Sept.

[35]"It's Been in Webster's Diksh since 1947," Spartanburg, S. C., Herald, 16 Sept. Since the new Merriam release gave a much earlier date, Winchell may have simply checked the publication date of a late printing of the second edition.

[36]Soon, however, Life joined the chorus of detractors, with an editorial "A Non-Word Deluge," 27 Oct., p. 4.

[37]The release followed the dictionary entry and specified that ain't I? was the most common use in standard English. Perhaps a wire service transposed the statements, or McDowell misread them.

[38]For a comparable situation, see Martin S. Shockley, "The Reception of The Grapes of Wrath in Oklahoma," American Literature, 15 (Jan. 1944), 351-61. Most of the hostile critics of the novel admitted that they had not read it and had no intention of doing so; but they were sure it was unfit to be shelved in a public library or read by respectable citizens.

[39]The American Scholar, Spring 1963, p. 176.

[40]E.g., Kurt Vonnegut, The New York Times Book Review, 30 Oct. 1966, p. 1.

[41]This dictionary was originally sponsored by the American Heritage Foundation, whose president, James Parton, made an unsuccessful attempt to purchase the Merriam Company; he frankly admitted that he wanted to suppress the Third. The editor, William Morris, had repeatedly assailed the Third and the caricature of "structural linguistics" in his column "Words, Wit and Wisdom." The usage panel contains such noteworthy adversaries of the Third as J. Donald Adams, Lincoln Barnett, Jacques Barzun, Theodore W. Bernstein, Sidney Harris, Dwight Macdonald and Mario Pei; only

Roy A. Copperud, of the 105 members of the panel, had spoken out
in Gove's defense. The items referred to the panel were, by and
large, those that had aroused the hostility of lay critics of the Third;
their number is well under three hundred, but the existence of the
panel undoubtedly helped make the American Heritage a best seller.
In 11 May 1970, Time appraised it, not under "Books" or "Education,"
but under "Marketing." That Americans know their dictionaries less
by their merits than by their advertising was pointed out by James H.
Sledd in "Toward the First International Alvearie," a paper presented
in 1968 at the New York City meeting of the Modern Language Association. In response to Sledd's observations the Association has taken
the first steps toward creating a center for lexicography of the English language, though the fulfillment of this dream is some years dis-
tant.

  The charge of "permissiveness," against both the Third and
the fancied "structural linguists" behind it, was reiterated in a popular article on linguistics in Time, 24 Feb. 1967.

  [42] "One of the ironies in Webster's position is that the aspects
of its content that were used for their news value in the early publicity releases were settled upon by a promotion firm and not by the
publishers." John Allen Reed (pseud.), "A New Big Dictionary: Its
Virtues and Faults." [Review of the Random House Dictionary], St.
Louis Post-Dispatch, 18 Dec. 1966, p. B4. The review is reprinted
in Gove, The Role of the Dictionary, pp. 63-65.

  [43] In "Auto-da-Fe," the first chapter of Gambit (New York
1962), Wolfe is depicted as burning a copy of the Third, page by page,
including the buckram binding. As the burning proceeds, he reiter-
ates the hackneyed charges: "subversive and intolerably offensive,"
"threatens the integrity of the English language," "a deliberate attempt to murder the language." At the end of the burning, Archie
Goodwin, Wolfe's factotum, observes, "You knew you were going to
burn it when you bought it; otherwise you would have ordered leather."

  [44] Disinterested is one of the key words in the great debate
over the Third. Critics have deplored the fact that the first (historically oldest) sense presented, 'apathetic,' is given without a restrictive label; they have not noted that the same is true of the entry in
the second edition. Actually, the Oxford had labeled this meaning
"obsolete?" when the letter D appeared at the turn of the century; however, the 1930 Supplement had removed the label on the strength of
good citations from reputable writing. The New International,

second edition, had presented the same order of senses as the <u>Third</u>, but did not draw the lightning; perhaps the qualification of the earlier usage as <u>now rare</u> was sufficient, however inaccurate; or are affluence and leisure necessary before Americans can concern themselves with lexicographical quiddities?

16 | Poor Whites and Rustics

In Collaboration with Sarah Ann Witham
In Honor of Margaret Bryant

From her childhood, Margaret Bryant has been aware of American social classes and of the epithets used to designate them. She grew up in Edgefield County, South Carolina, a meeting ground of three cultures — plantation, small farming, and cotton mill — and often a bellwether in state politics.[1] As a graduate of Winthrop — the state college for women, founded shortly before she was born — she encountered students from all parts of South Carolina, with their sensibilities and prejudices. Despite her long residence in New York City, she has never lost her Southern sensitivity to social differences and the words reflecting them. Consequently, it is fitting to offer in her honor a discussion of such designations as recorded in the Linguistic Atlas of New England (Kurath et al. 1939-43), and the Linguistic Atlas of the Middle and South Atlantic States (Kurath, R. McDavid, and O'Cain 1978-).

All of the linguistic atlases in the United States have sought the epithets for persons whose dress and behavior mark them as conspicuously rural. In addition, for the South Atlantic States the investigators sought epithets for poor whites, particularly in communities dominated by the plantation system; of these epithets, informants were asked to indicate which terms were used by whites and which by blacks.[2] However, up to now there has been only one general discussion of such names, dealing with the Upper Midwest (Allen 1958, recapitulated in Allen 1973)[3] and two which treat the specific terms hoosier and cracker, associated primarily with the South and South Midland (R. McDavid 1967, R. and V. McDavid 1973). This study summarizes the findings for the Atlantic Seaboard, from southern New Brunswick to northeastern Florida, plus a number of interviews

from Ontario (16), eastern Ohio (44) and eastern Kentucky (20) —
a total of over 1, 600 informants.[4]

For the purposes of this study the responses for the three
items are considered together: whites' terms for poor whites, blacks'
terms for poor whites,[5] terms for rustics. Although one may draw
some fine technical distinctions between rustics and poor whites,[6] in
fact the two groups and their designations overlap: a number of epithets — such as cracker and hoosier and their compounds — were elicited for all three items. Appendix A — an alphabetical list of all
designations recorded — indicates the applications for particular
epithets.

Interpretation of the data inevitably involves an appraisal of
the practices of field workers, especially where more than one participated in gathering the data. Kurath et al. 1939 (50-53) is ruthlessly honest about differences in the practices of those who did the
work in New England; R. McDavid et al. (in progress) does the same
for the Middle and South Atlantic States. In contrast, Orton et al.
1962-71 officially recognizes no differences, though they may be inferred from charting the data for particular items.[7] Sixteen field
workers participated in the investigations of the Atlantic Seaboard;
the most important differences are those between the two principal
investigators, Guy S. Lowman, Jr., and Raven I. McDavid, Jr.
Lowman did the largest part of the work in New England, conducting
interviews in every state except Connecticut and Rhode Island — and
all from the Mohawk Valley through North Carolina. McDavid did
most of the work in Upstate New York, Ontario, Kentucky, South
Carolina, Georgia and Florida. Between them they account for more
than four-fifths of the field work.

Although both Lowman and McDavid were generally successful as field workers, and enjoyed good rapport with most of their informants, there were certain differences in their procedures. Though
thoroughly courteous, Lowman conducted his interviews aggressively
— proceeding straightforwardly through the questionnaire, often suggesting responses, recording relatively few synonyms and few forms
from free conversation. Furthermore, in the South Atlantic States he
did not normally seek terms for rustics in the plantation country, or
terms for poor whites in the uplands. In contrast, McDavid worked

more by casual indirection, sought — but did not suggest — synonyms, and recorded many conversational forms.[8] Furthermore, he had certain predispositions. He was a native South Carolinian like Miss Bryant, though brought up in the inner city of an industrial community rather than in a small town. He had been early sensitized to the implications of these designations (he had heard a large number of them) and to the often subtle differences between close synonyms, and had been constantly reminded of them by his father, an active politician and successful industrial lobbyist. He thus had a greater interest than Lowman in these items, and would have elicited a larger number of responses. Thus more terms, especially more compound terms, are reported from Upstate New York, South Carolina and Georgia than from Maine, Pennsylvania or Virginia. Lowman's comparatively minor interest in these items — which are particularly treacherous for an outsider — is also reflected in the data from New England: there are only 15 designations for rustics reported by Lowman from Maine, where he did 73 interviews; in Rhode Island, Rachel Harris recorded the same number in 23 interviews. On the other hand, there are also cultural differences operating: even where the same field worker was concerned, as Lowman in Pennsylvania and North Carolina, in each of which he did 155 interviews, the Southerners offer more terms.

Of the 479 terms recorded in a total of 3,516 responses, the commonest is backwoodsman (355 responses) found in every state and province.

The next most common is countryman (349 responses) found everywhere except New Jersey. There are also 51 compounds of which country is the first element.

Third most common is hayseed (203 responses) or its variant hayseeder (38 responses) which together are found almost everywhere. In only Kentucky, West Virginia and Florida is this term not recorded.

Poor white trash, the fourth most common term, is used by both blacks and whites to denote rustics and poor whites. White respondents were recorded 131 times using this term about poor whites;

56 responses by blacks speaking about the same group were recorded. The term was used once as an epithet for rustics, making a total of 188 responses.

The fifth most popular single term, used largely to refer to rustics, is backwoodser (108 responses). Its distribution is not as extensive as backwoodsman, being recorded only in ten states: New Hampshire, New York, New Jersey, Pennsylvania, South Carolina, Ohio, Delaware, North Carolina, Maryland and West Virginia. There are 23 compounds in which back is an element, 17 of which involve the word backwoods in some form.

Hick (94 responses), the sixth most popular single term, appears in 13 of the 20 states under study. It is also the essential element of six compound terms.

As we have seen, many of the terms are compounds. There are 21 kinds of cracker (all but one associated with the South). There are also six kinds of hoosier, mostly confined to the South Uplands.

Certain adjectives appear congruently in these compounds. Poor, part of 37 terms, is not found in use north of the Mason-Dixon Line. Common as a component of 27 terms is also largely confined to the South and South Midland except for a few occurrences in New York. There are also 16 compounds using the word low, usually with down (lowdown). Mountain appears as the first element in 14 compounds. Sorry appears as an adjective in 11 compounds, largely in the South.

Of particular interest are the terms applied primarily to poor whites. Of these, 118 are described as used exclusively or primarily by whites. Described as exclusively used by blacks are 47 terms.

Buckra, of African origin, has spread into white speech. Such terms as poor barker, bucker and buckram are probably to be considered as variants.

Several terms are identified with particular localities. Cherston Hillers from Cherston Hill, New York, is an example. In

State	Most common term	Second most common term
New Brunswick	countryman	
Ontario	backwoodsman	hayseed/hick
Maine	countryman	hayseed
New Hampshire	countryman	hayseed
Vermont	hayseed	backwoodsman
Massachusetts	hayseed	countryman
Rhode Island	hayseed	countryman
Connecticut	hayseed	backwoodsman
New York	backwoodsman	hayseed
New Jersey	backwoodsman	backwooder
Pennsylvania	backwoodsman	hecker
West Virginia	mountain hoosier	backwoodsman
Ohio	backwoodsman	hillbilly
Kentucky	hillbilly	
Delaware	backwooder	backwoodser/forester
Maryland	backwoodsman	poor white trash
Virginia	countryman	poor white trash
North Carolina	mountain boomer	countryman
South Carolina	countryman	poor buckra
Georgia	countryman	common people
Florida	cracker	white trash

Connecticut, West Mountain, an imposing landform north of New Haven, has lent its name to the rustics living near it in <u>West Mountaineers</u>. A term used for any rural person in Rhode Island but which refers to a specific location is <u>Block Islander</u>.

The list above is of the first and second most frequently used epithets in each state. A blank indicates that there is no clear second term.

The term <u>hecker</u>, second most common in Pennsylvania, appears in only one other state, New Jersey, where it is the third most common term. Of greater interest is the uniqueness of the most popular term in North Carolina, <u>mountain boomer</u>, in that it does not follow the general pattern of shared usage of a few core terms. The term is also found only in North Carolina.

A comparison of these terms with those recorded by Allen is interesting. The Atlantic Seaboard yields far more than the Upper Midwest. This is partly due to the larger number of informants, 1,628 to 208, though the number of terms, as one might expect, does not increase proportionately. It is also partly due to the fact that class and cultural differences are more clearly felt in the longer settled regions; nevertheless, local terrain and events have provided a number of terms that do not occur further east, such as Kincaider, from the Kincaid Homestead Act, bronco buster, habitant, rail splitter and apple knocker.

Allen 1958 does not sort out the Upper Midwest terms by states, though Allen 1973 does, nor by field workers. His vocabulary check lists — multiple choice instruments filled out by respondents — yielded 24 terms not recorded in field interviews. Whether check list evidence would have been so productive in the Atlantic states is a moot question; the relatively small number of terms in Wood 1971 suggests, perhaps, that in the South there is more diffidence about writing them down.

This preliminary analysis leaves a number of interesting questions unanswered.[9] Do urban informants use as many of these terms as do rural ones? Are the terms used in a given region fairly constant for the various types of informants? Or do education and social class make a difference? Do men use the same epithets as women? How many of the terms recorded in the 1930's are now obsolete, and why (the 1945-56 records by McDavid suggest that the vocabulary of epithet was then alive and doing well)? And have new terms arisen, perhaps disseminated by mass media, like honky and whitey, current bywords among urban blacks and appearing in some of the last field records, but not in the earlier ones? There is room for a great deal of further investigation, both more intensive analysis of the Atlas evidence and by way of following up. As it stands, however, the list in Appendix A (like that in Allen 1958) provides interesting evidence of the prejudices of Americans toward their less affluent and less sophisticated fellow citizens.

APPENDIX A

Code: unmarked terms — rustic only; W — white term for poor whites; B — black term for poor whites; * — term also for rustics

Term	Frequency	Term	Frequency
Abolitionist	1	bucker W B	4
Algereen B[10]	1	buck farmer	4
back countryman	1	buckra W B	31
back hill	1	buckram B	1
back in the sticks	1	buckwheat	4
back streeter	1	buckwheat farmer	1
back squatter	1	buckwheater	5
back wooder	1	bunkin	2
backward cracker	3	bushman	1
backward fellas	1	bushwhacker	19
backward hoosier	1	certain class W	1
backwoods	2	certain class of people W	1
backwoods cracker	1	chaw bacon	1
backwoods farmer	4	cheap John B	1
backwoods fellas	4	Cherston Hiller	1
backwoods, in the	1	Chodyites	1
backwoods people	8	clay eater W B	4
backwoods person	1	clod knocker	6
backwoods tacky	1	clodhopper	14
backwoods Yankee	1	clown	1
backwoodser	108	codger	3
backwoodsman	355	common W B	18
backwoodster	1	common buckra B	1
barker W	6	common class of folk W	1
barren towner	1	common class of people W B	2
beater B	1	common class of white people W	1
Block Islander	1	common country children W	1
bog jumper	1	common cracker W	2
bohunk	1	common elements W	1
boob	3	common everyday people W	1
boomer	1	common farmer	1

Term	Frequency	Term	Frequency
common fellow W	2	country fellow	2
common folks W	6	country fogey	1
common land B	1	country folks	11
common liver W	1	country, from the	1
common man W	3	country gawk	2
common old cur W	1	country gawky	1
common people W B	81	country greenhorn	2
common persons W	3	country guy	3
common poor people W	1	country hick	8
common run of people W	1	country hick from Sunday crick	1
common trash W	2	country hoe buck	1
common white B	1	country hoosier	7
common white folks B	1	country hopper	1
common white people W	3	country jack	1
common white trash W	2	country jake	15
commoner people W B	2	country jay	1
commonest people W	1	country kid	1
coof	1	country lady	1
corn tassel	1	country people W *	57
cotton mill boy W	1	country person	2
cotton mill worker W	1	country pumpkin	3
counter jumper W	1	country punkin	1
country	1	country raised boy	1
country boob	1	country rube	1
country boy	7	country sager	1
country-bred man	2	country squash	1
country bump	1	country suck	1
country bumpkin	11	country tack	2
country chap	1	country tacky	1
country clod	1	country white people W	4
country clodhopper	1	country woman	2
country cob	1	countryman	349
country come to town	2	cow cracker W	1
country cousin	1	cracker W B *	108
country cracker W *	37	cropper W	1
country dude	2	damned carpetbagger	1
country farmer	1	damned Yankee	1

Term	Frequency	Term	Frequency
dirt digger	1	hick	94
dirt farmer	1	hicker	2
down cricker	1	hillbilly W B *	42
down easter	1	hilliboy	4
down east Yankee	1	Hiram	1
drifter B	7	honkey B	1
dude B	1	hoodlum	1
dummy	1	hoopy	3
factory people W	1	hoosier	30
farm people	1	huckleberry picker	1
farmer	50	hunky	1
Florida cracker W *	2	hosebird W	1
forester	8	ignorant	1
fur backer	1	ignorant people W *	3
gaping countryman	1	illiterate white W *	1
gawk	1	Italyites	1
gawkey	2	jackass W	1
Geechee	1	jackoak jumper	1
Georgia cracker W B *	9	Jackson whites	2
gillian B	1	jay	3
goober	1	jayhawk	1
goober grabber W	1	Jonathan	2
greenhorn	25	josh	1
greenhorn from the country	1	landlubber	1
greenman	1	linthead W	2
greeny	3	loafer W	1
greyneck W	3	low class W	2
hay pounder	1	low class of people W	1
hay shaker	1	low down W	1
hayback	2	low down people W	3
haymaker	1	low down white W	1
hayseed	203	low down white man B W	1
hayseeder	38	low down white people B W	2
heck	3	low down white trash B	1
hecker	28	low grade people W	1
hector W	1	low trash B	1
hermit	3	low white trash W B	1

Term	Frequency	Term	Frequency
lower class W B	4	old timer	1
mean low-life rascal B	3	old white rebel B	1
mean white people W	1	one gallus boy	1
mill children W	1	one gallus crowd	1
mill people W	1	onery B	1
mountain boar	1	ordinary W	4
mountain boomer	29	ordinary class of people W B	1
mountain boorker	1	ordinary white man W	20
mountain hoosier B *	112	outlaw W B	1
mountain hoover	1	outsider	2
mountain jack	2	outskirt	2
mountain people	2	pale face B	1
mountain ranger	2	pauper W	7
mountain tack	1	peapicker	1
mountain tacky	1	peck B	1
mountaineer	20	peckerwood W B	2
mucker	1	pine hawker	1
mud rooter	1	pine lander W *	3
moss back	8	pine lander people	1
mustang W	1	piner	1
Nassau Rangers[11]	1	piney	2
ne'er do wells W	1	piney woodsman	1
nigger lover W	1	pin hook tigers	1
no-count folks W	1	plain country folks	1
no-count white people W B	2	plain folks W	1
no-counts W	1	plain lousy folks B	1
no-good people B	1	plain people B	29
no-good persons W	1	the plainer class B	1
North Carolina cracker	1	the plainer people B	1
north woodsman	1	po-its B	1
not decent people W	1	poor Arab W	1
old country boy	1	poor backer W	1
old field sager	1	poor barker W	6
old pale face B	1	poor buck W B	2
old reb B	1	poor bucker W B	7
old settler	1	poor buckra W B	98
old time people	1	poor class W	2

Term	Frequency	Term	Frequency
poor class of people W B	4	renter class W	1
poor country people	1	reuben	4
poor countryman	1	revel B	1
poor cracker W B	7	rice eater	1
poor farmer	1	ridge runner	2
poor folks W	5	riffraff W	2
poor heater W	1	roog	1
poor ignorant people W	1	root	1
poor man W	2	rooze	1
poor people W B	34	rough neck W	1
poor reb W	1	rube	84
poor scrub W	1	ruby	1
poor tack W *	2	rustic	12
poor trash W B	11	sager B *	3
poor white W B	26	sand hill tack	1
poor white ashes W	1	sandlapper	2
poor white backra B	2	scab W	1
poor white buckra W	2	scalawag W	1
poor white devil	1	scrub W	1
poor white dog W	1	scum W B	2
poor white folks W B	15	scum of the earth W B	3
poor white hellions W	1	second class people B	1
poor white herrings W	3	shanty white W	1
poor white man B	6	sharecropper W	1
poor white people B	4	shit pitcher	1
poor white reb W B	2	shrimp dipper	1
poor white trash W B *	187	soda cracker B	1
punkin	1	sod buster	2
punkin chaser	1	sorry W	2
punkin thrasher	1	sorry class of white folks W	1
raglegs W	1	sorry people W	1
rascal W	1	sorry persons W	1
reb B	3	sorry white folks W	2
rebel B	1	sorry white man W	3
redleg W	1	sorry white people W B	2
redneck W B *	9	sorry white trash W B	2
renter W	3	squatter B *	2

Term	Frequency	Term	Frequency
stickman	1	way back farmer	2
sticks, the	10	West Mountaineer	1
swamp angels	4	wharfinger W	1
swamp boy	1	white Arab B	1
swamp rabbit W	1	white barker W	1
swamp rat	3	white buck	12
swamp Yankee	2	white buckra W B *	1
swamper	1	white cracker B	2
tack B *	5	white nigger	1
tacky	4	white soda cracker	1
tallow face B *	6	white sons of bitches B	1
tenant W	2	white trash W B	60
tenant farmer W *	5	whitey B	1
tenant people W	1	wood hick B *	20
that element W	1	wood rat	1
thin people B	1	woodsman	3
tit puller	1	woodster	1
Tivertowner	29	wool hat W *	2
trash W B	1	wool hat boy W	1
trash people W	1	working class people B	1
trash white people W	1	yank	1
up country	1	yankee	3
very sorry man W	1	yap	3
very sorry white man W	4	yellow barker W	1
way back 1	1	yokel	6

APPENDIX B

State	No. of Informants	Total No. of Terms	No. of Terms Unique to State
New Brunswick	8	6	2
Ontario	16	14	1
Maine	73	15	2
New Hampshire	51	16	2
Vermont	57	21	4
Massachusetts	138	38	10
Rhode Island	23	15	3
Connecticut	57	24	12
New York	181	65	31
New Jersey	47	22	7
Pennsylvania	155	18	1
West Virginia	111	24	6
Ohio	44	20	3
Kentucky	20	14	3
Delaware	13	13	4
Maryland	61	16	4
Virginia	147	68	42
North Carolina	155	51	19
South Carolina	144	174	113
Georgia	107	160	89
Florida	8	31	4

NOTES

Permission to use the materials examined in this study has been
given by the American Council of Learned Societies, sponsors of the
original scheme for a Linguistic Atlas of the United States and Canada
(which has developed into a series of autonomous regional surveys),
by the AMS Press, publishers of the reprinted (1972) Linguistic Atlas
of New England (Kurath et al. 1939-43) and (for the Kentucky records,
plus ten in Ohio and three in Ontario) by Albert H. Marckwardt, editor-in-chief of the Linguistic Atlas of the North-Central States (in
progress).

[1] As a result, Edgefield County has provided ten governors,
more than elected from any other rural county in America. Two of
these have been particularly active in fighting the oligarchy that long
dominated the state Democratic party: Benjamin Tillman (1890-1894)
and J. Strom Thurmond (1946-50), now senior senator from South
Carolina (1955-) and a Republican since 1964
[2] Designations for blacks, also elicited, constitute another
problem. Apparently, urban blacks use many of the same epithets
for rural blacks that whites use for rural whites.
[3] Allen's use of farmer as his general term is perhaps unfortunate: (1) many of his epithets designate part-time or marginal cul-
tivators; (2) in recent years the Middle Western farmer has competed
with the New York banker as a symbol of affluence and power.
[4] Marckwardt's North-Central materials have not been consulted, except for the eastern fringe, since it was desirable to set up
a sharp contrast between the primary settlement areas of the Atlantic
Seaboard and the tertiary areas surveyed by Allen.
[5] These include not only the items obtained from black informants but those which white informants associate with blacks.
[6] The poor white is characteristically a tenant — sharecrop-
per or renter. The rustic, such as the Southern mountaineer, tries
to obtain and keep title to his own land — even when he moves out of
the region to obtain work, as in the rubber shops of Akron (Udell 1966).
[7] Orton rigidly prescribed the sequence in which responses
were sought and the questions by which they were to be elicited. Most
of the introductory volume of Orton 1962-71 is devoted to the questions
used in eliciting. The American field workers were encouraged to

develop their natural ways of eliciting, and to adjust to the culture of the community. Their substantial differences were actually rather few. See Pederson et al. 1972, 1977.

[8]His procedures derived partly from personal diffidence, partly from an awareness of local sensitivities, partly from his training under Bernard Bloch, who made 88 field records and was himself skilled in getting responses in free conversation. As one soon finds out, free conversation is particularly important when dealing with grammatical items, about which even illiterate Americans have a morbid sense of propriety.

[9]The list is not exhaustive. For instance, Emmett, a familiar epithet in New Hampshire, was not attested (S.A.W.). Nor did South Carolinians offer Scopholites or Scovillites, originally applied to bands of Tory irregulars during the Revolution, and later to any kind of rural riffraff. (R.I.M.)

[10]In Maryland, Algereen was also used to designate the log pirates on the Susquehannah. Ultimately the term is derived from the Mediterranean naval campaigns against the Barbary pirates.

[11]Nassau county is the northeasternmost county of Florida. During the American Revolution the Florida Rangers (bands of Tory irregulars) harassed and pillaged the settlements in South Georgia.

REFERENCES

Allen, Harold B. "Pejorative terms for Midwestern farmers."
         American Speech 33 (1958): 260-265.
_____   Linguistic atlas of the Upper Midwest. Volume 1. Minnea-
         polis: University of Minnesota Press, 1973.
Kurath, Hans, Raven I. McDavid, Jr., and Raymond K. O'Cain
         Linguistic Atlas of the Middle and South Atlantic States.
         Chicago: University of Chicago Press, 1978-
Kurath, Hans, et al. Handbook of the linguistic geography of New
         England. Providence, Rhode Island: American Council of
         Learned Societies, 1939. 2d edition, with new material by
         Audrey R. Duckert. New York: AMS Press, 1972.
_____   Linguistic atlas of New England. 3 vols. in 6 parts. Provi-
         dence, Rhode Island: American Council of Learned Societies,
         1939-43. Reprinted, 3 vols. New York: AMS Press, 1972.

McDavid, Raven I., Jr.   Word magic, or "Would you want your
        daughter to marry a Hoosier?" Indiana English Journal 2:
        (1967): 1, 1-7.
_____ and Virginia G. McDavid. 1973. "Cracker and Hoosier."
        Names 21: 3 (September, 1973): 161-167.
_____, et al. Handbook of the linguistic geography of the Middle
        and South Atlantic States (in progress).
Orton, Harold, et al. Survey of English dialects. Introduction; 3
        vols. in 12 parts. Leeds: E. J. Arnold, 1962-1971.
Pederson, Lee A., et al. A manual for dialect research in the South-
        ern States. Atlanta: Georgia State University Bookstore,
        1972. Reprinted: University of Alabama Press, 1974.
Pederson, Lee A. A Guide to the LAGS Project. Atlanta: LAGS,
        1977.
Udell, Gerald. "The speech of Akron, Ohio." Diss., University of
        Chicago, 1966.
Wood, Gordon. Vocabulary change. Carbondale and Edwardsville,
        Illinois: Southern Illinois University Press, 1971.

Author's Postscript

Looking back over the three decades covered by these essays, I can see how many times chance has operated.

Like all Southerners I was aware of linguistic variety, but
was late becoming aware of it as an academic discipline. Attending
the 1937 Linguistic Institute at Ann Arbor, I met Wayne Tyler, then
a graduate student at Wisconsin, and through him was invited to be
the demonstration informant in Bloch's seminar in field methods.
The interest of Kurath and Bloch made me a field worker; uncertain-
ties of the job market, as well as my gratitude to them, made my
performance in the field, and later as an editor, the center of my
academic career. Disappointments in the local institutional situations
simply meant that without feelings of guilt I could spend time and energy on the Atlas projects and on keeping alive public interest in them.
My gratitude toward those who have helped me is reflected in my
work with students, whom I try to accept as junior professional colleagues, with their own intelligence and energy. Being somewhat of
a marginal person myself, I am willing, often delighted, to work with
students who do not fit neatly into the traditional program; a student
or a subordinate deserves the best chance to find out what he can do,
and it is the advisor's responsibility to provide that chance, even if
it means going contrary to the academic organization. Much of the
same scepticism about academic fashion carries over into my scholarship; my first reaction is to reject the new, the fashionable, the powerful — and the more highly it is touted, the more I am inclined to
reject it.

Many people have contributed to the making of these essays.
My father shared with me a great deal of his intuitive knowledge of

the culture I grew up in. I had more than my lot of responsive teachers: at Furman there were Rosser H. Taylor, the student of Southern cultural history, and Alfred T. O'Dell, who helped me learn how
to write; at Duke there was Sir Allan Gilbert, who guided me to a
degree as a Miltonist and then never reproached me when I concentrated my efforts in another field, and Paull Baum, protean and sensitive and frighteningly modest, who kept my interest in linguistics
alive until there was a chance for it to develop systematically; at the
Linguistic Institutes there were Bernard Bloch and Edward Sapir and
Leonard Bloomfield and Edgar Sturtevant, who offered encouragement
and wisdom beyond what I was ready to absorb but which kept me
going in the right direction; over the years there have been Hans
Kurath and Al Marckwardt in all kinds of relationships, whose generosity I can repay only by trying to get the job done as well as possible
and by giving of myself to my students as they gave of themselves to
me. I have had many colleagues who helped make life tolerable,
from Jim Harrison at the Citadel through Bill Austin at the Army Language Section to Al Davis at the Illinois Institute of Technology. I
have had secular friends such as John P. Grace in Charleston and
Tom Woodside in Greenville. I have had more than my share of good
students: some of them have become partners in my work, like Bob
Van Riper and Lee Pederson and Ray O'Cain and Larry Davis and
Tom Creswell; others have become warm friends, like Roddey Reid
and Bettie Wilson. I have been blessed with a wife who has provided
not only affection but honest criticism and deep understanding despite
my many failures and disappointments; I have found appreciation
from my kinfolk, and delight in the way my children have grown up to
be persons in their own right, with careers of their own making. I
have learned not only about American English but about many facets
of American life from the hundreds who gave their time to be interviewed for the Atlas project, and from those dozens of local contacts
who made it possible for the interviews to be conducted under natural
conditions. The essays in this volume are the creation of all these
people; I have been but the student observer who happened to set
these observations down. They show a prejudice toward data rather
than toward theory; but a field worker is obligated to write down what
the informant says, not what the informant thinks he intended to say:
to be equally ruthless in setting down the Ulster cow call <u>chay</u>! in the
Williamsburg area of South Carolina, where Ulstermen settled in the
eighteenth century, and the putatively Holland Dutch <u>stoop</u> 'porch' in

the Savannah Valley, where no Holland Dutch colonies ever existed.
Explanations can wait; the data cannot.

My teaching style also derives from my field work. My office hours are irregular, flexible, and generous; I could not work a
five-day nine-to-five schedule in the field, but had to suit my hours
to those when the informant was available; similarly, the time to answer a student's question is when it is asked. I have become less insistent on prerequisites and more tolerant of deficiencies in technical
training — even of arrogance and stupidity; informants are sought not
for their political views or knowledge of world affairs, but only for
their ability to use honestly the language of their community. I delight
in taking rejects and seeing them do well professionally — unlike
many of my colleagues, I shape my teaching in terms of the laboratory
rather than the lecture hall. Even before I became a field worker,
I liked to sort out my students as individuals, and work separately
with each of them, as much as the situation allowed. Field work made
this the most natural way of teaching. Course assignments, I feel,
are contractual arrangements between teacher and student, with the
teacher as a consulting partner on each paper from the preliminary
exploration of topics to the final evaluation. If a topic seems unlikely
to produce a reasonable body of classifiable data, I advise adopting
something else. This kind of ground rule assures the student that the
teacher's criticism will be based on knowledge. If students are interested in a theoretical stance or an ideology outside the teacher's
competence, they should take their concerns somewhere else. The
kind of partnership I am easiest in does result, most of the time, in
good performances — and fairly often in work of distinction.

Whoever reads these essays should remember their background and judge them for what they are — tentative analyses to be
modified or corrected as new evidence comes in. If they stir some
of the readers to add to the body of data from which conclusions about
American English are drawn, the collection will have served its
purpose.

Inevitably, editing has required changes — polishing, dele-
tions, a few additions. Few as they are, they have created problems
for Anwar Dil, but his understanding and patience and desire for excellence have resolved the problems. I thank him.

Bibliography of Raven I. McDavid, Jr.'s Works

Compiled by W. A. Kretzschmar, Jr.

List of Abbreviations:

AA	American Anthropologist
ADS	American Dialect Society
AS	American Speech
CE	College English
CJL	Canadian Journal of Linguistics (formerly Journal of the Canadian Linguistic Association; entries for both titles are listed as CJL)
IJAL	International Journal of American Linguistics
JEGP	Journal of English and Germanic Philology
JEngL	Journal of English Linguistics
Lg	Language
LSA	Linguistic Society of America
MMLA	Midwest Modern Language Association
MP	Modern Philology
NCTE	National Council of Teachers of English
PADS	Publication of the American Dialect Society
SAMLA	South Atlantic Modern Language Association
SCB	South Central Bulletin
SIL	Studies in Linguistics

1935   Milton as a political thinker. Dissertation, Duke University. (Unpublished)

1938   Review of Concerning Words: A Manual and Workbook, by J. E. Norwood. South Atlantic Bulletin 4.3.11.

1939   A Citadel glossary. AS 14.23-32.

1940 a. Low-back vowels in the South Carolina Piedmont. <u>AS</u> 15.
144-48.
   b. Towards a scientific attitude. <u>South Carolina Speech Bulle-
tin</u> 2.14-16.
   c. Mr. Johnnie. (Mimeo.)

1941 a. <u>Ain't I</u> and <u>aren't I</u>. <u>Lg</u> 17.57-59.
   b. <u>Ivanhoe</u> and Simms' <u>Vasconselos</u>. <u>Modern Language Notes</u>
56.294-97.
   c. SAMLA and Southern pronunciation. <u>South Atlantic Bulletin</u>
6.4.17-18.
   d. A plan for an American dialect dictionary. Paper presented
at the SAMLA Annual Meeting, Atlanta. (Unpublished)

1942 a. <u>Slow</u> and <u>fast</u> time. <u>AS</u> 17.113.
   b. A new meaning for <u>heave</u>. <u>AS</u> 17.284.
   c. Manning the guns. <u>Louisiana Schools</u> 19.6.3-4.
   d. Opportunities for dialect research in Louisiana. <u>Louisiana
Schools</u> 20.2.10-11.
   e. <u>Adviser</u> and <u>advisor</u>: orthography and semantic differentiation. <u>SIL</u> 1.7.1-2.
   f. Phonetic distinctness of unstressed syllables. <u>SIL</u> 1.10.1.
1-11.
   g. English verb inflection: addenda. <u>SIL</u> 1.10.2-3.
   h. Some principles for American dialect study. <u>SIL</u> 1.12.1-11.

1943 a. <u>Wardrobe</u> and <u>loose floor</u>. <u>AS</u> 18.17.
   b. Provincial sayings and regional distributions. <u>AS</u> 18.66-68
   c. Miscellaneous notes on recent articles. <u>AS</u> 18.152-53.
   d. /ízənt/ and /fdənt/: addenda. <u>SIL</u> 1.17.6.
   e. (With W.S. Cornyn). Causatives in Burmese. <u>SIL</u> 1.18.
1-6.
   f. Review of <u>The Phonetics of Great Smoky Mountain Speech</u>,
by J.S. Hall. <u>Lg</u> 19.184-95.

1944 a. (Collaborator). <u>L'Inglese Parlato</u>: <u>Corso Elementare</u>.
Vol. I, Unita I-XII; vol. II, Unita XIII-XXX. War Department Technical Manual TM 30-1503, TM 30-1504. Washington: U.S. Government Printing Office. x + 245, 247-722 pp.

1944 b.   The unstressed syllabic phonemes of a Southern dialect: a
          problem of analysis. SIL 2.51-55.
     c.   Phonemic and semantic bifurcation: two examples. SIL 2.
          88-90.
     d.   Review of Melanesian Pidgin English: Grammar, Texts,
          Vocabulary, and Melanesian Pidgin English Phrasebook,
          by Robert A. Hall, Jr. Lg 20.168-71.
     e.   Review of English for the Armed Forces, by A.G.D. Wiles,
          A.M. Cook, and Jack Trevithick. South Atlantic Bulletin
          10.1.5-6.
     f.   Review of Phonetics, by Kenneth L. Pike. SCB 4.1.6.

1945 a.   (Collaborator). Dictionary of Spoken Chinese: Chinese-
          English, English-Chinese. War Department Technical
          Manual TM 30-933. Washington: War Department. iii +
          847 pp.
     b.   Burmese phonemics. SIL 3.6-18.
     c.   Review of A Dictionary of International Slurs (Ethnophaul-
          isms), with a Supplementary Essay on Aspects of Ethnic
          Prejudice, by A.A. Roback. AS 20.131-32.
     d.   Review of Western Words: A Dictionary of the Range, Cow
          Camp, and Trail, by Ramon F. Adams. AS 20.288-90.
     e.   Review of Outline of Burmese Grammar, by William S.
          Cornyn. Lg 21.290-93.
     f.   Review of American Dialect Dictionary, by Harold Went-
          worth. SCB 5.1.7.
     g.   Review of A Pronouncing Dictionary of American English,
          by John S. Kenyon and Thomas A. Knott. SCB 5.1.8.

1946 a.   Patterns of fascism: Southern style. Christian Frontiers
          1.328-40.
     b.   Dialect geography and social science problems. Social
          Forces 25.168-72.
     c.   Report on the Linguistic Atlas of the South Atlantic States.
          Paper presented at the LSA Winter Meeting, Chicago.
          (Unpublished)
     d.   Progress of the Linguistic Atlas of the South Atlantic States.
          Paper presented at the SAMLA Annual Meeting, Tuscaloosa,
          Alabama. (Unpublished)

1946 e. South Carolina dialect areas as revealed by the Atlas fieldwork. Paper presented at the South Central Modern Language Association Annual Meeting, Austin, Texas. (Unpublished)

1947 a. Pure and applied linguistics. SIL 5. 27-32.
   b. Review of The American Language: Supplement One, by
H. L. Mencken. Lg 23. 68-73.
   c. Review of Morphology: The Descriptive Analysis of Words,
by E. A. Nida. SCB 7. 2. 6.
   d. Review of A Glossary of Virginia Words, by Phyllis J. Nixon.
SIL 5. 21-24.
   e. Review of The Loom of Language , by Frederick Bodmer.
SIL 5. 43-46.
   f. American dialect lexicography: present and future. ADS.
(Mimeo.)
   g. Numerical classifiers in Burmese. Paper presented at the
American Oriental Society Annual Meeting, Washington.
(Unpublished)
   h. Report on the Linguistic Atlas of the South Atlantic States.
Paper presented at the LSA Winter Meeting, New Haven,
Connecticut. (Unpublished)

1948 a. Postvocalic /-r/ in South Carolina: a social analysis. AS
23. 194-203. [Reprinted in Language in Culture and Society,
ed. by Dell Hymes (New York: Harper and Row, 1964),
pp. 473-81.] [In this volume, pp. 1-14.]
   b. In search of Southern accents. South Carolina Magazine,
November, 20-21.
   c. The Linguistic Atlas of the South Atlantic States: its history
and present status. Southern Folklore Quarterly 12. 231-40.
   d. (With Marmaduke Floyd). A note on the origin of juke. SIL
6. 36-38.
   e. The influence of French on Southern American English (evidence of the Linguistic Atlas). SIL 6. 39-43.
   f. Review of Practical Linguistics, by Dean Pittman. Language
Learning 1. 25-27.
   g. Review of An Introduction to Linguistic Science, by E. H.
Sturtevant. SCB 8. 2. 6-7.

1948 h. Review of <u>Australian Pronunciation</u>, by S. J. Baker. <u>SIL</u>
      6.46-47.

     i. Review of <u>American and British Pronunciation</u>, by Eilert
        Ekwall. <u>Word</u> 4.134-38.

     j. Initial /hw-/ in the Atlantic Seaboard States. Paper pre-
        sented at the LSA Winter Meeting, New York. (Unpublished)

1949 a. An extension of <u>bayonet</u>. <u>AS</u> 24.42.

     b. Grist from the Atlas mill. <u>AS</u> 24.105-14.

     c. Berlin Street in New Orleans. <u>AS</u> 24.238.

     d. (With A. L. Davis). <u>Shivaree</u>: an example of cultural dif-
        fusion. <u>AS</u> 24.249-55.

     e. American dialect studies since 1939. <u>Philologica</u> [Prague]
        4.43-48.

     f. Derivatives of Middle English [o:] in the South Atlantic
        area. <u>Quarterly Journal of Speech</u> 35.496-504.

     g. Application of the Linguistic Atlas method to dialect study
        in the South-Central area. <u>Southern Speech Journal</u> 15.1-9.

     h. /r/ and /y/ in the South. <u>SIL</u> 7.18-20.

     i. Comments. <u>Report of the Conference on Planning for the</u>
        <u>Dictionary of the American Dialect Society</u> (Greensboro,
        North Carolina: American Dialect Society), 12-14, 26-27.

     j. Review of <u>The American Language</u>: Supplement Two, by
        H. L. Mencken. <u>Lg</u> 25.69-77.

     k. Review of <u>Linguistic Interludes</u>, by E. A. Nida. <u>SCB</u> 9.1.20.

     l. Review of <u>Signs, Language, and Behavior</u>, by Charles
        Morris. <u>SIL</u> 7.67-70.

     m. Review of <u>Some Sources of Southernisms</u>, by M. M. Mathews,
        <u>SIL</u> 7.71-74.

     n. Review of <u>Language and Myth</u>, by Ernst Cassirer, trans-
        lated by Susanne K. Langer. <u>SIL</u> 7.86-88.

     o. Review of <u>Introduction to the Phonetics of American English</u>,
        by C. K. Thomas. <u>SIL</u> 7.89-99.

     p. Review of <u>Peoples of the Earth</u>, by E. R. Embree. <u>SIL</u> 7.100.

1950 a. Our initial consonant <u>h</u>. <u>CE</u> 11.458-59.

     b. (With A. L. Davis). Northwestern Ohio: a transition area.
        <u>Lg</u> 26.264-73.

     c. The way we talk. <u>New York Times Magazine</u>, April 23,
        pp. 44, 46-7, 49.

1950 d. Linguistic science in popular form. Review of <u>Leave Your Language Alone!</u>, by Robert A. Hall, Jr. <u>AS</u> 25.125-28.

    e. Review of <u>Plain Words</u>, by Sir Ernest Gowers. <u>JEGP</u> 49.266.

    f. Review of <u>Studies on the Dorset Dialect</u>, by Bertil Widén. <u>JEPG</u> 49.273-74.

    g. Review of <u>Africanisms in the Gullah Dialect</u>, by Lorenzo D. Turner. <u>Lg</u> 26.323-33.

    h. Review of <u>A Word Geography of the Eastern United States</u>, by Hans Kurath. <u>New York History</u> 31.442-44.

    i. Review of <u>The Well of English</u>, by W. H. Brodie. <u>SIL</u> 8.15.

    j. The linguistic atlases: an instrument of research in the social sciences. American Council of Learned Societies. (Mimeo.)

    k. The science of linguistic geography. Paper presented at the Colorado Archaeological Society Annual Meeting, Denver. (Unpublished)

1951 a. (With Virginia McDavid). <u>A Compilation of the Work Sheets of the Linguistic Atlas of the United States and Canada and Associated Projects</u>. Ann Arbor: Linguistic Atlas of the United States and Canada. iv + unpaginated. [2nd ed., revised, with Virginia McDavid and A. L. Davis (Chicago: University of Chicago Press, 1969), xvii + unpaginated.]

    b. (With Virginia McDavid). The relationship of the speech of American Negroes to the speech of whites. <u>AS</u> 26.3-17. [Reprinted in the Bobbs-Merrill Reprint Series in Language and Linguistics, No. 62 (1962).] [Reprinted with Addendum in <u>Black-White Speech Relationships</u>, ed. by Walt Wolfram and Nona Clarke (Washington: Center for Applied Linguistics, 1971), pp. 16-40.] [In this volume, pp. 15-33.]

    c. Midland and Canadian words in Upstate New York. <u>AS</u> 26. 248-56.

    d. Hidden <u>hell</u> in <u>Helena</u>. <u>AS</u> 26.305-06.

    e. Why do we talk that way? <u>Canadian Broadcasting Company Times</u> 3.30.2, 8.

    f. Two decades of the Linguistic Atlas. <u>JEGP</u> 50.101-10.

    g. The folk vocabulary of New York State. <u>New York Folklore Quarterly</u> 7.173-92.

    h. Dialect differences and inter-group tensions. <u>SIL</u> 9.27-33.

    i. (With Marjorie M. Kimmerle and Virginia McDavid). Problems of linguistic geography in the Rocky Mountain area. <u>Western Humanities Review</u> 5.249-64.

1951 j. Review of Morphology: The Descriptive Analysis of Words,
         2nd ed., by E. A. Nida JEGP 50.408-13.
     k. Review of The Australian Language, by S. J. Baker. SIL 9.
         13-17.
     l. An American castration myth. (Unpublished Ms.)

1952 a. (Co-editor). Structural Notes and Corpus: a Basis for the
         Preparation of Materials to Teach English as a Foreign
         Language. Washington: The Committee on the Language
         Program, American Council of Learned Societies. x +
         109 pp.
     b. (With Virginia McDavid). h before semivowels in the
         Eastern United States. Lg 28.41-62.
     c. (With Virginia McDavid). The Linguistic Atlas of New Eng-
         land. Orbis 1.167-75.
     d. Millay's sonnet on Euclid. Pi Mu Epsilon Journal 1.214.
     e. Review of The Phoneme: Its Nature and Use, by Daniel
         Jones. Lg 28.377-86.
     f. Nephew and vase: a study in prestige pronunciations. Paper
         presented at the LSA Summer Meeting, Bloomington, In-
         diana. (Unpublished)
     g. Africanisms in the Eastern United States. Paper presented
         at the Modern Language Association Annual Meeting, Boston.
         (Unpublished)

1953 a. Notes on the pronunciation of catch. CE 14.290-91. [Re-
         printed in Readings in Applied English Linguistics, ed. by
         Harold B. Allen (New York: Appleton-Century-Crofts,
         1958), pp. 167-69.]
     b. Oughtn't and hadn't ought. CE 14.472-73. [Reprinted in
         Readings in Applied English Linguistics, ed. by Harold B.
         Allen (New York: Appleton-Century-Crofts, 1958), pp.
         169-71.]
     c. Some social differences in pronunciation. Language Learn-
         ing 4.102-16. [Reprinted in Readings in Applied English
         Linguistics, ed. by Harold B. Allen (New York: Appleton-
         Century-Crofts, 1958), pp. 174-85.]
     d. A Southern version of the dream contest. New York Folk-
         lore Quarterly 9.129-32.

1953 e. Concordances and historical linguistics. SIL 11.23-25.
 f. Review of Orbis 1. IJAL 19.246-50.
 g. Review of An Outline of English Structure, by George L.
    Trager and Henry Lee Smith, Jr. JEGP 52.387-91.
 h. Review of A Questionnaire for a Linguistic Atlas of England,
    by Eugen Dieth and Harold W. Orton. JEGP 52.563-68.
 i. Review of Linguistic Survey of Scotland: First Question-
    naire, by Angus McIntosh, H. J. Uldall, and Kenneth
    Jackson. JEGP 52.568-70.
 j. Review of The Story of English, by Mario Pei. SIL 11.35-39.
 k. Review of British and American English since 1900, by Eric
    Partridge and John W. Clark. SIL 11.39-42.
 l. Review of The Other Harmony of Prose, by Paull F. Baum.
    SIL 11.42-45.
 m. Linguistic evidence from the 1549 Prayer Book. Paper pre-
    sented at the LSA Summer Meeting, Bloomington, Indiana.
    (Unpublished)
 n. Regional and social patterns in Southern pronunciation. (Un-
    published Ms.)

1954 a. Linguistic geography in Canada: an introduction. CJL 1
    [Preliminary Number].3-8.
 b. Miles L. Hanley. Orbis 3.576-77.
 c. Report of the Research Committee on linguistic geography.
    PADS 21.43-47. [Reprinted, slightly revised, in Orbis 3.
    400-05.]
 d. Samson Agonistes 1096: a re-examination. Philological
    Quarterly 33.86-89.
 e. Review of A Survey of Verb Forms in the Eastern United
    States, by E. Bagby Atwood. IJAL 20.74-78.
 f. Review of Down in the Holler: A Gallery of Ozark Folk
    Speech, by Vance Randolph and George P. Wilson. Journal
    of American Folklore 67.327-30.
 g. Review of An Introduction to a Survey of Scottish Dialects,
    by Angus McIntosh. Lg 30.414-23.
 h. Review of Words and Ways of American English, by Thomas
    Pyles. Lg 30.423-26.
 i. Review of Who Killed Grammar?, by Harry R. Warfel. SIL
    12.30-32.

1954 j. Review of The Cockney, by Julian Franklyn. SIL 12.42.
     k. The habitat of prepositions. Paper presented at the ADS
         Annual Meeting, New York. (Unpublished)
     l. Kentucky grammar and the Kentucky teacher. (Unpublished
         Ms.)

1955 a. The grunt of negation. AS 30.56.
     b. The position of the Charleston dialect. PADS 23.35-49.
     c. Report of the Committees on Regional Speech and Localisms
         and on Linguistic Geography. PADS 23.55-57.
     d. Review of The Miracle of Language, by Charlton Laird.
         AA 57.379-80.
     e. Review of The Norwegian Language in America, by Einar
         Haugen. AA 57.1339-41.
     f. Review of English Topographic Terms in Florida, 1563-
         1874, by E. Wallace McMullen, Jr. AS 30.53-54.
     g. Review of The Study of Language: A Survey of Linguistics
         and Related Disciplines in America, by John B. Carroll.
         AS 30.90-94.
     h. Review of Letters of Noah Webster, ed. by Harry Warfel.
         IJAL 21.80-81.
     i. Review of La Dialectologie, by Sever Pop. IJAL 21.81-83.
     j. Review of Die Sprache des Amerikaners, Band I, by Hans
         Galinsky. JEGP 54.167-69.
     k. Review of Die Sprache des Amerikaners, Bände I und II,
         by Hans Galinsky. Lg 31.461-63.
     l. Review of The Place Names of Franklin County, Missouri,
         by Robert L. Ramsay. Modern Language Notes 70.222-23.
     m. The place of phonemics in the introductory course. Paper
         presented at the Symposium on Introductory English Lan-
         guage Courses for Teachers, Ann Arbor, Michigan. (Un-
         published)
     n. Linguistic geography and teaching. (Unpublished Ms.)
     o. Review of Wordsworth's Imagery: A Study in Poetic Vision,
         by Florence Marsh. (Unpublished Ms.)

1956 a. Social differences in pronunciation: a problem in method-
         ology. General Linguistics 2.15-21.
     b. (With Virginia McDavid). Regional linguistic atlases in the
         United States. Orbis 5.349-86.

1956 c. Report of the Committees on Regional Speech and Localisms and on Linguistic Geography. PADS 25.24-27.

d. Review of Introduction to Descriptive Linguistics, and Workbook in Descriptive Linguistics, by H. A. Gleason, Jr. AA 58.946-47.

e. Problems in revising Mencken's American Language. Paper presented at the LSA Summer Meeting, Ann Arbor, Michigan. (Unpublished)

f. (With Virginia McDavid). Elimination of the alternation between a and an. Paper presented at the LSA Winter Meeting, Philadelphia, Pennsylvania. (Unpublished)

1957 a. (Abridged by Margaret Egan). Machine literature searching in various fields: the humanities. Information Systems in Documentation (= Advances in Documentation and Library Science 2), ed. by J. H. Sheara, Allen Kent, and J. W. Perry (New York: Interscience Publishers), pp. 141-46.

b. Tape recordings in dialect geography: a cautionary note. CJL 3.3-8.

c. Linguistics at Western Reserve University. Orbis 6.525-28.

d. Report of the Committees on Regional Speech and Localisms and on Linguistic Geography. PADS 27.24-27.

e. Review of Logic and Language, by Bernard F. Huppé and Jack Kaminsky. CJL 3.27-28.

f. Review of Language as Choice and Chance, by G. Herdan. CJL 3.28-29.

g. Review of The Category of Person in Language, by Paul Forchheimer. Journal of the American Oriental Society 77.63-64.

h. Review of Negro Folktales in Michigan, by Richard M. Dorson. Ohio Historical Quarterly 66.324-26.

i. Broad a in the Eastern United States. Paper presented at the LSA Summer Meeting, Ann Arbor, Michigan. (Unpublished)

j. Linguistic variations: standard and otherwise. (Unpublished Ms.)

k. Linguistics and the teaching of literature. (Unpublished Ms.)

1958 a. Job finding. [Reply to the questionnaire of Alfred Boersch] Graduate Student of English 1.3.8-12.

1958 b.   Linguistic geography and toponymic research. <u>Names</u> 6.
           65-73.
      c.   (With Virginia McDavid, cartography). Linguistic geography
            and the study of folklore. <u>New York Folklore Quarterly</u> 14.3.
            241-62. [Special issue in honor of Harold W. Thompson,
            ed. by Warren S. Walker.] Also published in book form:
            <u>Whatever Makes Papa Laugh</u>: <u>A Folklore Sheaf Honoring</u>
            <u>Harold W. Thompson</u>, ed. by Warren S. Walker (Coopers-
            town, New York: New York Folklore Society), pp. 82-102.]
      d.   Report of the Committees on Regional Speech and Localisms
            and on Linguistic Geography. <u>PADS</u> 29.44-46.
      e.   The dialects of American English. <u>The Structure of Ameri-</u>
            <u>can English</u>, by W. Nelson Francis (New York: Ronald
            Press), pp. 480-543.
      f.   Review of <u>Tarheel Talk</u>, by Norman E. Eliason. <u>JEGP</u> 57.
            160-65.
      g.   Review of <u>A Concise Dictionary of the American Language</u>,
            by Arthur Waldhorn. <u>Lg</u> 34.146-51.
      h.   Review of <u>Shakespeare's Pronunciation</u>, by Helge Kökeritz.
            <u>SIL</u> 13.46-49.
      i.   An introduction to George Trager. Presented at the LSA
            Summer Linguistic Institute, Ann Arbor, Michigan. (Un-
            published)
      j.   <u>Houses</u> and <u>oxen</u>: anomaly and analogy in the formation of
            noun plurals. Paper presented at the LSA Winter Meeting,
            New York. (Unpublished)

1959 a.   (With Virginia McDavid). The study of American dialects:
            I. <u>Journal of the Lancashire Dialect Society</u> 8.5-19.
      b.   Report of the Committees on Regional Speech and Localisms
            and on Linguistic Geography. <u>PADS</u> 31.34-37.

1960 a.   (With Virginia McDavid). Grammatical differences in the
            North Central States. <u>AS</u> 35.5-19.
      b.   A new look at Mencken's Vulgate. <u>Ball State Teachers Col-</u>
            <u>lege Forum</u> 1.39-42.
      c.   The second round in dialectology of North American English.
            <u>CJL</u> 6.108-15. [Reprinted in <u>Thought from the Learned</u>
            <u>Societies of Canada</u> - <u>1960</u> (Toronto: W.J. Gage, 1961),

pp. 229-36; revised, under the title, "The dialectology of an urban society," in Communications et Rapports du Premier Congrès International de Dialectologie Génèrale, ed. by A. J. Van Windekens (Louvain: Centre international de dialectologie génèrale, 1964-65), vol. 1, pp. 68-80.

d. (With Virginia McDavid). The study of American dialects: II. Journal of the Lancashire Dialect Society 9.13-28.

e. Current Anthropology. Orbis 9.570-72.

f. Hans Kurath. Orbis 9.597-610.

g. A bibliography of the writings of Hans Kurath. Orbis 9. 610-12.

h. Report of the Committees on Regional Speech and Localisms and on Linguistic Geography. PADS 33.16-18.

i. A study in ethnolinguistics. Southern Speech Journal 25. 247-54.

j. The urban explosion and dialect differences. Paper presented at the MMLA Annual Meeting, Lawrence, Kansas. (Unpublished)

1961 a. (With Hans Kurath). The Pronunciation of English in the Atlantic States. Studies in American English 3. Ann Arbor: University of Michigan Press. xi + 182 pp., 180 maps.

b. The role of the linguist in the teaching of reading. Changing Concepts of Reading Instruction, ed. by J. Allen Figurel. International Reading Association Conference Proceedings 6.253-56.

c. Social dialectology: a proposal. Current Anthropology 2.62.

d. Structural linguistics and linguistic geography. Orbis 10. 35-46.

e. (With W. R. Van Riper). Report of the Committee on Regionalisms and Linguistic Geography. PADS 37.17-21.

f. Review of The Origin and Meaning of the Name "Protestant Episcopal", by Robert W. Shoemaker. Notes and Queries NS 8.236-37.

1962 a. Dialectology and the classroom teacher. CE 24.111-16.

b. (With W. R. Van Riper). Report of the Committee on Regionalisms and Linguistic Geography. PADS 38.5-9.

c. Review of Language Change and Linguistic Reconstruction, by Henry M. Hoenigswald. MP 60.76-78.

1962 d. Review of <u>Webster's Third New International Dictionary</u>.
         <u>Quarterly Journal of Speech</u> 48.435-37.
     e. Discussion. <u>First Texas Conference on Problems of Lin-
         guistic Analysis in English</u>: <u>April 27-30, 1956</u>, ed. by
         Archibald A. Hill (Austin, Texas: University of Texas
         Press), pp. 7, 12, 16, 18-21, 23-24, 27-31, 44, 51, 53,
         68, 71, 79-80, 83, 87, 89-90, 93-95, 102-07, 111, 122-24,
         128-29.
     f. Discussion. <u>Preliminary Transcript of the Proceedings of
         the 1961 Conference on Dialectology</u>, ed. by Vernon S.
         Larsen, Lee Pederson, and Roger Shuy (Chicago: privately
         printed), pp. 1-6, 9, 11-12, 14-30, 32-34.
     g. Letter. [Anthropology and the humanities]. <u>Current Anthro-
         pology</u> 3.77.
     h. (With Lee Pederson). The speech of Chicago: an experi-
         ment in social dialectology. Paper presented at the LSA
         Winter Meeting, New York. (Unpublished)
     i. The Merriam <u>Third</u>: a confidential report to the Encyclo-
         pedia Brittanica. (Unpublished Ms.)

1963 a. (With David W. Maurer, ed.). H. L. Mencken, <u>The Ameri-
         can Language</u> (The fourth edition and the two supplements,
         abridged, with annotations and new material). New York:
         Knopf. xxv + 777 + cxxiv pp.
     b. The cultural matrix of American English. <u>Baltimore Bulle-
         tin of Education</u> 41.14-19. [Reprinted in <u>Elementary English</u>
         42.13-21, 41; in <u>American Social Dialects</u>: <u>Two Articles
         by Raven I. McDavid, Jr.</u> (Urbana, Illinois: NCTE, 1965),
         pp. 1-10.]
     c. (With W. R. Van Riper). Report of the Committee on Re-
         gionalisms and Linguistic Geography. <u>PADS</u> 39.17-19.
     d. (With Vernon S. Larsen). The 1961 Conference on Dialec-
         tology. <u>PADS</u> 40.20-38.
     e. A living language. <u>Panorama</u>, November 16, p. 7.
     f. Remarks on B. Robert Tabachnick's paper. <u>Reading and
         the Language Arts</u>: <u>Proceedings of the Annual Conference
         on Reading Held at the University of Chicago, 1963</u>, v. 25,
         comp. and ed. by H. Alan Robinson (Chicago: University of
         Chicago), pp. 110-12.
     g. Review of <u>The Beginnings of American English,</u> by M. M.
         Mathews. <u>CE</u> 25.58-59.

1963 h. Review of The Five Clocks, by Martin Joos. CE 25.233-34.
  i. Commentary on "The sociopsychological analysis of folktales," by J. L. Fischer. Current Anthropology 4.280-81.
  j. Webster's Third on dialect. Paper presented at the ADS
   Annual Meeting, Chicago. (Unpublished)
  k. The role of the linguist. (Unpublished Ms.)
  l. Review of the Thorndike-World Book Dictionary. (Unpublished Ms.)
  m. Review of A Functional View of Language, by André Martinet.
   (Unpublished Ms.)

1964 a. American English. CE 25.331-37.
  b. Mencken revisited. Harvard Educational Review 34.211-25.
   [Reprinted in Language and Learning, ed. by Janet A. Emig,
   James T. Fleming, and Helen Popp (New York: Harcourt,
   Brace and World, 1966), pp. 112-29.]
  c. (With S. R. Levin). The Levys of New Orleans: an old
   myth and a new problem. Names 12.82-88.
  d. (With A. L. Davis). Communication barriers to the culturally deprived: a description of the Chicago speech survey. Project Literacy Reports 2.23-25.
  e. Dialectology and the teaching of reading. The Reading
   Teacher 18.206-13.
  f. (With Virginia McDavid). Plurals of nouns of measure in
   the United States. Studies in Languages and Linguistics in
   Honor of Charles C. Fries, ed. by Albert H. Marckwardt
   (Ann Arbor: The English Language Institute, The University
   of Michigan), pp. 271-301.
  g. Review of Mississippi: The Closed Society, by James W.
   Silver. Bêtes Noires and Straw Men [Quogue, New York]
   1.4.10.
  h. Review of Southern Politics in State and Nation, by V. O.
   Key, Jr. and Alexander Heard. Bêtes Noires and Straw Men
   [Quogue, New York] 1.4.3,10.
  i. Review of American Political Terms: An Historical Dictionary, by Hans Sperber and Travis Trittschuh. CE 25.
   632-33.
  j. Review of The Emerging South, by Thomas D. Clark. Chicago Maroon, March 27, p. 7.
  k. Review of The Regional Vocabulary of Texas, by E. Bagby
   Atwood. JEGP 63.841-46.

1964 l. Review of <u>Swift's Polite Conversation</u>, ed. by Eric Partridge.
         <u>Philological Quarterly</u> 43.393-94.

     m. Commentary on "Nelson Algren came down Division Street, "
         by Park Honan. [<u>New City</u> 2.16]. <u>New City</u> 2.17.14.

     n. Commentary on "Structure and typology of dialectal differen-
         tiation, " by Pavle Ivic. <u>Proceedings of the Ninth Internation-</u>
         <u>al Congress of Linguists</u>, <u>Cambridge, Mass., August 27-31,</u>
         <u>1962</u>, ed. by Horace G. Lunt (The Hague: Mouton), pp.
         122-23.

     o. From theory to practice. Paper presented at the NCTE
         Spring Institute, Oklahoma City, Oklahoma. (Unpublished)

1965 a. Edition with an introduction. <u>An Examination of the Atti-</u>
         <u>tudes of the NCTE toward Language</u>. NCTE Research Re-
         port 4. Urbana, Illinois: NCTE. vii + 62 pp.

     b. (Edited with James E. Miller, Jr.). Linguistics Issue.
         <u>CE</u> 26.4.

     c. American social dialects. <u>CE</u> 26.254-60. [Reprinted in
         <u>American Social Dialects: Two Articles by Raven I.</u>
         <u>McDavid, Jr.</u> (Urbana, Illinois: NCTE, 1965), pp. 10-16.]

     d. Can linguistics solve the composition problem? <u>Chicago</u>
         <u>Schools Journal</u> 46.193-200.

     e. The cultural matrix of our language. <u>Modern Compdsition:</u>
         <u>Book Six</u>, ed. by Wallace Stegner, Edwin Sauer, and
         Clarence Hach (New York: Holt, Rinehart and Winston),
         pp. 3-38.

     f. Review of <u>A Linguistic Introduction to the History of Eng-</u>
         <u>lish</u>, by Morton W. Bloomfield and Leonard Newmark, and
         of <u>The Treasure of Our Tongue</u>, by Lincoln Barnett. <u>CE</u>
         26.324-26.

     g. Review of <u>The English Verb</u>, by Martin Joos. <u>CE</u> 26.654.

     h. Review of <u>The American Scene</u>, by H. L. Mencken, ed. by
         Huntington Cairns. <u>Chicago Tribune</u>, April 25, Section 9,p.5.

     i. Review of <u>Historical Linguistics: An Introduction</u>, and <u>Exer-</u>
         <u>cises to Accompany Historical Linguistics: An Introduction</u>,
         by Winfred P. Lehmann. <u>CJL</u> 11.127.32.

     j. Review of <u>American English: A Bibliography</u>, by Vito J.
         Brenni. <u>JEGP</u> 64.574-78.

     k. Review of <u>Milton's Grammar</u>, by Ronald D. Emma. <u>Lg</u> 41.
         674-76.

l. Review of <u>Whiz Mob</u>, by David W. Maurer. <u>The Nation</u>,
   March 8, pp. 261-62.
m. Review of <u>The Anatomy of Dirty Words</u>, by Edward Sagarin.
   <u>Philological Quarterly</u> 44.566-69.
n. (With Evelyn Gott). Recording with commentary. <u>Our</u>
   <u>Changing Language</u>. St. Louis: McGraw Hill.
o. (With Vernon S. Larsen). Mencken and the South: an ex-
   Southerner's evaluation. Paper presented at the MMLA Annual Meeting, Chicago. (Unpublished)
p. Report on Merriam-Webster: an informal evaluation. [Con-
   fidential report to William Benton] (Unpublished Ms.)
q. Whither the Merriam dictionaries? A formal confidential
   report to William Benton. (Unpublished Ms.)
r. Review of <u>Anti-intellectualism in American Life</u> (1963) by
   Richard Hofstadter, and of <u>The New Radicalism in America:</u>
   <u>the Intellectual as a Social Type</u> (1965), by Christopher
   Lasch. (Unpublished Ms.)
s. Review of <u>An Adventure in Human Relations</u>, by Muriel
   Crosby. (Unpublished Ms.)

1966 a. <u>American English</u>: <u>A Syllabus</u>. Madison, Wisconsin: Uni-
        versity of Wisconsin Extension. 101 pp. (Mimeo)
     b. (With William M. Austin). Edition with preface. <u>Communi-</u>
        <u>cation Barriers to the Culturally Deprived</u>. Department of
        Health, Education, and Welfare, Office of Education Co-
        operative Research Project 2107. Chicago: privately
        printed. vii + discontinuously paginated.
     c. (With Donald C. Green). <u>Workbook</u>: <u>The Structure of</u>
        <u>American English, [by] W. Nelson Francis</u>. New York:
        Ronald Press. 139 pp.
     d. Pinfeathers for the ruptured duck. <u>CE</u> 27.635-36.
     e. Social dialects: cause or symptom of social maladjustment.
        McDavid 1966b, 10 pp. [Reprinted in <u>Social Dialects and</u>
        <u>Language Learning</u>, ed. by Roger W. Shuy (Urbana, Illinois:
        NCTE, 1965), pp. 3-7; in <u>The World of Words</u>, ed. by
        Barnet Kottler and Martin Light (Boston: Houghton Mifflin,
        1967), pp. 158-63.]
     f. (With A. L. Davis). Gathering the data. McDavid 1966b,
        6 pp.
     g. The talk of the Midwest. <u>Inland</u> [Inland Steel Co.] 52.12-17.

1966 h. The impact of Mencken on American linguistics. Menckeniana
         17. 1-7.
     i. Ghostly congressman. Men 19.12.
     j. Dialect study and English education. New Trends in English
         Education, ed. by David Stryker (Urbana, Illinois: NCTE),
         pp. 43-52.
     k. Sense and nonsense about American dialects. PMLA 81. 2.
         7-17. [Reprinted under the title, "Sense and nonsense about
         regional speech," in Humanities in the South 24. 2, 5-7.]
     l. Usage, dialects, and functional varieties. Random House
         Dictionary, ed. by Jess Stein, et al. (New York: Random
         House), pp. xxi-xxii.
     m. Dialect differences and social differences in an urban so-
         ciety. Sociolinguistics, ed. by William Bright (The Hague:
         Mouton), pp. 72-83. [Reprinted in The English Language
         in the School Program, ed. by Robert F. Hogan (Urbana,
         Illinois: NCTE, 1966), pp. 185-96; in Language/Rhetoric
         VI, ed. by Albert R. Kitzhaber, et al. (New York: Holt,
         Rinehart and Winston, 1970), pp. 196-210; translated into
         Russian by G. S. Sčur, under the title, "Dialektnye i sotsial
         'nye razlichiia v gorodskom obshchestve," in Novoe v Lin-
         gvistike, Vylusk VII: Sotsiolingvistika, ed. by N. S.
         Chemodanova (Moscow: Izdatel 'stvo "Progress,", 1975),
         pp. 363-81.] [In this volume, pp. 34-50.]
     n. Commentary. Sociolinguistics, ed. by William Bright (The
         Hague: Mouton), pp. 112, 256-57, 320-21.
     o. Review of An Introduction to the Phonetics of American Eng-
         lish, 2nd ed., by Charles K. Thomas, and of The Pronun-
         ciation of American English, by Arthur J. Bronstein. Lg
         42.149-55.
     p. Review of A Phonology and Prosody of Modern English, by
         Hans Kurath. MP 64.182-84.
     q. Review of The Treasure of Our Tongue, by Lincoln Barnett.
         South Atlantic Quarterly 65.143-45.
     r. Herakles in Elis: the Merriam Third and its critics. A re-
         port for the Encyclopedia Brittanica. (Unpublished Ms.)
     s. On graduate advising. (Unpublished Ms.)

1967 a. Vizetelly. Encyclopaedia Britannica 23.92.
     b. Webster, Noah. Encyclopaedia Britannica 23.360-61.

1967 c. Worcester, Joseph Emerson. Encyclopaedia Britannica 23. 670-71.

d. Dialectology: where linguistics meets the people. Emory University Quarterly 23. 203-221.

e. Each in his own idiom. Indiana English Journal 1. 2. 1-8.

f. Word magic: or, "Would you want your daughter to marry a hoosier?" Indiana English Journal 2. 1. 1-7.

g. Historical, regional, and social variation. JEngL 1. 25-40. [Reprinted in American Dialects for English Teachers, USOE Project HE-145; SS-12-32-67, ed. by A. L. Davis (Urbana, Illinois: Illinois Statewide Curriculum Study Center in the preparation of Secondary School English Teachers, 1969), pp. 3-12; in Culture, Class, and Language Variety, ed. by A. L. Davis (Urbana, Illinois: NCTE, 1972), pp. 1-20.

h. John Kepke. Lg 43. 825-26.

i. The elusive Slahvish. Languages and Areas: Studies presented to George V. Bobrinskoy (Chicago: Departments of Linguistics, Slavic Languages and Literatures, and the Committee on Southern Asian Studies, University of Chicago), pp. 86-89.

j. Dialect differences and the teaching of English. Louisiana English Journal 7. 10-12.

k. Discovery. Menckeniana 22. 16.

l. System and variety in American English. New Directions in American English, ed. by Alexander Frazier (Urbana, Illinois: NCTE), pp. 125-39.

m. Mencken's onomastics. Orbis 16. 93-100.

n. Language, linguistics and the three cultures. Papers in Linguistics in Honor of Léon Dostert, ed. by William M. Austin (The Hague: Mouton), pp. 123-33.

o. Needed research in Southern dialects. Perspectives on the South, ed. by Edgar T. Thompson (Durham, North Carolina: Duke University Press), pp. 113-24.

p. Dialect labels in the Merriam Third. PADS 47. 1-22.

q. Foreword. American English Dialects, ed. by Carroll E. Reed (New York: World), pp. v-vii. [Revised ed., University of Massachusetts Press, 1977.]

r. (With John T. Muri). Recording and pamphlet. Americans Speaking. Urbana, Illinois: NCTE.

1967 s. Review of Linguistic Change in Present-Day English, by
         Charles Barber. AA 69.256.
     t. Review of A Dictionary of Canadianisms on Historical Prin-
         ciples, by Walter S. Avis, et al. CJL 13.55-57.
     u. Review of An Introduction to Transformational Grammar,
         by Emmon Bach. MP 64.390-92.

1968 a. Folk speech. American Folklore, ed. by Tristram Coffin III
         (Washington: U. S. Information Agency), pp. 257-66.
         [= Voice of America Forum Lecture]
     b. Variations in standard American English. Elementary Eng-
         lish 45.561-64, 608. [Reprinted in On the Dialects of
         Children, ed. by A. L. Davis (Urbana, Illinois: NCTE,
         1968), pp. 5-9.]
     c. Two studies of dialects of English. Leeds Studies in Eng-
         lish NS 2 [Studies in Honor of Harold Orton, ed. by Stanley
         Ellis]. 23-45. [In this volume, pp. 206-233.]
     d. Dialectology and the integration of the schools. Zeitschrift
         für Mundartforschung, Beihefte, NF 4 [Verhandlung des
         zweiten internationalen Dialektologenkongresses, ed. by
         L. E. Schmitt]. 2.543-50. [Reprinted in Transactions of
         the Yorkshire Dialect Society 11.65.18-27.]
     e. Review of The Social Stratification of English in New York
         City, by William Labov. AA 70.**425-26.**
     f. Review of Investigating Linguistic Acceptability, by Randolph
         Quirk and Jan Svartvik. AA 70.1041-42.
     g. Review of A World Elsewhere: The Place of Style in Ameri-
         can Literature, by Richard Poirier. Style 2.163-64.
     h. Dialects and varieties of language. English for Elementary
         Teachers: Creativity and Imagination in Language (Urbana,
         Illinois: NCTE). (Videotape in television series)

1969 a. Systematic features with social significance in North Ameri-
         can English. Actes du Xe Congrès International des Lin-
         guistes, Bucarest, 28 août - 2 september 1967, ed. by
         A. Graur, et al. (Bucharest: Académie de la République
         Socialiste de Romanie), vol. 1, pp. 635-38.
     b. A checklist of significant features for discriminating social
         dialects. American Dialects for English Teachers, USOE
         Project HE-145; SS-12-32-67, ed. by A. L. Davis (Urbana,

Illinois: Illinois Statewide Curriculum Study Center in the preparation of Secondary School English Teachers), pp. 62-66. [Reprinted in Dimensions of Dialect, ed. by Eldonna Evertts (Urbana, Illinois: NCTE, 1967), pp. 7-10; in Culture, Class, and Language Variety, ed. by A. L. Davis (Urbana, Illinois: NCTE, 1972), pp. 133-39.]

c. The English can't make up their mind. AS 44.234.

d. Report of the Lexicography Committee. AS 44.311-12.

e. Social dialects and professional responsibility. CE 30.381-85.

f. Social variety in American English: Raven McDavid at the Linguistic Institute. (Ed. by Robert Blake). The English Record 19.32-47.

g. A theory of dialect. Georgetown University Monograph Series on Languages and Linguistics 22 [20th Annual Round Table, ed. by James E. Alatis].45-62.

h. H. L. Mencken, The American Language. Landmarks of American Writing, ed. by Hennig Cohen (New York: Basic Books), pp. 261-69. [Voice of America Forum Series]

i. Dictionary makers and their problems. Language and Teaching: Essays in Honor of W. Wilbur Hatfield, ed. by Virginia McDavid (Chicago: Chicago State College), pp. 70-79.

j. Dialects: British and American, standard and non-standard. Linguistics Today, ed. by Archibald A. Hill (New York: Basic Books), pp. 79-88. [Voice of America Forum Series]

k. The language of the city. Midcontinent American Studies Journal 10.48-59.

l. The uniformity of American English. Modern Composition: Book Six, ed. and revised by Wallace Stegner, Edwin Sauer, and Clarence Hach (New York: Holt, Rinehart and Winston), pp. 397-405.

m. No ivory towers. Newsletter of the American Dialect Society 1.1-2.

n. Do you really understand what I'm saying? South Carolina Review 1.6-16.

o. (With Virginia McDavid). The late unpleasantness: folk names for the Civil War. Southern Speech Journal 34.194-204.

p. Hroþulf, Hengest and Beowulf. Studies in Language, Literature and Culture of the Middle Ages and Later, in Honor of

Rudolph Willard, ed. by E. Bagby Atwood and Archibald A.
Hill (Austin, Texas: University of Texas Press), pp. 230-34.

1970 a. Analysis of natural language. Computer-Assisted Instruction, Testing, and Guidance, ed. by Wayne H. Holtzman
(New York: Harper and Row), pp. 222-27.

b. Changing patterns of Southern dialects. Essays in Honor of
Claude M. Wise, ed. by Arthur J. Bronstein, et al. (Hannibal, Missouri: Standard Printing [sponsored by the Speech
Association of America]), 206-228. [In this volume, pp. 51-
77.]

c. On a hierarchy of values: the clinician and the dialectologist.
Language Behavior, ed. by Johnnye Akin, et al. (The Hague:
Mouton), 250-55.

d. The sociology of language. Linguistics in School Programs,
National Society for the Study of Education Yearbook 69.2,
ed. by Albert H. Marckwardt (Chicago: National Society for
the Study of Education), pp. 85-108. [In this volume, pp.
182-205.]

e. The teacher of minorities. Nebraska English Counselor 15.
3.5-16.

f. Some problems of over-all patterning. Proceedings of the
Sixth International Congress of Phonetic Sciences, ed. by
Bohuslav Hála, et al. (Prague: Academia Publishing House
of the Czechoslovak Academy of Sciences), pp. 631-32.

g. Native whites. Reading for the Disadvantaged: Problems
of Linguistically Different Learners, ed. by Thomas D. Horn
(New York: Harcourt, Brace and World), pp. 135-39.

h. Design, data gathering, and interpretation. The Second and
Third Lincolnland Conferences on Dialectology, ed. by Jerry
Griffith and L. E. Miner (University, Alabama: University
of Alabama Press), pp. 1-19.

i. Commentary. The Second and Third Lincolnland Conferences
on Dialectology, ed. by Jerry Griffith and L. E. Miner (University, Alabama: University of Alabama Press), pp. 99-100,
102, 104, 106-09, 112, 114, 116-17, 120-24, 128, 131-33,
141-58, 160-63, 171, 175-76, 187, 194, 198-201, 203-20,
222-23, 225-27, 230-31, 234-35, 237-40, 242, 244-47, 253-
56, 258-59, 261-62.

1971 a. Planning the grid. AS 46.9-26. [In this volume, pp. 234-256.]

b. What happens in Tennessee? Dialectology: Problems and Perspectives, ed. by Lorraine Hall Burghardt (Knoxville, Tennessee: University of Tennessee), pp. 119-29.

c. English language: American dialects. The Encyclopedia of Education, ed. by Lee C. Deighton, et al. (New York: Mac-Millan), vol. 3, pp. 373-81.

d. False scents and cold trails: the pre-publication criticism of the Merriam Third. JEngL 5.101-21. [In this volume, pp. 310-336.]

e. Review of American Place Names: A Concise and Selective Dictionary for the Continental United States of America, by George R. Stewart. American Quarterly 23.342-43.

f. Review of Speaking Canadian English: An Informal Account of the English Language in Canada, by M. M. Orkin. AS 46.287-89.

g. Discovering Language. Our American language, no. 3008; Our alphabet, no. 3010; How words are made, no. 3013; How English borrowed words, no. 3014; Our language today, no. 3015; How words get new meanings, no. 3019. Chicago: Coronet Instructional Films. (Filmstrip series)

1972 a. (With Guy Jean Forgue). La Langue des Américains. Paris: Aubier-Montaigne. 271 pp.

b. (Ed. with Lee Pederson, Charles Foster, and Charles Billiard). A Manual for Dialect Research in the Southern States. Atlanta: Georgia State University. x + 244 pp. [2nd ed., University, Alabama: University of Alabama Press, 1974]

c. Field procedures: instructions for investigators, Linguistic Atlas of the Gulf States. In 1972b, pp. 33-60.

d. Some notes on Acadian English. Culture, Class, and Language Variety, ed. by A. L. Davis (Urbana, Illinois: NCTE), pp. 184-87.

e. Carry you home once more. Neuphilologische Mitteilungen 73.1-2 [Studies presented to Tauno F. Mustanoja on the occasion of his sixtieth birthday].192-95.

f. Sandhi-alternation of attributive genitives in Milton's works. South Atlantic Quarterly 71.4 [Essays in the Renaissance in honor of Allan H. Gilbert, ed. by Philip J. Traci and Marilyn L. Williamson]. 530-33.

1972 g. (With Lawrence M. Davis). The dialects of Negro Ameri-
         cans. Studies in Linguistics in Honor of George L. Trager,
         ed. by M. Estellie Smith (The Hague: Mouton), pp. 303-12.
         [In this volume, pp. 78-91.]

     h. Review of Studies in Area Linguistics, by Hans Kurath. AS
         47.285-92.

     i. Review of "Linguistic Darwinism: H. L. Mencken's The
         American Language, " by Mark B. Ryan. Cahiers d'histoire
         mondiale 11(1968).484-95. Menckeniana 42.13.

1973 a. (Ed. with Audrey R. Duckert). Lexicography in English.
         Annals of the New York Academy of Sciences 211. 342 pp.

     b. At points in time. AS 48.159-60.

     c. (With Lawrence E. Fisher). Aphaeresis in New England.
         AS 48.246-49.

     d. (Under pseudonym M. B. Darwin). A footnote on the rebel
         yell. AS 48.303-04.

     e. The English language in the United States. Current Trends
         in Linguistics, ed. by Thomas A. Sebeok et al. (The Hague:
         Mouton), vol. 10, part 2, pp. 5-39.

     f. New directions in American dialectology. English Studies
         Today 5.53-85. [Reprinted in Studia Anglia Posnaniensia
         5.1-2.9-25.]

     g. Reverse index of LANE maps to worksheets. Handbook of
         the Linguistic Geography of New England, ed. by Hans
         Kurath et al.; 2nd ed., revised with new material by Audrey
         R. Duckert (New York: AMS Press), pp. 243-49.

     h. American social dialects. Indiana English Journal 7.4.1-8.
         [≠ McDavid 1965c]

     i. (With Raymond O'Cain). Sociolinguistics and linguistic
         geography. Kansas Journal of Sociology 9.137-56.

     j. (With Virginia McDavid). The folk vocabulary of Eastern
         Kentucky. Zeitschrift für Dialektologie und Linguistik,
         Beihefte, NF 9 [Lexicography and Dialectology: Festgabe
         for Hans Kurath, ed. by Harald Scholler and John Reidy]
         (Weisbaden, West Germany: Franz Steiner Verlag GmbH.),
         pp. 147-64. [In this volume, pp. 93-113.]

     k. (With Virginia McDavid). Cracker and hoosier. Names 21.
         161-67.

1973 l. Philip B. Gove (1902-1972). <u>Newsletter of the American Dialect Society</u> 5.2.8-12.

m. (With A. L. Davis). The Linguistic Atlas of the Middle and South Atlantic States: an editorial comment. <u>Orbis</u> 22. 331-34.

n. Go slow in ethnic attributions: geographic mobility and dialect prejudices. <u>Varieties of Present-Day English,</u> ed. by Richard W. Bailey and Jay L. Robinson (New York: Macmillan), pp. 258-70.

o. Review of <u>The Taste of Yiddish,</u> by Lillian M. Feinsilver. <u>JEngL</u> 7.107.

p. Review of <u>Slang and Its Analogues,</u> by J. S. Farmer and W. E. Henley, reprinted with an introduction by Theodore M. Bernstein. <u>JEngL</u> 7.107-08.

q. Review of <u>Place Names of the English Speaking World,</u> by C. M. Matthews. <u>South Atlantic Quarterly</u> 72.617-18.

r. Opening remarks and discussion. McDavid 1973a. Opening remarks, pp. 5-7; discussion, pp. 25, 67-68, 124, 143, 266.

1974 a. (With Sarah A. Witham). Poor whites and rustics. <u>Names</u> 22.93-103. [In this volume, pp. 337-352.]

b. (With Stuart Flexner). Slang: bibliography. <u>The New Encyclopaedia Britannica</u> 16.853.

c. Webster, Noah. <u>The New Encyclopaedia Britannica</u> 19.720-21.

d. Review of <u>West Virginia Surnames: The Pioneers,</u> by William E. Mockler. <u>AS</u> 49.149-51.

e. Review of <u>Class, Codes and Control,</u> Vol. 1: <u>Theoretical Studies toward a Sociology of Language,</u> ed. by Basil Bernstein. <u>School Review</u> 82.517-19.

f. American dialects. Cleveland: Windhauer. (Videotape series) [Abridged edition, 1976.]

1975 a. Napier Wilt, 1896-1975. <u>American Studies International</u> 14.51.

b. The nature and validity of field evidence. <u>Linguistics and Anthropology: In Honor of C. F. Voegelin,</u> ed. by M. Dale Kinkade, et al. (Lisse: Peter de Ridder), pp. 465-71.

c. Notes on the pronunciation of <u>Ohio</u>. <u>Names</u> 23.147-52.

d. The urbanization of American English. <u>Philologica Pragensia</u> 18.228-38. [Reprinted in revised form in <u>Jahrbuch für Amerikastudien</u> 16 [1971].47-59. [In this volume, pp. 114-130.]

1975 e. Review of <u>A Word Geography of California and Nevada</u>, by
         Elizabeth S. Bright. <u>AS</u> 50.110-15.

    f.   Preface. <u>Lexikalische und grammatische Ergebnisse des</u>
         <u>Lowman-Survey von Mittel- und Südengland</u>, ed. by Wolfgang
         Viereck (Munich: Wilhelm Fink), pp. 7-8.

    g.   On research and resources. Columbia, South Carolina:
         Linguistic Atlas of the Middle and South Atlantic States.
         (Mimeo)

1976 a. (With Albert H. Marckwardt, Richard Payne, Duane Taylor,
         and Evan Thomas). <u>The Linguistic Atlas of the North-</u>
         <u>Central States</u>: <u>Basic Materials</u>. Manuscripts on Cultural
         Anthropology 200-02, 205-07. Chicago: Joseph Regenstein
         Library, University of Chicago. (Microfilm) [Includes
         Wisconsin, Michigan, Ontario, Ohio, Kentucky, and Long
         Worksheet Interviews, respectively.]

    b.   (With Glenda Pritchett). <u>A Bibliography of the Speech of</u>
         <u>the North-Central States</u>: <u>Preliminary Draft.</u> Chicago:
         Linguistic Atlas of the North-Central States. 27 pp. (Mimeo)

    c.   Language learning and dialects. <u>Language Today</u> 2.3-10.

    d.   (With Raymond O'Cain). The name researcher and the Lin-
         guistic Atlas. <u>Names in South Carolina</u> 23.23-28.

    e.   An editor's request for help. <u>Newsletter of the American</u>
         <u>Dialect Society</u> 8.2.10-11.

    f.   Linguistic Atlas of the North-Central States. Basic Mater-
         ials (Unaltered field records). <u>Orbis</u> 25.20-21.

    g.   In memoriam: Albert H. Marckwardt (1903-1975) and the
         Linguistic Atlas of the North-Central States. A memorial.
         <u>Orbis</u> 25.176-86.

    h.   Dictionaries. <u>The Scribner Dictionary of American History</u>
         (New York: Scribners), p. 340.

    i.   Review of <u>A Dictionary of Modern American and British</u>
         <u>English on a Contrastive Basis,</u> by Givi Zviadadze. <u>JEngL</u>
         10.73-75.

    j.   The Humanist in the Woodwork: or, if Lions were Sculptors.
         [An address presented to the graduate students of English at
         the University of Chicago, February, 1966.] Columbia,
         South Carolina: privately printed. (Mimeo)

    k.   Harold Orton. [Obituary]. <u>AS</u> 51.59-62.

    l.   Review of <u>Our Own Words,</u> by Mabel Dohan. <u>AS</u> 51.84-86.

1977 a. (With Albert H. Marckwardt, Richard Payne, Duane Taylor, and Evan Thomas). The Linguistic Atlas of the North-Central States: Basic Materials. Manuscripts on Cultural Anthropology 203. Chicago: Joseph Regenstein Library, University of Chicago. (Microfilm) [Includes Illinois]

b. Guy S. Lowman, Jr. A Biographical Dictionary of the Phonetic Sciences, ed. by Arthur J. Bronstein, et al. (New York: The Press of Lehman College), p. 134.

c. Hans Kurath. A Biographical Dictionary of the Phonetic Sciences, ed. by Arthur J. Bronstein, et al. (New York: The Press of Lehman College), pp. 123-24.

d. Evidence. Papers in Language Variation, ed. by David Shores and Carole Hines (University, Alabama: University of Alabama Press), pp. 125-32.

e. (With Raymond O'Cain). Existential there and it: an essay on method and interpretation of data. James B. McMillan: Essays in Linguistics by his Friends and Colleagues (University, Alabama: University of Alabama Press), pp. 29-40.

f. (With Raymond O'Cain). Southern standards revisited. Papers in Language Variation, ed. by David Shores and Carole Hines (University, Alabama: University of Alabama Press), pp. 229-32.

g. (With Raymond O'Cain). Prejudice and pride: linguistic acceptability in South Carolina. Acceptability in Language, ed. by Sidney Greenbaum (The Hague: Mouton), pp. 103-32. [In this volume, pp. 131-163.]

h. How can English teachers deal with illiterate expressions? Questions English Teachers Ask, ed. by R. Baird Shuman (Rochelle Park, New Jersey: Hayden), pp. 179-80.

i. Review of Harper Dictionary of Contemporary Usage, ed. by William Morris and Mary Morris. JEngL 11.41-50.

j. Review of The Speech of Australian Adolescents, by A. G. Mitchell and Arthur Delbridge. Lg 53.679-83.

k. (With Raymond O'Cain). Review of The Study of Social Dialects in American English, by Walter Wolfram and Ralph Fasold. AA 79.947-48.

1978a. (With Raymond K. O'Cain). South Carolina county names: a study in unreconstructed individualism, Names 26.106-15.

1978 b. (With Albert H. Marckwardt, Richard Payne, Duane Taylor, and Evan Thomas). <u>The Linguistic Atlas of the North-Central States: Basic Materials</u>. Manuscripts on Cultural Anthropology 204, 208. Chicago: Joseph Regenstein Library, University of Chicago. (Microfilm) [Includes Indiana and Appendix, respectively.]

c. (With Raymond K. O'Cain). Notes on the pronunciation of proper names: <u>New Orleans</u> and <u>Louisiana</u>. <u>Mississippi Folklore Register</u> 11.76-92.

d. The gathering and presentation of data. <u>JEngL</u> 12.29-37.

e. Review of <u>The Linguistic Atlas of Scotland</u>: <u>Scots Section,</u> Vols. I and II, ed. with an introduction by J. Y. Mather and H. H. Speitel. <u>JEngL</u> 12.76-82.

f. (With Raymond O'Cain). Special issue of <u>Names</u> in honor of Claude Neuffer. <u>Names</u> 26.2.

g. Review of <u>Linguistic Atlas of the Upper Midwest</u>, 3 volumes, by Harold B. Allen. <u>MP</u> 75.427-31.

h. (With Raymond K. O'Cain). South Carolina county names: a study in unreconstructed individualism. <u>Names</u> 26.106-15.

i. Presidential terminology. [Under the pseudonym of Owen Hatteras III]. <u>AS</u> 53.39.

j. (With Raymond K. O'Cain, and George T. Dorrill). The Linguistic Atlas of the Middle and South Atlantic States. Geography and Map Division, Special Libraries Association, Bulletin No. 113, 17-23.

k. (With Raymond O'Cain). From field record to data retrieval: some questions. Germanistische Linguistik 3-4/77: Automatische Sprachkattographie, ed. Wolfgang Putschke (Marburg/Lahn: Forschungsinstitut für deutsche Sprache-Deutscher Sprachatlas), pp. 11-24.

l. (With Virginia McDavid). Intuitive rules and factual evidence: /-sp, -st, -sk/ plus {-Z}. <u>Linguistic and Literary Studies in Honor of Archibald A. Hill,</u> ed. by Mohammad Ali Jazayery, Edgar C. Polomé, and Werner Winter (The Hague: Mouton). Vol. 2, <u>Descriptive Linguistics,</u> pp. 73-90.

1979 a. Linguistic and Cultural Pluralism: An American Tradition. <u>Studia Anglia Posnaniensia</u> 9.225-240.

b. The Linguistic Atlas of the North-Central States — A Work of Salvage Dialectology. <u>Philologica Pragensia</u> 22.98-101.

1979 c. Dialects in Culture: Essays by Raven I. McDavid, Jr., ed.
by William A. Kretzschmar, Jr., with the collaboration of
James B. McMillan, Lee Pederson, Roger Shuy and Gerald
Udell. University, Alabama: University of Alabama Press.

d. (With Raymond O'Cain). Notes on Maryland and Baltimore.
AS 54.

e. (With Hans Kurath, Raymond O'Cain, George T. Dorrill, et
al.). The Linguistic Atlas of the Middle and South Atlantic
States. Fascicle 1- . Chicago: University of Chicago Press.

f. Varieties of American English: Essays by Raven I. McDavid,
Jr., ed. by Anwar S. Dil. Stanford, California: Stanford
University Press. xvi + 384 pp.

g. Social differences in white speech. Language and Society,
ed. by William McCormack and Stephen A. Wurm (The
Hague: Mouton Publishers), pp. 249-61.

h. New directions in American dialectology. [Revised version
of 1973f] [In this volume, pp. 257-295.]

i. The social role of the dictionary. [In this volume, pp. 296-
309.]

j. Confederate overalls; or, a little Southern Sweetening. In
1979c, pp. 282-287.

k. Folk speech. American Folklore Cassette Lecture Series,
ed. by Hennig Cohen (Deland, Florida: Everett/Edwards)
[recording with text].

l. American English: a bibliographic essay. American Studies
International 17.2.3-45.

m. History of American English. Britannica Book of Better English (New York: Doubleday).

n. Review of Language in the Inner City and Sociolinguistic Patterns, by William Labov. AS 54.

o. Linguistics: through the kitchen door. Toward a History of
American Linguistics: Papers from the Conference on an
Oral History Archive ("Studies in the History of Linguistics,"
No. 21), ed. by Boyd H. Davis and Raymond O'Cain (Amster-
dam: John Benjamins), pp. 1-23.

p. Author's postscript. [In this volume, pp. 353-355.]

McDavid, Raven I., Jr.   1911-
        Varieties of American English:
essays by Raven I. McDavid, Jr. Selected and
Introduced by Anwar S. Dil. Stanford, California:
Stanford University Press [1980]
        xvi, 384 p. 24cm.
(Language science and national development series,
Linguistic Research Group of Pakistan)
        Includes bibliography.
I.   Dil, Anwar S., 1928-   ed.
II.   (Series) III. Linguistic Research Group of Pakistan